MEDIA EDUCATION

MEDIA EDUCATION

H. D. Kamat

A. David

CRESCENT

PUBLISHING CORPORATION

Media Management

Edition 2024

ISBN 978-81-8342-040-0

Published by:
CRESCENT PUBLISHING CORPORATION
4806/24, Mathur Lane,
Ansari Road, Darya Ganj,
New Delhi - 110 002
Ph.: 011 - 23244131
Mob.: + 91 - 9711991838, 9999021668
E-mail: crescentbook@gmail.com
Website: www.crescentpublishingcorp.weebly.com

Printed at:
Roshan Offset Printers
Delhi

PRINTED IN INDIA

PREFACE

Over the past twenty years the media has grown significantly in the world because young people need to learn about the media. The book is produced specifically with the needs of students in mind and is a result of a wide consultation. All previous forms of literacy are vital, but are no longer enough. In our new world of interactive media networks, we are not functionally literate without a deep appreciation for media awareness and power of our global interactivity. In our schools and libraries we are most concerned with media, many resources which are used in teaching and learning. Educational technology is a systematic way of designing, carrying out and evaluating the total process of learning and teaching in terms of specific objectives, based on research in human learning and communication. In the present age, when scientific developments have made the human life comfortable yet complex, media education has gained much importance.The media play a significant role in forming and influencing people's attitudes and behaviour. The masses may not have the opportunity to go to school, but by and large through media they can be educated.

The media education promotes research and an understanding of, the role and the effects of the media upon society. It seeks new ways in which people can enhance their understanding in the political and cultural life of the general community through the media. With an expanding media worldwide, and with the increasing use of new information and communication technologies—particularly in education—the objective is to develop an awareness. Multimedia and software development continue to be one of the corner stones of the learning. Although there are certain problems with this form of education but adoption of innovating methods of media education in formal and non-formal education, societies can develop at a very fast pace never imagined before.

H.D. Kamat
A.David

Contents

1

Learning and Communication

Education may be looked upon in a total sense as a process of imparting new and increasingly complex capabilities to the student. In this sense, education is itself a process of communication, which can be analyzed into a number of subordinate functions to be carried out by designers of instructional materials and equipment, teachers and other. When viewed in this way, it is evident that there are several important channels of communication that are in need of study and improvement. For example, some years ago a panel of psychologists (National Research Council, Advisory Board on Education, 1958) identified the following channels as important to the educational process, and deserving of increased research efforts: (1) the channel from curriculum-maker to pupil; (2) the channel from psychologist to educator; (3) the channel from educator to adult public; and (4) the channel from counsellor to counselee.

The varieties of communication that enter into the process of education, globally, conceived, continue to be a fundamental importance to any more narrowly defined component of the educational system. Recent developments, for example have seen a heavy concentration of effort on curriculum, in mathematics, science, social studies, English, and many other areas. It is apparent that consideration of the outcomes of these efforts, and their effects on the total system, raises questions about educational objectives which properly involve the channel of communication between educators and the adult public. The design of curricula represents only one channel of communication, but the objectives which are sought inevitably interact with other channels when the system of education is viewed as a totality.

It will be useful to bear in mind these interacting components of the total educational system, as attention is focused in this chapter on those varieties of communication that are involved in the specific function of *instruction.*

Communication and its Role in Instruction

The typical model of school instruction appears to embody communication as an obvious and prominent component. This is the model in which a teacher stands at the front of a room containing thirty students and conducts various kinds of verbal communication with them. The teacher may tell things to students, orally, or write them on a chalkboard; he may elicit communications from the students in the form of oral or written answers to questions; or he may invite students to formulate more extensive communications to other members of the class in the form of oral or written reports. When conceived in this ..y seem to be simply a kind of directed and structured conversation. It is tempting, even, to consider the possibility that instruction is simply equivalent to communication.

Further reflection will show, however, that this model of instruction is far too simple for analytic purposes. Students learn much in situations that do not involve conversations with the teacher—they learn from observing events, natural or contrived; they learn from reading books, examining pictures, and watching pictures that move; and they learn from their own self-generated mental operations.

There is much interest nowadays in computer-assisted instruction. Here, too, however, those who are engaged in serious research with this new tool recognize that the conception of a computer as a means of storing and locating information to be presented constitutes only the simplest part of what must be accomplished. Programs and routines of various degrees of complexity must be designed to engage the human learner in activities that require him to accomplish many kinds of codings and transformations of the materials displayed. And these transformations, in turn, create needs for even greater varieties of units of information to be communicated.

It seems clear, therefore, that one cannot simply equate communication with the process of instruction. Communication in its broadest sense of an event involving apprehension of a situation may be said to be an inevitable part of instruction, but by no means the whole. Thorn-dike pointed out that a common error of the scholar, inexperienced in teaching was to expect students to know what they were told. "Telling," he said, "is not teaching."

Accordingly , a consideration of what communication has to do with instruction must properly begin with a description of the process of instruction itself. Particularly, one must consider what happens to the students, or learner, during the events of instruction.

Instruction and the Learner

The purpose of the process of instruction is to bring about a change in the capabilities (knowledges, skills, attitudes, and other dispositions) of the human learner. At some particular point in time, it may be determined that the student is not capable of executing some class of performances, let us say, adding sets of two-digit numbers. Activities that are called instruction are then undertaken with the aim of making it possible for the student to change his starting capabilities, including his inability to add two-digit numbers, to a new set of capabilities that includes this latter one, as indicated by his performance when given a sample of such numbers to add. The change that takes place as a result of the instruction is referred to as learning. Although he may frequently play other roles, the student is functioning as a *learner* while in the instruction situation. When he learns, his capabilities at time x are changed to a new set of capabilities at x + 1.

What is Learned?

To conceive of learning as change in human capabilities is a first step in understanding the process of instruction. Such a view accomplishes two major clarifications. First, it puts the emphasis for instruction where it must be—on the student. However elaborate or complicated the process of instruction may turn out to be, or may be designed to be, its outcomes must be referenced to the changes that take place in the student. Whether instruction involves a teacher, a textbook, a class a motion picture, a television set, or whatever, its ultimate function is to bring about a change in the student. As will be seen later, the kinds of communications that form a part of instruction must also be judged in relation to changes in the capabilities of students.

A second kinds of elucidation arising from this view of learning is that the outcome of instruction pertains to its emphasis on an inferred internal state, or capability. Sometimes, it is said that learning is a change in "students responses" or 'students performance." While this manner of referring to the outcomes of learning may be convenient as a shorthand. It cannot be correct in any strict sense. A number of kinds of events may affect student performance at any given moment, but it is the underlying capability that is changed by learning. To be sure, observations of performance are what convince the instructor that a change in capability has taken place. The difference between two performances in the same student is the observation employed to make the inference about a change in capability: at one time the student does not add two-digit numbers, and at another time he does. But the aim of the instruction is to bring about the change in capability, and the observations made on performance must be carefully designed to so that this inference can be made with confidence.

The specific capabilities that are newly formed by learning can be described and classified in several different ways. Adding number, for instance, can be categorized as part of a larger set of capabilities in "whole number operations," which, in turn, forms a part of "mathematics." Forming correctly structured English sentences may be classified as a capability belonging to the larger class of "grammar," or of "language arts." Accordingly, one can, if he wishes, design a technology of instruction that is broken down into such subject-matter categories, as in "mathematics instruction," "English instruction," "science instruction," and so on. But it is evident from common usage that there must be a set of instructional categories that cuts across subject-matters. Thus, one thinks of instruction designed to establish knowledge of facts, whether these be facts of natural science, history, or mathematics. Similarly, it is not uncommon to find consideration given to the learning of concepts, whether language concepts or science concepts; or to problem solving, whether in mathematics or social studies. Phrases of this sort imply that designers of instruction, and teachers, commonly think of categories of human capability as organized along dimensions which are independent of subject-matter. There seem to be different kinds of learning, each of which requires, in certain respects, a different kind of instruction.

The view that categories of acquired capabilities may be distinguished in terms of the way they are observed or measured (that is, the kinds of performances to which they lead), as well as in terms of the kinds of change they imply, has been previously described. It is of particular relevance here because these categories of learning set the bounds of what can be accomplished by instruction. Including the communications which form a part of instruction. In brief form, much of what is learned in school may be described in the following categories:

1. *S.R Connections :* These are simple unitary motor acts that are usually acquired very early in the child's life, but some of which may be learned during school years. Making a mark on a piece of paper is an example; as in pronouncing the letter "I." For the most part, early school instruction simply assumes such capabilities as these.

2. *Discrimination :* Often, several simple connections must be learned so that different responses are made to different parts of the stimuli impinging on the learner. The performance to be observed is that of *distinguishing* colours, brightness, shapes, sizes, sounds, or various other portions of the environments. For example, the child must learn that the printed letter d is associated with the sound "duh," and also that printed letter *b* is associated with the sound "buh,". He must not only acquire the two individual connections, he should not get them mixed up. Acquiring multiple discrimination is a matter of learning the capability of making a number of differential responses to an equivalent numbers of different stimulus categories.

3. *Motor chains :* Integrated motor activities such as tying shoelaces, printing letters, describing circles with a compass,

focusing a microscope, and many others, are frequently learned in school. A motor chain may be described as the capability of carrying out a sequence of movements leading to a specifiable class of. result in the environment of the learner. Printing a letter, drawing a circle opening a lock, pronouncing a previously unfamiliar foreign word, are all examples of motor chains.

4. *Verbal chains* : A good many verbal sequences are learned in school, and appear to underlie of more complex verbal and intellectual skills. The young child learns to say the names of the numerals one to ten in order, and he may also learn the alphabet as a sequence. In addition, he acquires many common phrases, such as "boy and girl," "back and torth," "yes I will," and many others. Even later, verbal chains such as "one point four one four" may be a small but useful capability learned in mathematics. Considerably longer verbal chains, such as verses of songs or poetry, may also be learned as a part of school instruction. As a capability, a verbal chain is reflected in the performance of reinstating a sequence of verbal entities (usually words) which in its totality represents a specifiable outcome (the alphabet, a particular phrase or stanza).

5. *Concepts :* The most basic kinds of concepts appear to be capabilities of classifying objects (chair, table); events (expanding contracting); or spatial and temporary relations up, down before, after into categories. What is notable about such classes is that the physical appearance of their members may vary tremendously (a table, for example, may be large or small, high or low, three-legged or four-legged, and so on, yet the concept makes possible an identical response to them. Many fundamental concepts appear to be acquired by direct interaction of the learner with members of the class of objects or events concerned, and with the use of language. Other more abstract concepts (like "uncle," or "symmetry") are apparently most readily learned by means of language which itself refers to simpler concepts. In other words, they are learned by definition.d

A large proportion of school learning is concerned with concepts. Learning to use language requires the student to require many concepts beginning with those of letter and word functions. Mathematics depends upon the learning of concepts pertaining to numbers and number operations. Science and social science are replete with new technical terms for a student to master, each of which is a concept. There are concepts of art and music, as well as concepts relating to bodily movement and physical development. One has only to attempt to acquire new knowledge by reading in an unfamiliar field to recognize at once the necessity for learning the concepts of that field before further learning can transpire.

6. *Principles :* Another large class of learner capabilities reflected in school learning consists of principles or rules. Generally speaking, principles are combinations of concepts. They may be represented by such simple sentences as "Water pours," or by such complex ones as "When a body is in equilibrium, the sum of the movements of force about an axis of rotation is equal to zero." It needs to be emphasized that a principle is an idea, or perhaps a set of ideas, but is not the verbal statement of the idea. The latter merely *represents* the principle. Obviously a verbal statement may be learned as a verbal chain, but this capability is different from the capability usually meant by "knowing a principle."

A great deal of systematic knowledge acquired in the school situation consists of principles. As the psycholinguists have frequently pointed out, the learning of principles governing the use of language begins in early childhood. The child does not undertake the learning of the principles of syntax deliberately, but learn them he does, as can easily be proved by his performance in using them to communicate. Many kinds of principles are acquired in much the same way during the ordinary lifetime of the individual, while many others are learned as a result of formally planned instruction in the school.

Principles are frequently arrived at by the individual himself, in a largely self-instructional manner, as a result of a kind of performance called *problem solving*. In this activity, the individual learner "discovers" a relationship among concepts or principles which leads to the acquisition of a "higher-order principle".

7. *Strategies :* Another kind of capability, which may be considered a variety of principle in its essential nature, is called a strategy, and is emphasized in the work of Burner, among others. A strategy is a principle governing choices of the individual's own actions. Thus, an individual may acquire a

strategy of solving algebra problems a strategy of persuading his parents, or a strategy of investing his money. This kind of higher-order principle is likely to be a highly generalizable capability (or so it is thought by many writers), and therefore to pervade a great many different aspects of his intellectual life. Behaving "creatively" may perhaps best be viewed as a matter of performing in accordance with certain previously learned strategies. Many strategies are acquired in connection with formal schooling, while others are learned outside of school.

Instructional Implications of What is Learned

There are, then, six or seven *different* classes of capabilities that are acquired by the human learner during the course of his lifetime. Not only do these differ in indicating the variety of things an individual can do, they differ also in terms of the *conditions required for their learning.* The conditions for learning any single type of capability vary in respect to both the internal conditions of the learner (the state of his nervous system, including memorial traces), and the external conditions surrounding him and impinging upon him. These external conditions as a whole constitute instruction and, accordingly, they are centrally involved in the question of how communication is related to learning.

It is easy to choose extreme examples to demonstrate that the conditions for learning one type of capability differ markedly from those required in the learning of another type. The learning of a motor skill like batting a baseball, for example, is markedly little influenced by verbal communications on how to do it, whereas it is strongly affected by a regime of practice with knowledge of results. In contrast, the basic rules of the game of baseball, although they could be incidentally acquired during long period of practice and watching, are most readily and rapidly learned by being verbally communicated. The sharp contrast provided by these particular instances of learning is not an exceptional one. Rather, it is a familiar illustration of the general rule that learning different capabilities requires different conditions. The external components of these different sets of learning conditions are what must be identified in exploring the role of communication in learning.

Components of Instruction

The external conditions of learning may be said to embody the various kinds of communication made to the learner during the period of instruction. In this context, communication is meant in quite a broad sense. It often takes the form of verbal statements delivered to the learner in a language with which he is familiar. Frequently, communication assumes the form of printed or written statements in the familiar language. It may be noted that either of these forms may be medicated by a teacher (speaking or writing on a blackboard), or alternatively, by a device (a tape recorder or printed book). Pictures constitute another major category of communication available to the learner. These may be still or moving; and there are many ways to present them (slides, film, television). A somewhat specialized form of communication is comprised of non-linguistic symbols, a form particularly relevant to the learning of such subject as mathematics, science, and music. Other types of communication, including gestures and visual arts, have even more highly restricted and specialized uses as part of instruction.

The important question to be answered about communication in relation to learning does not concern the medium that is used for communicating, but rather, what functions the communications serves. The various conditions required for different form of learning partake of communication in various ways. At any give moment during a period of instruction, the communication to the learner is fulfilling a function different from that of any other moment. It is necessary, therefore, to address the question of what these various functions might be.

In the broad sense employed in this chapter, communication enters into every variety of learning described in the previous section. It would be possible to describe the specific functions of communication in the learning of S-R connections, multiple discrimination, motor and verbal chains. However, since such a large part of educationally relevant learning comprises concepts and principles (including strategies), the discussion which follows will give primary emphasis to these kinds of learning.

It is possible to analyze the instructional event into a number of component stages, occurring in an approximate time sequence. The functions of communication may most readily be described for each of these stages separately. First, communication to the learner may have the function of *gaining and controlling his attention*. Next, the *stimuli for learning* are to be *informed of the required performance* he will be expected to exhibit after learner in *recalling previously learned capabilities*. Now the stage is set for the essential act of learning, but in achieving this, one must often make provision for communication which accomplishes the *guidance of learning*. Once the new capability has been initially attained, communication may *provide feedback* or confirmation of the learning. Finally, if the newly learned entity is to be broadly useful, provision must be made to *promote the transfer of learning*. The following paragraphs briefly describe how each of these parts of the instructional process may be influenced by communication.

Gaining and Controlling Attention

The idea that the learner must attend to relevant stimuli in the learning environment comes from an accumulation of instructional experience as well as from modern evidence about the functioning of the brain. Whatever stimulus objects are to form a part of the learning event, whether they be actual objects, pictures, symbols, or words, they must have an initial *registration* effect in order for learning to occur. Essentially this means that they must be perceived, or coded, in some way that makes it possible for them to mediate the neural events necessary for learning. As a simple example, a word such a *flower*, when occurring in a printed communication, must in the usual instance of learning be registered as the referenced concept "flower," and not as merely a printed word.

The young and undisciplined leaner must acquire a whole set of habits of attention in order to begin the process of learning. Original stimuli for the arousal of attention, which function also in the establishment of these basic attentional habits, are known to be such things as intense stimuli (loud sounds or bright flashes, for example); repeated stimuli, rapidly changing stimulation (movement or other forms of change); or objects which are associated with certain basic needs such as hunger and sex. As is well known, these same stimuli are widely employed as attention-gainers in advertising, in this case largely with mature and disciplined learners, whose attentional habits to certain products have become extinguished because these stimuli are encountered so frequently in the absence of need. Under these circumstances, the basic attention-getters are used again and again in great variety to re-establish the desired attentional habits for intervals long enough for the advertisement, or a portion of it, to be perceived and its "message" to be learned.

For these two classes of learners (those whose attentional habits are not yet established, and those whose attention has been extinguished), communication must take a particular form in order to arouse attention. It needs to be loud, varied, repeated, and perhaps associated with prepotent drives. For the young child, the state of arousal which leads to the establishment of attentional habits may take the form of relatively intense visual or auditory stimulation, supplied by a teacher of parent, or rapid movement and change as contained, for example, in a motion picture or television presentation. Actually, this kind of attention-getting communication may take many forms, too numerous to catalog here. In any case, the intention of such communication is to establish habits of attention which are eventually to be controlled by much less intense stimuli. Accordingly, when this purpose is being pursued, the intensiveness of the stimuli needs to be progressively reduced, in order that attention will be more readily controlled for purposes of subsequent learning.

For the student who has acquired basic attentional habits related to the kind of stimuli normally encountered in school, there is, of course, no need to resort to communications having this markedly intensive character. Similarly, the disciplined adult learner whose need for learning is unambiguous, presents no requirement for communication of the intensive sort. Attention can readily be aroused in such learners by brief verbal directions such as "Now notice ... ," or "Look at the diagram ...," or by symbols (arrows, etc.), or signals (beeps, etc.) which sometimes serve the same function in such media as motion pictures or recorded presentations. Under these circumstances, the maintenance of attention can generally be insured so long as the relation of the material to his wants or purposes is evident to the learner. Making this relationship clear to the learner is, to be sure, an important function of communication, which will be further discussed in a later section.

Presenting the Stimuli for Learning

An important component of the external conditions for learning consists in the stimuli or stimulus objects towards which the behaviour, once acquired, is to be directed. In some instances, the use of physical objects as stimuli is quite essential, as is the case when motor skills are being learned. One would not expect to learn how to adjust a microscope without actually including the microscope as a part of the learning situation, and the same is true for driving an automobile, tying a shoelace, playing tennis, and many other varieties of motor skill. There are also instances of learning in which the use of physical objects, while not essential, may be highly desirable. For this reason, many of the concepts of physics are best learned in the physics laboratory, and of biology in the biology laboratory. Basic concepts may turn out to be inadequate if they are learned without direct practice involving the class of objects to which they refer.

Ordinarily, one does not think of the learner's interaction with relevant physical objects as falling into the category of communication. Yet, conditions of learning that include physical objects are on a continuum with those that include pictures or demonstrations, and the latter may usually be classes as instances of communication. Provided the learner has acquired suitable attentional habits, as well as requisite picture-observing habits, the activity of observing demonstrations or pictures of demonstrations may be a highly effective substitute for reactions to real objects. For example, a well-designed demonstration (live or in motion pictures) of Archimedes' principle, or of the concept of a lever, may be quite as effective a condition of learning as requiring the student to manipulate objects directly, provided the student has had certain other kinds of prerequisite experiences.

An important function of communication, then, may be to substitute for reality in representing concrete stimulus objects or events of the sort that are the direct objects of the behaviour being learned. This function of presenting the stimulus, it may be noted, is only a single step in the set of external events that is necessary to bring about learning. Yet, the existence of communication media which can represent and provide a substitute for the real thing enormously extends the range of possibilities for learning. Many concepts of earth strata and rock formation can be learned via the communication of pictures; architectural features that characterize buildings in remote parts of the earth can be identified and classified by means of pictures. It would be of little use to attempt to multiply these few examples to emphasize a generalization that obviously applies to virtually every field of study. Learning is extended to great limits by the use of pictures as media of communication even when one considers these as performing the restricted function of presenting stimuli.

Similar considerations apply to moving pictures, quite irrespective of the system used to display them (movies, television, etc.). Moving pictures are important means for communicating stimuli that embody motion, as in the case of the operation of engines, the movement of water, or the behaviour of animals. As is well known, they can also marvellously extend the range of possible events to be communicated, as in the speeded-up display of plant growth, the motion of planets, or the representation of historical events.

The function of presenting the stimulus is also performed by communication which is verbal, using words and sentences. This is probably the most widely used method. The learner is presented with a sentence describing cell division, rather than with a picture or with the actual cells. The conditions of family life in colonial days are described rather than being pictured, and of source cannot be observed directly. The concept of potential energy is defined in sentences and equations, rather than being demonstrated or pictured. The verbal means of communicating the stimulus for learning is relatively easy to use, and has virtually no limits at all with respect to what kinds of stimuli can be displayed.

It may be noted that there are many media by means of which verbal communications may be presented. The human being in the person of an instructor or teacher comes first to mind, and in this case the representation of the stimulus is usually presented orally to the student in a direct, face-to-face manner. The same kind of stimulus presentation, virtually undiminished in effectiveness so far as this restricted function is concerned, may be carried out by speech recordings. In printed or written form, an even wider variety of media may provide the learner with symbolic representations of the stimulus. These includes the teacher's writing, printed pages of books or papers, and various forms of filmed or electronic displays of words and sentences.

The sophisticated learner has little difficulty in learning concepts and principles, in any content field, under learning conditions that include verbal representations of stimuli. But the inexperienced learner may have serious difficulty. This is because the experienced learner is well aware that words are *merely* representations of reality; that it is the referents of the words which are the true stimuli, not the words themselves. The inexperienced learner may not have acquired this basic strategy, and therefore may fall into the trap of learning mere words or word-sequences. The capability he acquires becomes that of a verbal chain, rather than a principle. He learns to give an answer to a verbal question, and is not able to respond correctly when confronted with reality. This is surely one important reason why pictures have advantages over words as representations of stimuli; they are less likely to lead the unsophisticated learner astray. This fact should probably not be used, however, as an argument against attempting to teach the unskilled learner to acquire the capability of responding properly to verbal presentations in learning.

Informing the Learner of the Required Performance

Another function performed by communication within a learning situation is informing the learner of what he will be able to be do once he has learned. If a student is to learn a motor chain for printing an E, he is first shown a printed E. If he is to learn to concept of *cell nucleus,* he is first shown examples of the class of objects which are called cell nuclei.

It appears that the procedure of giving the learner information about the expected performance (which he will be able to do after learning) may not be followed consistently in typical school learning. To the extent that this is so, a probably important function of communication is being neglected.

Suppose the learners confronted with a passage in a textbook reading as follows: "The kinetic energy of a body moving with speed v can be determined by calculating the work done in accelerating the body from rest to speed v. Since work W = Fs, we can show by newton's second law, $F = ma$, that $W = mas$, or $W = \frac{1}{2}mv^2$. That is, the work done in accelerating the body is equal to the change in its kinetic energy, or $E_k = \frac{1}{2}mv^2$. It is evident that this communication, by itself, does not inform the learner of what he is expected to learn. Several different requirements are possible, including: (1) stating that work done in accelerating a body is or is not equal to the change in its kinetic energy; (2) calculating the change in kinetic energy of a body, given the mass and velocity associated with the change; (3) demonstrating that the change in kinetic energy of a body is equal to the work done on the body.

In view of the fact that each of these possibilities requires the learning of a somewhat different set of principles, it is not difficult to understand the need for telling the learner which of the performances, or what combinations of them, he is expected to acquire. In practice, this kind of communication may have been given to the student at the beginning of a course, or in the early pages of a textbooks, so that it does not have to be repeated in connection with each new stimulus presentation. Too frequently, however, this kind of information is not systematically included as a part of the learning situation.

Recalling Previously Learned Capabilities

Arousing attention, presenting the relevant stimuli, and informing the learner about his expected performance, are all early events in the process of instruction. But there is still another communication function which may sometimes precede these in time. This is the stimulation of recall of capabilities that have been previously learned, and which are essential components of the new learning about to occur. Learning a concept, for example, requires the recall of discrimination which differentiate positive and negative instances of the class of objects conceptualized; learning the concept of a rectangle involves recall of the discrimination of inequality of lengths of sides. Similarly, learning a principle take place under conditions in which the learner recalls previously learned concepts or simpler principles. Before the learning occurs, communication may be necessary to arouse the recall of these previously learned entities.

Suppose the young child is learning about number qualities, specifically, that he is expected to learn that the quantity called eight is formed when a single member is added to the quantity (or set), seven. (Note that the kind of learning being described here is not merely that of acquiring the verbal chain "seven and one is eight.") To learn this principle, he must be able to recall four major things he has previously learned: (a) the quantity seven; (b) the single unit or member; (c) the operation of "add to"; and (d) the verbal response "eight." These things seem rather trivial to us as adults, but it must be remembered that this is kindergarten child. The teacher may use communication to stimulate recall, by means or an orally presented sequence such as the following; "Here we have a set of objects whose number is seven. You remember what seven is? Suppose we add a member to this set. What do we do when we add? How do we add a single member to this set?" This is part of the instructing is almost entirely concerned with the recall of relevant concepts that have previously been learned by the students. All of this precedes the statement which, together with the displayed objects, constitutes the stimulus presentation itself: "When we do this, we have a new set, which is called *eight.*"

Obviously, any of several media of communication may be used to perform this function of stimulating recall. In the example given, the oral communication of a teacher is combined with the display of a group of small objects. But it appears that these tasks could be done with the use of recorded message or a sound motion picture.

Guidance of Learning

At some point in an instructional sequence, communication may be employed to guide learning. Typically, verbal statements or questions are presented which determine the direction of the learner's internal intellectual processes, although there are occasions when pictures or symbols may perform this function equally well or better. The effect of such communication is to permit the learner to arrive at the new principle without wasting his time considering possibilities which are wrong in extreme degree.

The function of guidance is perhaps most strikingly illustrated under conditions in which the learner is expected to arrive at a new principle by problem solving. For example, in one of Katon's studies the learners were asked to learn to perform a card trick. The correct performance of the trick results in alternate red and black cards being placed in order on the table, when successive cards from the top of the deck are dealt alternately to the table and to the bottom of the deck. The principle being learned is one which makes possible the arranging of the deck so that this result will be achieved. In this study, a blackboard demonstration, the known and unknown ones being represented by question marks. Instructions were given which led the learners to examine each of these questions in a systematic order, until they discovered for themselves the principle involved in arranging the cards. The experiments showed that subjects instructed in this way retained the capability of performing the card trick, and variations of it, much better than did subjects who memorized the order or the cards.

The amount of guidance provided by instructions can obviously be varied within a wide range. When little is given, instruction is said to emphasize discovery . At the other end of the spectrum, the principle to be learned may be stated verbally, thus providing a maximum amount of guidance. Such a method of didactic instruction is one which is often used (most textbooks are written that way), and is usually one of the most rapid methods of learning for the experienced learner. Methods with intermediate amounts of learning guidance, called guided discovery, have been shown in some studies to yield better retention of learned principles.

Providing Feedback

The learner often needs a kind of communication that provides him with feedback, or confirmation that he has managed to acquire the new capability. If he is acquiring the concept of *gas* as a state of matter, he may need to be told the correctness of his identification of the bubbles arising out of a boiling liquid as a gas. If he is learning a principle relating potential energy to mass and velocity, he may need to be told the correctness of his identification of the amount of potential energy possessed by a specific body in a specific situation. Feedback has the effect of preventing the retention of incorrectly the learned acts. More importantly, in the view of many students of the learning process, it provides reinforcement, and thus tends to perpetuate what is learned.

Although, there are undoubtedly instances in which pictorial media could be used to some advantage for purposes of providing feedback, this communication function is typically conducted by verbal means, either printed or oral. One of the most important varieties of feedback communication is that which occurs during instructional periods that are dynamic in the sense that the feedback is graded and selected according to the degree or quality of correctness of the student's response. Intercharges between the individual student and the teacher are likely to have this characteristic, and such a quality of instruction is often aimed for in the seminar or free-discussion group. In dynamic instruction of this sort, the student's attempts at problem solving can be subjected to many gradations of feedback, and in this manner his newly conceived ideas can be refined and sharpened in a highly selective and individual manner. It seems unlikely that the personal interaction involved in this form of instruction can ever be fully supplanted by any combination of mechanical communication media. Most experienced teachers are highly cognizant of the peculiar value of this form of instruction. Such an evaluation, however, need not blind one to the fact that there is a great deal of necessary instruction which does not need to be of the dynamic sort.

Promoting Transfer of Learning

A final function of communication to be described is the promotion of transfer of learning from the immediate instructional situation to new tasks of learning both inside and outside of the school situation. Learned capabilities are useful to the individual to the extent that they can be generalized in their application to subsequent learning or to the performance of a variety of practical tasks.

In serving this function, communication takes the form of providing a variety of examples, or a variety of opportunities for application of newly acquired knowledge. A principle such as that of proportional representation in legislative bodies, for instance, may need to be demonstrated by the student in a number of specific examples pertaining to nations, states, and local governments, in order to insure its generalizability to subsequent learning or to the activities of a citizen. Most often, such additional instances are provided by verbal descriptions made by a teacher or textbook. Again, other media can perhaps be of value, but hardly of unique importance in the presentation of this kind of instruction.

It appears that oratory communication are of little value in "instruction for transfer." The student may be made aware of the necessity for generalizing the newly learned capabilities, but is unable to do so simply as a result of urging. General communications of the sort "Keep this in mind always," or "Be careful" have never been demonstrated to be effective in generating transfer to new situations. Practice in application to a variety of specific examples appears at least to constitute a long step in the proper direction.

Summary of Communication Functions

The preceding analysis is designed to make the major point that the relation of communication to the accomplishment of learning is by no means a single-faceted affair. *Communication has a number of different functions in the instructional situation.* The range from the attention-arousing function which occurs immediately preceding the actual learning event to the promotion of transfer which follows the event by a shorter a longer period of time.

Following this function-by function analysis, it will perhaps be useful to attempt a synthesis of an entire instructional sequence, in order to show how the particular kinds of communication fit together in some reasonable manner. The instructional sequence shown in Table I elaborates on a shorter example, previously employed, regarding the principle relating work to kinetic energy. With some rearrangement of the verbally presented material, it has been possible to illustrate all of the separate function of communication previously discussed.

Table 1 : Functions of Communication in an Instructional Sequence on a Principle Relating Kinetic Energy and Work.

Function	*Communication*
Controlling attention	Look at the formula below.
Informing the learner of required performance	Since work is a change in energy, the question is how work can be expressed in terms of kinetic energy, as follows: $E_K = 1/2MV_2$
Recalling previously learned capabilities	Remember that the kinetic energy of a body moving with speed V can be found by calculating the *work* done in accelerating the body from rest to speed V. Remember that work (W) = F_s
Guidance of learning	How can an expression containing the variables F and s be related to one containing F and V?
Recalling previously learned capabilities	By Newton's second law, $F = ma$
Presenting the stimulus	$W = F_s$ W = mas $W = 1/2MV^2$
Providing feedback	Thus, work is related to kinetic energy, or $E_k = 1/2\ MV^2$
Promoting transfer of learning	What is the work done in accelerating a body from a state of rest to a speed of 128 cm/sec?

It may be noted that a considerable portion of the total communication in this example is concerned with preparation for the learning act (controlling attention, recalling previously learned principles) and that a fairly substantial amount pertains to events subsequent to the learning itself (feedback, promotion of transfer). This leaves a relatively small portion of the total message to deal with presentation of the essential stimulus and the guidance of learning. Insofar as this division of function is concerned, this is probably a quite typical instance.

Certain kinds of communication of the sort identified in the table might be omitted for the experienced learner. For example, it might not be necessary to gain attention in such an obvious fashion. Direct reminders of what has been learned previously might not have to be given. In addition, guidance of learning might be omitted or at least reduced to the barest hint. The table suggests merely that these kinds of communication are necessary for *some* learners. When they are used, each is performing a different function in the instructional situation.

Media of Communication

Some implications of this analysis of the function of communication for learning may now be drawn. Of particular significance, perhaps, are the conclusions suggested regarding the important problem of choosing communication media for instruction.

Matching Media and Instructional Purposes

For a number of years, investigators of the uses and effectiveness of communication media in instruction have pursued certain research question vigorously. One of these has been the question: which medium, or combination of media, is best for teaching mathematics? or chemistry? or history? It is well known that these investigations have generally not yielded consistent findings. Sometimes motion pictures have been found to be advantageous as compared, say, to a lecture, and sometimes not. Sometimes recorded speech has been found to be effective for learning, as compared with a live teacher, and sometimes not. The answers obtained do not seem to be any more consistent with one kind of subject matter than with another.

The implication of the present analysis is clearly that dependable answers to the question of matching particular subject matter with particular media are unlikely to be obtained except in highly specialized instances. There are two reasons for this. This first is that a number of functions of communications in learning might be equally well performed by *any* medium. For example, it is difficult to think of a reason why stimulus presentation which requires verbal statement could be performed with differential effectiveness by a teacher's written statement on a blackboard, by a printed statement in a textbook, or by a printed statement projected on a television screen. Similarly, on what basis could one suppose an advantage for the oral reminder of a teacher, versus the pictorial reminder of a projected film sequence, in stimulating recall of previously learned concepts?

The second reason why matching subject matter and media seems an infeasible task resides in the fact be ill-adapted for a second and different function within the same instructional sequence. For example, in a lesson concerned with mechanical advantage, pictures may be well suited for the function of recalling to the learner previously learned concepts concerning the length of lever arms, but quite ineffective in presenting the stimulus and guiding learning for the principle $F_1 \times d_1 = F_2 \times d_2$. Thus, any advantage which accrues in learning from the performance of the first function pictorially may well be cancelled by a disadvantage of using pictures to perform the second function.

Highly similarly considerations would seem to apply to the related attempt to seek an answer to the question of matching media and learners. Generally speaking, the idea that "some people learn better from pictures" has by no means received any marked amount of confirmation from studies carried out over a period of years. Again, the possibility suggested by the present analysis is that while some communication *functions* may be better performed by particularly media for particular kinds of learners, other functions within a single instructional sequence may not be. For example, a highly verbal learner may be able to translate a picture into a verbal statement of the stimulus situation quite readily, whereas an individual of low verbal ability may not. Quite the reverse may be true, however, if the function to be performed by the picture is the recall of previously learned concepts. Thus, a consistent answer to the question of who learns best from pictures, where learning refers to a total sequence of instruction, may be unreasonable to expect.

Analysis of Functions for Media

The suggested route to the continued search for a match between communication media and effective learning is through a process of analysis of the sort previously described. In making such an analysis, several steps are necessary, which may be described as follows:

First, it is essential to determine what kind of capability is to be learned. Is it a verbal chain? a motor chain? a concept? a principle? a strategy? The characteristics of these learned entities have been briefly described in an earlier section, and more fully elsewhere.

Second, the requirements that each type of learning imposes on the process of instruction need to be described. Concept learning, for example, requires the recall of a different type of previously acquired capability than does principle learning. Practice means something quite different in verbal chain learning and in concept learning. A more extensive treatment of these points may be found in Gagne.

Third, the functions which can or should be performed by communication within the instructional situation must be differentiated, in the manner previously described, an exemplified in Table 1. An extensive discussion of this procedure and its relation to the choice of media is contained in a report by Briggs, Campeau, Gagne, and May.

Fourth, an instruction sequence incorporating these communication functions may be designed, identifying the medium or media which are best suited to perform each of these functions.

Finally, if a choice of a single medium is to be made, or a combination of media, this may be done by selecting the ones which can serve as vehicles for the various communication functions without having conflicting effects on the instruction to be undertaken.

The most general statement of the point of view presented here is that selection of media for instruction is a matter which has no single rationale, and can expect to have none, insofar as a match between medium and subject matter is concerned, or for that matter between medium and individual ability of the student. The basis of such matching needs to be sought in an elaboration and empirical testing of classes of communication functions, several or all of which are involved in every unitary instructional sequence, regardless of subject matter. On the basis of an analysis of such functions, decision can be made regarding the medium or combination of media most likely to accomplish the total purpose of instruction.

References

Berlyne, D.E. *Structure and Direction in Thinking.* New York: Wiley 1965.

Briggs, L.J., P.L. Campeau, R.M. Gagne, and M.A. May, *Instructional Media: A Procedure for the Design of Multi-Media Instruction, a Critical Review of Research and Suggestions for Future Research.* Palo Alto: American Institutes for Research, 1965.

Brown, R. and C. Fraser. The acquistion of syntax, in C.N. Cofer and B.S. Musgrave, eds., *Verbal Behaviour and Learning.* New York: McGraw-Hill, 1963, pp. 158-196.

Burner, J. S. The act of discovery. *Harvard Educational Review,* 1961, 31, 21-32.

Gagne, R.M. *The Conditions of Learning.* New York: Holt, Rinehart & Winston, 1965. (a)

—. The learning of concepts. *School Review,* 1965, 73, 187-196. (b)

—. The learning of principles, in H. Klausmeier, ed., *Conceptual Learning,* New York: Academic Press, 1966, pp. 81-95. (a)

—. Varieties of learning and the concept of discovery, in E. Keislar and L. M. Shulman, eds., *Learning by Discovery.* chicago: Rand McNally. 1966. (b)

—. Instruction and the conditions of learning, in L. Siegel, ed., *Contemporary Theories of Instruction.* San Francisco: Springer, 1967.

Gagne, R. M. and L.T. Brown. Some factors in the programming of conceptual learning. *Journal of Experimental psychology,* 1961 , 62 313-321.

Hoban, C. F. Jr. and E. B. Van Ormer. *Instructional Film Research* 1918-1950. Port Washington, New York: U.S. Naval Training Device Center, 1950 (Tech. Rep. SDC 269-7-19).

James, W. *Talks to Teachers.* New York: Norton, 1958.

Joncich, G. M. *Psychology and the Science of Education. Selected Writings of Edward L. Thorn-dike.* New York: Teachers College, Columbia University, 1962 .

Katona, G. *Organizing and Memorizing.* New York: columbia University Press, 1940.

Lindsley, D. B. Psychophysiology and motivation, in M. R. Jones, ed., *Nebraska Symposium on Motivation, 1957.* Lincoln: University of Nebraska Press, 1957, pp. 44-105.

Lumsdaine, A. A. and M. A. May. Mass communication and educational media. *Annual Review of Psychology,* 1965, 16, 475-534.

May, M. A. and A. A. Lumsdaine. *Learning from Films*. New Haven: Yale University Press, 1958.

National Research Council, Advisory Board on Education. *Psychological Research in Education. Washington* D. C.: the Council, 1958 (Publication 643).

Suppes, P. Plug-in instruction. *Saturday Review,* July 23, 1966, 25-30.

Wittrock, M. The learning by discovery hypothesis, in E. Keislar and L. M. Shulman, eds., *Learning by Discovery*. Chicago: Randd McNally, 1966.

2

Educational Philosophies and Communications

Our purpose here is to explore some of the implications of educational philosophy as they might relate to educational communications. This, of course, assumes that there *are* implications, and it would perhaps be advisable to begin by pointing out what the implications are *not*. It is not assumed that educational philosophy is to be applied to education communications to the enhancement of either philosophy or communications. To imply this would be to make the same mistake that is so often made when considering the implications of the newer and currently popular field of psychology; namely, that there are rules and principles that can be derived from psychology and applied to communication processes to that the process will work more effectively. If there are such rules and principles, they are indeed few and far too fallible to apply with assurance of uniform success across the tremendous spectrum and complexity of differences encountered in the real-life, day-to-day conduct of educational tasks. Rather, the implications of psychology and philosophy for education communications derive from their methods. The teacher can benefit by judicious borrowing from the methods of these disciplines as he makes his many decision in conducting his professional enterprises He makes, of course, view his problems and decisions through the eyes of the artist, as well as though those of the sociologist, the psychologist and the philosopher.

Henry Johnstone, in his excellent book, *Philosophy and Argument* has pointed out a distinction between science and philosophy which is particularly pertinent. Vastly oversimplified, it is that philosophy depends on rational criticism, internal logic, and consistency, whereas science depends on empirical proof and verifiability of predictions. One comes very quickly to the realization that science raises far more questions than it answers. In fact, an exceedingly larger proportion of the decisions that must be made in controlling any communications act must, if they are made on the basis of established scientific principles, go so far beyond the data available as to make the process seem ludicrous. Yet, this is not to imply that only when all else fails should the communications worker rely on philosophy. Rather, it underscores the utility of philosophy as a starting point—as, in fact the alternative to wild extrapolation from scientific data or to mindless improvisation based on incoherent impulses.

Perhaps, the choice delineated in the preceding paragraph is too harsh. What does one when he is confronted with a welter of opposing possibilities as to how to shoot a scene in a motion picture? or which camera position to use at a particular point in a television show? or what sequence of pictures to use in a filmstrip? or any of the myriad larger or smaller problems he faces? Clearly, since he cannot always or *even usually* call up a scientific principle to test the answer, he relies on his general ability as a communicator. And what is the source of this common-sense ability? It is a combination of intelligence and artistry based on a accumulation of ideas and convictions derived from his training and experience as a communicator. These ideas and convictions are shared, to a greater or lesser extent, with his colleagues; perhaps the extent to which they diverge is a measure of his creativity, if not of his naivete.

Could it be said that all teachers use philosophy whether they realize it or not? Probably so, if logic, consistency, and rigorous thinking are the hallmarks of philosophy. There are other necessary conditions, however. Have the basic assumptions, on which the solution of the communication problem depends, been subjected to critical examination? Is there an unproved but essential element at the heart of one or more of the assumptions? This is vital, since assumptions are often remarkably unobtrusive and elusive. It may often be the case that the best among many ill-supported solutions depends upon a number of assumptions that are difficult or impossible to validate; and it is necessary to identify these assumptions and make them explicit. In a like manner, the educational communicator must be precise and consistent in his definition and use of basic terminology and concepts—a task made more difficult by the fact that he works in a field where words fail. (The failure of words is a major justification for pictorial communication.)

One final word on the relative uses of science and philosophy for the educational communication worker. It could be said that the study of philosophy; social sciences basic to communication such as sociology, psychology, and speech; and the study of educational communications themselves, can logically be thought of as a hierarchy of disciplines. The continuum starts with philosophy which is concerned with ultimate or final causes or solutions, whereas sociology, psychology, and those elsewhere and predictions relative to practice. At the same time that philosophy that has greater generalizability and , some would say, intrinsic worth, communication as a field of study has greater practical and instrumental value in achieving the aims of mankind.

It is assumed that for the most part, the teacher performs his professional functions in concert with other people concerned with education rather than in isolation. He may be part of a group effort to prepare the communication media for some instructional or educational purpose, in which case he will find it to his advantage to be able to conceptualize the philosophical position and methods of his colleagues. To be able to do so, and to be able to work most effectively as a professional. No less importance may be attached to the uses of philosophy and philosophic method in situations where the media specialist assist others in the selection of media appropriate for particular purposes with particular groups of learners. Here, he functions, is essence, as a critic among critics of media, and it behooves him to have a clear understanding of the philosophic bases from which his colleagues are operating as they reject one medium or approach and accept alternative media and approaches.

Philosophy of education is concerned primarily with three questions: the nature of existence or being; the nature of knowledge or truth; and the question of value. The individual's beliefs in these three domains, whether the beliefs be verbalized or conceptualized, or whether they be tacit or assumed, ought to determine or at least influence his conceptions of education and the way in which he approaches and solves educational communication problems. The equivocation in the preceding sentence recognizes the unpleasant fact that in all too many cases the educator's actions and those of the communication specialists are consistent with a philosophical position that he would (and often does) roundly condemn and reject when he hears it stated. Be this as it may, the questions of being, knowledge and value have a deep and overriding significance for everyone involved in education.

Concepts of Communication and Reality

A basic question of reality is whether there is any reality at all apart from the physical senses of mankind. Do things exist in and of themselves, or do they exist only in relation to a human being who senses them and perhaps learns from them? If things exist in and of themselves in fixed and inalterable patterns, then it would be entirely appropriate for educators to express the aims of education in terms of enduring varieties, and it would be equally appropriate for the educational media produced to assist the learner to learn about these varieties and to recognize their immutable character.

A somewhat more pervasive notion is that the relations between things may change the very nature of the things themselves. If such in the case, change in the relationships that exist among things cannot fail to rob reality of its independent character. If, on the other hand, changes in relationships among things are viewed a independent and unchanging. In this conception of reality, individuals may be conceived of as the basic elements of all social phenomena.

The relevance of these opposing views to education and, therefore, to educational communication is related to, among other things, the content of education and, therefore, the content of communication. If reality exists beyond the power of modification due to changed interrelationships, then there must be facts, customs, and information that should somehow be taught or communicated. The problem, once these realities are acknowledged, is simply how they may be identified and communicated. The criterion of validity of the content of a given communication will have to be the extent of its conformity to reality. If, on the other hand, the nature of reality depends on interrelations among its various aspects (and the learner must, of course, be included among these aspects), then the validity of the content of education will depend, in large part, on the nature of the learners and their reaction to it. The referent for the educational communicator here is either reality itself or the perception of reality on the part of the receivers of the communication.

The sense of the preceding paragraph is set at a given point in time. But time goes on, and things change. Or do they? Is it that we are only now beginning to see more clearly the true nature of things—a nature that has been in existence throughout time and has only been awaiting our discovery? Or is it that things really have changed as our perception of them—our relationships to them—have changed? the fact of change is obvious. It can be seen in the seasons, the growth of living things and, over the eons, in the evolution of species. But it can be argued that all of these changes occur in accordance with cycles which are, themselves, stable. Education and learning presuppose change. If change requires new concepts of the nature of things, then education and communication media must be directed toward the exploitation of change. The processes of change and growth are, themselves, the goals, and nothing is more important than additional growth. The media specialist in such a system will not look forward to producing the epic; he will know there are no epics in the universal sense. There are only epics that individuals produce, and these are epics only to themselves.

More generally stated the opposing views of the nature of reality thus far expounded may mean this: Those who hold the view that change itself proves that the nature of reality depends on the knowledge of human must also believe that novelty and change are genuine. The value of a given communications medium is measured to a large extent by the degree to which it impels the learner toward creative activity of some kind. The products of this creativity are viewed as reality itself and, therefore, as having inherent, primary value. They are not viewed as discoveries or reasonable facsimilies of pre-existing reality but rather as essential parts of the real world. On the country, those who hold that reality *does* exist, and has existed unchanged throughout eternity, may confront their learners with challenges to solve problems, but they do so with the solution already in mind. The process whereby the right solutions are found in important because reality is not necessarily revealed to the inept or the unperceiving, but the *right* solution is waiting, always ready to be discovered.

The Nature of Learners and Communication

While the preceding paragraphs have obliquely referred to the nature of the human beings who are the receivers of the professional products of the educational communication worker, they have been more fully directed at questions relative to the nature of the world in which we live and communicate with one another. It might appear that in paying special attention to the nature of human beings we are departing from the philosophical field and encroaching on that of psychology of education. To a certain extent this is true, for, although there are no points of conflict here, it is intended that philosophers should go beyond the scientific description of the nature of mankind. All too frequently, educational psychologists appear to take the view that if a force or characteristics cannot be measured it must not be real. Such concepts as the soul, the will, and the mind should not be sacrificed simply because they are not neatly measurable (or measurable at all).

What is it to be human? One point of view is that there is an entity in human nature which, while it has the capability of learning and of relating itself to the environment in the time and space in which it finds itself, nevertheless remains relatively constant and unchanging. In this view, although the human being is constantly buffeted by changes of all sorts being possessed of a constant entity in itself, it is free to make choice among these changes relative to a predetermined and immutable good. The opposing point of view denies the constancy of the nature of the human being; rather, it holds that man is by nature but one component in a field of forces which is forever shifting and changing. As the field changes, so must the nature of human existence change, and, as a result, the constancy that can be attributed to human nature is proportional to, or rather a function of, the totality of the ever-changing environment.

A concomitant of the first view is the notion that the human being can be thought of as consisting of two separate and distinct parts: the mind and the body. Mental processes are paramount in this case because it is they that control activity. Therefore, the focal point of educational activities is the mind, and the educational or communications worker's major concern with the body is that it not interfere with the mind. Obviously, this view is hospitable to the possibility that mind and body may work at cross purposes. This is neatly avoided by the opposing theory which holds that mind and body are one rather than a duality. In this view, everything can ultimately be reduced to a concept of mind. The structure of the mind can be determined by analyzing it in terms of its elements. The entirety is the sum of the parts and their interconnections; therefore, learning consist in assembling the parts in proper sequence and in proper relationships among each other. Obviously, this view would be encouraging to those who are interested in advancing programmed learning, be it linear or branching, although this philosophical point of view is far from sufficient grounds for a complete justification of programmed learning.

The Nature of Knowledge— The Content of Communication

Points of view concerning the nature of knowledge have obvious implications for defining the curriculum which, in turn, have major implications for the materials and systems of educational communications. One basic question is whether the subject matter in the curriculum *is* knowledge which is independent of the "processing " of the learner as he works, or whether it becomes knowledge as it is used by the learner in solving problems or engaging in learning activities. If the former represents the truth of the matter, then a curriculum that is relatively stable can be set up in advance, and the major questions have to do with the ordering of knowledge. Such a procedure would be inconsistent with the view of subject-matter a data and information to be transformed into knowledge by the learner, through use. In this case, the problem or the inquiry is basic, and problems and interests are so heavily dependent upon the course of events and on the vagaries of chance that it is folly to specify far in advance what the curriculum should be. Perhaps this is a slight overstatement, since the relativist view would permit drawing up a list of areas of learning which, from past experience, could be considered as strong possibilities for inclusion. (The adversary of the realist point of view who nevertheless desires the security of predetermined scope and sequence in the curriculum can "cheat" a little by arranging the environment so that certain problems *will* come up and certain interests will emerge.) Beyond these general probability areas and those areas which can be "managed" into the environment, the day-to-day content of the curriculum will be determined by what problems come up. Subject matter will be selected which bears on these problems, and it will be learned as it is adapted to the solutions of the unique problems at hand.

In reality, there are three major viewpoints regarding knowledge. One is that one cannot ever know reality except in terms of one's sensory and mental reactions to it. Knowledge is found in the consistency of one's *constructs* of reality. This is the point of view illustrated in the second part of the previous paragraph. It holds that what is true is theoretically different for each person. The wise man seeks consistency between his ideas and those of others, and he is perhaps comforted when he finds it; but in the final analysis, reality and truth are what he, and he alone sees.

An alternative and opposed point of view is that reality is "knowable" and, although it may be "seen through a mirror, darkly" at a given point in time, human intelligence is ultimately capable of knowing reality. Truth may be defined as correspondence between the knowable and the known. (The former is immutable; the latter capable of error or incompleteness.) The curriculum ought to be based upon and selected from what is known.

Dewey's pragmatism largely ignores the two opposing views just stated; they are considered to be irrelevant. Knowledge is a by-product of successful adaptations to the environment. More precisely, knowledge is generated by problem solving and adaptation to (reconstruction of) the environment. It is indeed in the curriculum, but not as an end in itself, rather as a sort of data bank upon which the learner can draw for future inquiry.

Philosophy and Educational Objectives

In the previous section, it was pointed out that, in one philosophical viewpoint, the problem of curriculum making consists of the ordering of the known. As a matter of fact, of no less importance to teachers are questions of value, which are central in all matters of education and are dealt with in all systems of philosophy.

Major philosophic theories concerning values—what is good or worthwhile—can be divided into two fairly clear-cut points of view. The first of these holds that values are intrinsic. Whether an entity is valuable does not depend upon the use to which it is put, but rather is related to the entity. This is not to say that some things may not be valuable because they are instrumental in achieving or maintaining other values; rather it is to say that when intrinsic an instrumental values appear, the former take precedence. The nature of man is basic, and the objectives of education properly relate to the fulfillment of man's intrinsic and enduring potentialities. Self realization is the highest aim, and all other objectives of education ultimately take their direction and their validity from it.

An alternative view regards values subjectively rather than objectively. This view ascribes value to personal feelings *about* value; that is, that is valuable which is *believed* to be valuable. When entities appear to have values in competition with each other, that value is accepted that best promotes the purpose currently at hand. Therefore, there are no *intrinsically* enduring values because purposes change as times and conditions change. The aims or objectives of education cannot be set up for any significant period in advance, and there cannot be established a hierarchy of aims which will be equally valid for all times and for all occasions. While education and the advancement of education itself may be an ultimate aim or value, the immediate objectives of education are constantly emerging from the learning situation and from life.

Obviously, the latter view gives sanction to a form of teaching in which improvisation plays a central role. Such plans as are made in advance must be of an ad hoc nature, and, as such, subject to the availability of such resources as may be at hand for their fulfillment. This is because, if value depends on use and interest, learners can be expected really to study only that in which they are interested or that which they perceive as leading to result that they find intrinsically attractive. These desires and perceptions are influenced by social factors, of course; otherwise, complete chaos would result.

On the other hand, the conception of values as intrinsic and objective can be used to give sanction to the inclusion of and maintenance of subjects in the curriculum at considerable cost in motivation. An ultimate resort to force may be required, or, less distasteful but no less worthy, to a shift in focus from the motive to learn to the motive to achieve extrinsic rewards such as prizes or the approval of teacher or parents.

Clearly, the kind of instructional materials prepared to be consistent with the first view would, paradoxically, be relatively devoid of such motivational gimmicks as protagonists, story lines, etc., because they would be used in situations where the learner was self-motivated. The learners uses materials only as instruments or data to achieve ends that he himself desires to achieve.

In the latter case, materials of instruction would appropriately include a powerful dose of motivational content. The kernel of truth that constitutes the intrinsic value may be better, so it had better be sugar-coated!

By the same token, the view that holds values and aims to be objective and immutable includes a logical hierarchy into which the various kinds of values can be placed. Lowest in the hierarchy are those values that arise from the mindless satisfaction of desires and appetites. Next are those values rationally chosen for the result that they have achieved throughout the past and those that they may be predicted to achieve in the future. The highest values are values are those that do not depend upon results which themselves are considered good at any given time and place; these are intrinsic values, and their higher place is justified in terms of their stability, durability, inclusivity, and creativity.

Implicit in the hierarchy of values just elucidated is the notion that is best which is least materialistic. The more the value is concerned with form, the greater the value. By extension, the more abstract i.e., independent of matter, the greater the value. There is perceived a connection between somatic faculties and matter on the one hand, and between rational faculties and form or abstraction on the other. This consideration explains much about the academic pecking order—philosophy, logic, mathematics, physics, and so forth down to applied art, shop, and vocational subjects. It also explains the derogation of the pictorial and graphic and the exaltation of the verbal and linguistic. The principle of proceeding, in communication and education, from the concrete to the abstract is, however, entirely consistent with this philosophy, and it is this and the temporal deficiencies of verbal and symbolic language that forms one primary justification for audio-visual materials.

Some Application: The Curriculum

Two main streams of philosophical thought can be discerned in what has been presented up to this point. The first has been summarized by wild in terms of three theses of *realist* philosophy.

The Metaphysical Thesis : The universe is made up of real, substantial entities, existing in themselves and ordered to one another by extramental relations. These entities and relations really exist whether they are known or not. To be is not the same as to be known. We ourselves and other entities actually exist, independent of our opinions and desires. This may be called the thesis of independence.

The Epistemological Thesis : These real entities and relations can be known, in part, by the human mind as they are in themselves. Experience shows us that all cognition is intentional or rational in character. Every concept is *of* something; every judgment *about* something. The realist holds that this is a peculiar relation by which the knowing act becomes united with, in a non-material sense, or directly identified with, something really existent. The mind does not become physically one with its object. To know an explosion is not to explode. Nevertheless, cognition is not merely a matter of containing states within one's self. To have gray cells inside the cortex is not to know this fact. To know something is to become *rationally* identified with an existent entity as it is. This is the thesis of direct realism.

The Ethical Thesis : Such knowledge, especially that which deals with human nature, can provide us with immutable and trusthworthy principles for the guidance of individual and social action. All men share certain common traits which determine vague tendencies in every child. These tendencies must be realized together in an orderly way if human life is to be really fulfilled. In subhuman entities, such tendencies are determinate, inflexible, and realized automatically with the sole support of external natural agencies.

In man, this is not the case. He has not been endowed with an exhaustive array of inflexible instincts which automatically propel him to proper acts. Instead, he has been given very flexible tendencies together with the power of cognition by which he may rationally understand his needs and freely determine his conduct in accordance therewith. The invariable, universal pattern of action, individual as well as social, required for the completion of human nature is called *the moral law or natural law.* By self-observation, every individual has some minimal knowledge of it. By disciplined study of human nature and the events of history, the knowledge may be increased and clarified. Such knowledge is the only trustworthy guide for human action.

The opposing point of view which Butler calls the *idealist* philosophy is summarized in his interesting book, *Four philosophies and Their Practice in Education and Religion.*

The Idealist Metaphysics : The self is the prime reality of individual experience. Ultimate reality *is* a self. Ultimate may be one self, a community of selves, or a Universal Self within whom are many individual selves.

Idealist Epistemology : Idealism holds that the qualities we perceive in the world are rooted in existence. Either we have direct experience of the self i.e., that it is a self-evident fact, or the existence of the self is a necessary inference. Selfhood being what it is , and the surrounding world being to well tuned to the experience of self, it is believed by idealists that reality is a

Self. Since nothing can be conceived to exist without being in relation to other things, reality is a logically unified, total system—a Universal Mind.

Idealist Ethics : The values human beings enjoy and desire fundamentally are rooted in existence. The values of human life are what they are largely because there are individual persons to possess and enjoy them. One important was, in which individual persons can realize value is by actively relating parts and whole.

The curriculum of the common school is conceived of as being a function of aims or objectives, subject matter related to the achievement of these objectives, the materials and methods whereby the subject matter may be mediated with relation to the learner, the characteristics of the learners themselves (broadly speaking), and the concepts and principles that govern learning. Clearly, how one views each of these factors, and the relative importance one attaches to each, is at least partly (some would say mainly) determined by one's philosophical position. And the media specialist is required to work in an implicit or explicit framework of philosophical positions whether he is in a position to plan, produce, and control the utilization of media according to his own philosophical predispositions or whether, as is more likely the case, he is required to plan and influence their utilization more or less "on order" according to the philosophical predispositions of others—school authorities, individual teachers, etc.

Aims and Objectives

The realist position is that aims are fixed and relatively immutable. The idealist holds that aims would be flexible and subject to continual modification. The idealist believes that aims should emerge from individual and group experience; the realist considers such a source to be temporary and vacillating, and prefers the security of external aims which come from outside and above experience. Regarding the relationship of aims to other considerations in curriculum making, the realist gives first and highest place to aims. State the aims, then find the means of achieving them. The idealist would shuttle back and forth between aims and the other factor related in curriculum building because he would consider it impossible to establish aims intelligently unless the means of and constraints on achieving them are taken into consideration.

A closely related question is that of the authority to establish aims. The realist would be disposed to establish a hierarchy of authority. The communications specialist would likely find himself placed in the upper reaches of such a hierarchy, but distinctly below the top. The idealist would tend to give nearly equal voice in goal setting to students, teachers and administrators. Idealists tend to emphasize the importance of children's present interests and capacities, and are therefore threatened by ultimate aims, however well stated and well justified, because such aims are likely to be remote in time and to lack psychological intimacy. Such remoteness would make them seem unreal and unattractive to children; such aims would be largely devoid of motivating power. Better it is, goes the idealist point of view, to accept the more wavering and less valid aims that take into account the interest and capacities of children on the grounds that these will be accepted by the children and will consequently be more likely to result in growth. Present growth, the position goes on, is the best guarantee of future growth.

If the teacher or communications specialist looks wistfully at the realist position. It is understandable. He might prefer the stability of well-defined aims that are presumed to be relatively constant over time. Planning will be greatly simplified and operations can be more clearly routinized. His place in the planning structure is definite and assured. If, on the other hand, he views planning as the most exciting part of his work—if he thrives on encounters with the unexpected and enjoys improvization more than preplanned execution—he will be far happier if his colleagues are idealists. In this latter case, he will find himself on numerous committees, usually as a resource person interacting with supervisors, teachers, and students. He will find himself covering familiar territory time and time again as different groups identify for themselves the proximate aims of education and seek to devise some of the means to achieve them. He will have to learn to live with the fact that the individuals and groups decide about aims may be "old stuff" to some, but brand new to others. He will have to share in the enthusiasm of their "discoveries" and to avoid stealing these discoveries from them by telling them too much too soon. And he will have to be willing to let them make mistakes.

The teacher or communications specialist who objects to a work environment dominated by realist philosophy, it may appear, trades the tyranny of an established hierarchy with commensurate division of authority for the tyranny of the democratic process. Paradoxically, some may consider it the greater freedom to be permitted to work within a clearly established and well-defined set of external aims or goals than to be required continually to construct and reconstruct aims and goals in response to every real or perceived change in the human condition. Witness the school child who asked his teacher plaintively, "Do we have to do what we want to again today?"

Subject Matter or Content

Obviously, the teacher or anyone connected with instructional communications cannot plan media in isolation from message or content; therefore, it behooves him to understand the ground rules that are invoked in determining what content goes into the curriculum and what stays out.

It should be no surprise that conceptions of what the curriculum should be can be related to the philosophical position previously described. Taking the surface view, one could say that the process of education has two basic ingredients; something to be learned and someone to learn it. But this is the surface view. Is there really a discontinuity here between the learner and what is to be learned? or it is more logical to presume an essential continuity between the learner and the curriculum?

What has been called the realist philosophical position accepts the dualism posited in the preceding paragraph. The learner is viewed as the particular, the changeable, the temporal, while the curriculum is viewed as the general, the universal, the stable, the timeless. The learner is, therefore, in the final analysis, adapted to the curriculum, not the other way around. To be sure, what is known about the characteristics of learners plays a part in determining the sequence of the curriculum, but so also does the inherent logic of subject matter.

The alternative to this view of the curriculum could be termed "*learner centred.*" This view rejects the notion of curriculum "imposed from outside" in favour of one in which the content of the curriculum is the content of the experience of the race— which differs in degree rather than in kind from the experience of the child. As Brubacher puts it:

> The child's experience and his studies in school are but the initial and terminal aspects of a single reality or process— education, life. The one flows into the other, is continuous with it. It is one of the functions of method to discover the steps which intervene between the child's present experiences and their richer maturity in the social heritage. The curriculum is the social stuff out of which the self realizes itself. To think of these two as opposed to each other would produce the unnatural result of putting the nature and destiny of the child at war with each other.

There may have been a time, perhaps even in the memory of the older generation, when, by diligent effort sustained throughout the childhood years, adolescence, and early adulthood, one could hope to master at least the rudiments of all of the major disciplines. If this happy state did once pertain, it is new long gone. The so-called knowledge explosion grinds out new information at such a prodigious rate that true scholars complain of the difficulties of "keeping up with" their narrow speciality *within* their academic discipline or professional field. The advocates of the learner-centered curriculum may have the solution to the dilemma of what portions of this expotentially expanding volume of information should be included in the curriculum. They take their cues from child experience. Each new problem or situation calls for a selection of subject matter from a variety of fields. There data rechecked as relevant or irrelevant, and the problem is solved. To the extent that today's problem or experience has features or aspects in common with tomorrow's, there will be something to transfer and to apply; but the new problem is expected to have new features and these new features will demand a new synthesis of data from various fields and will result in a new integration of knowledge.

This solution to the curriculum problem has two major weaknesses. First, it calls for a kind of broad and flexible planning that is prepared for a wide variety of contingencies. The process of the child or group must inevitably be chancy if not downright idiosyncratic. The technique of planning only in terms of large units of work that require a long time to finish in reality begs the question, for if the curriculum is really an extension of the child's experience, the teacher must be everyday to drop everything and seize upon a contingent opportunity in the interests of exploiting its learning potential. Such a curriculum is likely to appear fragmentary, discontinuous, and unrelated. It lends itself to repetition and to overlap over the span of time. Experience begets experience, and teacher-pupil planning can all too easily result in children working on a unit on the Indians of the Southwest again and again—a development that may or may not bring the invigorating breeze of fresh challenges to their minds and spirits.

A secondly weakness of the learner-centered curriculum is that it is extraordinarily susceptible to corruption by the inept or the lazy teacher. If goals are subjective, who is there to challenge the goals that the class has ostensibly set for itself? If Miss Jones' fifth-grade seems to find its experience leading it to a compelling interest in Latin America, just as did each of its predecessors down the dusty corridors of twenty-seven years of time, who is there to say that the fact that Miss Jones has had the materials and organization for such unit pretty well in hand for the past twenty-seven years has had any influence?

The alternative notion of the curriculum, of course, calls for an ordered sequence of content selected for its inherent worth. Selected by whom? By those who have the authority? or by those to whom authority is delegated? This could be the local curriculum committee, the state department of education, the committee on Undergraduate Programs in Mathematics, or the or the American Society of Biological Science. The selections in such cases are likely to give only passing attention to the learner's viewpoint. The obvious difficulty is that learning may become sterile and so removed from real life that the enduring values attributed to the subject matter may not only be lost but actually replaced by anti-values and rejection.

The problem of the overcrowded curriculum which has been exacerbated by the knowledge explosion can, in this view of curriculum making, be ameliorated if not actually solved by invoking the slogan often trumpeted by communications specialists; namely, "more learning in less time." While it is clear that improved means and techniques of educational communication can indeed pack more into the curriculum, it is entirely possible that there are finite limits to communications efficiency, and , worse yet, that the efforts of the communications experts may result in teaching more effectively much of that which should not have been taught at all. In such a case, the errors of the now generally discredited survey courses are perpetuated. An approach that is clearly more promising and, at the same time, is consistent with realist philosophy is that of focusing on the structure of disciplines and on their methods. Thus, a problem may be viewed by the learner successively through the eyes of an economist, a geographer, an historian, and a social psychologist. Presumably, the result is that he attains, in part, the immutable essences of these disciplines.

The methods of the communications specialist differ in terms of the philosophical viewpoints that dominate the process of building and implementing the curriculum in his educational environment. Clearly, the learner-centered curriculum does not easily tolerate neat schedules of film use and single or double screenings of television programs. To consider April's schedule in October is laughable. Rich resources of materials within easy reach of the learner are required. This means classroom and building libraries, equipment in every room, and free access to both by teachers and students. Textbooks give way to individualized learning materials unless the books can be adapted to those ends. Production of materials is likewise decentralized. Teachers and students make their own learning materials—full of flaws and imperfections, but nevertheless, *their own*. Rarely is it worthwhile to expend sizeable sums for "slick" productions or for filmed series, regardless of how well made and how closely integrated. Television is used more as a medium for children to learn how to use knowledge and less as a source of organized knowledge. The children engage in such activities as broadcasting their own version of the news—whatever the content.

The communications worker in a system dominated by realist philosophy is more concerned with the right material in the right place at the right time, with the latter factor being considerably more negotiable than the first two. He emphasizes quality of materials and media, confident that the investment will prove worthwhile. He is greatly concerned with field-testing materials because he can predict that the film or textbook that produces the best results in the test situation will be applied in reasonably similar situations over time and thus indicate its selection. He views television principally as a device whereby excellent teaching and learning experience can be economically distributed. If he establishes building or room libraries, it is largely for reasons of economy; it is cheaper to have them near the scene of use than to transport them. Local production is viewed as a means whereby the supply of commercial material can be supplemented by those peculiarly adapted to bringing the immutable values of some sections of the curriculum to this particular school group in response to its individual needs.

Methods of Teaching

The communications specialist is likely to be concerned with method in a way which is intimately related to his concern with the curriculum, viewed as content. He will have to advise on the production, selection, and use of materials differently, depending upon the school situation in which he finds himself; the differences in these situations spring from the dominating philosophy of the school.

It is consistent with the realist view that aims are objective, external, and immutable—and that the curriculum consists of content which has inherent value and is to be learned, hopefully, with interest, but in any case, to be learned—that the method of teaching that prevails be characterized by benevolent authoritarianism. More accurately, perhaps, it should be said that an emphasis is placed on adult authority, not because of any desire to usurp the learner's freedom, but rather to establish it as an end, rather than as a means, of education. Efforts *will* be made to interest the learner, to motivate him to learn, to adapt method and, to some extent, content, to the relevant characteristics of individual learners, to pace instruction within the capabilities of learners, and so on. Ultimately, however, the children must learn, and the effective teacher adapts his methods so that this valuable insight is gained by all. Those who are unreachable by other means may be punished or, as a last resort, removed from the learning situation.

The learner-centered curriculum and the monastic theory of educational value calls for a different approach to method. In this view, the curriculum is stated in terms of child nature, and method is determined by conceptions of learner activity. Problems arising from the experience of the learner or learners establish the structure of "lesson." Beginning with problems perceived by the learners, the method of instruction is, in reality, the method of inquiry. The teacher encourages learners to seek answers to their own problems. He is tolerant of trail-and-error activities and interferes with student activities wit reluctance and only then to protect the learner from the more unfortunate consequences of his problem-solving activities. Since the problems *belong* to the learners, motivation and interest can be assumed. Interest will be the parent of effort, which in turn will be disciplined by the inherent difficulties of the problem." Punishment is therefore rare or non-existent. When it occurs, it is administered only for its educative value.

The communications specialist working in the situation governed by realist philosophy will find that the most appropriate materials are those that are well adapted to group use. They are largely didactic in nature and approach. If they do not include devices for motivating the learner, it is because the teacher conceives this as reducing his position of authority. The internal structure of the materials conforms to logical sequence based upon the structure of the materials conforms logical sequence based upon the structure of the subject matter being presented. "Discovery materials" are included, but they are in a somewhat separate category of use from the primarily conceptual material. By the same token, materials primarily for the development and reinforcement of attitudes are frankly emotional, ranging from the performances of great artist in music, drama, and literature, to contrived narratives designed to instill attitudes conducive to safely, health, and morality.

By contrast, the communications specialist working in a learner-centered school environment must provide must provide materials that lend themselves well to individual and small-group use. They are generally fragmentary in nature. Film clips, picture sets, realia, trade books, and the like are emphasized. While materials presenting outstanding performances of great artists are available, they are used primarily for individual enjoyment and individual analysis and study. There are relatively few 'well-organized' and structured longer presentation, and it is commonplace to use only selected parts of those that are furnished. Attitudinal materials do not appear as a separate category since attitudinal learning is conceived of as an integral part of learning concepts, attitudes, and methods of inquiry.

References

Broady, Harry, *Building a Philosophy of Education.* Englewood Cliffs, N. J.; Prentice-Hall, 1954.

Brubacher, John. *Modern Philosophies of Education,* New York: McGraw-Hill, 1950.

Johnstone, Henry. *Philosophy' and Argument.* University Park: Pennsylvania State University Press, 1959.

Modern Philosophies and Education. National Society for the Study of Education, 54th yearbook, Part I. University of Chicago Press, 1955.

Education for the Professions. National Society of the Study of Education, 61st Yearbook. University of Chicago Press, 1962.

3

A Learning-Systems Concept as Applied to Courses in Education and Training

Introduction

The term "system" has many applications and is often used to refer to such things as a telephone system, payroll system, transportation system, school system, etc. During and after World War II, researchers developed a special meaning for the term system which concerned man-machine relationships such that as a particular machine was designed, developed, and completed, the necessary training of personnel to operate and work with the particular machine was designed, developed, and completed simultaneously. A critical part in this "system" was the specification of the operational objectives or purposes of the machine, of the man or men working with the machine, and their interrelationship. It was not until after the advent of programmed instruction that this system concept could be applied to education with a meaning similar to that just described. Programmed instruction introduced the need for specifying educational objectives and the techniques for making general and ambiguous objectives more specific. Although education has been concerned with stating educational objectives for decades, these objectives were not specific and measurable. As a result, educators stated objectives, described educational activities, and then designed tests almost as three separate functions with little if any correlation between them.

In adapting the system concept to education, several differences must be noted. In industry, the end product or goal is a machine of some kind with trained people to operate and work with the machine; consequently, this system is often referred to as a man-machine system. In education, the end product, or gaol, is learning; consequently, this system is referred to as a learning system. Machines are the major emphasis throughout the man-machine system, whereas in a learning-systems concept, the importance of machines is dependent upon their contribution to the learning process. Although the man-machine system and the learning system differ in several respects, there are also similarities. In industry, quality control is built into the man-machine system to increase the effectiveness and efficiency of the developmental processes. Likewise, in education, quality control can be built into the learning system to increase its effectiveness and efficiency. In both the man-machine system and the learning system, all activities should be based on verifiable or measurable specific objectives, not on guesses, opinions, or other nebulous or ambiguous statements.

Why should educators consider the use of a learning-systems concept? What is wrong with the present educational system which has been used as an example for the whole world to follow? In order to answer such questions, let us look at our present educational system.

The Existing Educational System

Society expects educational institutions to carry out at least the following three functions:

1. prepare students in such a way that they will have an even happier and more successful life than their parents;
2. be sure that the experiences necessary for each student to achieve the first function happens by choice—not by chance;
3. develop each child to the maximum of his capabilities.

These three functions are stated in various ways in most educational institution charters or constitutions. They sound good, but their implied goals are often not achieved because those goals implied by the first function have never been specified precisely enough to allow absolute measurement. In fact, very few teachers have ever specified, in measurable terms, the terminal objectives which are the desired student behaviours at the end of a course. Various state departments of public instruction have tried to define the content of each course at each grade level in the form of guidelines for the teachers. Most of these guidelines describe activities for the teacher or for the students. Objectives that are listed are so general that the interpretation of any one objective is actually up to the individual teacher.

If teachers do not know specifically what the terminal objectives of their courses are, then how can students be tested for achievement that has not been defined? Consider the following questions:

1. Can you make a test that would *fail all of the students* in your class? (yes or no)
2. Can you make a test that would *pass of the students in* your class? (yes or no)

If you answered "yes" to both questions, then consider this question: If you can make up a test that could pass all of your students and you can also make up one that could fail all of your students, where do your find that magic something to help you select test items that will pass those who should pass and fail those who should fail? This magic something does not exist, so most teachers grade according to some kind of curve (normal or skewed) which indicates more about how a student learned in comparison to his classmates than in comparison to the objectives of the course. When grading "by the curve," a failing student in a class of smart students could be an "A" student in a class of not-so-smart students without any difference in the amount learned by the student.

If a teacher knows precisely what the student is supposed to learn, and tests are designed to measure the achievement of the specific content, then a student's grade should reflect his progress towards the course goals.

In a situation where the teacher is a "presenter of content", and the schools concentrate on moving students through the system *regardless* of learning, the system fosters "cumulative ignorance" (the cumulative effect of non-learning that inhibits subsequent learning). Cumulative ignorance is responsible for a majority of dropouts and discipline problems. Consider the following anomalies:

(*a*) Almost every tenth-grade teacher will agree that any given class of tenth-grade students will contain students with reading levels from fourth or fifth grade up to college level. Knowing this fact, teachers will give these students tenth-grade reading level materials in literature, history, geometry, biology, etc., and when some of the students are unable to comprehend what they are reading, they are failed.

(*b*) Students who go through the "fail one year, pass the next" cycle several times usually find themselves in a situation where they couldn't learn if they wanted to because they don't have the prerequisite knowledge and/or skills.

(*c*) If a "C" grade in addition and subtraction means that a student didn't learn everything he was supposed to know about addition and subtraction, then chances are that this student will get a "C" or a "D" in a multiplication and division, a "D" or an "F" in decimals and fractions, and an "F" in algebra, if the student elects to take it. Most educators would say that some students just are not capable of doing mathematics. Could the "F" in algebra be a result of "cumulative ignorance" rather than lack of innate ability?

The Learning-Systems Concept

To many professional educators, the notion of a system, approach, which has been borrowed from engineering and industry, may seem harsh and ominous in its implications for the management of instructional processes. But instructional planning in modern educational institutions cannot be conducted on a piecemeal basis without some effort toward a rational and efficient deployment of human and technical resources. Consequently, the use of the systems concept is intellectually and practically inescapable.

For the purposes of this chapter, a "Learning-Systems Concept" will be defined as follows:

(*a*) The requirements or objectives of the system will control the design of the system.

(*b*) The system will maximize learning effectiveness through procedures such that all, or almost all, of the stated objectives of the system are achieved i.e., 90 per cent of the student will learn 90 per cent of the material.

(c) The system will maximize learning efficiency by adapting the system to the learner rather than making the learner fit the system.

(d) The design and procedures of the system will reflect the educational philosophy consistent with the requirements of the system and society.

Learning can occur under almost any set of circumstances; in fact, a great deal of learning takes place without the assistance of formal instruction. Experience itself is learning. The contribution of formal instruction is to assure that the student's learning experiences will occur by choice and not by chance.

A learning-systems concept, when applied to educational or training courses, offers an opportunity to develop or redesign courses that will be significantly more effective and efficient in relation to the learning tasks and goals of students.

It is necessary to begin with two objectives that exist irrespective of course content. They are:

1. to utilize more fully available educational resources and enriched teaching techniques;
2. to develop course patterns so that students can pursue where both knowledge and the population are expanding at a ever-increasing rate. Educators must investigate ways of making our educational process more efficient and effective. Changes must be made in existing educational patterns.

The first objective is based on the following assumptions :

* Education's primary purpose is to facilitate learning by establishing an appropriate environment conducive to learning.
* In any program, it is necessary to find out where the student in on the ladder of learning and to proceed from that point without gaps or unnecessary overlap.
* Programs must be revised if it is found that learning has not taken place. Revision should be made after an examination of the learner, method, media, and environment.
* If the leaning objectives of a particular course could be definitely stated, and if all of the learners could achieve

these objectives, they would all receive an "An" or some equivalent symbol indicating 90-100 per cent achievement.

* Some learning objectives cannot be defined specifically, but can be described as a result of other specific observable and measurable behaviours.
* Grades based on undefinable objectives and temperament of the grader do not contribute to an effective and efficient educational system and should not be included as a course requirement for grading procedures.

The second objective of the learning-systems concept, as stated previously, is to develop course patterns so that students can pursue their education or training as much as possible at their own pace, on their own schedule, and at a convenient site. This objective is important because students taking educational or training courses are "individuals" with different abilities, interests, past experiences, and environmental limitations. Most educators subscribe to this concept of individuality, yet in our schools they continue to insist on uniformity in performance within scheduled slots of time and at specific locations only.

The second objective is based on these assumptions:

* As educators, we want *to help* as many students through high school and college as possible.
* Many capable ex-students would like to continue their education or training if they could proceed at their own pace. A higher percentage of students could graduate from high school, and from college, if education could be geared to individual needs.
* "Cumulative knowledge," which is best defined as a situation where a student learns 90 per cent of each unit before he can proceed to the next unit, can be self-motivating and rewarding.
* Teachers can utilize the time released from presenting information, to "individualize" and make meaningful the learning experiences of the students.

The learning-systems concept should be considered from two points of view: the development, testing, and revising of the software system which actually helps the student learn; and the design and development of the hardware system which will store, transmit, and present the software.

Learning-Systems Approach to the Development of Software

What is the student's greatest problem in a learning situation? All too often, students have to play a guessing game with teachers concerning the content of the course to be learned. If the students guess wrong, it is reflected in their grades. Most teachers probably believe that they have pointed out the learning objectives of their courses, but if the students do not perception as well. Of course, communication, in a sense, is teaching; and perception, learning.

In the process of communication, there are four levels of communication which can occur.

1. *Independent*

   This is a level of communication carried on by everyone in the form of self-communication (thinking to oneself).

2. *Physical Interdependence*

   This is a type of communication in which the communicator just needs a "warm body" to talk to. Illustrations of this level of communication were typified in recent television commercials in which man talks to his wife about his business and the wife talks about a new soap. Although both talk, neither one listens to the other.

3. *One-way*

   This is a type of communication which predominates the present educational system and is typified by the one-way lecture presentations or by most other instructional materials including books. Over the years, this one-way form of communication in education has been portrayed in cartoons by a teacher pouring knowledge from a pitcher into a student's head. With one-way communication, there is no way to know to what degree the student is attending to the message and learning, or even whether or not the student is capable of attending to the message and learning from it.

4. *Two-way*

   This is a type of communication that is typified by the tutorial approach to teaching and recent instructional approaches such as programmed learning and computer-assisted instruction.

Although all four of these levels of communication exist in education, learning which is a result of the association or interaction between teachers, of the association or interaction between teachers and students, or between instructional materials and students (fourth level), is the most effective and efficient. The major problem consists in the development of materials to be used at the third level which, through appropriate development techniques, takes on characteristics of the fourth level.

A brief review of David Berlo's communication model will be of value in laying the foundation for a learning-systems approach to the development of instructional materials. Berlo's S-M-C-R model breaks the communication process into the characteristics of four parts: the Source, the Message, the Channel, and the Receiver.

Source	*Message*	*Channel*	*Receiver*
Communication Skills	Code	Seeing	Communication Skills
Knowledge	Content	Hearing	Knowledge
Attitudes	Structure	Touching	Attitudes
Social	Elements	Tasting	Social
Cultural	Treatment	Smelling	Cultural

Fig. 3.1 : S-M-C-R *Communication Model.*

Three points should be kept in mind.

1. The most important feature of Berlo's model is that the characteristics of the Source and the Receiver are identical.
2. One of the most important assumptions of the learning-systems concept is that educators "*want* to help students progress through our educational institutions." This does not mean just to give the students good grades, it means to *help* the student learn what is appropriate and necessary.
3. In the communication process, the Receiver or learner can mentally "turn off or tune out" Source at any time much easier and faster than closing a book, hanging up the telephone, or changing a television channel.

In order to help the student learn, we must design messages that will motivate the learner to keep his communication channels open to teacher's messages. For example, if the *source* uses one language but the *Receiver* uses a different language, communication is impeded. In many schools, teachers using a sophisticated form of classroom English are teaching culturally disadvantaged students who speak and understand an entirely different form of English. The teacher must change the message to fit the students' needs. In other words, *instructional messages need to be learner-oriented.*

In presenting information, we often make the assumption that the students perceive the information in the same manner and with the same meaning that we do. This is especially true in regard to verbal information. For some reason, many of us are under the impression that words have meanings. Words *do not* have meanings. People give meanings to the symbols we refer to as words, and because each of us has had a unique combination of experiences, these meanings may be highly personal or they may be almost coincident the meanings held by other people.

Visual perception has a great deal to do with learning. It is of value, therefore, to consider the validity of what we see. In Fig. 3.2, does the line *AB* appear to be equal to the line *BC?* Measure them and you will see that they are equal.

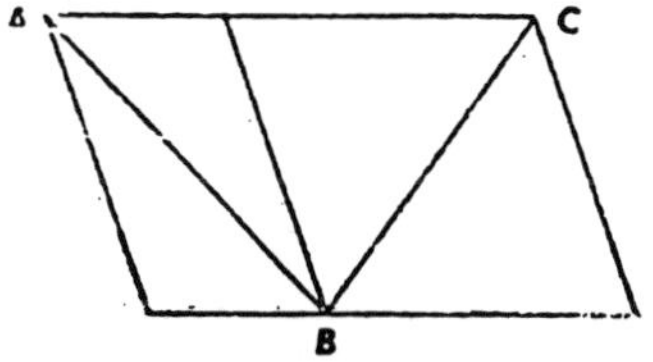

Fig. 3.2

Fig. 3.2 is disturbing to many people. The amount of disturbance appears to be in relation in relation to prior exposure to art, mechanical drawing, etc. Young children are not as bothered as are adults. In fact, some young children see nothing wrong with the picture. If you cover up one side or the other, the figure looks all right. It is the middle section that is distracting because prior experiences preclude a rationalization of the two extensions becoming three. The interpretation of information sent to the brain from the different senses are mediated by past experiences; consequently, perceptions of this information may vary from person to person. Therefore, if we are truly concerned that students perceive a specific message and have a meaning for that message that is coincident or at least similar to our own meaning, we must be willing to vary the mode of presentation until this condition occurs.

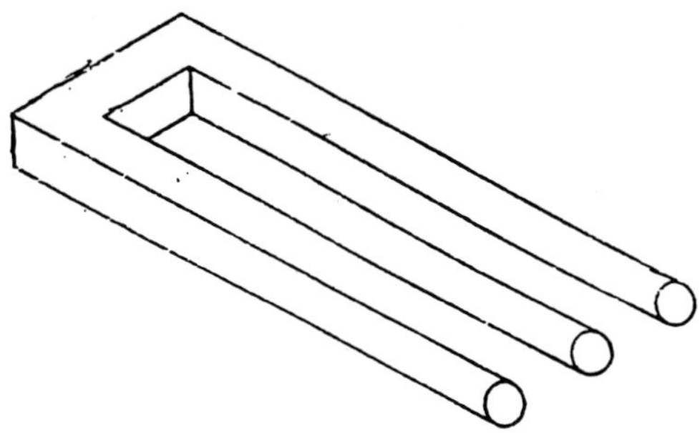

Fig. 3.3

Few people can see it right away. Some see the face only after hours of study and some never see it at all. In education, the learner is often expected to "see" a visual concept, or a situation with the same perspicacity as the teacher. If he fails to see this "something," he may not learn material that is important to his future progress. In the learning-systems concept, if the learner does not see what he should see, the stimulus is changed.

Usually, by increasing the visual clues, learning can take place, whereas initially, many would fail to achieve the objective (in this case a recognition objective).

Because of the restrictions of the printed medium, it is difficult to present actual examples concerning the problems of perception through our other four senses, but without too much trouble, examples of misperception in hearing, tasting, touching, and smelling can be demonstrated. An understanding of the communication process and how perception affects the fidelity of communication is vital to a successful use of a learning-systems approach to the development of instructional materials.

Development of a Course

The development of a course utilizing a learning systems concept includes the same steps that are followed when preparing materials for programmed instruction. A program consists of a sequence of carefully constructed items leading the student to mastery of a subject through self-study.

The change from programmed instruction to the learning-systems concept is a matter of a greater degree of sophistication. The name change is necessary because "learning systems" is more descriptive of the process involved and because the stereotype already established by those familiar with the term "programmed instruction" limits the mode of presentation to some kind of verbal format presented in a textbook form or by a teaching machine. People who are unfamiliar with the term often confuse it with computer technology. Extra steps are necessary, however, in order to apply a systems concept to the process.

Course development involves two major stages: (1) the behavioural analysis of the course content which is the preconstruction stage, and (2) the synthesis of learner of learner behaviours which is the construction stage. Learner behaviours are anything that a student does purposely in response to an appropriate stimulus and which results in observable and measurable activities; e.g., writing, speaking, performing, etc.

In the first stage, the task is to specify learner behaviour and learning objectives so that the nature of the behaviour can be discovered, past learning can be measured, behaviours to be modified can be identified, and objectives can be communicated.

The development of a typical course during this first stage follows a sequence designed to analyze and delimit the course content.

1. The first step in the analysis is the specification of the terminal behaviours (i.e., those behaviours which the course instructor wishes the learner to exhibit upon completion of a course). After each terminal behaviour (objective) is stated, the following three questions should be asked:

   (a) Why should the student learn this behaviour?

(b) What is the student supposed to do with the behaviour once he has attained it?

(c) How long should the student retain the behaviour after once attaining it?

Answers to the first two questions could affect the inclusion of the objective in the course content and answers to the third question could affect the design of the instruction materials.

2. The construction of a post-test is the next step and will enable the observer to determine whether or not the terminal behaviours can be exhibited by the learner. Usually, a slight change in the wording of the specified behaviour will result in the test item for this behaviour.
3. The third step is the specification of the assumed entry behaviours of representative learners (i.e., those behaviours pertinent to the course content that are exhibited by prospective learners of the course.
4. The fourth step is the construction of a pre-entry test that will enable the observer to determine whether or not he assumed entry behaviours can actually be exhibited by representative learners who would take the course.
5. The fifth step is the specification of learning objectives of the course content with will be achieved through learning experiences and convert the learner's entry behaviours into terminal behaviours.
6. The sixth step is the construction of a pretest that will enable the observer to determine which the learning objectives of the course content, if any, have been learned previously by representative learners.
7. The last step of the analysis is a preliminary tryout of the pre-entry test, pretest, and post-test on a sample of student that are representative of the intended learners for the course.

The tryout of the three tests is to verify the existence of assumed entry behaviours, the lack of terminal behaviours, and the lack of knowledge concerning the learning objectives which constitute the course content. Ideally, the learners would score 100 per cent on the pre-entry test and zero on the pretest and post-test. This would indicate that the entry assumptions made by the course instructor were correct

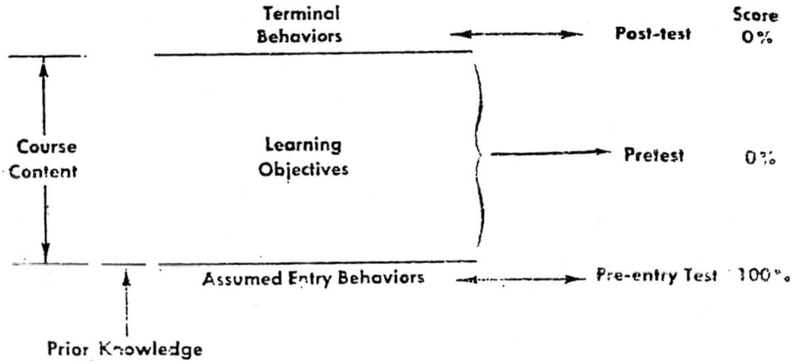

Fig. 3.4. *Ideal Assumed Entry Behaviour.*

The tryout test scores will usually vary from the ideal. If tho pre-entry test scores are less than 100 per cent, it is an indication that the course instructor's assumptions regarding student entry behaviours were overstand (see Fig. 3.5).

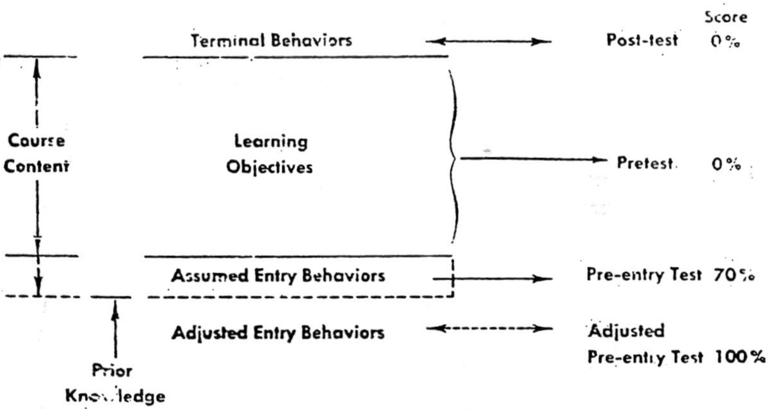

Fig. 3.5 : *Assumed Entry Behaviours—Too High.*

If one were to write programmed materials without testing for the existing entry behaviours of the intended audience, one would probably find many errors during the tryout of the complete program. Most writers would tend to expand the program by making the steps smaller and by overcueing the required responses to make up for the missing entry behaviours. Very seldom will a program developed under these circum-stances be successful; a high percentage of the dropouts will result because the steps will be too small and students working through the program will consider it very dull and an insult to their intelligence.

If the pre-entry test scores were 100 per cent the pretest scores greater than zero, it is an indication that the course instructor's assumptions regarding student entry behaviours were understated (see Fig. 3.6).

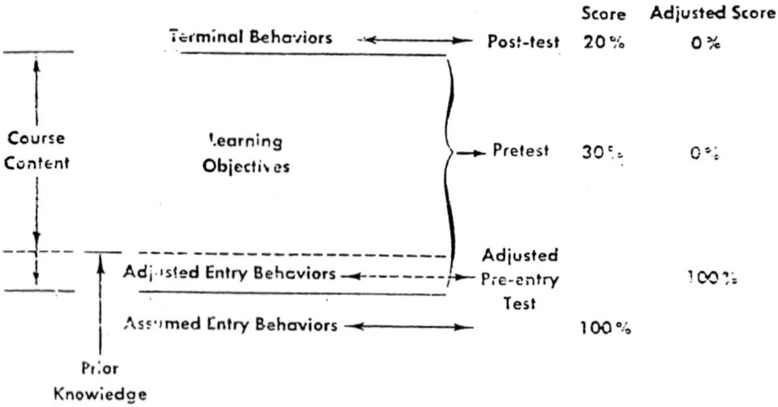

Fig. 3.6 : *Assumed Entry Behaviours—Too Low*

Programmed materials developed without testing for existing entry behaviours might enable learners to reach the terminal behaviours, but there is a built-in boredom factor which will inhibit positive growth of motivation as learning takes place during the program.

Program of this type are exemplified by situations where learners are able to score high on the post-test without going through the program. A review of the literature on research concerning programmed instruction reveals that many where the pretest data re given, indicates that students knew from 30 per cent to 75 per cent of the content of the program before even going through the program. Generally, if the program is written before the students are tested, the excess frames stay in. It is no surprising that many student make the statement about programmed instruction being boring and repetitious.

Often, when the intended audience is heterogeneous, students will be found in all three levels; above, below, and right at the assumed entry behaviours. Such data indicate the need for branching, and the same data can be used to locate and construct the appropriate branches.

This discussion has some rather obvious implications for the use of pre-entry tests and pretests in the classroom. If tests of this kind are not used, and subjective intuitive measures or traditional course limits are relied upon, the students' fund of cumulative ignorance grow because the material presented may be too far above or below them. Such a situation fosters low grades and/or potential dropouts.

In either of these two situations, overstated or understated entry assumptions, it is important to go back over the first six steps of the pre-construction stage and make appropriate adjustments in the behaviour analysis statements and the accompanying tests before going into the synthesis stage of the development of instructional materials.

The most successful programs start the learner from where he is. This gives support to a very important learning principle: *Paths of learning proceed most effectively and efficiently when from the known to the unknown.*

The analysis stage concerns the use of this principle in locating the beginning point for a course, but not necessarily the sequence during the course. The need for a specific sequence varies from subject to subject and from unit to unit within a given subject. The achievement of some learning objectives is more dependent upon prior learning than the achievement of other objectives. In determining sequence, the developers should remember that the best sequence is ultimately the one that result in the greatest progress for the learner. As a starting point, the sequence could follow tradition or an experienced instructor's best guess. To develop a sequence that will proceed from the known to the unknown, a matrix method can be used. This method becomes cumbersome with a large number of objectives. Therefore, it may be useful to perform the matrix method using units or groups of objectives when a great number of objectives are involved.

The Matrix Method for Sequencing

List the learning objectives (represented by number) across the top of a matrix and duplicate the list of numbers of down the left had side of the matrix.

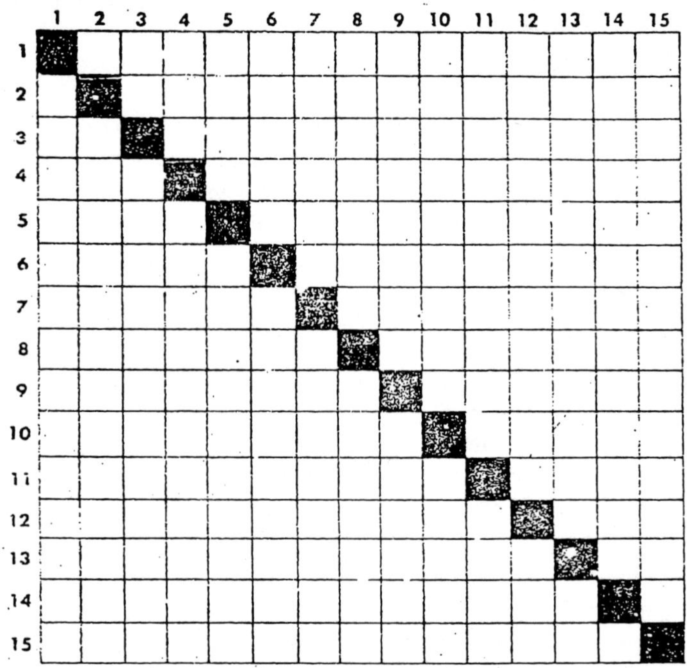

Fig. 3.7 : *Matrix Method for Sequence.*

Identify any and all relationships between the learning objectives by placing an (x) in the square representing the intersection between the objectives represented by columns and the objectives represented by rows. The diagonal from the upper left-hand corner represents the intersection, of the column and row designated by the same object number.

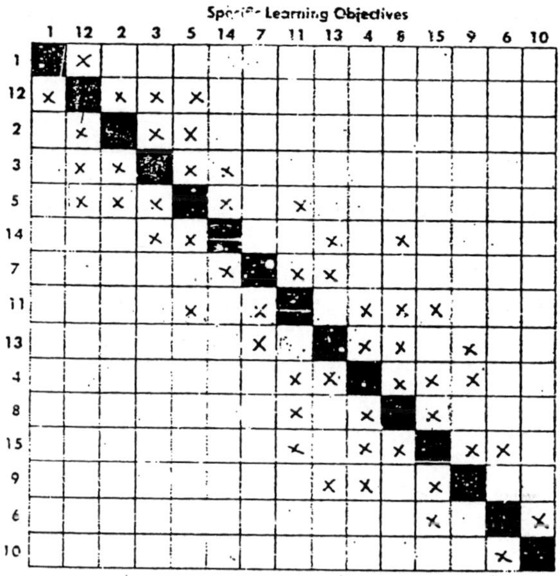

Fig. 3.8 : *Matrix Method for Sequence.*

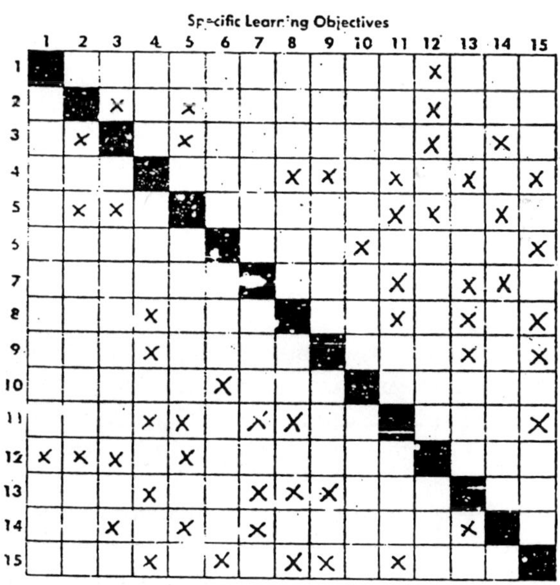

Fig. 3.9 : *Matrix Method for Sequence.*

Rearrange the vertical columns and the corresponding horizontal rows (some objective numbers; i.e., column 6 and row 6) in such a manner that the (X)'s on the matrix, indicating relationships between learning objectives, are brought closer and closer into an elliptical pattern with the matrix diagonal as the major axis. The ultimate goal of this step is to fill all the spaces adjacent to the diagonal with (X)'s. This would result in a particular sequence of objectives in which each objective would have some relationship with the previous objective and also with the subsequent objective or "the path of learning could proceed from the known objective to the unknown objective". The extra (X)'s not along the diagonal indicate relationship which can be used in testing, review, or for presenting content from a different point of view.

The second stage, the synthesis of learner behaviours, can start after all of the objectives have been defined, test constructed and tried out on representative students, and objectives sequenced. The synthesis of the course content should not be started until all necessary adjustment indicated by the result of the tryout of the tests have been made in the terminal and entry-behaviour lists and in the learning-objective list.

The first step in the synthesis or course-construction stage is the examination of the adjusted learning objectives to determine the most efficient and effective media and methods to be used in presenting the material associated with each objective, keeping in mind why that particular objective or terminal behaviour is desired, what the learner is expected to do with this behaviour, what budget is available, what the feasibility is of the media and method, how portable the course materials have to be, etc.

The second step of the construction or synthesis stage is the construction and preparation of the materials necessary to help the learner attain the learning objectives and terminal behaviours of the course, keeping in mind these four principles:

1. The content of the course is presented to the learner in small, single-concept steps or units that are appropriate to the learner's abilities, e.g., reading level, educational level, age, etc.

TERMINAL
LEVEL
GROUP
DEMONSTRATION
TRIP
ETV
FACE-TO-FACE
FILM
P.I.
AUDIO
MODELS
ENTRY
LEVEL

Fig. 3.10

2. For each step or unit, the learner is covertly or overtly involved, depending upon the behavioural requirement of that step.
3. In steps or units where the system request specific responses, immediate confirmation of the correct responses is *usually* available.
4. The course materials are self-paced to meet individual differences. This may necessitate a certain amount of branching from the main system to accommodate differences in the needs for the terminal behaviours of the course, the differences in learner abilities, or differences in entry behaviours.

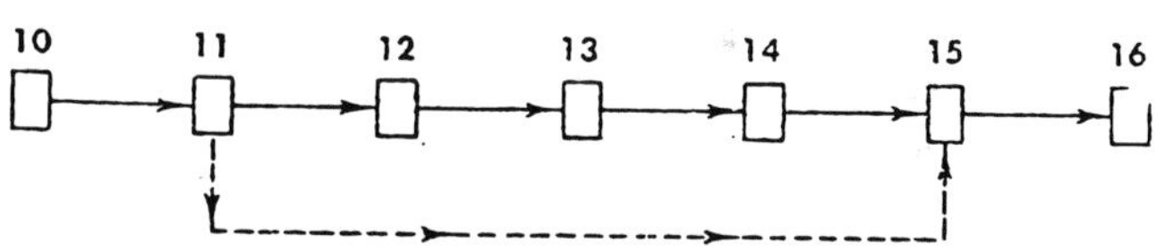

Fig.3.11 : *Modified Linear.*

The form in Fig. 3.11 allows check points from time to time, such that if a student answers frame II correctly he may be able to skip further redundancy by being advanced to frame 15. Another version of this form will send the student back to frame 11 for further review if he answers wrong on frame 15. In one case, redundancy is avoided, while in the second version, redundancy is increased.

Figure 3.11 illustrates another form that can be used in two ways. For the advanced and interested student, this form may allow him to pick up additional information relevant to the topic but not necessary for the terminal behaviours—an embellishment. For the slow student who was unable to answer frame 12 correctly, a variation of the previous frames may be used to present the particular topic or point from another viewpoint; i.e., frames *a* through *be* will be essentially the same as frames 8 through 11.

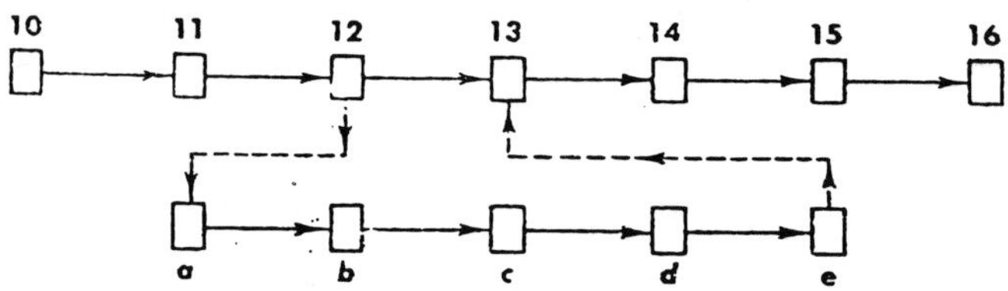

Fig. 3.12 : *Linear with Subroutines.*

For the student without some specific entry behaviours necessary to continue on with frame 13, the branch (*a to be*) could be used to teach the student the necessary material. In this instance, frame 12 acts as a testing frame or "gate keeper" to be sure the learner is capable of continuing the course successfully.

The third step is the assembly of course materials and examination of them for clarity, continuity, and subject-matter validity.

The fourth step, and one of the more important steps of the course development, consists of trying out the course materials on representative learners and revision of the materials based on learner comments and errors. This "tryout-and-revision" process is repeated enough times so that 90 per cent of the learners are able to exhibit 90 per cent of the terminal behaviours.

This last step is very important in the development of a course where materials are "learner-oriented" rather than "instructor-oriented," and will enable students to master the material to the appropriate level.

In testing out the units or total courses, the *developer* has to be especially aware of individual difference. The following learning variables should be kept in mind as being contributing factors to individual differences:

(*a*) rate of learning;
(*b*) amount to be learned;
(*c*) mode of learning;
(*d*) interpersonal relationships in learning;
(*e*) motivation to learn.

The fact that students *learn at different rates is* probably accepted by most teachers. The problem is that while most teachers agree that students learn at different rates, their teaching behaviours in the classrooms are based on techniques that require all students to learn at the same rate. If the students in a learning situation do not learn at the same rate both techniques and materials must be changed.

The *amount to be learned* varies from student to student. The amount to be learned can be identified through the use of pre-entry tests, and post-test.

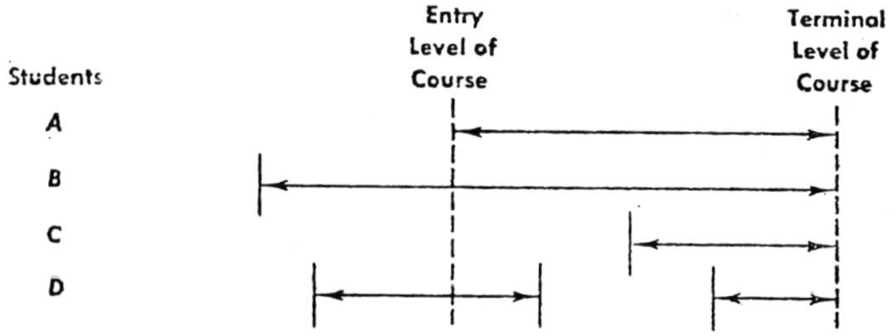

Fig. 3.13 : *Amount to be Learned.*

For example, student *A* has the right entry behaviours for the course and doesn't know any part of the course. Student *B* needs some remedial work before he can start the course. Whether or not student *B* takes his remedial work prior to the course or concurrently with the course depends upon the subject matter, the student, and the dependency of the course on the student's knowledge of prerequisite material. Student *C* knows most of the course and in most instance would be wasting his time if he were to go back through material he already knows. Student *D* is more typical of most of the students today. Even though he knows a considerable part of the material, he also needs a certain amount of remedial study. Some kind of branching is indicated in dealing with students like *C* and *D*.

Mode of learning is also an important learning variable. One's assumptions about how students learn will usually determine the teaching methods used. For the purposes of this chapter, a presentation will be considered a "simulation" of the real-life situation when the same set of related objectives can be learned from various methods of presentation in a synthetic situation or learned by chance in a real-life situation.

A better understanding of the concept of simulation will be assured by beginning with a statement of the assumptions upon which this concept is based.

(a) There is such a thing as a "life environment."
(b) There is such a thing as an "academic environment."
(c) The purpose of the academic environment is to prepare the learner for the life environment.
(d) The value of exposure to the academic environment is measured by the learner's performance in the life environment as a consequence of behaviours that have been transferred and adapted from the academic environment.

In real life, the learner's performance usually consists of perceiving certain stimuli and responsing to them appropriately. The learner's response generally is not made to one stimulus, but to patterns of stimuli. An objective of the academic environment is to present certain stimulus patterns that represents the appropriate specific experiences from which it is hoped the learner will be able to generalize when meeting real-life experiences. Transfer of learned response from the academic environment to the stimulus patterns met in life is referred to as "stimulus generalization."

Because the evaluation of the academic environment is measured by the learner's performance in life as a result of 'stimulus generalization,' it is important that the stimulus patterns in the synthetic situations of the academic environment be such that:

(a) they establish in the learner certain responses;
(b) the responses transfer positively to the real-life or operational situation; and
(c) the responses constitute the desired and appropriate reaction to the real-life stimulus patterns.

When there is a demand for transfer of learning to superficially different situations, some modes of learning which emphasize response to *patterns* of *cues* will be more effective than others emphasizing responses to *specific cues.* Learning which directs response to the total configuration of the life environment will therefore enable the student to cope with wider varieties of real-life situations, including transfer from synthetic to life environments.

The process of setting up a synthetic situation which enables the learner to learn responses, which through "stimulus generalization" are desired and appropriate in real-life situation, is called *simulation.*

As a process, simulation can be positive or negative. In the concrete-abstract continuum, positive simulation refers to the conditions wherein the synthetic situation (S_2) is *more concrete* than the real life situation (S_1). Examples of positive simulation are the three-dimensional models used in chemistry and mathematics as concrete demonstrations of abstract ideas or concepts. Negative simulation refers to the condition wherein the synthetic situation (S_2) is less concrete than the real-life situation (S_1). Examples of negative simulation are the simulated cars used in driver training, the simulated planes used in air-crew training, and the scenery in theatrical plays.

Simulation is made up of two components : physical simulation—the copying of that part of the real-life situation which is physically involved in the desired responses or behaviours of the learner; and psychological simulation—the copying of that part of the real-life situation which is psychologically necessary to obtain the desired responses or behaviours of the learner. Psychological simulation can be divided into three distinct types:

(a) the copying of that part of the physical environment of the real-life situation that is *not* physically involved in the desired responses of the learner but nevertheless does affect the learning of the desired responses. Examples of this are the use of films with, the driver-training simulators and the airplane cabins in the air-crew training simulators;

(b) the substitution of symbolic stimuli for physical realism based on stimulus generalization. Examples of this are the use of stubby wings on the flight simulators and the use of small hood on the driver-training simulator to symbolize the real thing;

(c) the use of symbolic stimuli (words and/or visuals) to retrieve from the learner's memory information concerning past experiences that will help in the setting up of a synthetic situation. An example of this is the use of directions give prior to role-playing (a form of simulation); i.e., "You are the owner of a toy manufacturing business doing three million dollars worth of business a year. You have 100 employees, etc."

Given the task of simulating a real-life situation, one may be tempted to produce a physical replica of the real-life situation, limited only by available budget and the state of the engineering art. There are kinds of behaviours and degrees of learning which may profit from a high degree of physical fidelity in the simulated environment, but other behaviours may be learned and may transfer quite adequately from synthetic situations having relatively little physical or functional realism.

Once it is recognized that there are degrees of both physical simulation and psychological simulation, practical decisions about the specifications for a synthetic environment will rest on economic and learning-objective compromises. From the standpoint of economy, the development of synthetic situation should rest on psychological simulation because as the degree of physical simulation increases, the physical environment (models, films, equipment, etc.) becomes more expensive to build and maintain. However, with low degree of physical simulation, the student will be making verbal responses and will be transferring to the real-life situation little more than identification of specifics, and perhaps, certain ways and means and means of dealing with these specifics. This is adequate only if learning such specifics is the objective.

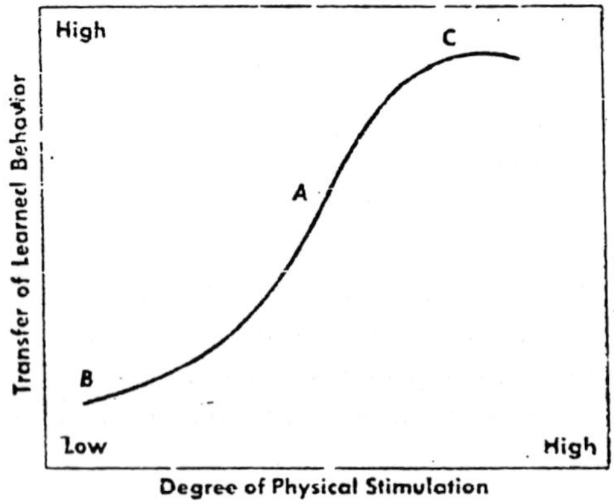

Fig. 3.14 : *Relationship between Degree of Physical Simulation and Transfer of Learned Behaviour.*

Up to a point, increased increments of transfer of learned behaviours result from increased degrees of physical simulation. Human receptor channels, like other receivers, have limitation in sensitivity. For any stimulus input, there will be ranges of physical differences in the synthetic situation which will not be matched with behavioural difference.

In setting up a synthetic situation, various instructional media and varied methods and degrees of utilization can be integrated providing flexibility in the desired simulation. It is important to remember that a particular synthetic situation (simulation) which involves a variety of instructional media should be designed in a accordance with the pre-determined learning objectives and not according to the characteristics of the instructional media. In other words, *fit the media to the objectives, not the objectives to the media.*

Figure 3.15 is, in a sense, a continuum ranging from abstract to concrete. The placement of a specific medium in a specific tier is based on the general use of the medium; the number of senses involved; whether a synthetic situation is perceived directly (or indirectly through media); whether the synthetic situation is observed, heard, or both; and whether the perception involved is a synthetic situation or a verbal description of a synthetic situation. It is relatively easy to affect the placement of a specific medium by incorporating some new features or characteristics that would relate to the criteria used for deciding placement on the diagram; e.g., adding sound to filmstrips would move the combined media to the next tier below.

Simulation in a specific synthetic situation can be evaluated for its effectiveness. *Perfect simulation* results in the performance of specified terminal behaviours in the real-life operational situations as a consequence of the transfer of learned behaviours from the synthetic situation. If some behaviours are not being performed adequately, it is an indication of a need for a greater degree of simulation.

For example, if, in the testing of learners who have taken a course or unit utilizing a specific media group or tier, it is found that only 50 per cent of the terminal behaviours are transferred to the operational situation (thus indicating 50 per cent successful simulation), then the course materials should be restructured utilizing the media represented in the next lower tier or group—increasing the degree of simulation. The testing of learners who have taken the restructured course should indicate an increased transfer of learned behaviours as a result of a greater degree of simulation which has been set up in the synthetic situation. In a similar way, if the testing for retention of learned behaviours over period of time, a decrease or loss is noted, increased simulation should be built into the course materials to increase retention.

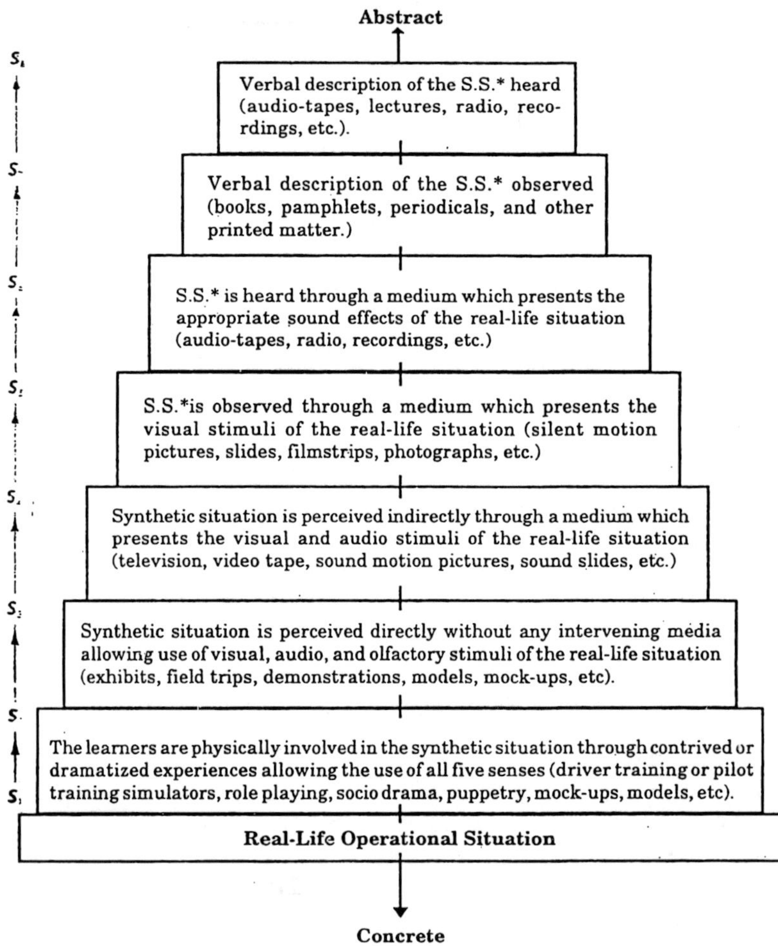

Fig. 3.15 : *Simulation through Use of Instructional Media (*Synthetic Situation)*

One of the reasons programmed instruction has been so successful is that it combines active involvement along with the verbal content. When programmed materials utilize records, films, or kits of materials, the resultant in even greater because the experiences are more concrete.

Throughout the research literature the reader is confronted with conflicting comments; i.e., students were bored—students were captivated; students learned faster through programmed instruction—students learned less; students learned better by branching programmed instruction—students learned better by linear programmed instruction; etc. Because of their varied abilities, interests, and prior experiences, some students will learn better and faster in certain subject areas through a different mode or combination of modes. The teacher should manipulate the learning environment for each student in order to facilitate learning rather than spend his time presenting the course content which limits the students to one mode of learning. This method necessitates the efficient utilization of a variety of media and materials for presenting course content: programmed instructional materials, for presenting course content; programmed instructional materials, films, slides, demonstrations, face-to-face lectures, etc. It is not an efficient use of learning time to have a student go through an hour of the stereotyped, textbook form of programmed material when the same learning objectives could be accomplished by having him read a regular textbook for ten minutes or view a five-minute demonstration; or have teacher and student lecture situation for an hour when the same learning objectives could be accomplished in fifteen minutes through independent study of programmed text.

The fourth learning variable, the *interpersonal relationship in learning*, has received increasing attention of late. Many people have been aware of this variable for years, but little, if any effort has been made to classify it as a learning variable and to take it into account in the learning situation. For instance, in a programmed instruction project, it was found that not all students like a particular programmed text; when given a choice of three programmed texts covering approximately the same content, each student was able to choose a text that he liked from which he could learn.

Why do we expect the learners to all like the same programmed text, textbook, or even the same teacher? *If our ultimate goal is learning, then whatever will facilitate learning should be a part of the system.* If a student is not learning and change in the textbook or a change in the teacher does result in learning, then why not do it?

The fifth learning variable, *motivation,* has been the topic of many conferences during the past two decades. For the purposes of this chapter, it is enough to say that, in general, educational institutions and educators are not paying enough attention to the need for motivation to stimulate learning. The concept of motivation is like the concept of individual differences almost all educators will agree that what will motivate one child will not necessarily motivate another. Yet, in the classrooms, it is continually assumed that all children are motivated in the same manner with no individual differences.

These five learning variables are not taken into account largely because the teachers are too busy presenting the content of their courses. When a teacher is presenting the content of a course:

1. the student's rate of learning is determined by the teacher's rate of presenting;
2. the amount the student learns is limited by the amount the teacher presents;
3. the mode by which the student learns is determined by the mode the teacher decides to use to present the course;
4. the interpersonal relationship between the teacher and student is restricted to the teacher that is presenting;
5. if the teacher is presenting, the teacher does not have time to worry about individual motivation.

In the typical classroom situation, the teacher is the presenter of information, and is generally the focus of attention. Courses developed in accordance with a learning-systems approach replace the teacher as the presenter of information. Learning now becomes the focus of attention, and the teacher, who has been relieved of the time-consuming task of repeatedly presenting the same information, can concentrate on the task of *teaching.* The teacher becomes an educational diagnostician, a director, or a guide to meaningful learning experiences, adapting available materials and environment to the needs of the learner.

Testing and Evaluation

Testing and evaluation are very important in the development of materials utilized in the learning-systems concept as well as for any significant improvement in learning.

In order to conserve time, energy and money, one unit that represents a good sample of the skills and knowledge to be learned from the entire course should be selected and developed first. Once the media and instructional methods which will bring about the desired transfer of learning of the specific unit have been determined and tested, the development of the balance of the course may be carried out with a minimum of restructuring.

The most difficult job in testing and evaluation is to define what is to be tested and evaluated; consequently, meaningful testing and evaluation should be based upon specific objectives measuring achievement of course content. Tests developed from non-specific or non-definable learning objectives tend to show a very low correlation between the course content and the tests. Learning objectives may be classified as shown in Fig. 3.16.

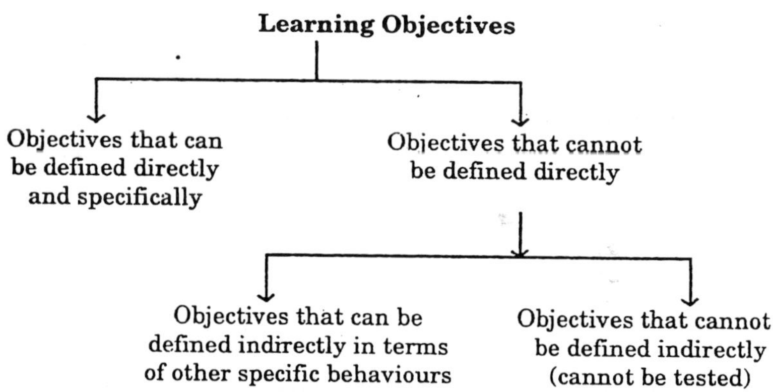

Fig. 3.16 : *Classification of Learning Objectives.*

A test made from definable objectives (directly or indirectly) may serve three purposes, depending on the point of view, without changing the test form. It may serve as:

1. a *teaching test,* to help the learner become aware of what be has already and what he may have to review;
2. a *measurement test,* to determine what the learner knows at a given time. The learner can then be placed in learning

situation which will enable him to proceed without either an unnecessary review, or a gap in his knowledge in going from the known to the unknown (pre-entry test, pretests, and placement tests);

3. a *mastery test*, to determine if the learner has achieved mastery of the specified objectives of the course content (post-test).

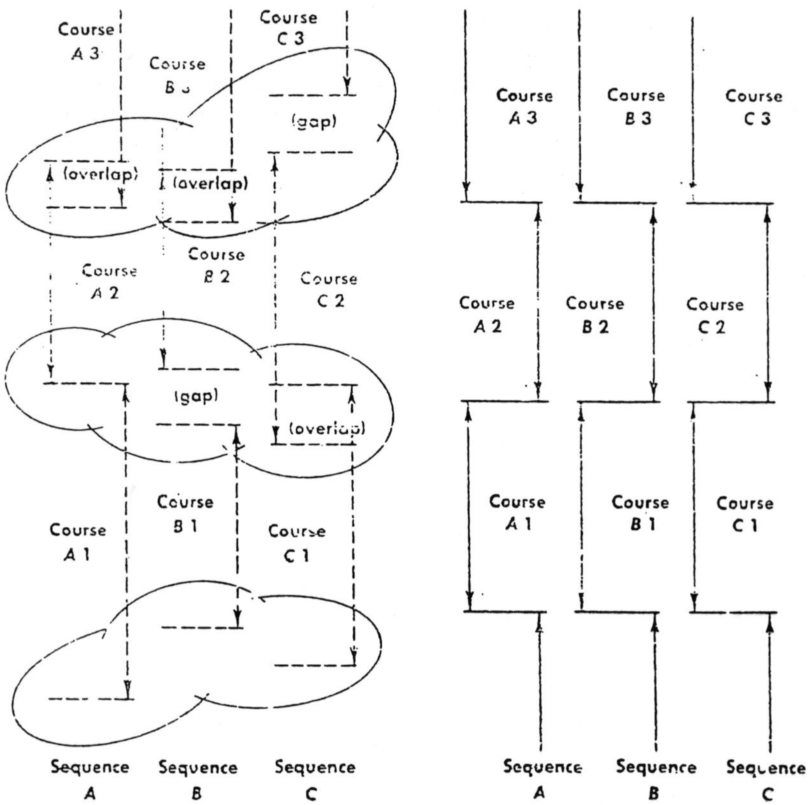

Traditional Patterns

Typified by obscure entry and terminal course behaviours permitting gaps and overlaps in a sequence of course.

Learning Systems Patterns

Typified by defined entry and terminal course behaviours such that the terminal behaviours of one course are the same as thee next course.

Fig. 3.17 : *Patterns of Course Sequences.*

It is useful to remember that the synthetic situation which has been validated by the transfer of appropriate learned behaviours to the real-life operational situation can be very effectively and efficiently used to evaluate student achievement. In almost all courses, some simulation other than at the verbal level is integrated into the course materials; e.g., films, models, artefacts, chalkboard, flanelboard, graphs, pictures, tapes, discs, and so on. If these materials are used in the teaching-learning process why not use them in the testing of learning? Verbal tests of behaviours which were learned in response to more concrete forms of simulation may not only be testing the learner's ability to correctly interpret the instructor's verbalization of the desired behaviours. The same general considerations which go into the decisions of what to include in a course also go into the decisions of what to include in an evaluation of the course.

Suggested Areas for Course Development

Several areas of education would benefit from courses that have been developed in accordance with the learning-systems concept: sequential courses having long-range goals such as those in elementary, secondary, and higher education; and non-sequential courses such as those found in continuing and adult education and in vocational-and industrial-education programs having short-range goals; e.g., learning of a psychomotor skill, gaining a finite unit of knowledge, etc.

In the area of sequential courses, it is important to point out one of the major differences between elementary, secondary, and higher education in regard to their developmental patterns. In elementary education, almost all students take the same content and follow the same pattern. In secondary education, almost all students follow one of four of five patterns. At the present time, the pattern which a student might follow in secondary education is determined to a large extent by the amount of "cumulative ignorance" acquired by a student in elementary school. One can only estimate the effects of the approach to elementary education which would enable 90 per cent or more of the student to learn 90 per cent or more the content :

1. The elementary curriculum would be completed by a high majority of students in a much shorter time.
2. Because of the decrease in learning time necessary to achieve the elementary curriculum, certain portions of the traditional secondary education curriculum would be transferred into the elementary curriculum.
3. Almost every student would enter and complete secondary education (only 71 per cent complete secondary education now).

Two approaches can be utilized in the developed of instructional materials for sequential courses. One approach is the development of a subject from its introduction to some finite level; e.g., mathematics from kindergarten to twelfth grade. This is essentially a *vertical systems analysis and development.* The second approach is the simultaneous development of all the basic subjects from their introduction to some finite level; e.g., grades one through four, or kindergarten through eighth grade. This is basically a *horizontal systems analysis and development.*

It would be most efficient to apply the systems design at the elementary level before any of the other educational levels, because almost all students follow the some curriculum patterns and there is need for interrelationships between basic subject areas. The horizontal systems analysis and development would be the best approach for a systems design at this level. It would allow the development of a continuous-progress type scale in each subject upon which a student's overall achievement profile could be recorded. The student, then, would experience a minimum of gaps and overlaps when transferring from school to school—or even from teacher to teacher. By varying the amount of time spent in each subject area in accordance with the student's needs, and by concentrating time and effort on the weak areas of the student's achievement profile, students should be able to complete eighth grade with solid background and foundation in all subject areas.

Although the required courses in secondary education provide a core of course content which lends itself to a continuation of the horizontal systems analysis and development, several curriculum patterns in secondary education would benefit more from a vertical systems analysis and development. The area of mathematics provides one good example.

Staff Requirements to Develop a Course

Course development is a complex process. As a general estimate, 25-150 man-hours of labour are required to produce on hour of instructional materials for the average learner. This estimate can vary considerably depending on such factors as the degree of competence of those involved in regard to their particular speciality and the complexity of the subject matter.

In order to develop quality courses in accordance with the learning-systems concept, the services of a number of specialists may be needed :

1. Subject-matter experts or analysts are specialists who have taught the course content and are interested in learning-system orientation and behavioural analysis. Their job is to specify the entry and terminal behaviours and the mediating learning objectives necessary. They also act as subject-matter editors for accuracy of content of the final course materials.
2. Media specialist or examiners must be acquainted with the advantages and disadvantages of various instructional media. Their task is to determine collectively the media to be utilized in the presentation of each step or unit for maximum effectiveness and efficiency, and to initiate the preparation of the necessary materials.
3. Subject-matter synthesists develop and synthesize the steps or units of the course on the basis of the behavioural analysis in the preconstruction stage. They are involved in the revision of those materials that have been tested with representative students.
4. Learning-system coordinators (behavioural technologists) must have a knowledge of a variety of media. In order to obtain the maximum benefits from utilizing the learning-systems approach in course development, their tasks are to conduct seminars; hold follow-up individual conferences; help define and analyze course content and accompanying tests as outlined in the preconstruction stage of the course development, and help in the validation of tests; make recommendations regarding the appropriate media for specified learning objectives; supervise the trial assembly of course materials; and help in the testing and revision of the completed courses.
5. Production specialists from television, radio, graphics, film, computers, etc., produce materials designed to maximize learning most effectively and efficiently from the student's point of view.

6. Publication editors edit the course materials prior to testing, after each revision, and prior to final publication for correct English, structure, continuity of format, etc.

Figure 3.18. indicates the sequence of events which might be followed in the implementation of a systems approach in education.

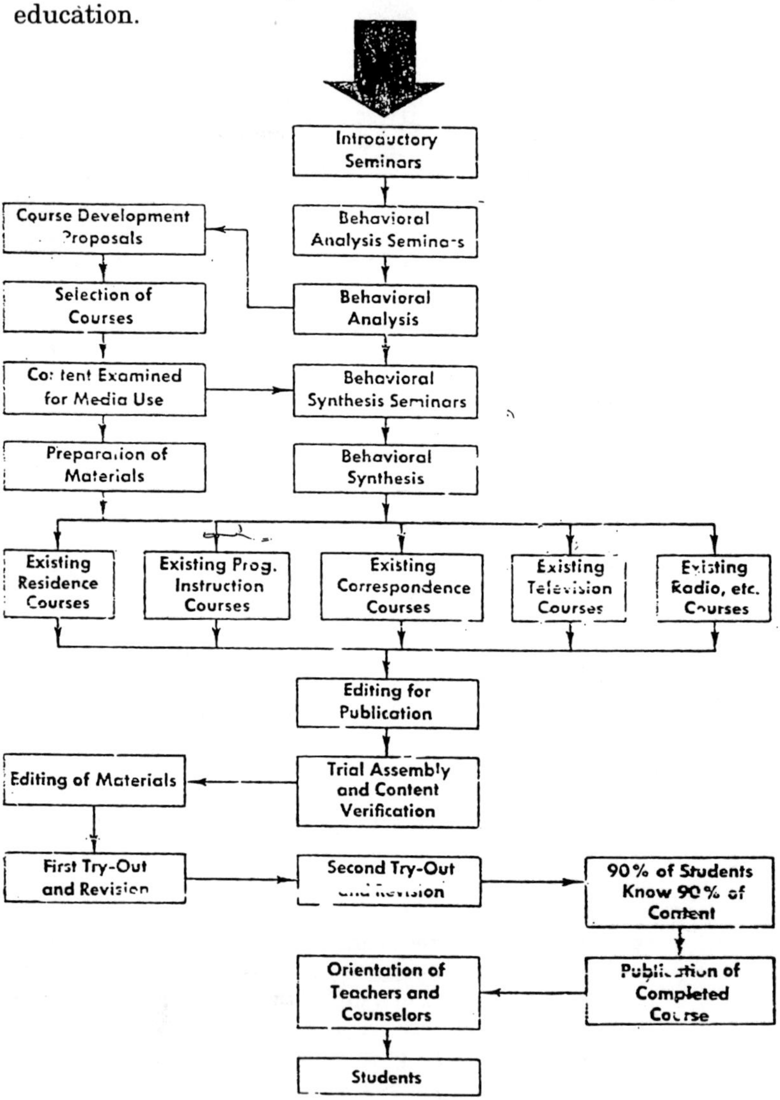

Fig. 3.18

Closing Comments

The use of the *total* learning-systems concept involves a lot of time, effort, and money. In order to facilitate educational innovation, several aspects of such an approach could easily be adapted into on-going courses as listed below :

1. Specify precisely the course objectives without using such vague and non-measurable terms as "understanding" "appreciation for," "familiarity with," "a knowledge of," etc. Robert Mager's book, on *instructional objectives,* has been helpful in the formulation of specific objectives. Just as it is possible to make test items out of specific objectives by a slight change of wording, it is also possible to make specific objectives out of tests items. At the very least, specify the "critical objectives" of the course. "Critical objectives" are learning objectives which if not achieved by the student, will inhibit or prevent learning in subsequent courses. Students should not be permitted to pass on to the next course without them.
2. Develop pretests which will clarify the student's standing in his class work, and indicate whether specific remedial work of advance placement is needed. A ready-made source of a pretest is a combination of a final examination from a prerequisite course or courses (just using the test items that are pertinent to the course for which your want the pretest) plus the first major test in the course itself (six- or nine-week examination). In this way, it is possible to measure whether the student has the necessary knowledge and skills to take the course and whether he already knows part of the course.
3. Look upon student's errors as indications of possible learning problems. Most students try to answer questions to the best of their ability. If a student's answers are incorrect, check into the learning situation. Maybe the objective was not taught right!
4. Make sure that tests are valid and actually measure the behaviours that represent the learning objectives of the course; test only behaviours which the student has had an opportunity to learn (no hidden objectives). For example, if a teacher wants a student to learn specific facts or to deal with facts in certain ways, a multiple-choice test may not identify whether or not the student has actually achieved these objectives. Multiple-choice

tests usually measure ability to discriminate between answers (process of elimination) rather than demonstrate knowledge of a specific item or skill.

5. Keep in mind the five learning variables discussed earlier in this chapter concerning individual differences.

In education, students come to teachers in order to learn. Generally, if the students does not learn by whatever method the teacher uses, he fails. The cumulative effect of failure cannot be measured in dollars and cents. Teachers have a moral responsibility to society to do everything in their power to help students learn to live.

4

Proficient Teaching : Communication in Process

Introduction

A learned philosopher once wrote the following poignant description of the function, role, and responsibilities of a proficient teacher:

> No man can reveal to you ought but that which already lies half asleep in the drawing of your knowledge. The teacher who walks in the shadow of the temple, among his followers, give not of his wisdom but rather of his faith and his lovingness. If he is indeed wise he does not bid you enter the house of his wisdom, but rather leads you to the threshold of your own mind.

Further, practice shows that it is not possible to *teach* anyone anything anyway! As the old saw explains, "You can lead a horse to water but you can't make him drink." So it is with children; you lead them through their lessons but you can't make them truly learn. Rather, the role of the teacher is more properly conceived as one which organises and provides essential learning experience for children. The process of learning does not occur until the learner interacts and becomes involved in the experiences which are provided.

Traditionally, teaching has been conceived as the act of imparting knowledge and selected skills; particularly those skills which our society has deemed necessary in order to achieve a fruitful life. It has also been traditional that the achievement of the teacher and the success of the students be assessed through determining each pupils's ability to answer selected queries posed by the teacher. However, this concept is not truly an adequate representation of the process of teaching and learning.

Teaching, when understood, implies a great deal more than the mere imparting of selected knowledge and skills; more than testing a student's ability to parrot back the facts and details of a lesson which has been presented. Fully understood, teaching implies content and a body of knowledge; it implies the activation and transfer of this knowledge from the unknown to one's storehouse of known; it implies relationships, associations and discriminations which bring one area of knowledge into close harmony with other areas of knowledge. Further, teaching implies discovery, excitement, and the joy of experience. And, perhaps most important, teaching implies communication; the means of transmitting that which has been learned by one learner to another. Succinctly stated, "the whole art of teaching is only the art of awakening the natural curiosity of young minds for the purpose of satisfying it afterwards."

Accordingly, and without question, it is the teacher who is the essential variable in the selection and presentation of the learning programmes found within our schools.

> Meaningful and skillful teaching is not an accomplishment of a teacher who views his task with misgivings and cloudy objectives. Rather, meaningful and skillful teaching is reserved for those who comprehend the great responsibility of their profession and who, day by day, conscientiously seek to improve their own personal inadequacies.

Further, proficient teaching relies upon communication as its vehicle for dynamism. Without such forces and energy, it is indeed questionable whether or not the process of teaching would exist at all, as all modes of teaching required some form of communication in order to achieve the transmission of knowledge from one learner to another. Notwithstanding, even meaningful watching requires communication!

The concept of communication, as an inseparable element of teaching is neither new nor esoteric. It is a common element which is usually well known to any conscientious student of the teaching process. However, to know and to understand teaching theory does not insure one of the ability to put it into practice. Why?

Teaching is a highly complex process involving an interaction among a potentially unlimited number of elements in rapid sequence. The speed of this process if often so rapid that it would appear that teacher presentations and pupil interactions are simultaneous. Not every one can teach; *teaching takes talent,* and only a few are so gifted.

The Communication of Knowledge

> Presenting information is an art; success depends on the teacher's insight into his pupils, his knowledge of the topic, and his use of a style suited to his personality. There is no single pattern or model to be followed....

The above statement rather ably identifies the qualifications necessary in order to achieve proficiency in teaching; except for one thing. It fails to take into account the means and devices available to the teacher in accomplishing his task.

For centuries, the only tool for the communication of knowledge and learning was verbalization. Men passed whatever they had learned from mouth to mouth in order that their further offspring and future generations might profit from their experiences. From these practices and procedures in instruction, we have inherited many legends and folk tales which advise and/or admonish the young toward certain selected modes of social standards or behaviours.

Generally speaking, it was not until the invention of printing that the verbal method of instruction was changed to any great extent.

The printing press provided, for the first time, an efficient means for reproducing and distributing man's knowledge in order that all men might become educated. However, few people today look upon the invention of the printing press as the initial use of media in the process of instruction.

From third modest beginning, teaching aids and instructional media have opened the way to a more efficient system of communication between teacher and pupil than had ever been known in recorded history. Instead of telling pupils what they are to learn, as they do in less developed cultures, or having to have students respond in a read, write, and recite session, the modern teacher is now free to teach creatively in meeting the various instructional needs of his students.

How is this done? What is the process of teaching and instruction which meets the needs of the growing child? In what ways does the process of communication facilitate the process of learning?

There is much to be learned before the process of teaching and the process of learning can be fully understood. However, it can be quickly said that teaching does not occur in the absence of students. Teaching might best be thought of as the generator of interaction between the pupil and the learning experience.

Logical examination reveals that teaching is but one half of the reciprocal relationship between itself and the process of learning. As such, proficient teaching requires effective communication with the learner. "The more effective the communication process, the more effective learning is likely to be."

Cassel has identified six independently organised phases of the process of teaching.

1. learner readiness;
2. pacing and individualising;
3. goal-setting and goal-striving;
4. affectivity and learner aspiration;
5. transfer;
6. evaluation.

He states that "each of these phases is closely related to the other five phases, and all six of the phases are an integral part of effective learning when it occurs".

In order to achieve effective communication with the learner, the teacher must clearly understand and appreciate the importance of each of the phases. For example, readiness is not something that becomes a part of a child when he reaches school age, not is it something which a teacher bestows upon a deserving pupil when he comes to school. Quite to the contrary, readiness is "the flame of knowledge that burns from within the learner, it cannot be imposed effectively by extrinsic manipulation.

It has been said that "telling isn't teaching"; all meaningful learning comes from within as the learner interacts with his environment. The skillful teacher presents problems, experiences, and activities which will serve to fan the flame of knowledge into a blaze of intellectual accomplishment. But, be ye warned! This is no simple task. To achieve the fire of enthusiasm, the proficient teacher must establish an open line of communication between himself and the learner. This is the first and most necessary step in promoting achievement.

When the bonds of communication have been forged, it is then imperative that the teacher concern himself with the pacing and individualization of the learning experiences. To illustrate, all horses have the capacity to run; the Thoroughbred is best suited for racing whereas the Clydesdale is better suited for work-type activities. So it is with children. Some can mentally run as fast the wind while others are more inclined to pled along, making good progress, but at a much slower rate of speed. It is only through effective communication that such individual differences can be ascertained.

The tasks of goal-setting and goal-striving can be independent activities, but, more often, group action is necessary. Were it not for the goals generated through social and intellectual interaction, man would probably have made little progress or improvement from his meager beginnings in the cave. In suggesting that goals are not necessarily self-originated, one must remember that goals are not necessarily self-originated, one must remember that man is a social creature as well as an intellectual being. From his various relationships and experience, man creates and/or innovates changes in his surroundings and environment which appear to him as being more desirable than what he has. These goals are derived, most often, through communication with others.

The teacher serves the role of an expeditious agent, telescoping the periods of time required for achieving the goals; i.e., skills and abilities necessary for a fruitful life. Instead of having each child learn the same things at the same speed that children in preceding generations learned; the proficient teacher, via communication, is able to condense and compress selected learning experience in order that children can learn more and faster than did the preceding generations. This task certainly is not for the incompetent or untalented.

Hopefully, a child will be able to apply what he learns in one area of study to the solution of problems which he encounters in other areas. This process is known as transfers. Some advocate that to achieve transfer of learning, a very formal, strictly intellectual curriculum must be presented, while others contend that learning which remains verbal and abstract; i.e., formal, only has negligible effect upon one's responses in real-life situations.

> The most imperative educational goal is to increase the pupil's ability to think, i.e., to replace trial and error or thoughtless response in a problematic situation with intellectual control of decisions. This outcome can be called many things—reasoning ability, intellectual power, mastery of the great disciplines, functional skill in problem solving—whatever the name, the aim is transfer.

As with the other phases in this discussion, communication plays an integral part in providing the means necessary for transferring knowledge from one to another. Further, it is not until the similarities and differences within a problem can be perceived that the learner can look back into his storehouse of experience and determine whether or not he has met a similar problem before. If he has, the alternatives to a solution may be at hand; if not he then has to communicate his insufficiency in order to get assistance. "Transfer of a behaviour pattern to a new situation is likely to occur whenever the person recognises the new situation as similar to other situations for which the behaviour has been appropriate." To accomplish this, purposeful communication is vital and must occur within the learner himself as well as between the learner and his teacher. Primarily, transfer is accomplished when the learner engages in evaluation of a problem with which he is confronted.

Evaluation, the final has presented by Cassel, is a process which is commonly not well understood. All too often, evaluation is conceived of only as a programme for testing or a means of measuring accomplishment. This, however, is not an adequate concept of the process of evaluation. Simply defined, effective evaluation is best perceived as feedback to the learner regarding a particular event, situation, or experience which he can use to develop more adequate perceptions about himself and his environment. Further, it should be understood that evaluation must serve two main purposes: (1) The purpose of assessment; and (2) the purpose of change, personal growth, and improvement. If growth toward greater personal adequacy is not the outcome of the process of evaluation, then time should not be wasted giving "lip-service" to this terminal element of the learning process.

A note of caution. Purposeful and effective learning, and thus the changing of behaviour, can only be accomplished through purposeful and effective evaluation. Again, as in the preceding phases of learning, the most essential ingredient in the process of evaluation is communication. Without communication, little can be accomplished toward promoting change in pupil behaviour and fostering a continuous experience for learning.

Thus far, we have examined the importance of communication in the process of education and, more specifically, the necessity of purposeful communication for affecting behavioural changes, i.e., learning, within the pupil. The next portion of this chapter will discuss selected patterns of communication and the affecting variable which are usually present to distort and/or prevent the learning message from being understood by the pupil.

The Communications Process Unmasked

Carefully examined, the process of communication requires the ex-changing and translating of knowledge into information, ideas, or view-points in order that other people can develop common understandings and mutually agreeable commitments. Accordingly, the key to successful communication is the concept of *commonness*. In order for one to fully communicate with another, commonness—a channel for understanding—must be established.

Most communication between people is of the "two-way" variety Many hours are spent each day at home, at school, and at the office sharing ideas and conversing with others. This is not the case within most of our school classroom today, however.

More often than not, communication in the classroom is of the "one-way" variety, epitomized by the dissemination of information without the opportunity, on the pat of the student, for discussion and verbal interchange.

In some situations, one-way communication can serve as an effective means of teaching; for example, for making known certain types of essential information in a brief period of time. However, in using one-way communication, the learner is usually not able to agree or disagree—his role is to accept that which is communicated to him. More cogently stated, in this mode of communication, the environment and circumstances surrounding the message to be learned are structured in such a way that the learner has only to pay attention and to heed the advice of the teacher. To illustrate this point, two examples of one-way communication are shown in Fig. 4.1.

Fig. 4.1

Obviously, it is possible for the teacher to convey the message, "Never run down the stairs," in many different ways. In the panel on the left, the teacher is pleasantly reminding the class that it is not safe to run down a stairway. On the other hand, in the panel on the right, the teacher is forcefully reinforcing the message. So it is in most of our verbal conversation. To change the emphasis upon the words within the sentences, or to change the manner in which the sentence is delivered, changes the meaning of the sentence.

A more graphic example of this phenomenon can be seen in the following sentence:

"I Did Not Say You Stole the Red Bandana!"

By merely changing the emphasis which is placed upon any one of the words in the sentence, the entire meaning and context of the sentence can be altered. Emphasis upon the word "I" gives the sentence an entirely different context than does placing the emphasis upon the word "not."

To extrapolate a bit from the example above, it is not difficult to gain some understanding of the pitfall which confronts a good many of our contemporary teachers in regard to their use of communication in the classroom. All too often, out of supposed necessity or ignorance, teachers rely upon one-way communication to teach their lessons. And what of this method? What are the results? With few exceptions, they are usually not very successful or rewarding.

Telling is not teaching! Many of the subject areas studied in school do not lend themselves to the one-way pattern of communication. Any subject that requires discussion, interaction, and/or' clarification is not appropriate for such a presentation. The study of ethical values within a cultural system, for example, is hardly an appropriate subject to approach via the technique of one-way communication. Values, in and of themselves, are relative in time, place, and culture, as well as in the understandings of the pupils studying them. Clearly, another means or design for communication is necessary.

In order to meet the requirements of an interactive discussion, two-way communication with "feedback" is required. Through the use of the feedback mechanism and the process of evaluation, a teacher can present an idea to a pupil and almost simultaneously determine whether or not it was properly understood. If it was, the teacher can then proceed to the next level of complexity. However, if the idea was not properly understood, the teacher can again present his idea to the pupil, perhaps with more explanation.

The student then can reinterpret the meaning of the idea and respond back to the teacher. If, upon this second examination of the idea, the learning is satisfactory, the teacher can proceed to the next step. However, if the student still fails to understand what the teacher is presenting, the idea, hopefully, can be presented in still another way in order that the student learn it.

In marked contrast to the process of two-way communication, a pattern of one-way communication is illustrated in Fig. 4.2. Note that there is no channel for feedback. Therefore, the efforts expended in explaining a concept (or in delivering a stern warning, as in the right-hand panel of Fig. 4.1) remain unassessed and, perhaps, unlearned by the pupil. It is only through two-way communication and the feed-back mechanism that one can know whether or not the task has been accomplished.

Element Which Inhibit Effective Communication

Thus far, it would appear that all is required for effective communication in the classroom is an adequate measure of discussion and feedback. In theory this is true; but in practice there are numerous variables which affect the process of communication.

Wittich and Schuller have identified six elements which they suggest interfere with the process of affective communication. These variables, although not impossible to overcome individually, do pose increasingly difficult problems when combined within the communication process. In fact, the problems encountered in achieving effective communication seem to multiply geometrically in relation to the number of variables present.

Among those variables identified, two distinct groupings seem to be present. Group One includes those factors which are likely to have their origins outside the classroom, or are attributable to physical causes. Group Two includes those factors which are more closely associated with a teacher's behaviour and his presentation of a lesson.

Group One (External Variables)	Group Two (Internal Variables)
1. Disinterest	1. Referent Confusion
2. Daydreaming	2. Imperception
3. Physical Discomfort	3. Verbalism

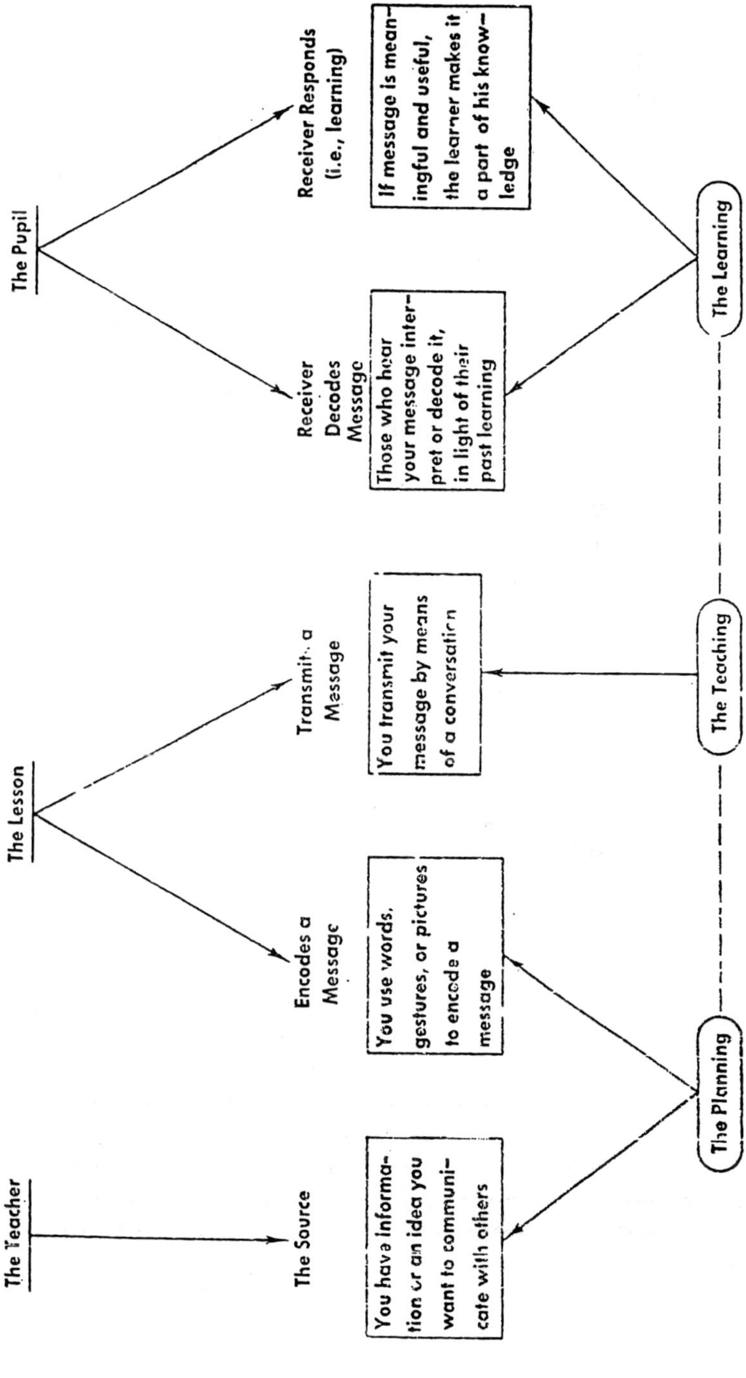
The Teacher
The Lesson
The Pupil
The Source
Encodes a Message
Transmit a Message
Receiver Decodes Message
Receiver Responds (i.e., learning)
You have information or an idea you want to communicate with others
You use words, gestures, or pictures to encode a message
You transmit your message by means of a conversation
Those who hear your message interpret or decode it, in light of their past learning
If message is meaningful and useful, the learner makes it a part of his knowledge
The Planning
The Teaching
The Learning

In addition to these variables, there is a third group of factors which must be considered in studying the process of communication. Categorically, these are best perceived as *intervening variables* within the learning process, in that they affect the behavioural habits of teachers as well as pupils. However, the intervening variables are much more subtle than those of the first two groups, and the often mistaken or overlooked. Accordingly, the student of classroom communication patterns should train himself to become sensitive to them and to their consequences.

Group Three

(Intervening Variables)

1. Prejudice
2. Experience
3. Cognitive Knowledge

More precisely, one is what one believes; one is what one has experience; and one is what one knows. what is likely to happen to the flow of an instructional message as it filters through the selected variables in the communications process.

Certainly, all possible variables which might interfere with communication have not been considered. However, the nine variables which are presented represent the major elements affecting communication within the learning process and hence, will serve as focal points for the subsequent discussion.

The intervening variables are perhaps the most difficult of all the selected variables to control within the learning process. For the most part, they are the products of psychological conditioning, opportunity for learning, and/or one's ability to assimilate that to which he has been exposed. In order to control these factors, one must really alter the attitudinal and behavioural patterns of an individual before much progress can be made.

Of course, radically changing the personality structures of students is not within the limits of a teacher's capacities or responsibilities. However, the proficient teacher is always sensitive to the effects of the intervening variables and is ready to deal with them and the challenges they present in the best way he knows how.

In sharp contrast to the intervening variables, the external and internal variables possess factors which the teacher can readily control. Disinterest, for example, may have its source either in or outside the limits of the classroom, but it can usually by controlled through the application of a small measure of *vividness*. All too often, the lesson to which we expect a pupil to respond is slow moving, lacking in luster, frought with up necessary repetition, lacking in the quantities of general interest, sometimes irrelevant to immediate needs, and worst of all, poorly taught. It is no wonder that students become disinterest and bored. It has always been a curious phenomenon that educators subject children to situations, conditions, and experiences that they would never apply when teaching adults. Certainly, children cannot be treated as miniature adults, but they can be treated as important individuals, possessing variables interests needs and abilities. Because students are a captive audiences, this does not mean that they should be treated as such. A simple but skillful application of instructional media—motion pictures, 35-mm slies, specimens, recordings, television—may be all that is necessary in order to transform a dry, uninteresting discussion into a dynamic and vitally alive experience for the learner. All that is required is a measure of *vividness*.

Daydreaming is an activity that everyone has engaged in at one time or another; it may be the source of our most potent and original thoughts. Generally speaking, however, the classroom is not commonly accepted as a place to daydream since the unaware student may miss essential information.

Again the solution to daydreaming at the wrong time or in the wrong setting lies within the classroom. More often than not, daydreaming occurs when the classroom lesson loses its vitality, its application to perceived needs, or breaks up in verbal confusion. The recollection of a more satisfying event or experience, held mentally ready, then usurps the attention of the student. What is the solution?

The skillful teacher can eliminate daydreaming by conveying a sense of *immediacy* through potent lessons that are applicable to students' need and geared to their appropriate levels.

Physical discomfort is likely to be either the most difficult or the least difficult variable with which the teacher has to cope. It is most difficult to deal with when the source of a child's discomfort stems from a chronic illness or a physical handicap. Here, the teacher can usually do very little in the way of removing the cause of the discomfort and hence, must rely upon building a warm and understanding relationship between himself and the student in order to overcome this limitation.

The discomforts which can be more easily handled usually originate right inside the classroom. Because a teacher is active and mobile, often he may not feel or be aware of classroom conditions which cause discomfort for children. When constrained to a particular desk in a particular part of the classroom, such things as a lack of adequate ventilation, too much or too little heat, improper lighting, a poorly fitted desk, or a rigid policy concerning lavatory and drinking mountain privileges can interfere with a student's academic efficiency. All that is required for the elimination of the "in-class" discomforts is the development of a mental sensory-thermostat. When it is stuffy, open the windows; when it is too bright, pull down the shades; when it is too cold, turn up the heat, etc. With practice, regulating the environment within a classroom can practically become a conditioned response.

In contraposition to the external variables just discussed, the internal variables present quite another problem in working out suitable control for the improvement of communication. Commonly, the internal variables, *referent confusion, imperception,* and *verbalism*, are products of a teacher's pedagogical style rather than inadequate skills in communication alone. These problems generally result from what the teacher does, or not do, when he presents a lesson.

Referent confusion can be the result of hearing a new meaning applied to a word for which a prior (different) meaning has been established:

> ...on crossing the state line into Vermont a geography teacher's son expressed great surprise at seeing forests of trees instead of the never-ending forests of chimneys which he had "learned" characterized heavily industrialized New England.

Or it can be the result of hearing similar sounding words:

> A second-grader reported that she had ridden up and down on an alligator (escalator-elevator) on a field trip.

Thus, it is possible for two people to hear the same presentation yet for each to come away having an entirely different understanding of what was intended.

Imperception is the result of inaccurate observation which bring about inaccurate understandings. The terms "to see" and "to understand" are usually taken as synonyms. "To see is to believe" is a familiar expression which is based upon the assumption that what one sees, he understands.

The fallaciousness of this logic is easily shown through the presentation of an optical illusion or legerdemain. In addition, it is demonstrated in the mirage phenomenon which is common to most hot deserts and equatorial oceans. So it is with imperception; to see is not necessarily to understand.

Perhaps the best example of imperception is illustrated in the old parable of the blind men examining the elephant. The first blind man said, "I see, the elephant is very much like a tree"; he felt the trunk. The second blind man said, "I see, the elephant is very much like a wall"; be felt the elephant's side. The last blind man said, "Ah, the elephant is much like a rope"; for he had felt the tail. All three blind men were correct to a very limited degree. However, an elephant is not like a tree, or a wall, or a rope; in fact, it in no way resembles these entities. Imperception, thus, is the result of inaccurate perceptions based upon inaccurate or insufficient information. The result: misconception and confusion.

Verbalism, the final element to be discussed, is probably the most common variable which interferes with communication and the process of learning. Simply defined, verbalism is the practice of using too many words, thus confusing the issue, or too much dependence upon words alone to get one's message across. As a prime example, Wittich and Schuller make the following comment:

> This point is well illustrated by one teacher's report: "During the first five or six weeks of schools, pupils listen to me; they seem very interested in my description. Then comes a curious change. As week follows week and more words follow more words, interest lags, and finally even I realise that it is time for

> a change, a change in the methods I use to get across the ideas I so urgently seek to teach.

What happens? Why do words, the very ingredients of communication, inhibit the process for which they were created? Perhaps the answer can be found in reversing the familiar expression, "A picture is worth a thousand words." A thousand words are not always worth a picture! Sometimes only three hundred are enough, and anything more would serve only to confuse or be repetitive. The following poem very sueeinctly yet fluently, describes the metamorphosis of a leaf with the coming of autumn:

To An Autumn Leaf

As if the gods of Nature
Know that you must die
So soon
They've changed your once green face
To rich ripe gold.
Your last attempt at gaiety
Has come
To give to all, who do behold
Your loveliness
A lasting memory before you did
So soon.

A thousand words could be said regarding autumn and the turning of the leaves, but it is doubtful that any more words would render the statement more eloquent.

The effective use of words is an art an a skill. However, it would be insufficient to suggest that teachers too much or are not very skilled in communication, although, in many instances, this is true. As a counterpoint to the need for clarity and sueeinctness, L. J. Cronbach offers the following comment in support of a certain amount of repetition in teaching:

> The teacher should guard against the temptation to "cover ground" rapidly. This phrase itself reveals a false conception of teaching. Exposing the pupil to an idea is not teaching; the exposure must be thorough enough that he comprehends and retains the important part of the presentation. Information can always be presented more rapidly than it can be grasped; language is a highly distilled extract of the speaker's thought.

> ...The pupil who misunderstand one part of the communication, either through inattention or because some word is unclear to him, can catch his error if the same thought is echoed in several sentences.

Verbalism, then, can be an extreme. The redundancy of a repeated message does not help the learner to grasp an idea; rather, unnecessary repetition thwarts a learner's attempt to grasp the concept being presented. How much is enough, and how much is too much? Only experience can tell. Classes vary as do individual children; what is extreme for some may be entirely correct for others. Perhaps the best advice which could be offered here would be to *know* the material, have the essential points outlined, and stick to the point; i.e., avoid tangential remarks which may tend to detract attention or obfuscate the concepts which are being presented.

Summary

Communication is the heart of teaching and its process the veins and arteries through which knowledge flows. Further, the concept of *class-room communication* implies a great deal more than merely achieving common understandings through verbal interaction. To really communicate with students, it is necessary that a teacher acknowledge and accept six essential ingredients in the process of teaching. The teacher must:

1. capture the interests and desires of his students;
2. select and present purposeful experiences which are within the intellectual abilities of his students;
3. choose problems of sufficient merit and value that they will evoke discussion and critical thinking on the part of his students;
4. present credible and acceptable experiences in order that his students can relate new experience to earlier learnings;
5. reinforce learning in order that his students will remember what they have learned; and
6. promote socially constructive behaviours among his students.

Indeed, this is a large task—perhaps for some, an impossible task. Nonetheless, in order to achieve affective instruction, each one of these elements must be dealt with competently.

The simplest place to start in organising for meaningful instruction is with the students. Certainly, proficient teachers are familiar with the following principle; *Begin where the students are; use their existing interests and learnings to broaden old concepts and to help in developing new ones.* Instructional programmes which are planned and developed apart from the interests, desires, and needs of the students are most likely to end up in failure, or, at best be only minimally effective.

Instruction should be personalised by such qualities as genuine interest, warmth, understanding, empathy, and an alertness on the part of the teacher to non-verbalizes, personal learning needs of the student. In this way, the teacher can transform an ordinary in-class activity into a very real and significant experience. Most important, whatever is taught must be credible and worthy of the attention of students. Time permits neither teachers nor students the luxury of aimless floundering in hopes of acquiring an education. Instruction must be well planned and well presented.

Accordingly, effective communication and instruction does not just happen! *It is planned* Similarly planning is not a haphazard activity either. Definite precepts are required and must be followed in order that confusion and the variables which spawn misunderstanding are eliminated or are reduced to an absolute minimum.

Traditionally, teaching has been perceived as a verbal experience between the learned and the learner. However, this conception and approach is severely limiting and a most inefficient method of instruction due to the many complex variables which interfere with the process of communication. To teach is to communicate; anything else is a deception! Meaningful communication is only achieved in the common ground of mutual understanding. In this attitude, affecting variables can be known and controlled, the instructional needs of students can be accurately perceived, and the presentation of vivifying experiences can be accomplished. Herein lies the challenge.

5

Visual Communication

Visual communications bombard civilized man most of his waking hours. Visual symbols that are neither literary not scientific range from the symbolic meaning expressed in monumental architecture to children's drawings. The structures of visual symbols range from the simplest stereotypes of objects which have been abstracted from visual realism (highway signs, for example) to the symbolization of the complex culture of a people as expressed in national capital buildings, monuments, and surrounding landscape.

In contemporary society, non-verbal visual symbols are used to transmit ideas; express qualities, feelings, and emotions; note varied rank, status, and social roles; and to persuade changes in behaviour and decision-making. Advertising, package design, publishing layout, clothing and jewelry, furniture and household accessories, motels, drive-ins, amusement centers, housing, business buildings, main streets, and cities all communicate values and ideas depending upon the quality of the symbolism used. Mass media extend this communication multifold.

In education, we diagram, graph, and organise symbols to express relationships. We build two-and three-dimensional models to help student analyse complex problems. We use the newer mechanical and electronic instructional media to expose students to more varied visual experiences and learning process than can be achieved through written and spoken symbols. Non-verbal symbolic communication plays a major role in interpersonal and intergroup communication, particularly since the development of the mass media. However, too few teachers or students are educated in how to use this communication to best advantage. In our traditions of education, most emphasis has been on learning through written languages and mathematical and scientific symbols.

Design is the grammar of the visual world. It is the ordering system that makes the symbol more or less readable. It helps the content come through to the viewer. If the symbols have no background referent for the viewer, they will have little meaning for him. For example, in written language, an elegantly designed poster in Greek will communicate an excellent design to someone who understands design but not Greek. For those who read Greek, the message will be enhanced by the design and made clearer by the arrangement and design of the letters. The same message in Greek, read by a Greek could be poorly designed and hard to read. Symbols and the quality of their visual arrangement are reciprocally related—they can enhance or deter the function of the other; thus, they are in large part interdependent.

Bohannon, an anthropologist analyzing art and communication, suggests that art is one of the modes of creating cultural images to improve subtle appreciation and increase communication. He says that part of the process of maturation for humans is learning to communicate what one perceives. Symbolizing from our experience with sensory reactions and things, we develop the images for social interaction, communication, and patterns of culture.

By contrast, learning to read the symbols of our culture helps us to understand the culture. But the content and the form of the message must both be understood.

Aspects of Transmission

Design has several aspects in message transmission. Out of individual or collective experiences, symbols are invented to express the nature of experience. The symbols are expressed through visual design to project the meaning, and the meaning is responded to in terms of the readiness of the viewer. For example, a curving line with an arrow point at the top means curving road ahead to most drivers. The symbol illustrated the problem of driving on a curving road—it communicates a shared experience. But to people who don't drive, or have had experience in driving only in flat, open country, or have not seen such a sign, or have had very threatening experiences with such driving situations, the symbol will communicate somewhat different things. A visual symbolic message is not a direct transfer of one person's experience to another person, but is mediated through each step from the initial experience of the sender to the response of the receiver. The teacher in the classroom may assume that the same message, either verbally or visually symbolic, will be received in the same way by all of the students in the class. But even if the teacher and the pupils share the same background of experience (which would be rare), other difference in readiness to respond will occur.

We are faced with the rather practical evidence that the elements of designs, form, line, colour, texture, and their "gestalt"—the overall interacting impacts they can be made to produce—affect people differently. Why is it that some combinations of the visual elements create images of chaos for some people, while for other, order, or excitement, or monotony? Why do some people find an arrangement pleasing, while other people find it repulsive? Some designs and art forms have symbolic meaning to some segments of society and have little or no meaning to others. Some retain their meaning for centuries, others only transitionally. Yet, even with all this diversity, there must be some common denominators that enable us to respond to art and craft forms of cultures whose value and attitudes vary widely from our own.

The structure in Fig. 5.1 is an attempt to identify a hierarchy or factors that are involved in individual responses to the visual environment, and, thus, to message design. It starts at the lowest common denominator of visual information handling which appears to be cross-cultural and evidences in some degree in all the arts of all periods. The next level is cultural—the perceptual conditioning and symbolic meaning that evolves within a given society in terms of its values and attitudes. Third are personality variables that, at least in Western culture, differentiate between individuals within the various sub-cultures in Western civilization, and, finally, the immediate situation in which an individual is responding. The message designer uses cultural symbols, appeals to personality, but basically he works at the level of visual information handling.

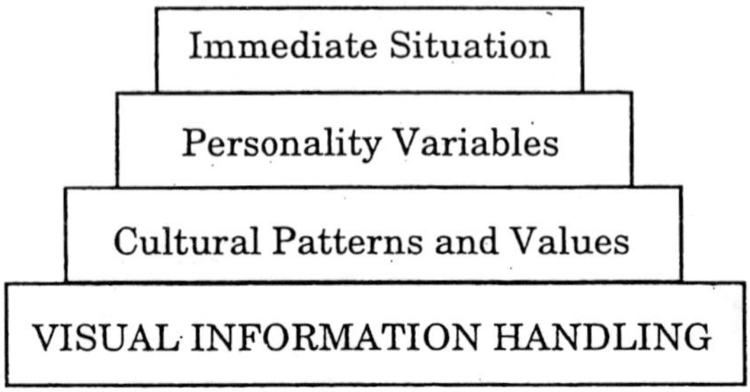

Fig. 5.1.

The message designer mediates between raw data—visual information before it has been organized by the viewer—by doing some of the organising for him. To communicate to other people, the designer has to structure both the content, the "what is said" and the design, the "how it is said" so that there is a closer relationship between the intended message and the one received by the particular audience for which he is designing. Since this chapter is concerned with making design more effective as an instrument for communication, the discussion will focus mainly on the questions: What is there about the design of the message that can help the message that can help the message designer mediate ore effectively between the sender and the receiver? What will such knowledge do to help the message designer get the information through in a better way than if the individual had responded to the experience himself? How can experience be clarified through design? In other cases, how can message design create for the nonparticipant the essence of an experience he can have only vicariously? This last process is involved in much of education—learning about prior to, or instead of the actual experience.

Research on these complex questions is meager. By operating rather broadly, the writer with background both in design and the psychology of perception will posit some perimeters of the behaviours involved, referring to applicable research where possible, and drawing upon experiences in teaching design when little research is available.

Visual perception itself is not a direct "image in the mind" of an outside stimulus. Rather, in very simplified terms, the visual-perception process involves a cognitive response to a sorting or ordering process from the "mosaic of retinal stimulation" which is in turn, a reaction to the stimulating objects. Non-physical properties enter the sorting and cognition processes as well. These include past experience and prior learning. Gregory suggests that information from the other senses in past and present perceptual tasks are involved as well—"touch, taste, smell, hearing, and perhaps temperature or pain." The author in her Perception-Delineation Theory includes success and failure, fear and anxiety as modifiers of the information-handling process. Fig. 5.2 symbolizes the simple process, but does not identify all the points where individual differences would operate.

Fig. 5.2

The message designer may be able to design for a particular subculture of the society where identifiable tradition can be used to play upon the familiar. A teacher, knowing the cultural background and aptitude of his pupils can vary the symbolism and complexity level to their readiness. But all designers can use the common denominators of *visual information handling* to reach more of the population.

Visual Information Handling

At any given time, an individual responds cognitively with conscious awareness to only a small part of the visual information that is reflected on the retina of the eye. Look across the room—or whatever space you are in. To become aware of everything in your visual field, even if the room is very barren, takes considerable time. Most of us start our visual training by *identifying* thing. Apparently, this is as far as many people go.

If the room is a study, you would fairly soon be able to categorise books, maps, pictures, hanging coats, pens and pencil, drapes, rugs, chairs, etc. But, if you were to look for all the variations in colour as changed by light and cast shadows, changes in forms in terms of their relation to your view, textures, lines, spaces, and planes—you could spend hours just looking at one view. Many people probably do not attend to the visual qualities unless specifically asked to do so.

In music and in all non-verbal sounds, as well as in written and spoken language, systems of categorizing and systematizing information are necessary in order to conceptually handle the complexity. Apparently, man's capacity to differentiate between discrete things in single instances is much greater than his ability to handle them when he must respond to a great deal of information. In the latter case, he stereotypes and categorizes information, making it simple enough so that he can respond. In a study of colour names, Chapanis estimates the number of colour variations that the normal human can differentiate. By multiplying the recognizable 200 different hues by the 450 different steps between black and white and the degrees of saturation (strength of colour) which range from 15 to 65, a figure close to 7,000,000 is achieved 5000 colour names, but in usage there is little or no standardization. On the basis of his study of colour naming of subjects, he finds about 52 usable colour names, which in common English is usually reduced to about 12 names.

The message designer is a mediator, in this case with colour, between the diversity to which man can physically respond and the ordinary name-categorizing of colour.

The same is required with responses to objects. For example, if we have a box of conglomerate objects and are asked to tell someone what is in it, we have to put the contents in *order* to do so. If these are nuts, bolts, nails, pins, paperclips, and tacks, we have to sort them into some kind of order to identify and quantify them. We have a *use* classification already—fasteners. But this is often not definitive enough. We can order them by differences in fastening functions, or in terms of size, shape, or colour. Colour coding of manufactured parts is often used to denote a specific size of a given type of object that differentiates it from another similar object of different type and size. Colour coding can be a quick recognition of differences, giving order to complexity.

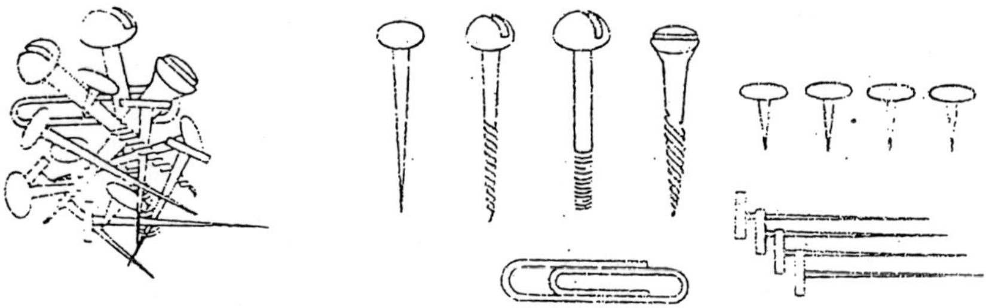

(a) **Fig. 5.3** (b)

Visual ordering in designed messages has to use visual ordering as well as conceptual ordering or categorizing, unless all things in a concept category look alike visually. For example, in Fig. 5.3, the objects pictured in part (a) are presented under the concept of fasteners but are visually confusing. In part (b), they are not visually confusing because they are analysed by size and shape. Visual ordering makes the messages of content easier. Much of our responding is so fast that we are unaware of the processing we do. One of the tasks of the message designer is to make the sorting process easier; he selects and organises visual information so that it is easier for the viewer to assimilate.

The writer had been teaching design for some years before being exposed to the theories of Gestalt psychology. The pattering in that theory—proximity, similarity, and closure—began to make sense as to why some designs "worked" and other "didn't". Experimentation with teaching methods indicated that some people apparently used the organization of perceptual information at what the psychologist, Attneave, calls a pre-cognitive level of awareness. Students called this "intuition" about what leads to a good pragnanz or sense of overall form. Some students were consciously aware of perceptual organization and its underlying functions in design, but were generally unable to achieve a sense of design by "feeling". After becoming aware of the perceptual dynamics of visual information handling, these non-intuitors became aware of the elements of design. They could recognise the diversity of impact upon themselves of the various combinations. They also seemed to develop more feeling sensitivity to what was going on.

One of the most difficult problems for the intuitive designer is to realise that other people do not respond as he does. The approach to message design developed here is to help the intuitive designer understand the ranges of response among those for whom he designs, and to help the less intuitive designer understand some of the phenomena that appear to be going on in visual organization which underlie the design process.

Visual Ordering as Design Principles

Some of the Gestalt concept continue to be useful even though explanations as to why they operate vary.

People need to make order, to group or pattern visual information so they may see objects. Figure 5.4 illustrates one's need to organise. Each of the dots is the same in size, shape, and distance from the other dots. If you look at it awhile, you find yourself trying to make lines or squares, but the *images* do not last long because all the alternatives are equal, and your tendency to continually search for order keeps you busy reordering.

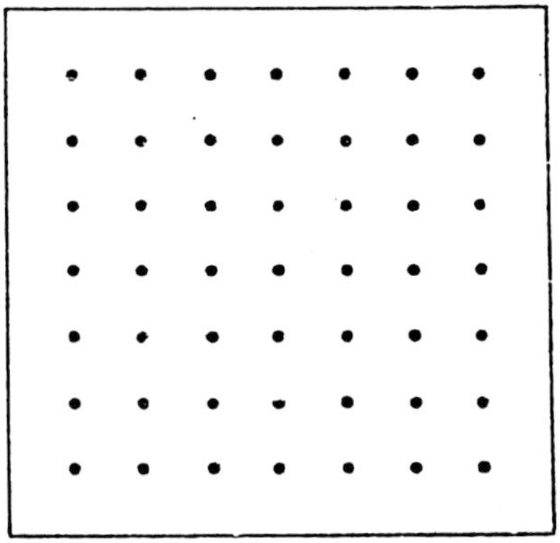

Fig. 5.4

Grouping by the Principle of Similarity

Figure 5.5*(a)* is different from *(b)* because they involve different alternatives. In both, alternative rows of circles have open and solid centers. Figure *(b)* is the same as *(a)*, but rotated 90 degrees. The circles are all equidistant so there are no "real" rows, but you see vertical lines in part *(a)* and horizontal lines in part *(b)* because you are sorting the visual information into

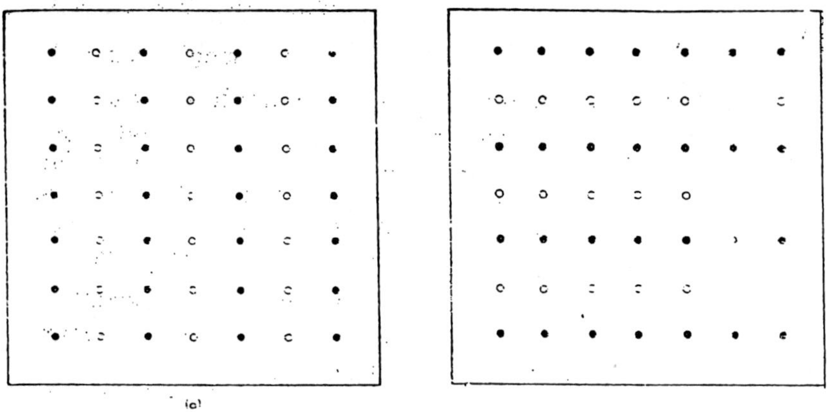

Fig. 5.5

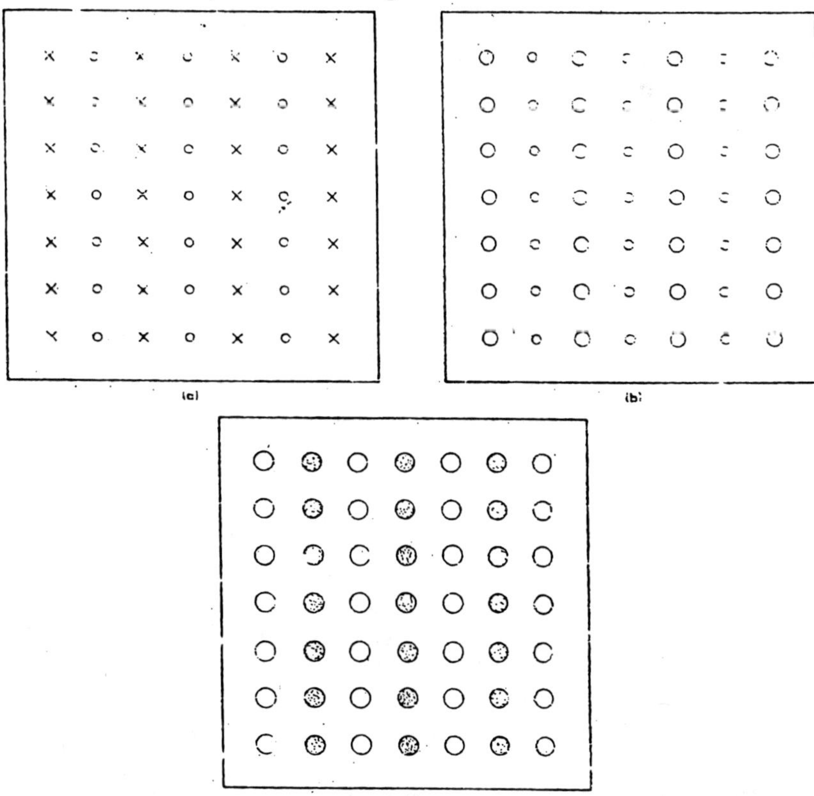

Fig. 5.6

similarities in this case, open or solid circles. This same principle operates if the circles, or other objects used are varied in any way. Figure 5.6 is another example. In part *(a)* the shape is varied, part *(b)* varies the size, and part *(c)* varies the texture.

Colour, value and intensity can all be used in the relating process. *Color* is the hue, the red, blue, blue-green, etc; *value* is the lightness or darkness of the color; and *intensity* is the strength of the colour, such as the amount of pigment in a wash. By varying any of these colour dimensions, the designer can direct the viewer to find order by grouping those things that are similar. He can also create lines and edges between groups of things by such simple transitions.

Grouping by Proximity

Another way the organising system sorts information is by the response to the grouping presented by the design of the outside stimulus.

Fig. 5.7

In Fig. 5.7, most people see three pairs of lines and an extra one on the right. Try to make yourself see three wide pairs with one on the left. This is very difficult to do. Proximity is a tool of the designer. If he wants things to be seen together they need to be grouped together. If too much space is left between things, the viewer will try to find other ways of ordering.

All the systems of ordering are open to the viewer. The designer needs to analyse what he is doing to see if he is providing the choices he wants. He may assume that he has ordered by proximity; however, similarities of colour in two distinct groups may be the stronger pull, or, perhaps, two similarities in shape.

In Fig. 5.8, the two clusters of small outlined figures are clearly separate, but a tension between group *(a)* and *(b)* is produced by the two *circles* which the organising system is relating by similarity.

In Fig. 5.9, similarity of shape appears to be the strongest relationship even though the two different shapes are superimposed in one case. Proximity is functioning but not as strongly as is similarity. If one were to make the two figures on the left red, and the superimposed figures on the right blue, using line along to differentiate shape—then similarity of colour and proximity would strongly outweigh similarity of shape.

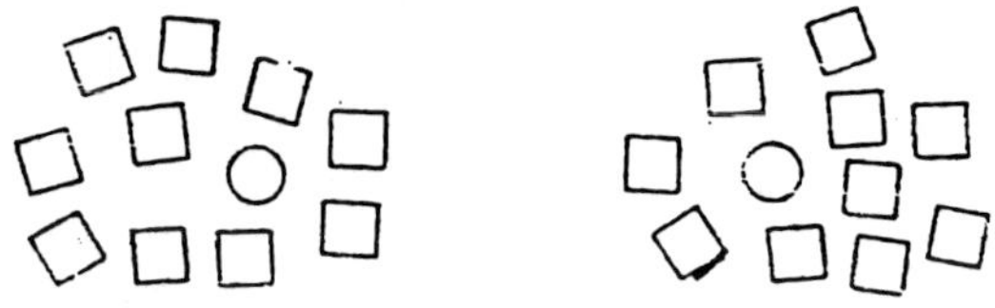

(a) (b)

Fig. 5.8

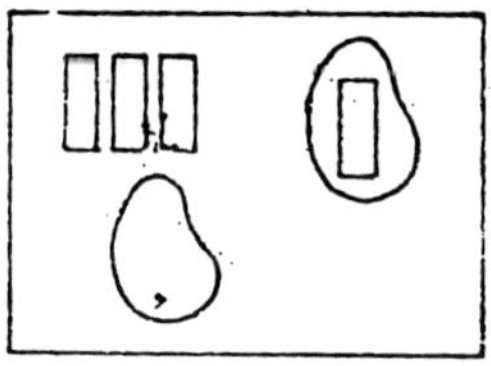

Fig. 5.9

Similarity and proximity can be used by the designer to solve difficult problems with very diverse objects. Differences in size, shape, and texture can be muted by grouping objects together or by ordering them by one common factor such as colour. These principles also apply to designing messages in words or symbols.

In design, things do not exist as single entities but rather as *interacting factors* within the whole. Color, shape, texture, space, and lines have traditionally been used as the elements of design. Balanced, rhythm, and emphasis are considered key design principles. Each of these has a basis in perceptual organizing. That which is balanced, creates rhythm, or stands out as emphasis depends on how both the designer and the viewer organise the visual information. In terms of organising processes, the elements of design are not the colour, the shape, or the texture; they are, rather, the ways these ingredients are used to create an ordered stimulus to which the organizing observer can respond. In other words, the designer plays upon the observer's tendencies to group things—the grouping tendencies become the principles of design.

We have seen how similarity and proximity operate. We will now explore the implications of other grouping tendencies.

Closure

Closure has two aspects: (i) a tendency to complete a form when part of it is presented and past experience with it leads one to respond as if it were completed; and (ii) a tendency to complete an abstract or geometric form though the nature of the directions suggested by lines created by the forms.

Completion due to the continuity of known relational concepts can be shown in Fig. 5.10. In part *(a)*, both symbol and mental closure give us clues as to the whole. In part *(b)*, we add a chin and other features to a face.

Fig. 5.10

Completion also operates with abstract forms. Figure 5.11 is an examples. Part *(a)* is organized on a vertical line that is not drawn, but created by the relationship of the shapes. Parts *(b)* and *(c)* are made up of repetitions of the same shape, but their relationship to each other create different wholes.

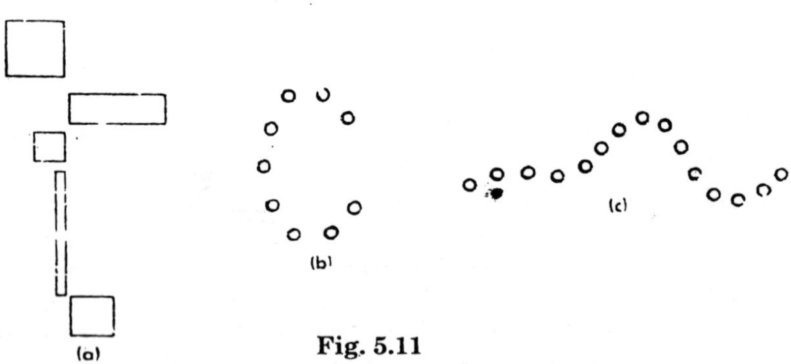

Fig. 5.11

Good Continuation

"Good continuation" is defined as that arrangement of line separation of figure and ground, or symbol edge, that produces fewest interruptions or stopping points for the eye. Figure 5.12, parts *(a)* and *(b)*, compares two continuations, one better than the other. In part *(b)*, a short mediating line at all extreme angles produces a smoother effect, the eye is helped past the angles.

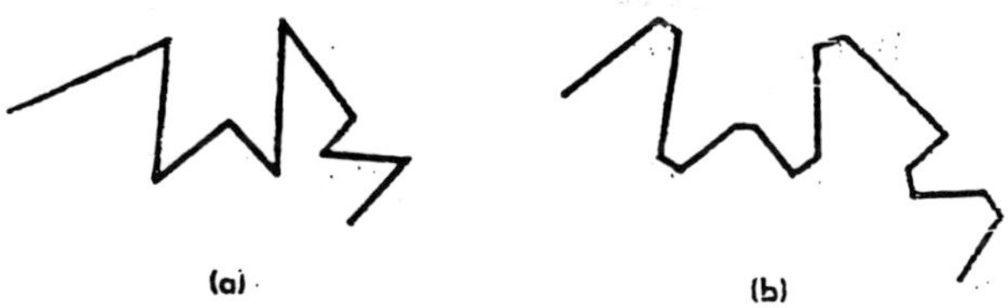

Fig. 5.12

Figure 5.13, part *(b)*, is the easiest to read; the same curvature is repeated. In part *(a)*, there are four different wave sizes varying in width and height, and in part *(c)*, size, height, width, and shape are all varied.

Fig. 5.13

Averaging Processes

Attneave has demonstrated that one of the key visual sorting processes is taking an average of complexity—another process of ordering so as to respond to the complex environment. When we see similar but diverse objects, we group them in terms of their likenesses, and we stereotype variations in shade and intensity in colour into single colours. When we see textured surfaces, we tend to respond more to the average colour or value the texture creates than to all the details of the texture over all the surface we are observing. This may be what operates in design when directional angles interact; we respond in terms of the average impact. In Fig. 5.14, part *(a)* the direction is singular and down right; in part *(b)*, the left and right angles point in two directions down; and in part *(c)*, a state of equilibrium is suggested because the angles counteract each other.

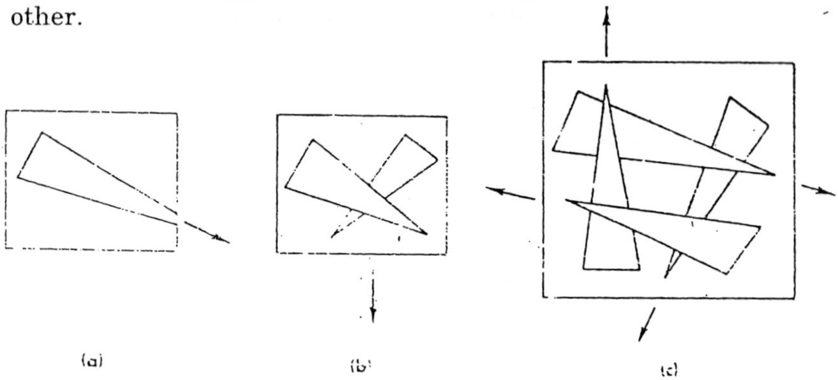

Fig. 5.14

Part of this symbolism is our reaction to gravity. Ozeefant suggests that single lines at angles are less strong than verticals as the force of gravity *we* experience we project to the lines; the angle receiving more force to move to a horizontal position. As more and more people take off in jets and see rockets resist gravity, the symbol for falling may become the symbol for taking off.

Information Points

Contrasted with "good continuation" is the sorting of information by focusing on information points. When subjects were asked to reproduce a form by using only ten dots, Attneave found they placed the dots at the points where the greatest changes took place in contour or angle. Salome found that fifth-grade children who were taught to utilize these key information points significantly improved their drawings over children who had the same drawing experiences but not the perceptual training. Hochberg found that, to reproduce a form, the individual needed information most on the number of different angles and the number of different line segments of unequal length. This would lead to the conclusion that change points are key factors in design.

One of the challenges to the designer is to produce enough good continuation to produce stability, but not so much that *no* averaging in scanning processes is needed. Too much stability would produce boredom and the viewer would look away. On the other hand, the designer should not create so much visual information that the viewer is lost in changes and detail. McWhinnie suggests that continuation is related to what designers call order and variety. The scanning organism needs visual work to do, but not so much that it can't find order.

Figure and Ground

A final way of grouping to overcome complexity is to separate figure from ground. In this aspect of information handling, it is more difficulty to separate what is a common denominator of perception from personality and learned values. We tend to look at form a and listen to sounds that have meaning to us. In most perceptual experiences, we attend to some things and not to others. This is one reason we get varied reports of happenings from honest people who looked at the same incident and perceived different things; what one brought into figure, another left in ground. This is part of the ordering process through which the individual finds meaning in his visual experience.

Part of attending is recognition of what is familiar; another part is attending to what is important or valued, or, conversely, what is feared or arouses anxiety-laden associations. Considerable research has been undertaken estimating the recognition threshold of words that arouse emotional responses as compared to mental words. There are identifiable figure over ground factors in the viewed objects that tend to make one figure, the other ground. Krech and Crutchfield indicate that what is figure tends to be better, more solid, to have clearer outlines; what is ground is less so. Camouflage is based on this principle; with false patterns, it difficulties the solidity, structure, and outline of the object which melts visually into the background.

Colours and value contrasts are stronger in figure than ground.

When the spaces between letters are used more strongly than the letters which are the figures, visual confusion or figure-ground reversal can result.

Fig. 5.15

When the same line is used to separate two areas, one becomes figure and the other ground with different properties. The same line divides them. The area at the back are the same, but two distinct figures result depending upon which is figure and which is ground.

Fig. 5.16

When the visual field is complex, the overall structure will tend to determine. In other words, the strongest organisation force will relate its elements as figure whether it be proximity, similarity, closure, or continuity.

Illusion effects that come with the interaction of ground on figure can be used by the designer to make things look or shorter rounder, or flatter. The well known Mueller-Lyer illusion can make the same line shorter or longer. In part *(a)*, the lines are the same length, and in part *(b)*, the rectangles are the same size, but the ground lines in both figures give the illusion that one line or rectangle is longer than the other.

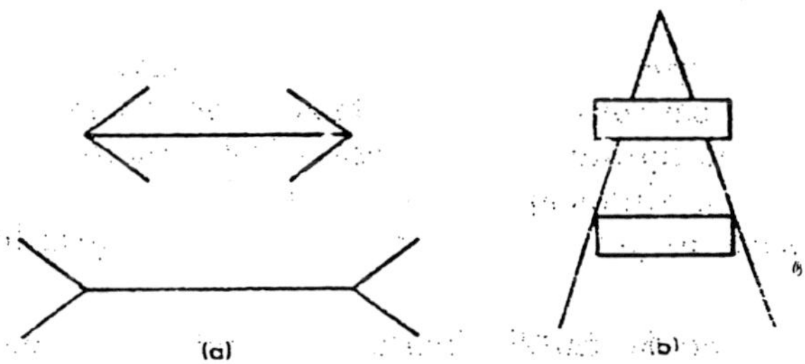

Fig. 5.17

Competition between Grouping Processes

Only in a vary simple stimulus is just one organising process evoked. In most cases, similarity in some degree, proximity in sonme degree, closure, and figure-ground relationship are used in handling the visual information. In some cases, the systems compliment each other. Proximity of objects, similarity of objects as to size and shape, and value reinforce the two groupings. In Fig. 5.19, part *(a)*, the proximity is probably strongest, but the similarities of shape set up cross tensions. Proximity and closure counteract when lines suggesting closures are added to part *(b)*.

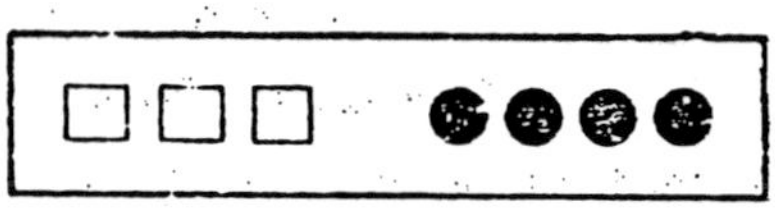

Fig. 5.18

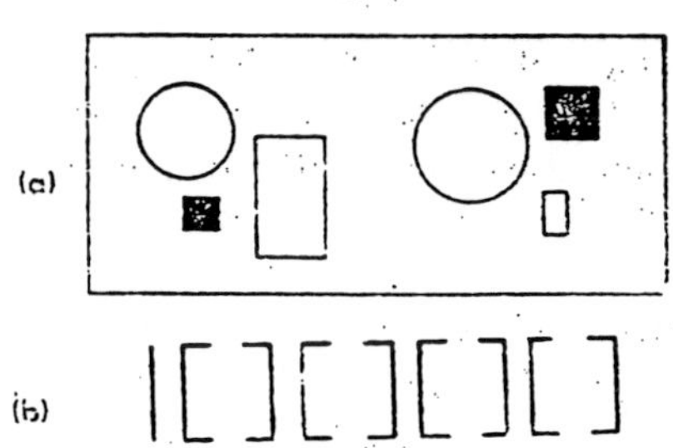

Fig. 5.19

Examples of Problem Solving in Design

The following problem-solving examples show further ways the grouping principles interact.

Using the concepts of proximity, the designer works from exact repetition in close proximity within a given field (Fig. 5.20) to the farthest reaches the perceiver can respond to and still see relationships. For example, the two forms in Fig. 5.21 are related because they are bounded within the same field, but they are different in shape, size, and colour, and weak in proximity. We can increase the cohesiveness of the design by making both figures the same colour or value (Fig. 5.22); by making them the same in size, which of course, increases the proximity; keeping the sizes different, but using the same shape (Fig. 5.23); or increasing the proximity within the bounding field, with enough space so that nothing else distracts or changes the interaction of the rectangle and circle (Fig. 5.24).

If we introduce another circle in reasonable proximity, then the likeness of the circles and the difference of the square set up a new pattern (Fig. 5.25). Even though the left-hand circle is closer to the rectangle, it relates more to the other circle. This is the way the message designer creates suggestion of tension to his viewers—two systems working unequally in different ways.

Tension is also produced when forms are almost identical, but not quite; an overall flutter effect takes place (Fig 5.26). Direct repetition is static; if the forms are all exactly alike, no movement takes place (Fig. 5.27). But if one rectangle is changes in value, size, or perspective, the organiser is stimulated to make a new organisation and interest increases (Fig. 5.28, 5.29, and 5.30).

Operational Explorations in the Dimensions of Design

To help students become involved in problem solving in message design, the following tasks are suggested to explore the interaction of elements in the organising processes.

1. Task: *Make order out of assorted unlike things.*
   Cut assorted sizes and shapes out of varied coloured and textured papers.

Similarity:

Search for ways to organise in terms of *size.* Create groups according to similarities in *colour.* Group with clearly identifiable similarities in *texture.* Group according to similarities in *shape.*

Proximity:

Without using similarity, group assorted things by *clustering* and *spacing.*

Closure:

Without using similarity, group assorted things using both *proximity* and *closure.*

2. Task: *Create order with variation.*

   Cut rectangular shaped pieces of coloured paper. Keep the size, shape, and spacing the same—*vary the colour.* Keep the colour and shape the same—*vary the size and space.* Keep the shape the same—*vary size, colour, and spacing.* In each case, analyse to see which of the perceptual organisation processes you are using: *Similarity* of size, space, shape, or colour; *proximity* of sizes, spaces, shapes, colours; *continuity* by creation of line; *figure* and *ground* by creating some areas that come forward and others that recede.

3. Task: *Create a free form* so that:

   None of the parts one too large or too small to relate to the whole. None of the angles suggested are parallel to any other angles. None of the spaces created dominate the space.

4. Task. *Using free forms, create colour and variation.*

   Keep the size, shape and colour the same—*vary the space.* Keep the colour and shape the same—*vary the size and space* as necessary. Keep the size and spacing the same—*vary the colour.*

5. Task: *Keeping the basic shape the same, create as complex a design as possible, varying all other elements to create variety, and using proximity, some degree of similarity, figure-ground, and continuity-closure to make order.*

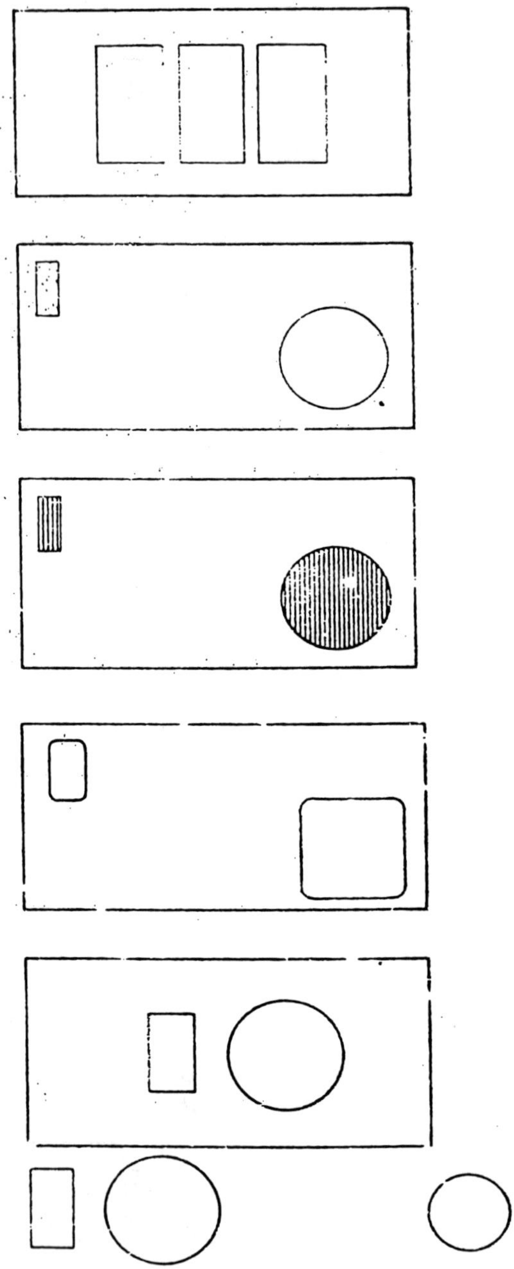

Fig. 5.20 to 5.25

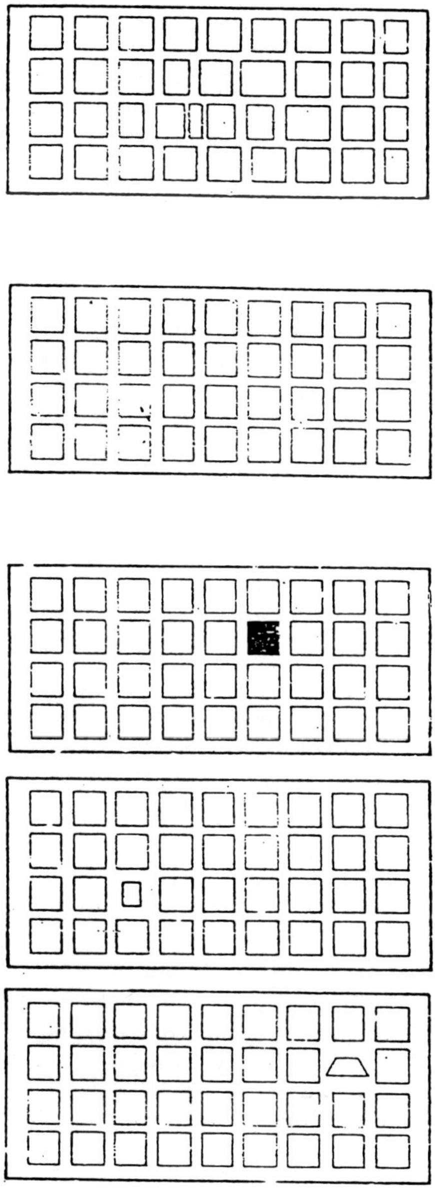

Fig. 5.26 to 5.30

Summary

Too much order produces monotony. Rows of unmodified cement called "housing" creates an environment that can depress the quality of living of people who try to make these their homes. Institutional drabness can contribute to the defeat of purposes such as learning and creative problem solving, physical or mental restoration, and social rehabilitation. Monotonous educational materials in whatever from can slow the pace and intensity of response.

Overly complex visual stimuli can lead to confusion on the part of some viewers. Others will abstract from the environment or the message only what is familiar, or what is valued. If the purpose is educational and *all* the material is needed for adequate understanding, then the ordering and varying of the information is critically necessary to make learning possible.

To get the message through to specific viewers, or groups of viewers, the designer must understand the ingredients of his communication system. These include the variables in the sender, the message, and the viewer. Culture, background, and personality vary from person to person. Perceptual literacy ranges widely. Individual response to different kinds of viewing situations should be considered.

When the design is for large and diverse groups of people, the common denominators of information handling—similarity, proximity, closure and good form, and figure-ground relationships—can be used to direct the viewers attention and get the message across. These processes underlie all organising of message designs, but in the case of messages to diverse groups, they are of primary importance.

Symbolic visual communications are everywhere. The designer has much competition for the viewer's attention. The more appropriate the design is to the message and the audience, the clearer will the content come through.

6

Concomitant Learning : An Anthropological Perspective on the Utilization of Media

Cultural anthropologists study two complementary aspects of social behaviour: ideal behaviour and real behaviour. One of the distinguishing characteristics of the anthropologist as a field worker is his attention to what people actually do as well as to what they say to. While information about what people feel is ideal (preferred, best, proper, good), and can often be gathered with some ease through the use of interviewing or questionnaires, the anthropologist will make every attempt to observe real or actual behaviour as well. His most important field technique is participant-observation; it provides the basis for his accounts of what "really is" as well as what people tell him "ought to be." The fact that ideal and real behaviour are often disparate is not disconcerting to the anthropologist as long as he is satisfied that he has adequately described them both. He is not compelled to make judgements on discrepancies between real and ideal behaviour any more than he is compelled to judge a culture as good or bad.

The purpose of this chapter is to take the perspective and methodology of the anthropologist to explore the real behaviour of teachers and pupils in selecting, utilizing, and learning from instructional media. The emphasis here is not on *ideal* or *normative* aspect of teacher behaviour—how teachers should act, the kinds of goals or objectives towards which they should strive, the best ways to organise for instruction, or the right ways to select and use media—but rather on such questions as: What actually goes on in the classroom when teacher avail themselves of media. Are the only lessons learned the ones the teacher intends to teach? Are audiovisual aids and other media an unmitigated blessing? or can they also produce stress and conflict in teacher behaviour and unintended lessons for pupils?

This discussion and the accompanying accounts of classroom behaviour deal with instances in which instructional media, particularly the most frequently used audiovisual aids, are utilized. The implications of these comments are not limited only to such situations. Every classroom lesson, independent of whether the teacher supplements the instruction by using media, provides the opportunity for ideal behaviour to be at variance with real behaviour, for ideal teacher purposes to be pre-empted by accompanying learnings which provide a lesson of different consequences for the pupil. A lesson never looks exactly the same to the learner as it looks to the teacher.

Actual classroom behaviour is far more complex than phrases like "good teaching" or "proper use of instructional media" imply. There are aspects of instruction which are incidental to or even antithetical to the intended or ideal purposes. These incidental or unintended aspects are here called *concomitant learnings.*

Observing and recording protocols of the actual verbal behaviour in classroom is one of the assignments of a course titles "School in American Life" taught by this writer. Students practice the techniques of observation in the college classroom before proceeding to the public schools. From hundreds of protocols of classroom behaviour made by students over a period of two years, examples have been selected with illustrate the concomitant aspects of intended and unintended consequences in classroom instruction where teachers happened to be using instructional media when students came to observe. The protocols are quoted verbatim in this chapter, as submitted by the students. While it is impossible to appraise the accuracy of any protocol, the very divergence among the students and their naivete as classroom observers should preclude systematic biases or errors. The observations were not made in "demonstration" classrooms. Students were extended an invitation to observe in several schools each term, and they were also free to make arrangements for visits at other schools. Thus, most teachers did not know that they would be having an observer until a student entered the classroom.

Intended Learnings

In his instructional role, at least part of a teacher's behaviour is consciously directed toward producing some change in a learner, whether it be the acquisition of a new fact, a reorganisation of existing information, or a reinforcement of or shift in values or attitudes. In its most formal aspect, such behaviour by teacher reflects their intention as expressed in lesson plans, courses of study, and the whole concept of curriculum. In addition to any preplanned and structured meeting out of facts, concepts, and generalizations, teachers also consciously take the responsibility for instructing their pupils in attitudes and values as opportunities arise, particularly values concerning punctuality, cleanliness, courtesy, aesthetic appreciation, and love of learning—those which we often associate with the "middle-class bias" of schools. While we can easily think of some examples of intended learnings, it seems unlikely that a teacher can explicitly identify the totality of learnings he intends to impart. Each of us internalizes his "culture" to the extent that he takes for granted much of his own behaviour, his reactions, and his expectations for others, including the expectations which teachers hold for their students.

Instruction in the classroom presents problems in the *selection and accuracy of content* and in the determination of *how much information* to introduce and *which information to emphasize.* In the following protocol of a fifth-grade class during a science lesson, for example, the teacher appears to be getting the lesson across just as she intends it. Further, she is using certain pedagogically approved techniques (eliciting class response, developing an outline on the chalkboard, relating discussion to experience). Yet, the scope of the lesson suggest a superficiality in dealing with content which may not be as uncommon in the classroom as we might like to imagine.

Observation No. 1

T: What are some metals which we use every day? [*No response*] Let's start with some of those mentioned last time. [*As the students answered she wrote the words on the chalkboard.*]

P: Quartz.

P: Gold.

P: Silver.

P: Copper.

T: And what do we use copper for?

P: Pennies.

T: Is there anything else we should add to our list?

P: Lead.

T: [*Pointing o list*] Do you know that our bodies contain all of these? Using your element charts, what are some other things we use?

P: Gases.

T: Which ones?

P: Oxygen to breathe with.

T: Do you see why these things are so valuable to us? It's their properties. What are properties? [*No responses*] Well, which would you rather fall into, a tub of iron or a tub of cotton?

P: Cotton.

T: Why?

P: It's softer.

T: [*Writing "Soft" on board*] All right, what are some other properties of any matter then?

P: Hardness.

Other pupils, one after another: Sweetness. Cold. Sourness. Heavy. [*Some time is devoted to a discussion of examples of matter which possessed the properties written on the board.*]

T: These properties are very important, then. Now, what are some other gases?

P: Helium.

T: What do we use helium for?

P: Weather balloons.

T: What else is important to us?

P: Iodine.

T: Why?

P: We need it in our bodies.
T: Any other thing?
P: Uranium which we use in bombs.
P: It kills with radiation.
T: Let's get off war. How do we use it for peace?
P: For power.
P: We can use it for power and not build dams.

This protocol illustrates that even when the lesson proceeds simply and directly in the way the teacher directs it, the problems of selecting and presenting content to accomplish teaching purpose are never simple. In this illustration, what the teacher intends to accomplish is not easily discernible. What the children *may* be learning includes not only a vague notion of properties, or the fact that we are surrounded by the elements, but also how to give the teacher the answer she wants, learning not to explore questions to any depth, or learning that to be a teacher all one has to do is write what pupils say on a blackboard.

The protocols which follow provide date for exploring classroom behaviour in which the actual lesson perceived by the learner may be far removed from the ideal intent of the teacher.

Accuracy of the content present a problem in intended instruction. In the following example from a high school biology class, the student observer, a former laboratory technician who has returned to the university to prepare for teaching high school science, included in her observation notes two parenthetical comments identifying misinformation in the teacher's instructions.

Observation No. 2

T: What else might happen that could contaminate our cultures?
G: Dirty test tubes.
T: That's right, but ours were sterile. Open tubes and currents of air flowing in can sweep bacteria right into it. What else?
B: Coughing or sneezing on it.
T: That will do it, too. Remember how to hold the tube? Hold the open and down [*Teacher holds agar tube upside down. Observer shudders at technique!*] so air won't go

in and stuff fall into it. [*Good trick if one can hack it. What you really do is hold it horizontally and not vertically!*].

T: Question number four: "How can contamination be prevented?" I think we've pretty well answered this. [*Teacher explains why it is necessary to flame loop after transplanting bacteria. Demonstrates loop and how to use it to students. Shows how students make mistake of laying loop down on table with bacteria still on it.*] Bacteria are all pathogenie, so remember that. [*Whoops! Error number two. I hope they don't remember that statement!*]

The observer's first comment calls attention to one of the most common assumptions regarding the use of instructional aids or equipment in classrooms—that teachers have the skill for using the materials with which they are provided. The observer's second comment questions the accuracy of the teacher's knowledge. Faced with the growing number of instructional aids for individual classrooms—the new "hardware" of educational technology—and the popular concept of an "explosion" of knowledge, we may suspect that it is the teacher's lack of ability or interest in acquiring new skills and knowledge that provided the major constraint in attempts at curriculum change. Further examples of this problem are provided later in the chapter.

Teachers are not required to be experts in all field. In confronting problems in the scope of their studies and in providing accurate up-to-date information, teachers have the resources of both specialist personnel and specially developed media, with perhaps educational films firmly entrenched as the favourite source of instructional assistance. Yet, in the following protocol taken in a first-and second-grade classroom, the instructional value of the first of two films shown (a film presenting land and water forms) seems to have been negligible when evaluated by the discussion that followed it. The problem with the second film—that it was not the film originally ordered—has implications that will be discussed later concerning the unintended aspects of instruction.

Before the observer entered the classroom, children from two other first-and second-grade classed had come to the room to see the film on land formation and bodies of water. Children were watching the film when the observer arrived.

Observation No. 3

[*Pupils are quietly watching film.*]

[*film ends, pupils clap.*]

[*There is to be another film, so pupils sing a song about speckled frogs, waiting for the projector operator.*]

[*The teacher asks whether the children know anything about the name, Washington. I couldn't hear their replies.*]

[*The film is supposed to be about Washington but it is the wrong film. It is a film about service stations; it is shown anyway.*]

[*Film gets underway. The pupils whisper or giggle occasionally.*]

[*Special announcement over the intercom interrupts during the film: Would all cleanup members come to room five right now. Two pupils leave.*]

[*Film ends, pupils clap.*]

[*The two visiting classes line up at door and leave. Remaining children relocate furniture, raise blinds, and take down the screen.*]

[*The teacher goes to the front of the room, and the pupils gather around her.*]

[*Last of visiting teachers leaves with projector.*]

T: We don't have too much time left. We will talk about the film on land and water. What kind of land is a mountain?

P: It's rocky and steep.

T: Very good.

P: Land is dirt, and—

T: Yes, but what *kind* of land?

P: It is cole in the mountains.

T: Why?

P: Clouds and rain make it cold.

T: Ok, good.

. . . .

T: And is a hill different from a mountain?

P: They aren't as steep and not as high.

P: They have a round top.

P: Hills are flatter.

P: Hills have grass and mountains don't.

[*Similar discussion takes place about valleys and plans.*]

. . . .

T: So what kinds of land have we talked about?

P: ...[*Observer couldn't hear the reply.*]

P: Valleys, mountain, hills, and plains.
T: OK. [*Directs discussion to water.*] What else did you notice about a stream?
P: ...smaller.
P: Streams are kind a heading down hill.
T: What kind of water stays in one place?
P: Mud puddles.
T: Good.
P: Lakes.
T: Yes.

. . . .

T: What lakes do you know of that we have around here?
P: Crater Lake.
P: Diamond Lake.
P: Pacific Lake.
P: Oh! That's an ocean.
T: I can tell that you did a good job today watching the movie.

From the teacher's closing comment, one might assume that the comments of the children measured her that her instructional purposes were accomplished. Although the protocol of the discussion is not complete, the samples which the observer recorded suggest that the film provided little more than what some administrators refer to as a "time-killer," a suspicion supported by the showing of the second film.

Polyphasic Learning

Another aspect of intended instruction adds to the complexity of what teacher attempt to accomplish in class. This is a consequence of the tendency in formal education (more obvious in the lower grades but evident at all levels) to derive more than one lesson from any "learning experience." The anthropologist Jules Henry has suggested the term *polyphasic learning* to describe this process of learning more than one thing at a time. He contracts polyphasic learning with monophasic learning, the hypothetical case in which only one thing is learned at one time. It is hypothetical, Henry insists, because it is a human inability. Henry describes the extent to which polyphasic learning is emphasized or de-emphasized in an instructional setting as a cultural variable, and his observation in public schools lead him to conclude that American teacher *emphasize* the polyphasic aspects of learning. Here is Henry's discussion and a protocol he uses for illustration:

> Polyphasic learning is the process of learning more than one thing at a time. Normal human beings cannot learn only one thing at a time; rather they learn a pattern. This capacity to learn more than one thing at a time—to receive complex inputs—is exploited in different ways in various periods in our own culture. The present tendency in elementary school education is to *exploit consciously such polyphasic learning capacities.* In simple societies the storage processes often handle but very little information at a time; and even when information is relatively complex, the input process is not specifically developed with this complexity in the minds of the teachers. That is to say, for example, that while food-sharing among the Pilaga Indians ends up being not only the process of giving away one's food, but also a way of operating a scale of social distance, food-sharing *as information* is not consciously taught as a social distance scale. It is the difference between saying, "Give food to people," and saying, "Give food to your first cousins through your mother." In the first instance the individual simply learns that he has to share food, in the second he is required to master a social system in connection with the giving of food. It is the second instance that is polyphasic in *intent.*
>
> The present tendency in elementary school education in the United States is to exploit polyphasic learning capacities consciously. Thus a painting lesson becomes not only one in art, embodying the use of colours and brushes, learning the names of colours and how to mix them, and so on, but also a lesson in geography and human relations. A painting of the Sahara Desert becomes a vehicle through which to communicate information about Africa, Arabs, and the Mohammedan religion *all at the same time.*

The following extract from a protocol of observations in a fifth grade classroom will further illustrate the point.

Teacher: What does art do for us?
Student: It cheers us up.
Teacher: It cheers us up. Yes, beautiful things will cheer you up when you're feeling bad. What else does it do?
Student: It express yourself—I mean it's not just copied
Teacher: What does it express about yourself?
Student: How you feel.

> Students go on to say that a happy artist draws bright colours, and unhappy artists use dark colours or gray. Teacher points our exceptions: when the artist is producing a scene in which the subject is dark or gray. She says, "if a person is not disturbed, mentally or nervously, he tends to like bright colours, doesn't he?" Teacher announces she is going to play records which a student has brought, and the class is to listen to them, get the feel and the rhythm—whether it is active, soft, soothing, or what—and then express themselves in a picture. She says, "You know, the more intriguing your picture is the more valuable it is. You may have a five-hundred dollar picture when you get through." [*Both sides of the record are waltzes.*]
>
> Teacher stops the record, says, "Some of you are drawing before you feel the rhythm. You are bound to have a picture in your mind, but I'II make a bargain with you. Listen to the rhythm of the music, and then just cut loose and express yourself this time and we'II draw the old-fashioned way another day this week." Teacher stops the music and says, "If you were in New York in an art class, you'd be paying ten dollars for this lesson, and if you talked, out you'd go. It's selfish to disturb your neighbour—now just be quiet." Plays more music.

From this example we see that what is ostensibly an art lesson is exploited, as a polyphasic learning experience for the purpose of attempting to teach among other things the following: (1) The immorality and even disease of being unhappy; (2) notions of economic life and the market; (3) the myth of the pot of gold at the end of the rainbow ("You may have a five-hundred dollar picture when you get through"); (4) the importance of "cutting loose,' but under the proper circumstances; (5) the relationship (?) between music and painting on the one hand, and "self-expression" on the other. We observe also efforts to control children's spontaneous expressiveness (dark colours should not be used), and above all, we can see that this art lesson is used to maintain level or organisation in the American culture as a whole.

Henry's discussion of polyphasic learning is included here because the utilization of any special media in a classroom introduces additional stimuli into the learning situation. External stimuli tend to increase the polyphasic nature of instruction; thus, the content of an educational film shown to a class may be only one facet of a complex lesson in which the teacher concomitantly gives (intended) instruction in courtesy

("Who remembers how we act when we watch a film?"), care, and use of equipment ("Be careful with that screen, boys"), allocation of privileges ("Who would like to take the film back to the office?"), management of time ("We'II have to hurry because another class needs the projector"), and so forth.

As the significance of the media increases (reflecting such criteria as uniqueness, duration, cost, relevance to the instructional programme), there is a tendency to increase the polyphasic aspec. of the lesson. Thus the amount of "readiness" instruction and the number of intended lessons which the teacher draws out of a regularly viewed TV programme may seem minor when compared to the effort expended in preparation for a special visitor or for a classroom field trip. As an example, consider the following protocol taken in a fourth-grade class planning an ambitious field trip to explore tidepools at the distant seashore.

Observation No. 4

T: Before we take our field trip, we have to get ourselves organises. [*The noise has not yet subsided.*] Class, I'm waiting on you. [*The class becomes quieter.*] Now, I think rather than having me tell you what we are going to do at the beach—which would make it may trip—I'II let you decide what we are going to do so that it really will be your trip. So let's divide into committees, and each committee would be responsible for planning the action for one thing. For example, we would need a committee for clothing; the committee would then decide what kind of clothing we will need.

B: Swimming suit.

T: Mike, you had your hand raised.

B: No.

T: Can someone else think of another committee? Roger.

B: A committee for clothing and lunch. [*Teacher writes on blackboard: "I, Clothing and food."*]

T: What other committee?

B: Games.

T: Yes, activities. [*She writes: "2. Activities."*]

B: Can we run out in the water?

T: [*Evidently she didn't hear this question.*] Oh yes, before we forget, there is a law that says we can't we take things out of the tidepools.

B: I'm gonna.

T: [*She ignores this remark.*] What other committee?

B: A committee to decide on behaviour on the bus, because it's a long trip to the coast.

T: Very good, yes, behaviour on the bus. [*She writes: "3. Standards on bus."*]

G: Yea, a list on no-no's.

T: [*Laughing*] No-no's. I guess you might call them that.

B: We'II some guys to keep order on the bus. [*The majority of students start giving ideas all at once.*]

B: People don't push in lines on the bus.

T: Roger.

B: We could use the same people on the beach that are on the bus for standards.

T: Yes, very good Roger. We will need a committee for standards on the beach, too. [*She writes: "4. Standards on the beach."*]

G: Yes, I think we'II need two committees.

T: OK, now, we have four committees. I think that is enough. Number one is for clothing, what to take, wear, remember it might be raining. Number two, activities—this committee will think of things to do at the tidepools and on the beach. [*Students start yelling out things they think of like bats and balls, surfboards.*]

G: Can we take—

T: Why don't we let each committee decide for each thing? Now think for a minute about which committee you want to be on. [*Pause*] We will also need a chairman for each group. OK, who wants to work on clothing and food? [*Many hands come up.*] Steve, James, Cynthia, and Jimmie. Steve, will you be chairman? OK, for activities. [*Many hands come up.*] Mike, Brian and Dave. OK, standards on the bus. [*Two hands come up.*] Richard, Roger. We need a few more people.

B: Aren't there supposed to be two? Can we work on two committees?

T: No, if you work on one that will be enough. Mark, why don't you be chairman. [*She points to the rest of the people to be on the committee.*] You're going to want to meet in discussion groups. [*She points to certain places in the room and designates which committee will meet there.*]

[*Each group runs to its designated place, there is a great deal of noise. Two girls remain at their desks.*]

T: You have 15 minutes and then we'II meet back in our seat's [*She walks over to me and says: "You're now going to see the fourth grade at its peak in interaction."*]

It is hardly surprising to find extensive classroom attention in preparation for a field trip. The point is that the introduction of outside media may have a tendency to provide so many "teachable" aspects that the instructional impact of the lesson gets lost. Teachers are seldom conscious of their inclination to make complex lessons out of simple ones, drawing attention away from the intended lesson. In the class-room cited above, the presumed focus of the trip—the content of the tidepools—has at least temporarily been obscured by the extent of the other preparations.

Thus far we have considered classroom behaviour concerning the use of media from the perspective of the teacher's intent. Henry's notion of polyphasic learning—that we learn more than one thing at a time—invites another consideration. The lesson as perceived by the learner is not restricted only to those elements which the teacher intends. In the same way that the introduction of instructional media creates a variety of learning situations on which the teacher may draw, so, too, the media create sometimes uncontrollable or unanticipated consequences that provide concomitant learnings.

Unintended Learnings

The teacher's intended or stated purpose for introducing education media is usually to increase the basic information of the students or to help them reorganise information they already possess. We have already noted how ideal purposes can be compromised by problems related to the scope, accuracy, or relevance of introduced material and by an inclination among teachers to overload or overwork educational experiences. These problems were introduced as functions of the intent and skill of the teacher; the educational consequence were related to the teacher's competence.

We now explore some possible stresses for the teacher who augments his instructional programme by introducing media. The utilization of any media may force compromises in the way a teacher attempts to fulfill his ideal role. Media may become a variable external to the teacher and, therefore, not subject to his control. The result may be a learning that is incidental or antithetical to the intent in instruction.

Media as Sources of Stress in the Teachers' Role

The Preview Problem

Ideally, the teacher in the classroom is the instructional leader for his students. He is also responsible for their demeanor while in the classroom. Media can compromise him on both counts. For example, as instructional leader, a teacher is expected to be familiar with the material he presents to his class, so that he can select material that is appropriate and can guide his pupils in the use of the material. In the case of audiovisual materials, this necessitates previewing.

No teacher will argue against the desirability for previewing, but this is often impossible. The demands on a teacher's time are great, and the demands placed on the beginning teacher (the very teacher least likely to have prior information about available audiovisual material) are literally overwhelming. Even experienced teachers know the difficulties sometimes involved in coordinating a projector, a classroom, and a film along with the time to view it on just one occasion. Previewing requires this operation to be carried out twice. Consequently, beginning teacher either restrict their use of media to what they can examine beforehand or they use media in a way which has been described in their teacher-training courses as irresponsible. Seldom are aspiring teachers made aware of the idealistic nature of their training.

Media as Teacher Surrogate

If the teacher has not previewed the film, scouted a field trip, briefed himself on the TV lesson of the day, or conferred previously with a guest speaker, he abdicates his leadership—he puts his instructional programme in someone else's hands and literally takes potluck on the outcome. The compromise may not be a comfortable one. The increasing use of TV instruction in classrooms, such as the short daily programme in foreign language instruction common in upper elementary grades in some areas, represents a case where the teacher abdicates his position as instructional leader of the classroom every day. The result is that the teacher is left with no role to perform or with only the role of disciplinarian. The following protocol from a sixth grade illustrates the passive role taken by one classroom teacher while the TV teacher "takes over" the class. One wonders if the remark of the teacher at the conclusion of the telecast is a reaction to pupil behaviour or to the fact of the television itself.

Observation No. 5

[*The teacher turns on the television and sits down in the back of the room. The TV instructor is a woman and is indicated by "TV." She uses a chalkboard.*]

TV: Today were going to work on complete factorization. Does anyone know the difference between factoring and complete factorization?

T: Who knows?

P: Complete factorization is when you work the number clear down to its prime.

T: How many agree? [*The student's hands go up, and it looks as if everyone agrees.*]

TV: Can two times two to the second power (2×2^2) be reduced any farther?

T: Can it be?

P: No.

TV: Let's use the number 84 for practice. I want the boys to begin with 4×21, and the girls to begin with 6×14. I want both groups to work these down to their primes. [*The students are now busy working out the problem. They have all finished in two minutes.*]

TV: Okay now, you should all be about finished about now. We'II start with the boys first. We can factor 4 into 2×2 or 2 to the second power. We can factor 21 into 7×3. Our answer now should be 2 to the second power times 7 times 3. These are your primes. Okay girls. We can factor 6 into 3×2. Now we can factor 14 into 7×2. Our answer now should be 2 to the second power times 3 times 7. Now you can see that no matter how you go at it your always get the same primes if your answer is right. By dividing the class into boys on one side, and the girls on the other, we can get better arguments.

TV: Will the number 12 have more than one complete factorization?

T: Will it?

P: No.

TV: By now you should know that there is only one complete factorization. This is the Unique Factorization Property.

....

TV: I want you now to try to complete this fraction. [*She writes the number 36/48. The students are busy working out the problem.*]

TV: your can reduce 36 down to 2 × 18: 2 × 18 = 2 × 2 × 3 × 3 = 2 to the second power times 3 to the second power. We use the same unbrilliant approach to 48: 2 × 24 = 2 × 2 × 2 × 6 = 2 × 2 × 2 × 2 × 3 = 2 to the fourth power times 3. [*The classroom teacher gets up from her seat to check on one of the pupils work. The pupils has some pictures drawn on the paper, but there are no number written down I couldn't hear what she said to him.*]

TV: For your assignment tomorrow, I want you to read exercises 5-5, and do exercises 5-5c, 9-28. Practice up on your factorization at home tonight because were going to have more of it tomorrow. Goodbye. [*The classroom teacher comes to the front of the room and turns off the television.*]

T: I want you to be quieter for me that you were for her. Let's work 45/75 down to its prime...

The recorded remarks of the classroom teacher during the telecast: "How many agree"? Can it be? and "Will it"? do not provide the teacher with a very important instructional role in the presence of the television instructor. Actually, the teacher has only repeated the TV instructor's question, presumably as a sort of self-appointed audience prompter for the students. Whether pupils *need* a prompt is questionable, although the protocol suggests that in the classroom being observed pupils expect a prompt to precede any response they will make. Acting as a prompter is not a highly satisfying task for most classroom teachers; rather, it is a potential source of role stress and conflict.

Mechanical Problems

Studies of the adoption and rejection of new media provide interesting cases of persistence and change within the educational institution. For many teacher, introducing audiovisual equipment into the classroom also introduces an element of tension or excited confusion.

Some teacher refuse to incorporate newer media, particularly the electromechanical innovations, in their classroom for this very reason. Other teachers accept new innovations as part of the inevitable march of progress, but they relegate the operation of equipment, frequently depending on their students for any prerequisite technical skills. Indeed, some teacher never learn to operate even the simplest of projectors or machines with any apparent confidence.

Coping with mechanical difficulties and breakdowns in equipment, or with organizational problems such as the sharing of equipment among colleagues, sometimes leads to unintended learnings because such situations catch the teacher off guard. Not every teacher reacts to mechanical difficulties with the calm observed in the following situation, but few teachers have as small a class as this one of seven students in an eighth-grade class in French. Note that the student observer included her personal reaction to the use of the film being presented, both for its content and its appropriateness in a language class.

Observation No. 6

T: Is there anyone who would violently object to having the written dictee tomorrow so we can see a film today?

Class: [*In unsion]* No.

T: Maintenant, le cinema pour aujourd'hui est concernee de Monseiur De Gaulle. II s'applle *France and the French People.*

[The film is black and white and is in English. Most of the French is translated by the narrator of the film. I certainly feel that this particular film would be of much better use in a social studies class. It gives a fairly idealistic view of France under De Gaulle, but the worst part of the film is that it is entirely in English, thus not really benefiting those in the French class who want to extend their speaking and understanding and understanding abilities of the language. The film greatly exalts and glorifies De Gaulle.]

[All seven students seemed to be interested, because they were all watching the screen. The teacher got up from her desk after the first few minutes of the film and walked over to a file cabinet at the other end of the room by the sink. She remained there for 5 minutes and then left the room via the back door.]

[The boys suddenly burst into laugher when someone discovered that the takeup reel was not operating. The takeup reel had been put one the wrong way, and there was a huge pile of film on the floor beneath the projector. The girls started to laugh too.]

P: I guses we had better do something about it.

[The student got up from his desk and walked over to the projector. Since he couldn't find the of-on switch, he pulled the cord out of the socket on the wall. Just then the teacher came back into the room, noticed all the students out of their seats surrounding the projector, and she turned on the lights in the room.]

T: Oh, no What's happened? Oh, why do these things always happen to me? *[All the students help to put the film back on the reel correctly.]*

P_2: Wouldn't it be awful; if the film was all over the room?

T: We are going to have two more films tomorrow. I certainly hope that this doesn't happen again.

The Problem of Availability

Frequently, the use of media compromises the teacher's efforts to provide continuity in his organization for instruction. The teacher does not necessarily have access to people transportation, or materials when he needs them. Conversely, the availability of resources such as a special exhibit or a frequently requested item from an instructional materials center often dictates the time and conditions when media can be used. The compromise arises because teachers attempt to organise be used learning experiences systematically, building on experience through a planned "scope and sequence" of curriculum organization. The seemingly capricious way in which orders for instructional aids sometimes arrive at the classroom finds teachers faced with a dilemma. They can fragment one lesson with vestiges of an earlier one, or they can elect not to introduce some additional source of information with the rationale that if it is not available at an appropriate time in an instructional sequence, then there is no point in using it all. In the following example, a teacher has just concluded a science lesson with his ninth-grade class and he has explained to the student observer why be felt the lesson (about snakes) has not been successful.

Observation No. 7

[After class I talked with the teacher who had by this time taken out the snake and put it around his arm again. He indicated that the class which I had just observed had been completely unprepared in that they were not due to discuss snakes for about a week. But another teacher from another school had brought the snakes over to him that morning, so he decided to use them for the class, as he would only have them for that one day.]

In a comparable illustration, a sixth-grade social studies lesson about Rio de Janiero is interrupted when a pupil comes to the classroom to announce the arrival at the school of an exhibit of to live farm animals sponsored by a local dairy company. As the observer notes, the exhibit is visited by every classroom in the school. Teachers do not customarily decline "invitation" for instructional experiences regardless of the immediate relevance of such experiences.

Observation No. 8

[There is a knock at the door during the discussion of Rio de Janiero, One of the pupils gets up and goes to the door.]

T: I'II get it. [*The teacher goes to the door and then returns to the room after talking to the messenger.]* The Dairy Display is here and we have been invited to go through it. This is the [name of local milk company] Story Book Barn. Shut your books and line up at the door. [*The students, teacher and observer leave the room and go outside to the display. The display consists of a pick-up truck pulling a trailer. Inside the trailer are two pigs, a rabbit, a rooster, a horse, a cow, and a goat. Every classroom in the school visits the display.*]

T: When you get through the display go back to the room and start work on your social studies. [To observer]: These kids are real good about keeping busy when I'm gone.

The Problem of Advertising

A display such as the free one sponsored by the local dairy presents yet another dilemma for the teacher. The dilemma pits pragmatism against idealism, for in the use of "free and inexpensive materials" in class (a practice of such scope that it supports the publication and sale of an annual catalogue of material), the teacher must measure his comments about the material between the extreme of endorsing the blatant advertising motives of the industries that provide them, and that of failing to extend the courtesy of recognition and appreciation for useful instructional material. From the teachers point of view the problem does not have an easy solution unless district policy provides strict guidelines for the use of free materials (in which case the school-board members have had to argue whether free materials handed out by the Bell Telephone Company differ from those handed out by the Red Cross of the Audubon Society). If the school board does have a policy, the teacher is compromised because he is denied the right to use his professional judgement in a matter which he may feel is properly within his domain.

The relationship between the teacher and the profit-making, political and religious activities of the community are tenuous. School people as a group are careful not to aggravate either local norms or national stereotypes in this regard; the evidence suggests that professional educators continue to act more conservatively in regard to community expectations than the members of the community actually feel they should. Thereby, pupils are witness, at least indirectly, to a kind of don't rock the boat behaviour which reinforced another unintended lesson—that teachers are relatively cautions, conservative, sometimes peripheral members of the profit and issue-making activities of the adult community.

The Teacher as a Learner

Another source of stress introduced through the utilization of media derives from the ideal that the teacher be both well informed and a disciple of learning. The ideal teacher is thought of as one who brings knowledge to his pupils at the same time that he, himself, is forever an enthusiastic seeker of knowledge. Classroom observations suggest that teacher behaviour as it relates to the utilization of media can teach other lessons instead, for not every teacher can juggle the role of humble, inquiring learner with the all-knowing role of sage. Not all pupils recognise that one reason their teachers appear to be so knowledgeable is that the teacher controls both the content and direction of class activity. The teacher teaches that which he can—that which he knows.

The teacher who includes external sources of information in his instructional programme risks losing control of the content and direction in the lesson. The content has been pre-packaged for him in the vedio-tape, the film, or even in the comments which an uncoached resources person may make in speaking to a group of students. The teachers reaction to information which he does not control and which is unfamiliar to him may teach a love of inquiry, but it may also teach that learning requires too much effort, is too time-consuming, too boring, too difficult, or that it is an activity suitable for children but of no consequence for adults.

In the following protocol, a fourth-grade teacher demonstrating with slide projection may be teaching far different attitudes toward learning in general, and specifically toward scientific names, than those she intends to teach.

Observation No. 9

[*During the showing of the slides it was hard to take notes since the teacher was showing me things and then sometimes the other teacher would ask her questions. But here is an except from the slides while the teacher was narrating.*]

T: Myitods [?] do thousands of dollars worth of damage each year. Pinworms are found on fresh fruits. So don't eat fresh fruits and vegetables from the market without washing them.

Tom, would you please shut the door and sit down?

Horsehair worms—Now you kids probably have never been around this but when I was a girl someone told me to put a horsehair in water and we would get a horsehair worms. So we went out where the horse was kept and got a horsehair. We put the hair in water, but after several days of waiting and watching, we found out they had played a joke on us. [*The children laughed.*] But now this is a true story. [*The teacher read the background of the horsehair worm—the story was printed on the slide which showed on the screen.*] In the barn-yard we used to find them 15 inches long but this says the average length is 6 inches.

This one, the Arrow Worm, Phylum... Wow, I can't pronounce this one kids [a long Latin name that I didn't get copied down] is a free swimmer among the plankton we studied about.

[*Two boys walks around the room. Three boys talk together in a little group. One girl plays with the window-shade string.*]

T: You know, if some of you kids were quiet back there, I wouldn't need to read as loud.

These look like cherries, but they are lamp shells. I won't even try to pronounce this word [Latin name], because I won't put the accent in the right place.

Whether the teacher should have read these particular Latin names in this particular class's moot. The important point is that the way in which teachers confront new or unfamiliar information becomes a part of what they teach. Not all teacher even subject themselves to the same instructional programme that they provide for their pupils. One wonders what concomitant learning results when teachers turn the attention of the class to a telecast, broadcast, or film and then *leave the classroom.* In the following *example* from a fourth grade, the teacher did not return to the classroom until the conclusion of a fifteen-minute radio broadcast turned on at the office after recess.

Observation No. 10

[*It is recess time. The teacher leaves the back of the room, where she has been talking to me, and walks to the front of the room to get her purse.*]

T: [*To observer*] Would you like to go for office? [*I said I would stay in the classroom., She left the room. Some children remained in the classroom recess in order to work an arithmetic papers.*]

Time: 10:15

[*The rest of the class comes in from recess and promptly takes seats. One girls does not head for her seat but instead walks up to the teacher's desk and picks up a stack of papers. From observing, I guessed the paper were the corrected math assignment from the previous day.*]

Time: 10:18

[*The intercom now comes on in the classroom with a radio broadcast. Four different voices are heard. These are the voices of a frontier man and wife and their two children. I would estimate the age of the boy to be 9-12 and the age of the girl to be 5-8. About half of the students lay down their pencils and turn towards the intercom while the other half seem to be listening but continue to write. The story is about frontier life and the problems the early settlers were likely to encounter. In the story, the husband is forced to leave his family because of his participation in battles outside the settlement. The young boy has been given directions by his father to take care of the family and the farm. One day his little sister disappears. With the aid of an Indian boy, they find her safely. This incident reduces the tension between the two fighting groups, the settlers and the Indians. The radio then goes off. Shortly thereafter the teacher walks in.*]

T: Ok class, hand in those math papers. [*The students get out of their seats to deposit their papers at a common point on the side of the room.]*

Administrative policy varies between districts and schools as to whether a classroom can be left without supervision. In schools where the teacher may not leave the class unsupervised, he can still escape by not subjecting himself to the message of the media. Thus, we observe teachers who use the running time of film or broadcast to dust the room, arrange bulletin boards, correct papers, or handle administrative details. Such behaviour on the teacher's part does not necessarily teach pupils anything antithetical to the teacher's stated purposes, but a teacher who ignores the instructional content of the media he introduces would do well to consider the question: What does my behaviour in the classroom teach my pupils about learning? Curiously, when it is the pupil who ignores the media, teachers have a host of labels by which they characterize him: daydreamer, disinterested, inattentive, reluctant learner, and so forth.

Media as Moralists

As a final example of how media produce comprises in the ideal teacher role, consider the normative content of much school instruction, the "shoulds" and "oughts" through which models of proper behaviour are presented to the young. Through the place he allocates to various normative aspects of behaviour, the teacher can circumvent discussion about those norms with which his own behaviour conflicts. Thus, a teacher who "smokes" and "drinks" may be less inclined to speak out against such practices than the teacher who abstains, even though providing at least token instruction in health, safety, and morals is mandatory in most school districts. The health, safety, conservation, and patriotic films available for classrooms are typically hortative. While they are consistent with a moralizing tradition characteristic in American education, they may compromise the teacher as a model of good behaviour, with the unintended consequency of making him less effective in other aspects of the instructional programme. Not all teachers are able to find themselves guilty as easily as the eight-grade teacher in the following illustration from a class in health and safety.

Observation No. 11

[*The teacher arises and walks over to the overhead projector. He removes the paper he had previously laid there.*]

T: You have five minutes to complete the assignment. If your don't finish, come in the first thing in the morning. The books will be here for you. [*The teacher walks to the side of the room and picks up a podium and sets it down near the overhead projector. He inserts a paper into the machine and turns it on. On seeing that it works, he immediately turns it off. The teacher then walks out through the open door into the hall where he talks to a fellow teacher two or three minutes. The teacher enters the room.*]

T: OK, let's put the books away. [*The students leave their seats and take their books back to the bookshelf.*]

T: Get your notes out. Today we have a picture on the overhead that is a little elementary, but it has four important points that are worth remembering. OK, let's book at it. What's wrong in this picture?

P: That broken ladder rung.

T: OK, we should keep equipment in repair. How many of you can think of an example of equipment at home that is being used but is in need of repair? [*Two boys replay by raising hand.*] I don't think we thought about that one long enough. [*He shows the next picture.*]

P: That man is getting out of the car on the wrong side of the road.

T: How many of your parents are guilty here? [*About half of the class respond by raising their hands.*] Good, because I'm guilty of it too. Here I am trying to teach you something that I don't even do myself.

Several concomitant learnings may result from this or from any of the other protocols. Here, the eighth-grades may have learned that they should not get out of a car on the "wrong side of the road". They may have also learned that many adults, including their teacher, engage in such unsafe behaviour. Or they may have learned, instead, that safety discussions, like the pictures teachers use to initiate them, are a "little elementary".

Some Non-Instructional Aspects of Media Use

Introduction or Entertainment: The Delicate Compromise

Particularly in selecting and using films, teachers face another compromise of their ideal self-image. They ask themselves the rhetorical question: Are we teachers, or are we just babysitters? The "right" answer is, of course, that teachers are specialists who blend their knowledge of the universe with their knowledge of human beings as learners to produce desired changes in the behaviours and attitudes of their students. A teacher is not a paid entertainer who does from Monday through Friday what TV and "real" movies do on the weekend. Yet, we argue that school should not be dull. We search for variety in lessons for more effective ways to extend children's experiences, and for ways to win and reinforce their allegiance to school. The question of just how pleasant and "fun" to make school is crystallized for many teachers in the question: How many films shall I show, and how relevant do they have to be? If a film is entertaining but not very instructional is it shown anyway? The answer is often Yes. Recall an observer's comment cited at the beginning of the chapter. "The film is supposed to be about Washington but it is the wrong film. It is a film about service stations; it is shown anyway". In the following protocol, the instructional value of both short films which these seven and eight year-olds had come to watch seemed questionable to the observer.

Observation No. 12

T: You boys and girls are to line up and go to Room Two for a movie. Table One may go. Jennifer, you can do that later. Put the glue down.

Time: 12:25

[They went into the next room and sat in a semicircle. There were sixty-five children. Thirty-two of them sat in chairs, and the others sat on the floor in front of the chairs.]

T2: This is a film called Snuffy, Smokey Bear's Pal."

[Two girls walked in after the film started. The teacher, who was sitting next to me, said the children had been learning about conservation. Snuffy was a dog that spoke to the children about building fires and leaving a clean camp. The dog was watching some children on a picnic. In this five-

minute movie Snuffy said four times that he liked children who were good woodsmen and good campers, who would never be careless and let a fire start in the woods.]

P: Do we have another one?

T: That was fast. We have two.

[*There were three teachers in the room. One of them tried to quiet the students.*]

T3: Boys and girls! [*The room got a little quieter.*] *All boys* and girls! [*She waited for quiet.*] I think you can help Mrs. — most by talking softly, because when your voices get very big and loud, it bothers. We have a second film, and if you will talk softly, Mrs. —will have it ready in just a minute. The next film is from the Forestry Department. Do you remember when we had Smokey the Bear?

[*The second film stated just as this teacher finished speaking. The film was titled, "Junior Raindrop". It was a cartoon about a raindrop that started out as a nice little boy, but became a juvenile delinquent, then a gangster, when he was mixed with other raindrops in a flood. The narrator spoke too fast, end the sound was fuzzy, Five or six students in the back of the room were stretching and twisting. The movie was oever at 1:15, and the children went outside for recess.*]

The conservation theme of both films may have justified their classroom use, although the observer seemed unimpressed by the content of either one. With the questionable educational value of many classroom films, it is not surprising that some educators dogmatically insist that teachers refer to such media as films rather than as "movies," hoping to minimize the association with entertainment. It is not too easy to enlist every member of the school staff in this linguistic plot. I recently overheard a school custodian explain that a classroom that appeared to be unoccupied was not deserted at all. "They've just havin' a show," he explained.

While audiovisual departments in large school districts try to devise ways to inform teachers of their *other* services and resources, the use of classroom films is so frequent in some schools and classrooms that it cause administrative uneasiness. In addition, upper-grade elementary school teachers disapprove of a practice of some primary-grade teachers who show all the films that come to the school, creating for the upper-grade teacher the frustrating moment when pupils make the comment that is the epitome of audiovisual sophistication: "Oh, we've already seen this."

Media in the Reward-Punishment System of the Classroom

Media can also be viewed as part of the reward-punishment system of the classroom. Filmstrips, field trips, records, films—all are intricately involved not with instructional content, but also with pupil-teacher interaction. Because of the popularity of films, literally any film has value as a reward which a teacher can confer and as a weapon with which to counter pupil misbehaviour or lack of endeavour: " If we have time" (i.e.; if class assignments are completed), or "If you are 'especially good' this afternoon," then the conditions have been met for the film.

In some classrooms, the good behaviour that is a condition for seeing a film includes student acceptance of the film (or speaker, or exhibit) as a favour or privilege granted by the teacher rather than as an instructional sources to be weighed and considered. In the following protocol from a high school class in economics, the class had just seen a film on international trade. The three-word appraisal of a student ("It was dumb") provoked a diatribe by the teacher in defense of the film, rather than a probing for the meaning of his comment.

Observation No. 13

[*A film has just been shown.*]

T: All right, what did your think of that film?

Richard: It was dumb.

Girls: It was pretty colour.

T: [*Addressijg Richard*] Your said it was dumb?

Richard: I did.

T: Why?

Richard: I don't know, it was just—

T: I thought it was a good film for economics. It was [good] because it showed...[*Observer could not keep up with the teacher*] and because of international trade. It was easy to see why we can't live without one another now. We actually can't. We need the things in foreign countries. [*Teacher started listing all the things she could think of form foreign countries. We started checking tings up to see just how many things we had—my sweater that I had on*

> *from Hong Kong; the coffee that we were drinking that came to us from South America; etc.*]This was a real good picture. The magnesium from Norway that goes into the making of suitcases—the Volkswagen from Germany coming to America...This was a good story in economics had your tried to get this out of the picture; and it didn't make you realize it all, Richard? And isn't that strange, I thought you would enjoy it.

The teacher's response suggests that she regarded Richard's remark as an affront to her personally. She did not let Richard explain his reaction, and he may be less inclined to comment next time a film is shown in that class—that is, of course, if another film is shown.

Pupils generally recognise the reward element of media, especially films ("Oh boy, a movie") used in class, and teachers take advantage of peer group pressures to keep everyone in class well behaved in order to "earn" an audiovisual reward. Students often react with such enthusiasm that the effect is disconcerting to the teacher who interprets the response as a lack of commitment to the customary classroom tasks. Not every possible instructional aid elicits an overwhelming response, however. Opaque projectors seem low on the popularity scale, and the excitement generated over the use of recordings of music or of filmstrips varies widely among schools.

Students are aware that the introduction of an instructional medium often has a "cost" in terms of consequent pupil effort. The use of a film may presuppose a subsequent assignment, frequently a written one, and particularly if there has been no prior bargaining for good behaviour. These assignments are often efforts, on the part of the teachers, to keep students fro identifying films and television used at school with commercial movies and commercial television; suspicious pupils may try to assess the terms under which the reward is being bestowed, ("Are we gonna' hafta' make a story about it after") An extreme example of this is suggested by the remark of a sixth-grade boy attending a week-long camp in outdoor education, a regular part of the sixth-grade curriculum in that school district. As a group of pupils and their adult leader approached the top of a ridge on a morning nature walk, the boy advised his friends, "Don't look at it. If you do, you'II have to write about it."

Media as Vehicles for Conveying Cultural Stereotypes

Some media, particularly artefacts and films concerning peoples in other parts of the world, provide the stimulus for another kind of concomitant learning. These learnings, usually unintended, reflect the attitude that our own way of life is the only right and proper way, and that the way any other people live is inferior. This attitude may be accompanied by the concession that no one is really at fault because not everyone has access to all our advantages. Anthropologists refer to this an ethnocentricism. It is an attitude that is antithetical to many stated teaching objectives, particularly in the social studies, concerning inter-group understanding, the dignity of all human beings, and the concept that there are countless variations in meeting and resolving the problems of human societies. The unintended aspect of instruction arises when teachers introduce artefacts from other cultures and present them to students out of cultural context, and with the expressed or implied notion that the culture under discussion is exotic, but, at the same time, impractical and second-rate. For example, in one ninth-grade social studies class, the teacher opened with the following comment:

> The afternoon class is very fortunate in having two students whose relatives have traveled all over the world. In the back of the room are several artifacts from Egypt and India. In the middle of the room are things from Iraq brought to Dave by an exchange student who is living with his family while he attends the University. We have some jewelry and bowls. Here is a light fixture which they put over lights. We tried it yesterday in my afternoon class and it is just beautiful. Do you know what these are? They're camel bells. [*She rings them.*] Wouldn't they make a beautiful sound around a camel's neck. Here we have a beautiful Egyptian tray. Dave asked us to be especially careful with it. And do you know what this is? It's a camel saddle. Isn't it funny looking? Dave said his little brother has so much fun sitting on it and pretending he's ridding a camel. [*A few students laugh.*] Now if any of you have interesting things to show please bring them.

By her comment, "Isn't it funny looking?", the teacher added a tiny increment on the side of cultural stereotyping. She lost an opportunity for her students to explore form and function which she might have fostered by asking such questions as, "Why do you think this saddle is shaped as it is" or "What would be some of the problems to overcome in designing a saddle for riding a camel?"

The tendency toward ethnocentricism is as prevalent in the content of many of the commercially prepared instructional media as it is in the incidental comments made by teacher.

Conclusion

In this chapter, the instructional content of the classroom has been considered from the perspective of the learner as well as from that of the teacher. While we can discuss, with some certainty, at least part of what the teacher intends to accomplish (we can both ask him to describe his intent and observe his behaviour in implementing it), we cannot do more than conjecture on all the possible dimensions of the lesson as perceived by the learner. The purpose of the discussion has been to alert the teacher or prospective teacher to the fact that the end product of the human teaching-learning interaction is seldom restricted to a unilateral transmission of an isolated unit of information. Lessons contain both intended and unintended elements, regardless of the sincerity, effort, dedication, or skill on the part of the teacher. Indeed, if teacher and pupil do not share a similar cultural heritage, there may be no intended learning at all.

We have used the term *concomitant learnings* to include all the learnings other than the central purpose of the lesson as intended by the teacher. They also include the incidental lesson as intended by the teacher. They also include the incidental lessons which a teacher would acknowledge as consistent with his intent, but which are not the focus of the lesson.

A lesson looks different from the bottom up than it does from the top down. From his point of view at the "top" of the lesson the teacher asks. "What did I intend to accomplish in this lesson?" and "How well did I succeed?" The teacher who seeks an awareness of his impact must also contemplate the lesson from the perspective of the learner. This leads him to ask: "How did my pupils perceive this lesson?" "What are the possible unintended consequences of my instruction?" With this approach, the teacher should be able to utilize educational media more effectively in the instructional process.

References

Eichholz, Gerhard, and Everett M. Rogers. "Resistance to the Adoption of Audio-Visual Aids by Elementary School Teachers: Contrasts and Similarities to Agricultural Innovation," in Matthew B. Miles, ed., *Innovation in Education,* Teacher College, Columbia University: Bureau of Publication, 1964.

Fordsdale, Louis. "S mm Motion Pictures in Education: Incipient Innovation," in Matthew B. Miles, ed., *Innovation in Education,* Teachers' College, Columbia University: Bureau of Publications, 1994.

Henry, Jules. "A cross-Cultural Outline of Education," *Current Anthropology* Vol. 1, July 1960, 267-305.

——. "Culture, Education, and Communication Theory," in George Spindler, ed., *Education, and Anthropology,* Standford University Press, 1955.

Sady, Rachel. "Teaching About Ethnocentricism," Occasional Paper No. 3. Anthropology Curriculum Study Project, Chicago: the Project, 5632 Kimbark Avenue, n.d., 15pp., mimeographed.

Spindler, George, "The Transmission of American Culture," in George Spindler, ed., *Education and Culture—Anthropological Approaches*, New York Holt, Rinehart & Winston. 1963.

7

The Media Service System in Each School

The one question frequently asked by new practitioners of media methodology is: How can I promote the use or instructional media in my school? Instead of answering it at once, we should counter with some questions of our own. The implication that is obvious in the original question is that the existing media-use program hasn't prospered, teachers haven't changed along desirable lines of action. We ask, "Why?" What learning-space media facilities have been provided? Do teachers get the assistance they need in changing to technological methods? Have they had reasonably good opportunities to develop a feeling of security with unfamiliar methods? In short, how effectively has the media-service program in the school been organised? We program in the school been organised? We must hasten to point out that *promotion* is hardly the world for the kind of *change process* that should be carried out in every school building in the country today. What media program directors must be able to do is to work with all concerned in establishing the fundamental conditions under which teachers can make use of media naturally and conveniently.

It has been emphasized repeatedly in previous discussions and in illustrations that media-service spaces are and have been included in new schools around the country and have also been provided when remodelling old schools. The reason is obvious, namely, the burgeoning of technology and in increased understanding of the roles that media play in modern education. In view of the essential character of a school's media-service system, this chapter is intended as a handbook for planning and implementation by innovators not only in each school building, but by the prospective school-system media program director as well.

Give Teachers the Help They Need

If we have learned anything about the process of facilitating media use, it is that we as change agents must give teachers the help they need in adjusting to new conditions. Of course teachers must also be motivated to the point of being willing to make innovations, but such efforts are likely to fall unless they can experience success in the new processes and be recognised and given attention along the way. The climate for such success is generated in large, part by the service system that is functioning in support of effective teaching.

It can be readily seen that as facilities for technological media are developed in the various learning spaces, teachers need technical and clerical support. For example, as teachers grow dependent upon the electronic learning laboratory as the means of teaching specified operations, such as learning the pronunciation of words or the operation of a microscope, and as such laboratory sessions are scheduled with regularity in the teaching process, technicians will simply have to be available throughout the day to keep the units operating. On the more professional side, it can also be seen that as teachers plan and write scripts for tap-recorded instruction, they need in-service education programs to develop new skills in pinpointing objectives and identifying appropriate pupil responses that will accomplish them. But then as the volume of writing builds up, teachers need additional clerical services. Thus we see that teachers have need of an array of in-school services, from professional skill-building activities and clerical and technical assistance to the ordering and scheduling of materials and mobile equipment.

Some Specific Kinds of Help Needed by Teachers: In the light of conditions already described we can list a number of important kinds of help commonly sought by teachers in carrying out their plans to use audiovisual media effectively.

The list that follows would of course vary as the program in each school varies from meagre to comprehensive. Teachers ordinarily seek help in:

1. Obtaining up-to-date information about locally owned materials.
2. Locating and scheduling needed materials from local and remote distributors.
3. Transmitting orders to local distribution headquarters.
4. Arranging for pre-use examination of materials.
5. Arranging optimum conditions for learning when media are to be used.
6. Learning to operate equipment.
7. Obtaining delivery to and pick-up of media equipment at classroom.
8. Obtaining the assistance of trained equipment operators whenever needed.
9. Finding what the trouble is when physical difficulties with materials and equipment arise.
10. Avoiding conflicts with plans of other teachers for material and equipment.
11. Obtaining supplies and equipment for the personal preparation of audiovisual media such as slides, transparencies, tapes, automatic sequences, and TV programs.
12. Obtaining media materials that are to be prepared by others for specific purposes.
13. Planning classroom presentations that are to be supported by special media productions.
14. Planning equipment installations in learning areas such as libraries, auditoriums, gymnasiums, and in school corridors for both general and highly specialised purposes.
15. Organising cooperative efforts with other teachers in preparing and exchanging, needed media to save time, effort, and expense.
16. Developing special professional skills for making effective use of media in both small and large groups.

A Cooperatively Formed Plan by School Principles and Media Program Directors: Giving such help is no easy matter, and if school principals and the school-system media program directors turn their backs on these needs, their best efforts to have an impact on the learner through modern media contributions fail. Therefore, the media director and principal must cooperatively establish a system of teaching services in each school building—elementary and secondary. The efficiency of this service program depends on a key person, an audiovisual media leader, working at the school-building director level. Although this position has been given many titles, such as *Vice Principal in Charge of Media* or *Audiovisual Building Representative,* the ones most common presently are *Audiovisual Building Coordinator, Instructional Media Coordinator.* It must recognised that the help teachers need cannot be given by the principal on an unorganised, unsystematised basis. Therefore, the first step in establishing his essential media-service system is to select a qualified individual to work with the principal and the media program director in setting up the service system. In the section that follows we discuss each of the essential operating facilities and conditions under which this school-building media leader can supply the necessary services.

The Availability of Media Equipment and Materials

Assign Equipment Units to Each Building

We frequently blame teachers for not making use of media equipment when we should put the blame instead squarely where it belongs on school leaders for not meeting the minimum standard of reasonable convenience. Equipment units should be obtainable with ease according to a well-organised service system. We cannot seriously charge teachers with dereliction of duty in carrying out their methodologies when they cannot make arrangements for using media at the right time and place for optimum learning. The bulk of the equipment needed for classroom use in any school building should be assigned permanently to the building. It has come to be axiomatic that centralisation of the most expensive materials is economical and feasible, but that centralisation of *equipment* is unwise and impractical because trucking it to the schools subjects it to merciless pounding and, most important, generally puts it beyond the reach of teachers for convenient, frequent use. Another reason if that equipment units need to be on the spot for training students and teachers to operate them. Although decentralisation of equipment in every school unit is a clear-cut goal of the media-service program, it may be necessary to establish a central pool of certain kinds of special-purpose equipment that may not be needed continuously and which, if permit a more rapid build-up of the inventory of more commonly used equipment such as motion picture projectors, filmstrip projectors, and tape recorders.

In the light of recent technological developments, we now have to emphasize the essential need to locate in each school building a number of permanently installed equipment units. We certainly will not find it feasible to transport television receivers to and from schools, nor would we wish to deliver hundreds of headsets for an auditorium or library listening-response laboratory. The fact is that we see more clearly in both old and new roles of media the vital necessity to equip each school building with the amount and kind of media that teachers need, for now we think less frequently of enrichment, and we think instead of the accomplishment of clearly recognised basic objectives that cannot be achieved without modern methods.

Kinds of Equipment Usually Assigned to Each School: In a well-developed media-service program, one or more of the following equipment units are likely to be found in every elementary and high school building in the school system in reasonably adequate quantity:

1. 16mm sound motion picture projectors, with a special auditorium model, or regular model with booster speakers if the public address system is not designed for projector sound connections.
2. 8mm cartridge-type projectors, both sound and silent models for both group (possibly rear-projection screen) and self-instruction uses.
3. Filmstrip and 2 × 2 inch slide projectors (combination model).
4. Automatic and remote-control 2 × 2 inch slide projectors.
5. Slide projectors, 3¼ × 4 inch models.
6. Slide or filmstrip projectors for short-exposure projection exercises.
7. Sound filmstrip projectors, for both disk and tape recorded audio components.
8. Record players, both monaural and stereo, for scheduled audio listening exercises in music rooms and libraries.
9. Overhead transparency projectors, both light weight and heavy duty, the latter for large-group learning spaces.

10. Tape recorders, both monaural and stereo, equipped with packaged headsets and plug-in boxes as accessories.
11. Classroom and auditorium TV receivers.
12. AM/FM receiver, depending on audio programming in the area.
13. Microprojectors.
14. Opaque projectors.
15. Portable projection screens, both front and rear-projection types, for learning spaces not having permanently wall-mounted or other fixed screens.
16. Mobile projection stands, ample for moving each heavy piece of equipment on assignment.
17. Copying cameras, 35mm, in preparation of materials spaces, and related graphic supplies.
18. Polaroid cameras and copymaker stands, and related graphic supplies.
19. Transparency-maker equipment, and related graphic supplies.

Such equipment units will make it possible for teachers to plan for a variety of teaching methods in reaching their objectives, hopefully right in their own well-equipped classrooms. Some of there units will be used so frequently that they should be located in each classroom permanently, and others will be on call from the school's service headquarters. Still other media equipment may be needed on a loan basis for special purposes and such equipment may be centralised at the school system media program head-quarters.

Nature of the Centralised Media Equipment Pool : Let us now take note of several kinds of media equipment that individual schools may have need of on a loan basis. We should recognise, of course, that the degree of local development may tend to limit or increase the size of the following list:

1. Magnetic sound, motion picture projector, for recording and playing back, school-make sound tracks.
2. Motion picture cameras, both 16mm and 8mm, necessary lighting equipment, and film exposure meters.
3. Flash-meters for filmstrip and slide projectors, for short-exposure work not covered by specialised equipment units.
4. High-fidelity record and tape playing components.
5. Portable public-address systems.
6. Portable TV display system for special learning space uses.
7. Large-screen TV projection system for large-group uses.

Some Fixed Media Equipment Installations : In a school where pupil groupings are flexible and learners learn by themselves under optimum conditions part of the time, additional media equipment units and installations become necessary. The following are among those frequently referred to in remodeling and new construction plans:

1. Electronic learning laboratory rooms as special separate learning spaces, or provided in instructional materials centres, in libraries, or in divisible auditoriums. Also referred to as listening and responding centers and as foreign language laboratories. May have broad or specialised scope through dial-access techniques.
2. Individual electronic study stations or carrels, located in libraries, classrooms, and special learning areas. Equipped with manual control devices, or with dial access to central, local, and remote sources, both audio and videotape, and small projection screens for flexible programing in multimedia format.
3. Closed-circuit television studios in each school or in one school serving a cluster of schools, by means of cable or other transmission system.
4. Television image magnification and display systems in large learning spaces, as fixed equipment.
5. Teaching machines in fixed positions in large or small learning areas. Such teaching machines may possess various kinds of media-use and display capability, and they may or may not be linked or associated with computer terminals for analysis and/or activation.
6. Fixed, remote control projection stations built into classroom, both large and small, and into teaching auditoriums. Projection stations may be at rear of rooms of behind rear-projection screen installations.
7. Learner-response devices at each student desk, connected to group presentation and analysis equipment, in teaching auditoriums, and in large and small classrooms.

It can be readily seen that the media equipment units appearing in the preceding list are special installations designed for use in modern programs that possess the capability to delegate to media new roles in the teaching process. Such roles demand unusually talented teachers who know how to analyse the teaching process into the various aspects of pupil and teacher action that will produce optimum achievement in any given situation. Such action must not be subjected to the capricious difficulties that frequently attend the borrow-and-return process, where a delay in arrival of a specific film or film-strip or an emergency failure in equipment, can be readily adjusted.

Amount of Equipment in Each School: The problem of formulating standards or guidelines for the amounts and kinds of media equipment units that should be purchased and made available to each school building is a difficult one to solve. Many national groups have worked on solutions to this problem, and from time to time and results of such earnest and arduous deliberations have been published. We must be clear on the point that although guidelines are often helpful to school program planners and to all who prepare budgets for adoption by local boards of education and finance, they may also tend to place lower limits on the thinking of school leaders, and actually may then focus attention on the devices themselves rather than on the learners' needs and the required instructional programs. It is essential to recognise that it is the nature of the school's program in relation to valid objectives that determines the need for the particular kind or amount of instructional equipment.

We must, however, in the face of an urgent need to make estimates of financial support for media-service programs, turn to the help of the excellent statements of guidelines (notwithstanding their shortcomings). This is especially true in the preparation of proposals in connection with state and federal grants for instructional programs. We shall for the present purposes stress the need to assign to each school the media equipment required for optimum use by teachers under favourable conditions. Then in Chapter, in connection with budgeting and finance, we shall make use of published standards, and use some of our own judgments as well.

Development of Media Equipment in Each Building

If we bear in mind the basic principles for the organisation and development of a media-service program that were stated in Chapter, the kinds of action demanded leave us little choice. The potentially important roles that audiovisual media can play can only be realised when sufficient equipment and materials in good repair are maintained in each school building so that teachers can put them to them to use with a minimum of time and effort. As we have already indicated, this kind of availability is indeed one of the first essentials of the desirable media-service system in each school building. We shall now examine the several aspects of the problem of deploying equipment.

Equipment at Each Teaching Station: As school leaders and their boards of education work towards adequate support of instructional programs, they will come to realise that audiovisual media utilisation is vital and basic to teaching processes, and that thus each classroom, special learning area, and most teaching stations, wherever they are, need permanently assigned media equipment units, either fixed or portable. Various teaching stations may require different equipment units. One particular teacher or classroom may, in addition to equipment units assigned to all teaching stations such as an overhead projector, require a remote-controlled 2 × 2 inch slide projector for daily use. Another teacher in a larger-group teaching situation might require the same equipment plus a 16mm motion picture projector, two tape recorders, a record player, and six TV receivers. Still other special learning spaces may require electronically equipped listening and response carrels accommodating up to ninety students. Teaching auditorium spaces may be equipped with a permanently installed multimedia rear-screen projection system and dial-access equipment for videotape and audio programs accommodating 300 or more pupils. For the present we should emphasize the principle that teachers ought to have equipment for use at the optimum time for maximum learning impact. One of the ways, then, for deploying audiovisual media equipment is to assign urgently needed and frequently used units to each classroom.

Equipment at Media-Service Centre Substations: Some effectively organised media-service systems incorporate a plan that locates frequently used equipment units close to clusters of teaching stations. Such decentralised location points throughout a school building can be called substations for media equipment. Thus a group of social studies, science, shop, or business studies classrooms, or a cluster of first and second grade classrooms, for example, may be served by a media equipment pool from which a specific piece of needed equipment can be drawn upon request by simple scheduling procedures.

Deployment of media equipment in this fashion cuts red tape to a minimum, and reduces the equipment delivery time from school headquarters, or cuts pick up and return time if teachers are handling the details. In some of the sprawling, one-floor schools, it is readily seen that wheeling a loaded projection stand a third of a mile on wobbly, noisy wheels is an unpleasant task, even when a pupil on duty does it. Certainly no school principal or school superintendent would expect a teacher and a motion picture projector in the other from his office on the first floor to a third-floor classroom. So deploying frequently used media equipment or instruments on their own mobile projection stands or carts to substations close to the teacher is another of the desirable possibilities.

Equipment Units at the School Media-Service Center: Conservation of time in preparation for classroom learning activity is a crucial matter for teachers. Those activities that are clerical or menial in nature should not be permitted to take precedence over those that are professional, insightful, and innovative insofar as communication with pupils and the guidance of their responses are concerned. Thus we need to make it possible for teachers to obtain their media materials and equipment with minimum interruption of class routines and pupil activity. If, for example, a teacher who wishes to project a seven-minute motion picture clip show fifteen slides, and three overlay transparencies, has to spend and hour locating and setting up the proper equipment, those in charge of the school's instructional program are causing an unfavourable balance between nonprofessional and professional activities. What we want to do is to provide the time for planning the presentation, formulating questions for guiding student reactions to content, and preparing and sequences the media materials that are vital to the objectives being attained. Therefore, it media instruments cannot be placed in the classroom on long-term loan, or assigned to substations serving clusters of classrooms, then they must be deployed in the school's service headquarters and an effective system of ordering, delivery, and pick-up established. When equipment units are so deployed several conditions must be created, namely: (i) that each heavy and bulky equipment unit must be in a state of readiness for delivery on its own mobile projection stand; (ii) that teachers may order such equipment with a minimum of red tape and advance notice; (iii) that the equipment may be made available on the day preceding carefully planned utilization and thus made ready at times most convenient for the teacher; and (iv) that teachers who obtain such equipment will have other needed facilities in their own classrooms or other regular teaching stations that will permit easy use of the equipment after it is delivered. We shall of course deal fully with these matters again later in relation to organising the school's media-use facilitation headquarters.

Assign Some Collections of Media Materials to Each School

Lest we focus too much attention on equipment and thus detract from the true reason for its existence—the content in the media materials—we ought to refer again to Chapter 5 in which we gave proper emphasis to the effective distribution of media from centralised collections. We must emphasize again at this point that good equipment services for teachers must go hand in hand with optimum availability of the materials. Having already introduced this subject in other contexts, we need merely to point out here that in recent years there has been an increasing tendency in well-developed media-service programs to built up collections of filmstrips, 8mm cartridge motion pictures, study print sets, maps and globes, recording, magnetic tapes, and other special-purpose and repetitively used media materials in each school building. This decentralisation of the less expensive kinds of audiovisual media will doubtlessly facilitate their use, but unless teachers select such materials with due regard for their frequent demand, inefficient usage, will result. Some media materials used for self-instruction and other special purposes doubtlessly should be in the teacher's full-time possession or kept at the school's media headquarters, for issue to the various learning laboratories, or located in dial-access resource banks. With the decentralisation of media equipment and materials a service center in each school is essential, and the organisation and development of such a center are dealt with in the following sections.

Organising an Effective Program of Media Services in Each School

In the preceding section we emphasised the importance of having media materials and equipment close to the teacher to facilitate their use at the optimum time in the teaching process. Now we are confronted by another group of problems that have to do with maintaining conditions that will provide for the continuing flow of media materials and equipment at maximum-use levels with a minimum of inconvenience, and at the same time provide at least a desirable minimum of help that teachers need in order to carry out their work with media efficiently. The goal is clear, but the requirements for that kind of operation are many and are often complicated by inadequate personnel and money, by ineffective operational procedures, and by poor administrative arrangements. We shall therefore discuss these basic conditions and seek to point out some solutions to problems common to school people everywhere.

The System of Services in Operation

First let us take an overall look at a hypothetical service system as it is functioning in a given school building, and then proceed to deal with some basic questions about the nature of organisational problems. The school-building system in a thriving citywide media organisation with good leadership and financial support may be in operation under the following conditions:

1. All classroom and other learning activity spaces have been equipped with facilities for audiovisual media use.
2. Equipment units needed by teachers have been assigned to the school for quick, convenient use upon request.
3. Collections of frequently used, less expensive materials have been assigned to the school by the central headquarters.
4. A school building media-service center has been organised and is open for business. This center is the clearing house for all orders for media materials and equipment for the school.
5. A responsible staff of professional media specialists, trained technicians and clerical workers, supplemented by a crew of student assistant has been organised and is on hand to carry out the day's media-use schedule as needed.

6. A professional leader, the school's coordinator of the media-service program, has been appointed and is available to consult with teachers, organise in-service education programs, and coordinate the flow of service from both the school building and the school-system headquarters. The coordinator has the necessary professional prestige in the school, and his importance is recognised by top-level school authorities. He sees to it that the system is set up properly and functions efficiently. The school principal helps him accomplish his mission by providing leadership and financial support. The principal has also appointed a media advisory committee to help plan the school's program of service. The services of other teachers have been elicited to help with the media-service work load as needed.

Under such conditions there will be a ceaseless flow of materials in and out of the school according to a well-worked-out system, and teachers will make their plans for suitable learning activities with confidence that they can be carried out without distraction or interruption.

Such an operation in broad outline appears to be workable at a high level of efficiently, but the fact is that several important questions need to be raised to point out the nature of decisions that both the principal of the school and the citywide media program director and possibly other administrative officers have to make. The first question we shall ask has to do fundamentally with the nature and scope of the services to be given. Will the media-service center for the school building be broad and comprehensive in its instructional media service, encompassing the school's library facilities as well, or will its services involve audiovisual media only? Every school principal in the country knows how difficult the answer to this problem can be. He knows full well the need for competent librarians, and he also knows that when teachers want, or are required, to use sophisticated technological methods, both professional and technical assistance are indispensable. In this case, just what do the principal and the citywide media program director do? Although a number of people have taken a firm stand on both sides of this issue as basic methods for organising school service programs, we can say that local conditions—that is, the sum total of local experience and conditioning, including qualifications and potential of present staff, present operational efficiency of existing media-services facilities, the nature and degree of media use envisioned, and the nature of services needed by teachers—ought to be taken into account in making the decision. But this situation leads us to examine this problem further as we explore the topic of organisational patterns for media services next.

Some Organisational Patterns for School Media Services

Because the media services to be given in any single school building vary in complexity, and because some programs of media use are far more comprehensive than others, there are many possibilities for setting up workable service organisations. We shall of course deal with the problems of providing staff members for any given type of organisation and planning and equipping school-building media-service centers separately, in later sections.

In discussing the various organisational patterns for media services, we must focus on the needs that have to be met and the duties that have to be performed. Professional duties should be performed by individual with professional preparation. If teaching experiences is required for certain duties such as for in-service education programs involving instruction in teaching methods, then only those individuals who have the required experience should be given this responsibility experience should be given this responsibility. On the other hand, when technical duties are paramount such as maintaining equipment in operational readiness, and when clerical and secretarial duties are called for, then it is essential that such duties be performed by supporting staff members at their respective non-professional levels. Some professional librarians have never had teaching experience in the true sense of the term, but they have taught groups of students to use library facilities. Other librarians have had years of experience in regular classrooms, and in addition have been thoroughly prepared for work in the field of audiovisual media. It is asserted that when trained audiovisual media specialists are assigned responsibility for library activities, they ought to undertake special training courses in the field of library science as well, or library specialists should be provided to carry out these aspects of the service.

Media-Service Leadership in Each School: There is general agreement among school people that media-service programs in school buildings prosper when the leadership function is placed in one person who is sufficiently free of other duties and responsibilities to concentrate a major portion of his time and energy on the media problems that have been identified. Occasionally, school principals and others claim that a media-service-building coordinator, as a media specialist, is not being used. These people have probably developed other plans for providing services, using, for example, a vice principal, backed up by a head technician, and one or more teacher aides as in a team teaching program. It is true that a number of the identified duties that appear in any listing are clerical and technical in nature. Yet, we assert that school principals themselves are too far removal from the specific media services needed by teachers duties themselves. To be sure, school principals, as we shall point out later, are the key administrators in their schools. They themselves are the first and foremost media-use facilitators, through their active support for methodological innovations. Thus, throughout the country, in both large and small cities and towns and in both large and small schools, ways are found by good school leaders to provide qualified, professional personnel to carry on the media-service program where it matters most and where it succeeds or fails—close to the teacher at his teaching station. In a later section we shall treat the problems of staffing, but at this point we assert that to provide qualified leadership at the school-buildings level is one of the most commonly agreed-to, though not always achieved, patterns of action the country over.

This media-program leader, operating as an audiovisual media specialist or as an all-media generalist, seems to be the key to successful technological services for teachers at the day-to-day instructional level. Every existing statement of duties of the school media coordinator that the writer has observed includes the job of helping teachers use media more effectively, a professional supervisory function, as well as organising and overseeing the purely physical and mechanical details of the building's service program. Actually, this makes the media coordinator a unit director working with and for the school-system but appointed by and responsible to the school principal.

In a very real sense, therefore, the audiovisual or all-media building coordinator also plays the roles of educator, executive, supervisor, technological expert, and equipment technician. Everyone recognizes the absolutely essential nature of the coordinator's service in the realm of physical details, but some school superintendents and principals are apparently afraid of the implications for higher salaries if they recognise and utilise the services of a talented school coordinator in more professional ways, for example, in supervisory and consultant capacities. School superintendents and other key administrators should "go all out" in attempts to discover talented teachers on their staffs who, through their valuable experience working with colleagues, form a cadre of school-curriculum leaders. Willingness to express open appreciation for this service is shown by Curtis Davis, Assistant Superintendent of Schools in San Jose, California, who wrote the following Foreword in a manual for school coordinators:

Effectively used audiovisual materials represent one of the great advancements in education during the past few years. As a school coordinator, much depends on you as to how well these materials are used. The extra work required and the many co-ordination duties are well known and appreciated by all.

When you get discouraged at machines breaking down and the schedule going haywire, just stand back for a moment and think about the importance of what you do. It takes you to make the program click.

** Curtis Davis*
Assistant Superintendent

We would do well to consider the following listing of the major duties and responsibilities of audiovisual media coordinators in the Grosse Pointe, Michigan, school as part of an adopted operational plan.

Major Duties and Responsibilities

1. Counsel teachers in the wise selection of audiovisual materials.
2. Work with teachers to improve utilization and production of audiovisual materials in the instructional program.
3. Compile teacher's monthly orders for audio visual materials and forward them to the instructional materials center.

4. Train teachers in the use of audiovisual materials.
5. Organise the scheduling and use of AV materials in the building.
6. Be responsible for the care and maintenance of AV equipment.
7. Serve on the central audiovisual committee:
   (*a*) Attend monthly meetings with the curriculum assistant in charge of the instructional materials center.
   (*b*) Help make decisions for the expenditure of the yearly budget for new materials.
   (*c*) Help select materials that will be purchased.
   (*d*) Evaluate the function of the AV program in the instructional programs of the entire school system.
8. Maintain an effective liaison between the school and the instructional materials center for the efficient operation of the AV program:
   (*a*) Inform teachers of available materials.
   (*b*) Promote participation by teachers in previewing materials for purchase.
   (*c*) Prepare materials daily for pick-up and return to the center.
   (*d*) Notify teachers when AV materials arrive.
9. Work closely with and advise the principal on all phases of the AV program.
10. Demonstrate and interpret AV materials and equipment to the board of education, PTA's and others.
11. Be on call on an emergency basis to assist teachers with equipment.
12. Participate in local, state, and national audiovisual programs and conferences.

We would also do well to study the following listing of duties published by the Los Angeles City Schools, Instructional Services Branch, in its celebrated handbook, revised and reissued in 1965. The listing follows:

An effective audiovisual coordinator makes certain that

The principal is kept informed about the operation of the school's audio-visual program.

Teachers are kept informed about development of new audio-visual techniques, technology, and research.

Teachers are notified of availability of new material.

There is effective liaison among teachers, administrators, and the Audio-Visual Section.

Teachers receive advice and instruction in the proper utilisation of audio-visual materials.

Teachers are assisted in selecting materials in their subjected areas which will enhance learning.

School film orders are properly processed and sent to the Audio-Visual Section.

Teachers are informed of the identity and content of materials present in the school or scheduled for delivery.

Teachers have a convenient, established procedure for previewing audio-visual materials.

Films are scheduled to appropriate classroom.

Equipment is scheduled for maximum utilisation.

Films are skilfully projected by qualified operators.

Films and other materials are returned on time and in good condition.

School audio-visual equipment is inventoried, conveniently stored, and properly maintained.

Another statement from the same publication that shows these duties and the relationship of the audiovisual coordinator to the principal and the central media headquarters.

It has been repeatedly emphasized that duties such as those listed, together with the additional professional and technical knowledge required by television, dial-access and other self-instruction systems in education today, leave no room for doubt as to the need for school-building leadership and supporting staff for the services that have to be given on a continual basis. The title conferred is not so important, but the abilities and insights possessed by those who are responsible are crucial.

Certainly as has been pointed out, leadership personnel at the professional level are essential. This designated professional person may be a part-time teacher or supervisor, or a vice-principal who is devoting specified portion of his energy on solving instructional media utilisation problems. It may well be that this leadership will be supplied by a professional working on a full-time media-supervisory job in the central office who devotes a portion of his time and energy to a cluster of schools, working under the cooperative jurisdiction of two principals, or under a combination of administrators such as the system-wide media program director and the principal of the school that gets his services for a portion of the weekly work schedule. As the job of being an audiovisual building coordinator takes on a new urgency in the face of new technologically supported programs, the leadership personnel together with the necessary supporting secretarial and technical stall members will have to be located close to the teachers in every school or be assigned an intermittent schedule in the schools, but be based in a central office or in a cluster of schools, both elementary and secondary. The work has to be done; services have to be given. But we must be mindful of the fact that in many schools both principals and teachers have not yet created in their own minds the image of working effectively in a technology environment. The day when such images will have to be developed is rapidly approaching.

In the light of recently published standards that we shall quote a little later on, we can insist on the need to employ the following staff for each 500 students in a school: two media specialists (including print and audiovisual media capability), two clerk-aide assistants, and two technician-specialist assistant. When in the next organisational pattern we discuss the audiovisual media center, we must recognise that the need for audiovisual media leadership personnel is in addition to the library organisation.

We should not hesitate to assert that unless the right media personnel are provided, the media-services job is simply not done. If school principals claim that the only personnel needed are secretaries and some technicians, then the job of developing professional skills will not be carried out. If the school system provides only central office leadership, the various close-to-the-teacher assistance procedures simply will not be performed because the district-wide media program director cannot cope personally with the specific activity plans in each school. He must therefore expedite action through his administrative and supervisory activities that affect the programs of all schools at or nearly at the same time.

There are many ways to solve the leadership problem, not all of which are as good as others. We shall deal with these problems more fully in another major section to open up a number of possibilities. However, some of these are implicit in additional patterns for organisation to which we now turn.

The Role of the Audio-Visual Coordinator

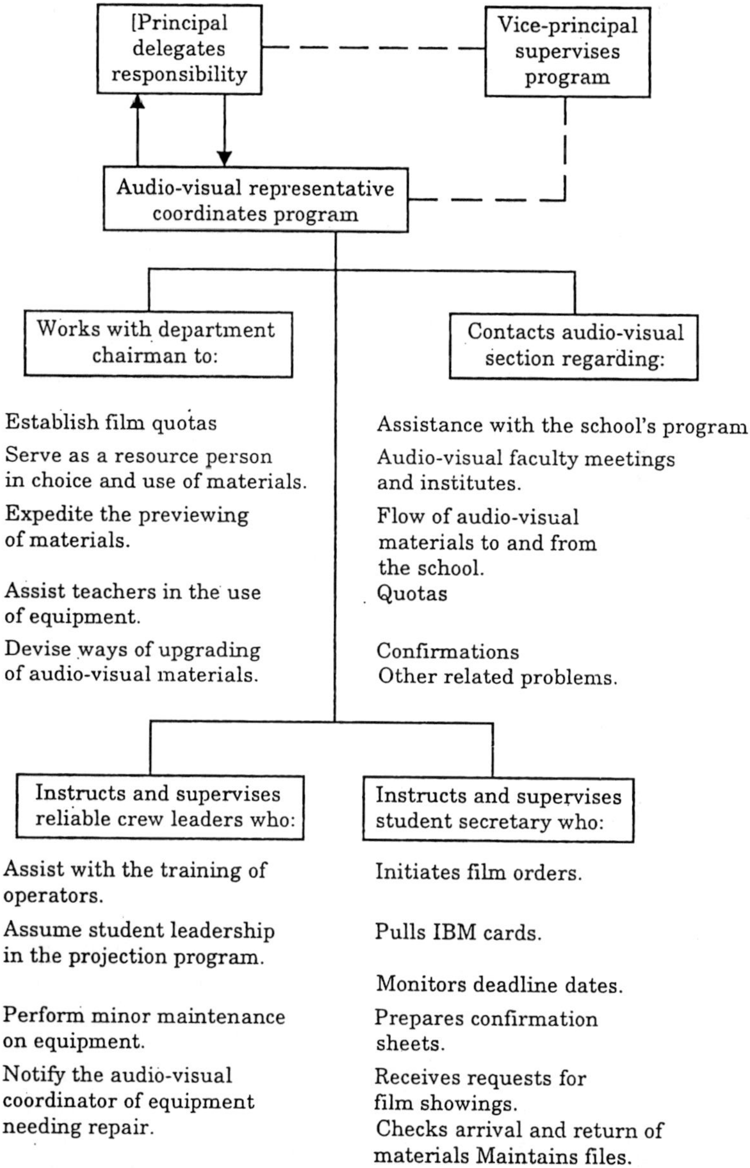

Fig. 7.1 : This analysis of the role of the school's audiovisual media coordinator is a clear-cut statement based on the Los Angeles organisational relationships between school centers and the district center. Courtesy Los Angeles City Schools.

The Audiovisual Media Center Pattern: One has but to examine the various names for school-building media-service centers to note the organisational emphasis. Some of the names applied to the centers are actually misnomers, for although some names may mean one thing in terms of specific operational scope, they may also refer to something else. Regardless then of the name applied, let us identify a widely known pattern of organisation that includes in its scope all technological media, all media materials and equipment and related processes except the medium of print. This means specifically that libraries and librarians, and audiovisual media-service centers and their media specialists in individual schools are organised into separate organisation although they may work closely together and may actually complement each other's activities. And, as we have already pointed out, libraries may possess specialised instructional media facilities, such as listening response centers and electronic carrels variously equipped, and may be engaged in carrying on a number of specified media services such as cataloguing, storage, and the delivery of information to teachers about available media in local and district collections.

The most commonly used names for a media-service center that is separately organised from the library are the Audiovisual Service Center or the Instructional Technology Center. Other names, such as Educational Media Center, Learning Resources Center, Curriculum Materials Center, Instructional Materials Center, or Instructional Media Center, refer to more broadly based media programs that include all media. Not to include the print media under service center names such as these is to mislead all who have broadened their insights into the roles that media play in teaching. This may or may not be a serious matter. It may even be justifiable. The logic underlying the organisational separation of services, however, is that audiovisual media and their related processes, call for such complex and specialised facilities and for such unique applications to teaching and learning that it is more simple and effective to concentrate professional and technical effort on the tasks that have to be done.

According to the Audiovisual Media Service Center pattern, each individual school would possess a headquarters suite that would be not less than a conventional size classroom in area, with such supporting operational spaces as are needed around the building. Such spaces may include equipment substations on each floor or in the vicinity of clusters of classrooms, electronic learning laboratories, teaching-machine laboratories, teaching auditoriums, listening centers libraries, television studios, projection spaces with rear-screen projection equipment centers, and multimedia storage spaces for valuable mobile television and video-taping equipment. If we return to Chapter 3 for a look at the items included in a hypothetical audiovisual media-service system in operation, we can see that the nature of the program will demand certain minimal conditions, and as a program waxes in importance and scope of its technological applications, the service organisation—from space allotments to personnel and equipment demands—will increase accordingly. A principal may say, "We do not need anyone in our media program besides myself to work with teachers in teaching methods," until he gets involved in a large-scale television production responsibility. Then it is not only the technical engineer that matters, but also the designer and curriculum worker who understands the roles that media can play, who can break the teaching process down into its components and then advise and guide teachers in using the television medium wisely. When teachers need professional advice in preparing and using audiovisual media, principals—despite their being key curriculum workers and administrators—do not always have the necessary technical skill to help them.

As we look to the future we can see that the technological development of audiovisual media and related processes may become so complex that it may be wise (except in situations where the personnel have the required qualifications) to maintain a separation of the print and non-print media services insofar as supervisory and administrative organisation are concerned. This is particularly true because a head librarian who is carrying on in-service education in television programing, or working with teachers in developing media preparation skills and planning teaching systems for special objectives, will obviously have to be a media-service generalist and have a staff of media specialists working under his supervision. In such cases the librarian may be more an audiovisual media specialist than a print medium specialist.

In the pattern under consideration, it can be readily seen that the service headquarters leader will be in most cases fully responsible to the school principal, but in the light of good central media leadership, this school-building co-ordinator would also be a cooperating colleague of the system-wide media program director. It is in fact one of the primary concerns of a district wide media administrator to lead all involved in the formulation of media program policy, and see to its execution. It is at this point that principals and other decision makers work together to implement changes or carry out old plans. We must take care not to conjure up the image the service programs of by-gone days, dating from the turn of the century, when a single city-wide media program leader with a tiny office, and perhaps one clerk, operated a central slide or film lending library. We have instead entered a new age where filmstrips, videotapes, color TV, computers, and electronic study carrels are no longer a novelty. We must not forget either that schools are being designed for teaching that is vastly different—or ought to be—than it was in the Middle Ages, and that schools as units are larger because more pupils are being taught better than over before at minimum cost.

But such considerations make possible, and point the way to, other new and effective arrangements for providing vital services. Hence there has been an expansion in the development of another pattern for giving comprehensive media services to teachers. This is the pattern we may call the *Instructional Media Center* service pattern. We shall explore and illustrate this pattern next.

The Instructional Media Center Pattern: The symbol IMC has come to mean Instructional Materials or Media Center, and as such, is the symbol that indicates another of the principal patterns for organising a school's media-service program. Under this pattern we combine the school's provisions for handling the print medium, usually administered out of the library facility, with a complete audiovisual media-service program. Such school libraries may or may not be assigned the responsibility for text-book selection. Almost universally, however, they provide whatever services exist for circulating books and documents to students and teachers and, even more importantly, they arrange for the short-term assignment of classroom reference libraries as needed during a given period of special need. The symbol IMC has thus come to represent a comprehensive media-service program that has grown out of an expanded concept of the library function. Thus the library with its former limited focus on the print medium has broadened its service to include all of the so-called audiovisual media from a model to a CCTV telecast. Virginia McJenkin and Bruce Miles have discussed the new library concept in this way:

Virginia: Also, the IMC person is quite aware of the total program and must participate in all types of activities related to curriculum, scheduling, selection of materials, in-service education, and so on. She works closely with teachers, department heads, and the administration as well as with students in producing a more effective program. In short, the IMC has become a vital part of the overall teaching-learning picture.

Bruce: IMC's will differ widely from one school system to the next and, as a matter of fact, will differ within a given school system. Such differences may stem from philosophy, the unique needs of a school or school system, and always from the budget. Budget is often necessary to accomplish the goals set for a program. Thus, possibly the best thing to say about the difference between traditional libraries and the modern concept of the IMC is that the new service is one dedicated to the necessity and opportunity of providing a wide variety of critical learning resources to many people within the community served. It may be that the word "service" is the all-important word in such an attempt to define this difference.

Regardless of whether the school-building instructional-media center is in an elementary or secondary school, one of its main aspects of service will be the print medium, and hence its existing library facility will serve in whole or in part as the media-service headquarters. The library may be only one of the units along with its workrooms for print medium operations. The spaces for audiovisual media services may be located elsewhere such as in a separate technological center where both professional and technical services are controlled. In some instances, the librarian with the rank of vice principal would head the program, especially when he or she possesses the required expanded media skills, professional and technical, and would presumably have an expanded staff of library assistants or media aides, one or more technicians, and one or more professional assistants. Of the professional assistants, one or more would specialise in nonprint such as television and others would carry out print-medium duties. In other instances, instructional-material centers may be headed by a school-building audiovisual media leader with the rank of vice principal who, if he has considerable insight into print-medium problems and procedures, may supervise the library and all other media service as well. However, his main concerns should be the advanced in-service education programs and other technological systems in the school. This variation of media program organisation is but another instance of the instruction materials center pattern. We are not concerned here with who is in charge of the school's media services, but rather with the nature and scope of the services that are brought together under unified leadership. If the library, as it has been organised in schools before the need for other communication media developed, is the organisational hub, or is an integral part of the school's media-service organisation complex under unitary leadership, the school's media-service organisation may be properly classified under the Instructional Media Center pattern.

Patterns of Media-Service Organisation: It is not a simple matter to choose an organisation of a particular type. School principals working with their staffs and their administrative leaders and the school-system media program director must make this decision in the light of local conditions. What any local group must undertake before reaching this decision is to identify the services that have to be rendered and to find out what changes in personnel need to be made to reach the goals stated.

If there are elementary schools that have not library facilities whatever or if secondary schools or elementary schools have weak library facilities, the decision for action should be deflected toward the unification of all services in the school with new leadership. If, on the other hand, the existing leadership status of the library in any given school seems unreceptive to, or incapable of, expansion into other media efforts, then it would seem best to exert pressure for the development of both print and audiovisual media-service aspects along the lines of separate organisational patterns. As we have emphasized before, the educational need that has to be met is primary. Decisions have to be made as to what means will be employed to achieve the desired ends, and such judgments may not be easy to make.

Relationship of the Media Service Organisation to the School-System Organisation: A problem of large scope faces the school-system media program director when he plans with principals and other key administrators the best public policy for adoption by the Board of Education. We have reiterated this basic insight repeatedly. As schools are presently organised, individual school principals occupy uniquely powerful leadership positions in their own schools and therefore principals must help make the plicy with regard to leadership for the media-services program in each school. It may even be desirable to institute several different patterns of organisation throughout the schools of the system, but each of the school-building media program leaders should have the kind of relationship to the central media headquarters that will expedite the flow of leadership forces as well as the flow of media materials and equipment. Thus there ought to be a wide, open line of communication and leadership force from the school-system media director to each school-building media director, yet it ought to be recognised that staff members in any given school may also have to be more directly under the jurisdiction of the school's principal as the school's chief administrative officer.

We should explore one other possibility that changes the nature of the principal to school-building media-coordinator control. This is the case where a principal does not assign one of his own staff members to the media leadership job, but instead holds for himself the jurisdiction of technical and clerical personnel and takes charge of the supervisory and professionally creative aspects of media-use developments. In this case the line of control and jurisdiction from the central media program director becomes tenuous. In some cases, and this was not cited as a basic pattern of organisation for media service, the central office staff is expanded to include additional supervisory personnel to move among the various schools on either a flexible or fixed schedule—for example, a professional media supervisor working in a given school two days each week. Many arrangements are thus possible and the need for additional services on a full- or part-time basis will have to be determined in light of the needs in a particular school. It is certain that the more technically complex teachers' uses of media materials and equipment become, the more necessary it will be to add additional supervisory and technical staff members to whatever system of organisation has been developed.

We have repeatedly referred to the need for professional and technical staff members, and in the next major section of this chapter we shall deal at considerable length with the problems in the arrangements for giving needed assistance to teachers in carrying on their media-use activities. We have been discussing two considerably different patterns of organising and grouping the various services that constitute the prime reason for having a school-building media headquarters. Up to this point we have generalised both teachers' needs and the scope of services rendered, without regard to the level of instruction. Principals of elementary schools are confronted by different problems that confront principals of secondary schools. We now turn our attention to these problems and recommendations for the solution.

Media-Service Problems in the Elementary School

There is little doubt that elementary schools, as a class of schools, are less likely to have well-instructed and organised media-service programs than secondary schools. We need not overemphasize this condition, nor should we overlook the fact that in a number of schools outstanding programs have been developed. In some cases the existence of these programs has led some observers to make generalisations that were not true. However, it cannot be said that all secondary schools have good media-service programs. Most curriculum leaders and analysts imply in their writings and speeches that elementary school teachers, working as many do with groups of pupils all day long, tend to focus their attention on the learner and his needs instead of on the act of teaching a subject per se. Perhaps this belief about elementary schools has led some observers to say that the leader in the self-contained group can handle her own visualisation, projection, and presentation problems, and on a more informal basis can manage with whatever audiovisual equipment is available. Many school principals have through sheer necessity appointed one teacher to take care of the record players, another to look after the filmstrips, and still another to handle a cataloging project. The truth is that in any formal or informal survey conducted on a statewide basis, the facts about organisational procedures are often shocking. Many so-called media-service coordinators have little or no time in which to carry out their duties. Moreover, some principals resent the assertion that audiovisual media coordinators should be anything more than equipment clerks or technicians. Yet they themselves in many cases do little to organise and give leadership for needed development. Actually this is understandable in the light of a principal's generally heavy work load. But should they not then do some creative planning, exert a little more administrative leadership in guiding other professional people on their staff to do media work under their supervision? We answer, of course, in the affirmative, but obtaining staff for this program of service poses real problems in the elementary school. Obviously we need to take a look at some of the more serious problems that face the elementary school principal and then make some recommendations as to several possible solutions for them.

The Problem of Obtaining Leadership Services: We have already pointed to the urgent need for additional manpower hours to carry on media-service programs. We assert that despite a few voices to the contrary, what is needed is professional leadership activity for implementing innovations. Yet, some principals and some school-system media program directors, probably in desperation, settle for one or more people to do the work of clerks and technicians. What is a greater pity is that many times teachers who are freed for hours of service, or even other part-time or full-time personnel of professional caliber who are assigned to school-building staffs, are completely taken up with nonprofessional duties. In both cases the effect is to weaken the potential to move to creative and more mature levels of media utilisation. Now, just what is the problem? The trouble seems to lie in the difficulty of finding or arranging for professional people to be freed from their teaching duties on a part-time basis. Many principals have resorted to such expedients as relieving teachers from such nonteaching chores as play-ground supervision during daily recesses, daily cafeteria duty, transportation surveillance before and after school, and other dreaded but necessary chores, and also have assigned media chores to teachers whose classes are instructed one or more sessions per week by special teachers, as is often the case with art and music activities. When we discuss the secondary school situation in the next section, we shall find that there are many possibilities for freeing competent teaching personnel for professional media-service responsibility that do not exist in the conventionally organised elementary school.

We shall direct our attention first to the *conventionally* organised elementary school. Each teacher in such schools is pinned down, by and large, for the entire day at work with the same group of learners. This type of organisation is often referred to as the self-contained classroom method of grouping and teaching learners. It is obvious that under this condition teachers cannot be rescheduled for part-time assignments as a part of the professional work load. What are some possible solutions to this problem that we can suggest to elementary school principals who wisely place a high priority on media-service development? We shall list a few of the possibilities, but we shall also make suggestions that are applicable to those situations in which pupils are not scheduled all day in one room and taught by the same teacher all of the available time. Our suggestions follow:

Under Conventional Classroom Organisation

1. Using funds from school allotments, appoint a full-time coordinator for the instructional media-service organisation, and provide the necessary supporting staff of media specialists, clerical workers and technicians. The coordinator should be in charge of school library services as well, undertaking training in this field. This position could or ought to be rated as a vice principal, especially in large schools.
2. Where a librarian is already on the staff, but is not qualified by experience or training for audiovidual media responsibility, employ a media-use coordinator for full or part-time

duties along professional technological lines. Some of the professional distribution duties may be assigned to the school librarian.

3. Appoint the current full-time librarian to the position of coordinator of instructional materials center services, and assist him or her in obtaining audiovisual media skills as needed, in order to carry out a well-balanced program of services. Support this effort by additional media specialist, technicians and media aides.
4. Employ an additional professional staff member and assign to him the responsibility for audiovisual media, and also the responsibility of inaugurating a school library service. Employ also a supporting technician and a media aide.
5. Invite (and assist him a procuring support for the policy) the citywide media program director to assign on a part-time basis, a professional audiovisual media specialist who would serve as an organiser and implementor for the use of media by teachers, thus sharing professional media leadership with one or more elementary schools in a given area of the district. Appoint one or more full-time media aides and technicians to support the leadership activity.
6. Find ways to combine extra-teaching responsibilities in the lunchroom, playground, and so forth, in order to free teachers for a specified number of hours to perform professional duties with media-use tasks working under the supervision of the principal or a vice principal. Support this professional activity by a technician and a media aide.
7. Proceed as in item 5, but assign the responsibility for clerical and technical duties in maintaining good control of flow of equipment and materials to specific teachers, with the regular vice principal carrying on in-service education for implementing media-use activities.

Under Newer Pupil Organisation Plans

1. Employ an instructional media specilist as a vice principal to take charge of the professional media-use responsibilities, and support this person with media specialists, technicians, and media aides according to need. Assign some of the leadership responsibility to the leaders of teaching teams, and some of the media-use duties to the teachers' aides.
2. Where a full- or part-time librarian is already on the staff, assign media duties to that person, if he is qualified; or employ an audiovisual media person and separate the functions accordingly, on a full- or part-time basis.

3. Employ one or more additional teachers as specialists in science or mathematics, or to meet other needs, and assign these persons on a part-time basis, to carry out media-service duties of a professional nature under the principal's supervision and coordination. Because of the flexibility in scheduling instructional activities under newer organisational plans, one or more teachers in a given team may be scheduled so as to devote up to half-time to a media-use supervisory position. One of these people might well be designated as the school's Chief Media-Use Coordinator, with administrative control over the assignments to one or more part-time media-service professionals. Technicians in media preparation, and for more complicated technological installations such as television and electronic study carrels, would have to be provided according to need.
4. As in item 3, invite a central office media- use professional to provide organisational and innovational services as valuable school-district media-center contributions. School-building staff members may support this effort by carrying on continuing assignments according to local technological needs and developments.
5. Plans of action patterned after items 2 through 6 listed previously under plans for conventionally organised elementary schools.

Providing Technicians and Clerks for Media-use Purposes: The level of accomplishment of educational goals is diminished when professionally trained workers spend their time on nonprofessional tasks. Obviously it is necessary to employ the necessary technicians and media aides and, on the basis of an adequate task analysis, to assign them duties in line with their training and capabilities.

As the nature of the educational process changes in the direction of technological emphasis, needs for personnel will change—and in fact have already changed. Principals should unite their efforts with those of school-system media directors to exert pressure on other key administrators to increase citywide budgets for an increase in technical and clerical personnel. The existing situation is deplorable, but as we have said, it should be solved in good balance.

Many schools use students as a whole or partial solution to the problem of providing media aides and technicians. We shall discuss this procedure more fully later, but we ought to relate the use of students, possibly from fourth grade up, to the need for a non-professional work force. Of course, the wasting of professional potential may be due to a lack of administrative insight and organisational ability, but in cases where principals are forced to use teachers as clerks, they may also have to turn to the organisation of student work crews. There can certainly be little if any harm done, and very probably a lot of good may come from from using student workers. The students will get a chance to practice being a responsible individual, relating their developing personalities to adults, settling conflicts with peers, and budgeting their study time. Special arrangements may have to be made with specially trained and highly qualified high school juniors and seniors to pay either a token sum or a full hourly wage for their services. This is understandable in an age where material wealth has become so highly prized.

The use of student assistants required close supervision, careful planning, and hence demands a professional person who understands the role of the contribution of work and personal service to the total learning process. We must find ways to avoid overloading students with work that should be organised and carried on in other ways—and here is where the principal and media coordinators must show their administrative imagination in wise decisions. We must never miss the point that students are not being sent to school to do the menial and clerical tasks of the professionals, but to engage in a continuing stream of learning experiences, the specifications for which must not be altered for selfish ends. At any rate, we can point to the fact that in elementary schools organisation is generally such that pupils are not scheduled for study halls or free time with any precise regularity, and furthermore, almost all of the youngsters in our kindergarten-through-grade-six schools can learn to turn on switches volume controls, and manipulate knobs and push buttons for self-instruction purposes. However, it is not generally feasible to organise them into working crews that carry out a schedule of assignments for moving projectors or players, or for operating equipment outside of their own classrooms. Elementary school students may actually serve the teacher best by helping in each classroom situation rather than being organised as an external group operating during the school day. Older pupils may assist after school with mechanical and clerical chores, and help get equipment into classroom locations for the following day.

There is a definite relationship between an adequate equipment inventory and the need for technical services for teachers. There aren't many teachers who would not be willing to learn to operate and use audiovisual equipment units located in their teaching areas. What most teachers object to is moving out of their class-rooms for walks to other spaces, or having to go to an equipment center to pick up and return heavy or even mobile equipment units. Although operating the equipment is a non-professional activity in one sense, it may be quickly accomplished once the skill is developed, and moreover, when teachers are in operational command of their situations, they may plan the timing and carry out special uses of equipment in the stream of their teaching decisions. Thus we ought to point out that as the number of equipment units approaches the optimum amount, the need for additional technicians may be reduced. For example, if thirty teachers in a given school are using audiovisual equipment units of one kind or another at the same time on a self-operation basis, one trouble-shooting technician and a clerk for handling communication and note-taking jobs may suffice for surveillance and control; and thirty operators would not have to be at their posts in classrooms. We have already stressed the developed of optimum media-use environment in schools, and now we have seen another reason why this optimum condition is desirable.

Lack of Provision for School Libraries: Another possible deterrent to the development of better media-use service programs in elementary schools is the lack of formal library facilities, especially in the older schools. (See Chapter for detailed discussions.) In one sense the difficulty of inaugurating a school library service is almost as great, from the standpoint of obtaining professional staff and financial support, as it is to inaugurate new audiovisual media-service programs. Adding them both simultaneously poses an even bigger problem. Some elementary schools have regrettably solved the library staff problem by adding non-trained, or technically unqualified, "librarians" to their school organisations as a stopgap measure. Thus the principal has a decision to make as to the direction along which to move in solving his problem of providing what we may again refer to as comprehensive instructional materials center services. Some school principals solve this problem by assigning duties for both audiovisual media and library services to the audiovisual media leader, and other principals start with a part-time librarian and add the audiovisual duties. In either case, leadership for the media services ought to go to the most professionally qualified person. As we have said, expansion of both print and audiovisual media services needs to be accelerated.

Lack of Available Space in Elementary Schools for Media Services: We must refer again to the self-contained classroom concept as it has been applied to school-building in the past. Since the program was based on a teacher for a specific grade group of a definite number of pupils, schools were made up of just the number of rooms for the predicted enrollment. Occasionally an all-purpose room and an auditorium, and more recently a cafeteria and a gymnasium, were added. Under limited so-called extra or flexible space there was and still is no room to use for media headquarters. A principal in one of these situations is hard pressed to come up with a solution that does not require an addition to the building, or involve shifting pupils of other schools, thus compounding the problem elsewhere. This may be the reason why so many principals operate their audiovisual media programs right out of their office suites, with the equipment under lock and key and almost inaccessible to teachers when desired. In any school of ten teachers or more, where such space limitations exist, it appears that the only solution is to find ways to take over one of the existing classrooms, and to develop a media resources center of a comprehensive nature, or to undertake a remodeling job and add the kinds of facilities for media and other purposes. When we develop the image of modern education and what essential components are mandatory, we will no longer be content with improvised teaching methods.

Media-Service Problems in the Secondary School

Just as we explored media-service problems in the elementary school we shall also identify some characteristics that generally exist in secondary schools, and we shall study them to ascertain their influence on media-program development. Such explorations are essential for the assessment of plans to organise, inaugurate, and implement media-service programs director working cooperatively.

Just what are the basic conditions in high schools that have a bearing on the developing of media services? We shall list them first and then proceed to make some recommendations.

1. High schools are large schools, larger by far than most elementary schools and fewer in number in a community.
2. Their instructional programs are vastly more diverse and flexible than in elementary schools.
3. High school programs are departmentalised, and thus by means of the scheduling process, class enrollment may be shifted, and sections combined, thus making possible the rearrangement of work loads of staff members.
4. Students are sophisticated, independent, and mature.
5. High school principals quite frequently occupy positions that are higher up in the power structure of a community than do elementary school principals.
6. High schools have, by and large well-developed and long-established library facilities.
7. High schools generally possess staff members often acclaimed as expert in subject-matter fields, and therefore subjects per se tend to receive great emphasis.
8. Great value is placed on cumulative records, transcripts for college entrace, and satisfactory job applications. A sense of high priority tends to develop from the immediate link with adulthood responsibilities. Financial support for extra services in such schools is easier to get, generally.
9. In the high school environment there is likely to be more movement of teachers to and from facilities because of shifting class sessions. Hence more contracts during any given day, better communication, more action class to class, more activity between administrators and teachers and learners, making a high school more closely knit as an organisation.
10. In large high schools there are generally available what we may refer to as flexible-use spaces, even a ground floor area that can be taken over for special uses, multiple-purpose areas that by rearranging the schedule of space use may

free a classroom adjacent perhaps to a main library, or a space between classrooms that lends itself for a media-service office or an equipment distribution substation.

11. In our modern high schools there is a sense of urgency to keep people in school, by means of interesting, lifelike, highly practical, and worthwhile activities.
12. Students are often available for special work as a club member or as an after-school paid worker. Independent study and work periods and study halls may thus help in making available a student technical and clerical work force of considerable proportions.
13. High schools universally have a number of electronic installations that require technical services. Electronic learning laboratories for foreign languages, electronic carrels supplied with both videotape and regular audio program recordings, extensive public-address systems central sound systems, television facilities for CCTV production and distribution and for reception via master antenna systems, and automatic projection equipment.

Having identified several of the major characteristics of and conditions in high schools, we should now proceed to an analysis of the bearing that some of these conditions have on the media-program development.

Size of building and Scope of Program: Programs in large high schools are so diverse, and the need for media services is so great, that the media leadership, staff support, and equipment inventory are sometimes incredibly large. Such programs may have one or more full-time professional media coordinators and specialists, a staff of technicians and secretaries, together with a crew of projectionists and clerical and media-preparation assistants. The principal may decide to keep the library and staff operating as a separate agency, with new media installations in the library being serviced by the audiovisual technical maintenance staff. In this case the audiovisual media coordinator will have his own service spaces and will work coordinately with the head librarian. In cases where all media services are combined under one head, the principal would be likely to secure the appointment of a media coordinator at the vice principal rank. As we have said before, high schools usually have highly structured organisational patterns, and well-organised staffs. Their media coordinators are generally certifiable and hence possess special qualifications for the jobs. A sizable staff is an essential for the work that has to be done. It is, however, a fact that even though many schools have incorporated television in their media-service programs, they still have far too little service space in which to work. Moreover, some sizable programs are administered on time borrowed from other classroom activities. Extensive developmental action needs to be taken by principals, superintendents, and the school-district media director working together to arrive at sound operating policies.

Finding Suitable Spaces for Media Head-quarters: The problem of locating space for an instructional materials center, or for a separate audiovisual media center, in a large school is always difficult unless this problem has been met in plans for new construction. The nature of the space needs is determined as usual by first mapping out the program itself. When the audiovisual media center is to incorporate electronic learning laboratories or remote-controlled resource centers involving videotape recording and audio programs, to say nothing of media preparation, equipment maintenance, storage and distribution areas, areas must be extensive. The problem is even more acute when in the case of instructional media centers, spaces for a complete library service, which now also generally includes listening centers, electronic carrels accommodating a ceaseless flow of students, are also included in the plans. We shall deal in considerable detail with the problems of planning media-service headquarters and show in the illustrations the nature of spaces and operation in both old and new schools. At this point we should emphasize the hope that because of the flexibility that exists in the high school program and because of several of the other factors identified, principals can find—on a stop-gap basis—spaces that are more or less suitable to operate sizable media service programs. In situations where space is severely limited, it will be necessary to locate storage areas and equipment substations out of which equipment may be deployed to the classrooms.

Obtaining Professional and Technical Staff: In the next major section we deal with staff arrangements in schools for media-service duties, but we must point up this problem here as a crucial one that needs more extensive action. Since high schools are so universally departmentalised, and since newer pupil organisation methods with increasing emphasis on independent study by learners necessitate a flexibility in scheduling that may free some teachers for other duties, obtaining a professional work force for media service may not be overlay difficult. On the other hand, because the program is so complex in most high schools, and because the work load carried by most teachers is heavy, principals and school system media leaders cannot expect to superimpose extensive, additional media duties of a permanent school wide nature on these people. Hence, a solution to the problem of procuring a full-time media-use leader for the school plus the additional media specialists, media aides and technicians needed should be assigned a high-priority designation. We need technicians to maintain equipment, and also graphic technicians to assist teachers with the preparation, of slides, transparencies, and film-clips. Media-service programs in modern high schools can no longer operate as they did decades ago mainly by student work crews and a teacher as a media leader with two free periods a day and a $250 annual bonus. Now, with adequate leadership and support staff, teachers can be led to cooperate in the preparation of materials, working together on programing for television and electronic carrels, for example, and thus participate in increasing the effectiveness of instruction through media. Under such leadership, student assistants may be recruited and trained for making reasonable though significant contributions to the program of services.

The General Climate for Change in Media Organisation in High Schools: We have noted several conditions that appear to be characteristic of a most high schools, and some of these have a direct bearing on the development of media-service organisations. Other conditions have indirect relationships, but so far as we can observe, it appears that in schools that lay claim to having an effective instructional program, a well-organised and expanded media-service system is indispensible.

Possibilities for Solving the Media Leadership Problem: In preceding pages we listed several possibilities for action by principles of elementary schools to procure and deploy media leadership personnel in their schools. We presented two lists, one applying to old schools with conventional classroom organisation and the other to newly designed schools. Rather than refer to that list we provide here a tersely stated summary of those possibilities that apply as well to the principal of a high school that is in general characterised by flexible scheduling and departmentalised operations. We assume when we discuss leadership arrangements that other staff members such as technicians and clerks will be provided, or other stop-gap arrangements made, until the needed financial support is available. Our brief list is arranged in order from most desirable to least desirable, in our view.

1. Appoint a full-time coordinator for the comprehensive instructional media-service organisation, including all library facilities and operations, expanding the existing position of librarian to include full media-program leadership, or make the existing librarian position a subsidiary one in case audiovisual media insight and skills are lacking. Establish the rank of the position at the level of vice principal. Title the position Vice Principal in Charge of Instructional Media, Coordinator of Learning Resources, or Coordinator of Instructional Media. This person would be directly responsible to the high school principal, but would work through him with indirect lines to other key media and curriculum experts at the school-system level.
2. Appoint a full-time coordinator for the audiovisual media-service center, and organise such services and library services as separate agencies in the school.
3. Invite (and bring pressure to bear in support of the position) the school-system media director to supply a full-time or part-time audiovidual media consultant to work with school-building media specialists in two or more schools.
4. Appoint a qualified teacher to serve as an audiovisual media-service coordinator on a part-time basis. Provide him with one or more part-time qualified teacher assistants who will take charge of specific aspects of the service program, such as in-service education in television programing; in designing slide sets, transparencies, and tape-recorded instruction; electronic carrel installations; the library's listening center; student part-time projection and clerical crew; media procurement and distribution; or, equipment readiness and distribution.

5. Add media aides to the school librarian's staff, and assign all clerical functions of procurement and distribution of media, cataloging processes, and communications with central media headquaters for the school system, and appoint from the teaching staff a qualified part-time audiovidual media coordinator to take charge of the full-time technicians and to carry on all in-service education activities and consulting work.

As we have emphasized, all such plans require technicians and clerical assistants proportionate to the technical complexity of installations in the school, the volume of service given, the degree to which teachers need to prepare their own materials, and the need for extensive television, electronic-carrel, and self-instruction programs. The need for change agents in implementing innovations in the years ahead seems staggering. The logistics will have to be worked out at an ever-increasing pace until higher levels of efficiency and teaching skill with new media have been reached.

Principals and Their Media-Use Decisions: Principals of schools need to develop a penetrating insight into the nature of learning products and activities and the ways in which media contribute to the effectiveness of learning. Insight into the dynamics of the teaching process whereby components involving specific teacher acts, pupil responses to stimuli, pupil efforts, specific media and their relation to both teachers and pupils, will determine in large part the level of priority that principals place on media-use development. Because principals know so little, by and large, about technical matters, they appreciate the emergency services of a technician. When a microphone is out of order they seem to lay undue stress on the need for a technician—but they sometimes exclude or underestimate the importance of the professional person who helps teachers. School-system media program directors also sometimes make this mistake. Principals need to differentiate between the technician-clerk activities and those activities of professionals who may lead a school staff to use media to achieve educational goals at high accomplishment levels. Principals also must be the ones to develop an insight into the possibility of stratifying talents of their personnel if maximum efficiency is to be achieved. Professional personnel ought not to be permitted through negligence or incompetence to waste time and energy in the face of great need to carry out regularly assigned tasks of menial and clerical nature. Each of us needs to take this responsibility to heart. We must not, in addition, fall to envision the growth and development that will take place in the years ahead in the use of technological media in all phases of instruction. In the fact of this burgeoning developing, the stratification of talents among many people, each with his valuable potential contribution to desirable educational results, should be planned and implemented. As we have emphasized again and again, principals are key administrators. They are agents of change, and school-system media directors must unite with them in arriving at sound policies to recommend to chief administrators. The process of change need not be carried out at a snail's pace when readiness for a sound plan of action has been developed and when the people involved in the change understand it and support it. Moreover, such processes of change will demand equally extensive plans in both old schools and new.

Staff for the School-Building Media-Service Program

We have made already many detailed references to the need for both professional and technical staff members in carrying out a modern media-service program in each school building. We have based such discussions on the principle that assistance for facilitating innovation and for unleashing the potential of technology in the teaching-learning process has to be located close to the teacher and should be continuously available. We have also indicated that the physical environment in each learning space must be favorable. We need now to define somewhat more specifically the nature of the work that has to be done in a given school and then emphasize the use of various kinds of personnel that have to be obtained and deployed for accomplishing it. First we shall indicate what has been set up as national minimum standards for providing the professionals who are called upon for guidance in matters of teaching methods and curriculum in each school-building unit.

Minimum Standards for Professional Personnel: We shall point out first that the minimum standards to which we refer were first published as *Tentative Guidelines for*

Audiovisual Personnel and Equipment, by Gene Faris, Chairman of the Department of Audiovisual Instruction of the NEA. The quantitative guidelines, published as a part of the Gene Faris-Mendel Sherman study under the auspices of USOE, NDEA, Title VII, Part B Program, were officially adopted by the DAVI Board of Directors in October 1965, and also by the Association of Chief State School Audiovisual Officers of the same year. The personnel guidelines specify leadership personnel only, and the recommendations for elementary and secondary schools are stated separately, and further evaluated as *weak, good,* and *superior.* The person is described as an *instructional materials specialist,* and is defined as a person with training in both audiovisual communications and library science:

Elementary Schools

> One instructional materials specialist per 35 teachers *(Weak)*
> One instructional materials specialist per 25 teachers *(Good)*
> One instructional material specialist per 15 teachers *(Superior)*

Secondary Schools

> One audiovisual specialist per 60 teachers *(Weak)*
> One audiovisual specialist per 40 teachers *(Good)*
> One audiovisual specialist per 20 teachers *Superior)*

In another official publication of the Department of Audiovisual Instruction of the NEA based on the same study, personnel guidelines were stated in more direct fashion with additional reference to a number of different categories of professional and nonprofessional staff members needed for school services. These guidelines, as restated, are quoted as follows:

In schools with 15 teachers or less—half-time audiovisual specialist (specialists may serve more than 1 school).

In schools with 16 to 30 teachers—1 full-time audiovisual specialist.

Add one audiovisual specialist for each additional 40 teachers or major fraction thereof.

One, or the equivalent, semiprofessional assistant (technician, graphic artist, clerk, photographer, etc) for each 30 teachers.

In schools where audiovisual and library responsibilities are combined (the instructional materials concept), the amount of staff required will be determined by adding the above audiovisual requirements to the personnel standards for libraries set by the American Library Association. It is recommended that the first specialist hired be an instructional materials specialist with training in both audiovisual instruction and librarianship.

Every multiple unit school district with at least one high school and four elementary schools shall employ a district or system audiovisual specialist.

We thus observe that directors of school-system media programs as they look toward the fulfilment of new roles by media must exert great effort to implement teacher-assistance plans at two levels working in each school building. They must seek ways to provide professional help in designing and carrying out media-supported and media-controlled teaching plans, or components of such plans, and they must provide clerical and technician services so that teachers themselves may devote their talents and energies along professional lines for maximum effectiveness. The personnel guidelines just quoted reveal that this action has been given full consideration.

To reveal the need for a multi-level staff for media services, we present at this point a statement of duties usually carried on by school-building audiovisual media coordinators together with an analysis indicating the nature of professional and nonprofessional activities.

The Need for Professional and Non-professional Staff Services in a School Building

The Nature of the Media Coordinator's Duties: Since media-service programs vary from school to school, the following list of duties performed by audiovisual media coordinators is intended to be representative rather than exhaustive. We should note, however, that the reason for this particular listing of duties is to make it obvious that a variety of personnel are needed if media are to be used effectively to play important roles in the teaching process. Duties in the following list generally apply to both elementary and secondary school situation.

Group 1

1. Design the physical layout of a school building media service suite.
2. Devise a complete media-services program, provide leadership and guidance for its implementation, and evaluate its effectiveness.
3. Write a proposal for decision by the principal and other key administrators and curriculum leaders to carry on an in-service education program for teachers to teach them to prepare their own teaching tapes and guidesheets for large-group, self-instruction processes.
4. Write job specifications, procure qualified personnel, teach them to carry on desired duties as needed, assign responsibilities, and supervise their work with both teachers and students, and as needed carry out the same performance with student work crews.
5. Design a media preparation workroom for teachers, obtain authorisation to spend funds, make decisions as to kinds of equipment needed by teachers, identify needed supplies, develop teacher-assistance programs, maintain inventory of supplies on a continuing supply basis, and teach teachers, visualisation skills.
6. Organise and conduct in-service education meetings to teach teachers the relationships of media to valid educational objectives.
7. Discuss and demonstrate before teacher groups how to plan and design slide sets, tapes, and television programs to accomplish specific educational objectives as a part of a self-instruction program in both large and small groups.
8. Plan and supervise the installation of electronic learning laboratories, and work with teacher groups as grade and subject-matter specialists in deciding how best to use them in programs of instruction.
9. Work with teacher groups in his school to assist them in planning what special media they need to prepare as a part of a system-wide cooperative exchange program with other teachers of similar subjects and grades.
10. Teach teachers how to prepare scripts and continuities for audio and television programs on tape for repetitive use in classrooms.
11. Design and make self-instruction plans and materials with which to teach teachers to operate equipment to both use and make media.

12. Assist teachers in the selection of media for use in specific teaching situations, for specific teaching objectives, including supervision of teacher evolutional activities.
13. Assist and advise the school principal, teachers and departmental heads as to the proper application of new technological developments.
14. Serve as a media consultant in advising principals and teachers in preparing media specifications for remodeling old and building new classrooms and other learning spaces.
15. Manage the school's budget for media expenditure in the light of central or local allotments.
16. Devise and implement an effective plan for controlling the flow of incoming and outgoing media, from local sources as well as from sources outside the school system, including the proper ordering, scheduling, and confirming actions, and the delivery of materials and equipment.
17. Carry on liaison activities with school-system media headquarters personnel, making reports, conducting surveys, analysing media needs of teachers, and preparing budgetary estimates for long-range planning.

Group 2

18. Make slides and transparencies for teachers for which design and content have been determined.
19. Maintain inventory records of the school's media collection and equipment units.
20. Inspect and maintain high-quality condition of the school's media materials and equipment that flow in and out of classrooms.
21. Maintain in operational readiness the school's electronic learning laboratories and other fixed technical installations such as CCTV studio production, transmission, and receiving equipment, and both individual and group responding systems.
22. Assist in carrying out promotional activities such as preparing special listings, visual presentations for the principal, and typing, duplicating, and distributing announcements.
23. Keep adequate records of the use of media equipment and materials and maintain work records of personnel who contribute service to the media program.

Analysis of the Duties : Now we suggest that the reader analyse the performance in the foregoing listing and take particular note of those activities that are characterised by (a) design and planning, (b) responsibility for sound decisions, (c) need to evaluate objectives and the means to achieve them, (d) teaching teachers how to apply operational techniques, (e) judging the contribution of teacher efforts in relation to the school's instructional program, (f) perceiving application of technology to instructional systems, (g) leadership activity, and (h) laying out work patterns and activity to be done by others. Such activities are the responsibilities of professionals.

Freeing the Media Coordinator for Professional Service: Such an analysis indicates that the items in *Group 1* demand a concentration of the leadership and design action. Obviously these kinds of performances cannot and should not be permitted to be undertaken by any but professional people. But let's note further that the issue is whether or not the professional because he has no choice in the matter has to work at a nonprofessional level. This will be the case when he has to check off the return of equipment and media, change lamps in projectors, type forms and run off copies of reports make and post schedules of equipment delivery to classroom, clean tape heads in electronic learning laboratories, show teachers how to perform simple equipment operations, answer phone calls, type letters, put out supplies in the teacher workrooms, make slides and transparencies for teachers, copy audio programs on tape or operate a CCTV camera. Thus if we analyse the performance in *Group 2,* we will see the need for both clerks and technicians. We can assert with confidence that so long as the school-building media coordinator is forced through lack of supporting personnel to engage in the types of activities just listed, he or she will be unable to carry on the kinds of performance listed in *Group 1.* Moreover, if we carry the need still further, we can readily observe that in almost any one of the *Group 1* activities the assistance of secretarial and technical staff members would make significant contributions. When clerks and technicians are present and at work under the guidance of a competent professional worker, the school and pupils will gain because more of the leadership and design energy will flow into and through the media-service program to the growth of teachers in their ability to use media in newer and more important roles.

Kinds of Nonprofessional Services Needed for Mature Programs: We have already pointed out that as media programs wax in importance in every school building, highly trained technicians of various kinds will become a necessity. We mention in the following list a few of the kinds of technical workers that will be required as the school-building media service program reaches maturity.

1. Electronic and electromechanical equipment repair and maintenance technicians.
2. Television cameramen.
3. Television engineers, licensed and unlicensed.
4. Videotape and audiotape recorder operators and studio and studio technicians.
5. Film inspection technicians.
6. Graphic technicians, and media production assistants.
7. Photographers, and photo-lab technicians.

Coordinators May Need the Assistance of Specialists: When we consider the professional worker in the media field, we look for certifiable individuals who have gained experience in the classroom and who have undergone a program of preparation in the media field. Such individuals may also be highly specialised as in the field of media design working specifically in television, in designing teaching materials for visual presentation by means of slides and transparencies, either partially or fully automated, or for use by teachers in their face-to-face groups. A full-time media generalist may in fact be supported by professional assistant, and by other specialists who are not in the strict sense professional, for example, a television program assistant who may be working closely with teachers in the design of their TV presentations, serving as an adviser in TV techniques for effective communication.

As we have already pointed out, individual schools and school systems have found a variety of ways to get the required man hours of work during the school day needed to assist teachers with their media-supported teaching processes. Sometimes the central media headquarters staff is supplemented by several additional professional and technical persons who work part time at headquarters carrying out assigned duties, and then these people move into the schools to carry on assigned technical duties there under supervision of the school's media coordinator. Many times a staff of pupils handles the clerical work and routine equipment-handling duties that are carried on by adult technicians on a full or part-time basis in schools that have more mature programs in operation. Since students in both elementary and secondary schools play such elementary and secondary schools play such important personnel roles in media-service programs, a special section is devoted to common problems in their organisation and control.

Obtaining the Services of Qualified Media Coordinators: In the face of a critical shortage of media professionals at all levels of instruction, many school principals and school-system media program directors are forced to select teachers who, though they posses excellent reputations in the classroom and are interest, are not technologically prepared for leadership in this field. School media coordinatorship in this field. School media coordinatorships, of course, are or may become, the stepping stones for qualified individuals to system-wide contracts with teachers and citizens, to prestige, and to new jobs as school-system media directors, school supervisors, and principal. No media director or principal should shrink from seeking the most capable teachers that are to be found on the staff for this purpose. They have a duty to select the best obtainable personnel and to bring every professional influence and argument to bear upon getting this leadership. They may have to take less than the best teacher available, but they must select and secure the appointment of a person who at least shows promise to a marked degree, and they must then assist that person to undertake needed training in the media-use field. The reader has but to turn again to the listing of representative duties of the professional media coordinator in a school building with a mature program to realise the need for knowledge and skills in both teaching methods and media technology. In the recently revised *Handbook for Audio-Visual Representatives, Secondary Schools* of the Los Angeles City Schools, this brief description of a media coordinator and his qualifications appears.

The audio-visual coordinator is in a position to exert lively educational leadership. His is a unique place in the secondary schools. To varying degrees, he is a curriculum specialist, in-service training specialist, and media specialist. There is an increasing demand for him to be familiar with an ever-widening field of audio-visual resources ranging from study prints to educational television...To be successful an audio-visual coordinator should possess certain qualifications. First and most important, he should be an expert teacher and should have a genuine desire to serve as a resource person. He must be familiar with audio-visual methods and have the ability to share his knowledge and skill with others. It is also important that he be able to work harmoniously with teachers, administrators, and pupils. Organisational ability is a key to the success of the audio-visual program. Mechanical aptitude is an asset but not absolutely essential. The audio-visual coordinator must be able to accept criticism and to evaluate it objectively.

Today in a number of states, such as Connecticut and Pennsylvania, a media coordinator who is to devote half time to his duties may not be employed by a school department unless he has become certified, or, shall we say, is *certifiable.* Thus in an increasing number of cases principals and citywide media program directors turn to qualified personnel outside of their own school staffs. Therefore it is imperative that those who seek to fill such positions prepare explicit job descriptions and specify the levels of preparation and other qualifications that have to be met by applicants. A more detailed discussion of the problem of preparing job specifications is provided in Chapter.

It is expected that one of the duties of a city-wide media program director will be to advise school principals as to the present and future nature of duties envisioned for school-building media-use leaders. It is revealing to read a set of specifications written for a high school media coordinator that includes the sentence, "*...Must be able to repair and maintain audiovisual media equipment.*" If the list of specified duties had stipulated instead "*Devise and supervise an effective equipment maintenance program,*" a candidate for the position would have been able to sense a greater concern for the professional aspects of the service system rather than preoccupation with technician's duties. When we deal with the school-system media program headquarters we shall discuss in detail the nature and importance of equipment-maintenance programs. If technicians are urgently needed, and they will be in all advanced programs, they will have to be employed, deployed to service stations, and supervised. No professional media-use leader should spend his valuable time on maintenance work, except in an emergency.

Remuneration Policy for School Media Coordinators: Individuals who have established their reputations as outstanding teachers, who are capable organisers, and who exert significant professional influence on the teaching ability of other staff members deserve more than letters of appreciation and their own personal professional satisfaction in return for their services. The fact is that in far too many schools, remuneration policies are still woefully inadequate. The city-wide media program director as one of the educational leaders of the school system, together with the various school principals, who are themselves respected key school administrators, must put their good influences to work to formulate acceptable local policies governing the remuneration of school-building audiovisual media coordinators for service rendered. Care should be taken in formulating such policies to include an agreed-upon statement of major duties and responsibilities (samples of which have been presents earlier), and to involve school principals, teachers to be served, and other curriculum leaders in the process of developing effective plans of action. It will not be easy to obtain the adoption of adequate remuneration policies, but even though unsuccessful, the campaign to do so must be continuous. The combined weight of the opinions of principals, teachers, and other curriculum people should be formally reported to school authorities, and as needed, community support should be enlisted through PTA groups or other local school-community organisations. Reports and requests for action on this matter need also to describe the extra work load normally involved, and to provide the evidence and results of the duties performed.

Because school-building media coordinators are professional workers, they should be paid as such. Therefore, they should be paid not only as a regular teacher, which they were at one time, but as teachers who give special services that influence the work and results of other teaching personnel. This means that as a vice principal, or as a special teaching consultant, and because of special skills and knowledge, they deserve additional remuneration. Many are the ways in which media workers in schools are paid, some of them, unfortunately, receive small token bonuses at the end of the school year, in additional to their teacher's salary. Schools with advanced or mature service programs will recognise the values in an adequate staff; other schools may somehow arrange for a technician to be on duty to help teachers with equipment problems, but provide no professional service whatever. The following levels of remuneration are presented from inadequate to highly desirable.

1. Reduce teaching load or release from required school routine assignments.
2. Annual bonus payments as salary, starting at $300, in combination with reduced teaching and extra-duty loads.
3. Full-time media-service assignment with rank of teacher.
4. An additional salary payment equivalent to one or two months of extra pay when the coordinator spends two extra weeks at school after school closes in June, and two weeks prior to the opening of school in September on significant service projects.
5. Full-time assignment as an instructional materials specialist, ranking as an assistant principal, or the salary of a regular teacher plus a differential of 10 per cent as a minimum.

We can not and should not ignore the fact that many individuals are indeed willing to accept additional responsibility for unique reasons. Such incentives may be the means of inaugurating service programs, but they rarely serve successfully as a continuing basis for worthwhile and long-range programs.

Employment and Remuneration for the Nonprofessional Media Worker: Although it is common to employ a wide variety of workers at well-developed city- or countrywide media-service centers, it is not so common to find film inspectors, projectionists, electronic technicians, graphic technicians, secretaries, and illustrators in every school building of a given system, but this is rapidly becoming a prime necessity. Again as before, it is imperative that citywide media program directors work with school principals in preparing job descriptions and specifications, and all school administrators know that it pays to study applicants and their records before, not after, they are employed. Since levels of training and experience different vastly between professional and nonprofessional personnel, their salaries and wages differ also. Secretaries and clerical workers may carry on a wide list of important duties, and men, who generally demand higher wages for their marketable skills in media-service centers may frequently possess combinations of skills that are very valuable. Some electronic repairmen have been known to possess graphic skills as well, of they may be taught to use cameras and media-preparation equipment. And of course, if skilled technicians are available, women may be employed to operate electronic film-inspection machines. As we shall point out in the next section it is also possible to employ skilled students as part-time workers. Such students working on an after-school basis receive varying hourly rates of pay, however not often lower than $1.50. A combination of club activity and a work experience program on a no-pay basis as a part of the school's course work may work to the advantage of media coordinators. The pay range we present for technical workers may prove helpful for purposes of long-range planning but of course the figures indicated may very considerably across the country according to experience and economic factors. The following are starting-salary estimates for non-professional, technician-type media-service personnel:

1. Television engineer or chief technician in a school television studio and transmission facility: $6,500-$9,000.
2. Electronic equipment installation and maintenance technician, with skill in designing systems of components: $5,500-$8,000.
3. Electronic repair and maintenance technician: $5,000-$7,000.
4. Electro-mechanical repair and maintenance technician: $4,500-$6,500.
5. Film inspection and service worker, both men and women: $3,500-$6,000.
6. Graphic technician and media preparation assistant: $6,000-$8,000.
7. Photographer and photographic laboratory technician: $6,000-$8,000.
8. Television cameraman and videotape and audio-control technician, and other studio assistants: $5,500-$8,000.
9. Instructional programing design assistant for school studio operations (nonprofessional or semi-professional): $6,000-$8,000.

We are well aware that in larger organisations supervisory personnel may also be nonprofessional in category, as for example, a chief film inspector, and in these cases, additional pay for additional responsibility is well worth it to free the media-use leader from the time-consuming supervisory work of setting up standards of workmanship and planning work schedules and checking on their completion.

We have pointed out previously that school-building media-program leaders, in the absence of financial support for full-time technical and clerical workers, rely heavily on student media-service clubs and work crews. As service programs develop, there should be a steady stream of dependable and continuous assistance by trained, full-time workers. Even though it may be necessary to make use of some student helpers—as long as it is beneficial and not harmful to the pupils—the largest percentage of the needed man-hours of service should come from regular employees. Until that goal can be reached, various kinds of students service organisations will be needed. Therefore, we turn to a discussion of this topic in the following section.

Making Effective Use of Student Assistants

A Rationale for Using Voluntary Students Work Crews

We should bear in mind that although donating service to their school may be a rewarding experience for pupils, both and educationally, it is for special service to teachers and media coordinators that student work crews have to be recruited, trained, organised, and supervised. Because of their frequent presence in classrooms and laboratories, media coordinators and school principals should persuade the most dependable and capable pupils or those with acceptable potential for accomplishment, to donate their time and energy to school-building media service. If we were considering in a major way the particular needs of pupils, we would then select those who could profit most from the work experiences, and some or many in that category may bring discredit one way or another on the total service organisation, and in addition require unusually large amounts of training and supervision.

Thus, on the one hand we face the personality-development needs of pupils who are recruited for work on media-service clubs who are recruited for work on media-service clubs and squads, and the need of a media program coordinator to extend highly efficient and well-organised technical and clerical services throughout the school day. A balanced decision will have to be reached on this and other problems. The school-building media coordinator should work with his school principal and also with the school-system media director in formulating and implementing policies and procedures. In fact, we must emphasize that meeting the need on the part of the citywide media director to implement an operational plan for school-building services becomes one of his primary problems. Therefore, the school-district media leader must be prepared to advise and teach, through the cognizant principal, of course, each school-building media leader how to organise and maintain student operational crews. The problem then is both a school-building problem and a school-district problem. The basic assumption underlying the stated rationale is that selected fourth-and fifth-graders and above, both boys and girls, may under favorable conditions be motivated to donate time and energy without detriment to their academic standing and health. It is also important to note that the less the degree to which teachers possess technical self-sufficiency, and the more sophisticated and the greater the volume of media use is in any given school, the greater will be the requirement for student work crews and other full-time technical and clerical assistants.

This student-crews aspect of the total media-service system involves the school-building media coordinator in solutions to the following important problems: (1) selection of crew members; (2) training the crew; (3) organisation for efficient service; and (4) developing morale. All these are interrelated, but each needs a separate discussion.

Selection of Crew Members

When selecting members for the crew, the coordinator must formulate local policy, but he should bear in mind the following suggestions:

1. There is a need for balance between members at various levels to facilitate progress in capability from year to year. This policy provides a number of top-ranking, capable students for the most difficult jobs, such as training and supervising other workers, and inspecting equipment. For example, strike a balance between a number of fourth-, fifth-, and sixth-graders in elementary school; between

seventh-, eighth-, and ninth-grade pupils in junior high school; and between tenth-, eleventh-, and twelfth-graders in senior high school.

2. Superior students are needed for crew members, but above all, students should be capable of excellent workmanship or they should never be accepted, or if they cannot succeed, they should be eliminated. But sometimes membership in the crew, as has already been pointed out, will be good for a student who is maladjusted, and here a real problem exists in balancing the good of the service against what might be good for one or more individuals. Thus, in the selection of crew members, the coordinator should incorporate the advice of his colleagues through the offices of the principal and the guidance counsellor.
3. Teachers and current crew members may help in recruitment, although it is imperative that a scale for judgment be formulated for all who make recommendations; that is, a brief, workable scale involving such items as appearance and poise (or capability to develop it), health, character, academic capability and study habits, interest in media equipment, and technical aptitude.
4. Final acceptance of new members should be made only after a specified provisional status period which ends as soon as an elementary though important examination has been passed satisfactorily.

Many times, teachers in both elementary and secondary schools may organize supplementary classroom services by asking interested students whom they themselves train to perform valuable kinds of work in the interests of more efficient use of media materials and equipment. In this era of technological sophistication, many youngsters in third grade know how to operate several kinds of media equipment in self-instruction programs for themselves and for the teachers as well. Everyone knows that in modern day school teaching, the teacher herself has need for technical and clerical support that is rarely adequately met, so it is not only the media program leader for the school who needs and deserves sympathetic consideration.

Training the Media-Program Service Crew

Training the crew demands an organised teaching program with study materials and laboratory practice sessions. The coordinator should bear in mind the points made in the following paragraphs as he builds a training course for his own situation.

An equipment handbook for each student is an essential. Directors of media-service programs should prepare suitable handbooks as a direct form of assistance to each coordinator. Such a handbook should contain threading diagrams and explanations of how equipment should be set up and handled. An interesting example is the mimeographed *Manual for Student Projectionists,* prepared by the Division of Instructional Materials of the San Jose Unified School District of California. In the front of this manual there appears a Foreword by the Assistant Superintendent of Schools. Similar manuals including appropriate additional materials have also been prepared for teachers and for elementary and secondary school coordinators by the San Jose department. Los Angeles provides another example. The audiovisual department there has prepared an attractively printed and illustrated manual for school coordinators that contains excellent materials for training programs. Many schools follow this practice. In this connection equipment operation manuals and textbooks may be used as a source of content for preparing materials for local use.

Scheduled training-practice sessions are essential. The best training programs are organised on the basis of sessions complete with instruction sheets and practice in an equipment laboratory. Such instruction should be carried on in groups for specific topics and machines and should involve only those who have not passed the required operational tests. This procedure demands a record system that shows on a card, to be carried by the student, the extent of the trainee's qualifications. For example, at the Bloomfield, Connecticut, High School, the operator's qualification card bears the signature of the school's media coordinator and of the school principal. All major pieces of equipment are checked off on the card as performance tests are passed.

Personnel for carrying on training are essential. The school-building media coordinator may not be able to find the time to accomplish the required training on a personal-instruction basis. He should take the necessary steps to obtain assistance from colleagues through the principal's office, or he should organise a teaching crew among his best student operators, thus putting the training program on an apprentice basis, or he should turn the training and handling of the crew over to an assistant.

Projectionist Checksheet

Audio-Visual Projectionist Performance Rating

Central High School

Name——————————Date——————————
Projector Make and Model ——————————

	Meets Performance Standards	Below Performance Standards	Needs Further Instruction
Operate Projector			
Set up equipment			
Thread film			
Adjust focus, sound, framing			
Start and stop during showing			
Disassembly equipment			
Service Projector			
Change projection lamp			
Change exciter lamp			
Change fuse			
Change metal belts			
Clean lens, film gate, and film guide			
Splice Film			
Make overlap splices			
Make permanent splices			
Know How To Care For Film			
Explain common types of damage			
Explain common causes of damage			
Explain ways to prevent damage			
Know How To Solve Common Projection Problems			
Loss of loop			
Jumpy picture			
Dim picture			
No picture and no sound			
Picture but no sound			
Distorted sound			
Sound but no picture			
Sound not synchronised with picture			

Fig. 7.2 : Many media centers that depend on student service organisations to carry out projection and other operational assignments at teaching stations on schedule, develop and use rating sheets. Such checksheets may be highly specific to check on certain kinds of performance, others are more general. The particular checksheet shown deals with operation of the motion picture projector. It was developed at Central High School, Los Angeles, *Courtesy Los Angeles City Schools.*

Implementation of programs of instruction designed to develop specific abilities is an essential. The nature of a crew member's duties, whether secretarial or technical, and the standard of efficiency desired, will determine the specific nature of the instructional activity. Objectives, identified as kinds of performance, ought to be written out and then developed by appropriate means in optimum order so as to build one skill on another to facilitate the learning process. For example, from a filmstrip projector to a motion picture projector or from an audiotape recorder to a videotape recorder, thus making use of knowledge learned in preceding steps. Some student crew members may work in electronic learning laboratories, or operate listening centers in teaching auditoriums and libraries. Their work may be operational only and not include maintenance. Other student assistants may be film inspectors and splicers, work in the school's CCTV studio, or clean and inspect equipment for readiness for the next assignment. Training programs may therefore very greatly. Many media coordinators are visualising and taping instructions for crew members and thus are moving toward media-supported training systems. Even though the design and preparation of such systems is an arduous task, the eventual economy in time and energy and the subsequent facility with which future training sessions are handled are astounding. Kenneth G. Skinner, one of the author's students has inaugurated a teaching system of this sort for his crew members in the Manchester, Connecticut, High School. Instruction is presented by means of 2 X 2 inch slides calling for small- step responses. This self-instruction system is designed to teach skill in preparing classrooms for effective projection. See Figure. Illustrated booklets may also be prepared for similar self-instruction purposes. It is hardly necessary to emphasize the importance of continuing evaluation of crew-member performance by means of tests, checksheets, and teacher reports of action while on assignments.

Organisation of the Student Crew for Efficient Service

Organisation of the operator crew for efficient service is another matter of great importance, and the following suggestions in the following paragraphs should be considered.

Leadership Force: Each school-building co-ordinator will have to determine how to organise his operational crew so as to maintain control at all times, either on a personal basis, or through students who have been designated as crew leaders. Even when media coordinators have no teaching assignments in regular classrooms, a leadership structure may serve to free him from excessive direct personal control. A word of caution is in order, since some of the drawbacks in having students give technical and clerical services that full-time personnel could be held responsible for, are the possibilities of absenteeism, irregular performance, and having to use pupils who are neither qualified nor properly trained. It is necessary to understand the nature of the problems involved and to be alert to what is going on. Strict control and full and continuous knowledge of performance is of the greatest importance. A supplementary leadership structure is, therefore, vital tò any student organisation. In this case, the service of the operator crew could function with the help of a top-ranking, capable crew member as a captain, together with one or more assistants who could take over during scheduled periods of the school day or when the captain was absent from school. This leader would have specific duties of a supervisory nature, checking on attendance, orders, routing, and so forth. The media coordinator will then have to check up in detail on a fewer number of workers.

Teams or Squads: The organisation of crew members into teams or squads for the coverage of floors, or for morning or afternoon sessions, or for certain days of the week—depending on the volume of service and the size of the school—may prove to be helpful. Each team or squad would, of course, have a leader who could separate the coordinator or to the crew captain.

Office Force: Any operator crew should be supported by an office clerical crew; these workers may never go out on classroom assignments, but may process orders, check schedules, prepare materials and route slips, and get equipment ready. Office forces are easier to organise at the high school level, but modifications of such procedure in elementary schools is not impossible. In the case of high schools, students may conveniently report to the audiovisual headquarters during study periods or under other arrangements. In elementary schools when the school media coordinator has a part-time teaching assignment, care must be taken to locate the coordinator's classroom near the headquarters suite to facilitate office-force work under surveillance before and immediately after school. The system for accepting and processing orders may thus have to be restricted to specified periods in advance of the date that materials and equipment are needed. Greater emphasis may also have to be place upon teacher operation of equipment and the training of operators within each class, fourth grade and above, in order to cut down the frequency of separating the same student from his class for a projection assignment elsewhere.

Developing Morale in the Media Service Crew

A highly important factor in developing and maintaining the efficient service of a crew of projectionists is morale. Morale develops as a result of favorable conditions, and although not all these conditions can be covered here, those discussed in the following paragraphs should receive close scrutiny.

Operating according to a well-known, clearly defined set of procedures and commitments develops morale. When working with either youngsters or adults, it pays to inform them about their responsibilities. We need to spell out important requirements in broadly stated rules and regulations. If such statements are too detailed and lengthy, they are likely to be neither learned nor heeded. Rules will make their maximum contribution to morale when they are formulated in a spirit of mutuality and then agreed to by all concerned. Morale grows through understanding and respect for an organisation and its leadership and goals.

Check-up and accurate recognition of quality workmanship is important for morale. Coordinators must know what is going on and what is being done by each worker. Unless work is being checked, a sense of disregard for good workship is likely to ensue. Morale is influenced by the knowledge that what is done will be checked and due recognition given.

Belief by crew members that the work is important develops morale. This belief can be most effectively instilled by expressions of appreciation by someone other than the immediate leader. School principals, teachers, and top-level school authorities can speak the right words. The impressive Foreword in the San Jose school system Manual for Projectionists was signed by the assistant superintendent of schools. It is a strong case in point and we quote it here in full:

You are a member of a select group that gives much service to your school.

The morale of your group and the services performed have always been very high. You should always strive to fulfil your obligations, and maintain the highest standards of performance. Your first consideration must be satisfactory service rendered.

A projectionist must become familiar with each piece of equipment, and well trained in its use. Following is a manual that will give many useful and practical hints to help you do a better job of showing audio-visual materials.

Curtis Davis
Assistant Superintendent of Schools

Example 7.1

Audio-Visual Section
Los Angeles City Board of Education

Date——————

The undersigned has completed a course of instruction in the operation of the 16mm motion picture projector or projectors named below.

Authorisation is hereby given to operate the projector when all rules and regulations of the Board of Education, and all laws of the city, county, and state governing motion picture projection, are fully met.

This card shall be revoked upon evidence of incompetence or for violation of city, country, or state requirements.

Make——————	Name——————
——————————	School——————
Model——————	Instructor——————
——————————	Approved——————

Club or organisation procedure and appropriate insignia develop morale. Making a club out of the crew, with elected leaders chosen by carefully taught criteria for judgment, together with appropriate membership cards and badges, is a good pathway to morale. School coordinators may set up a strict procedure for application for a membership card of their own design of the club may become affiliated with the Projection Club of America, using standard cards and gold pins. As we pointed out earlier, projectionist cards should show special qualifications as a matter of record. The standard student projectionist card as used by the Los Angeles City Schools is shown Example.

As a club, the operator crew frequently engages in interesting group activities such as trips to nearby university audiovisual centers, theatre projection rooms, and audiovisual production centers, thus adding variety to the training activity that must characterize most of the club sessions. Expenses for such all-day trips, including charactered buses, are frequently paid out of school funds budgeted for the purpose.

School awards and formal personal recognition develop morale. Such awards go beyond school newspaper accounts and over-all recognition by school authorities in publications. At appropriate times, a book award, or some other prize, could be offered in school assemblies to the most outstanding technician of the year. Other awards, such as certificates of service and letters by school officials stating the period of service and the overall rating assigned by the coordinator, should go to all participating students annually. Plaques with engraved names of leaders, or with names of crew members who serve a specified number of years, have also been effective in this regard. A tribute could also be given the school's crew by arranging a special exhibit of pictures of members using or delivering equipment. Details such as these should, of course, be discussed with other coordinators in meetings with the director of media services for the school system.

Limitations on Student Responsibility

Having given rather detailed suggestions relative to the implementation of student-assistance programs, we feel compelled to point out that limits should be placed on the kinds of performance that are expected of students. We media people are prone to move ahead in our plans to inaugurate our innovations, and we are many times sorely tempted to work on a shoestring basis until we can establish a better set of support circumstances. Thus we place some of our student workers in critical situations, in which, if unfortunate accidents took place, we could be greatly and perhaps permanently embarrassed. Take, for example, the use of minors as messengers, or the assignment of high-school-age technicians on a volunteer basis to make videotape recordings of telecasts during the evening hours. Suppose some of these highly respected workers met with an accident route to or from the school. Or suppose that youngsters left doors unlocked, or had impressions made of keys on loan to them, or brought uninvited guests to the media headquarters suite or to the work places, while they worked late. What might the consequences be for the school officials? For the students? For the media-service program?

We raise these doubts in line with earlier suggestions that we use adult, full-time technical employees to handle the bulk of our critical assignments, especially those that involve the need for stable adult judgment. We should not place our volunteer workers in those situations where embarrassment may occur either to them or to ourselves. When such special assignments are necessary. When such special assignments are necessary, the school's media leader ought to arrange for on-the-spot supervision by regular, full-time professional or technical employees, and to take any other precautions that seem to be called for.

Planning and Equipping the School-Building Media-Service Center

When school buildings that were built many years ago lack complete media-service facilities, they must be remodelled to include them. Influenced by media technology, new school structures, as has been pointed out repeatedly, are virtually complete with service suites—some, of course, more extensive than others. School-system media program directors shoudl encourage school planners to increase the media-use potential of all new buildings in order to provide the best possible service to teachers. When old buildings are devoid of up-to-date media facilities, such facilities must somehow be planned, constructed, and equipped. However, we direct this discussion to both school media leaders and principals, prospective and practising, and to school-system media program directors as well, because it is an urgent topic to which too many school officials continue to assign a low priority.

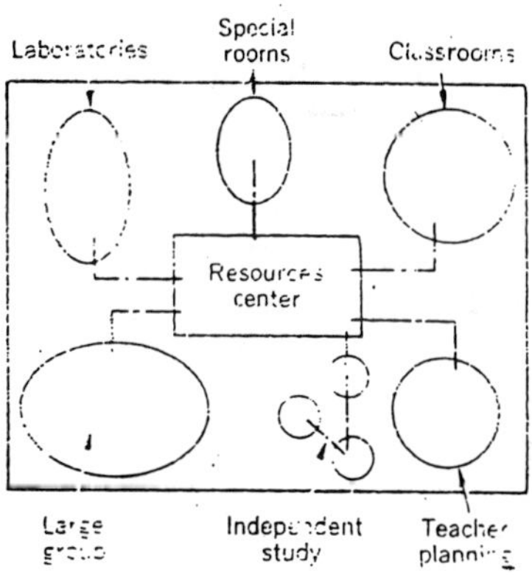

Fig. 7.3 : This spatial relationship chart indicates the kinds of teaching stations and special facilities that use the services of a school building media or resources center. The sketch is form the book, *Educational Facilities with New Media*, published by the DAVI of the NEA in 1966. *Courtesy Center for Architectural Research, R.P.I., Troy, New York.*

Because of the flood of new school construction across the land we will first discuss the nature of space needs. Then with these needs in mind, we can suggest how they may be met in old school buildings. We shall refer to illustrations of school-building media headquarters spaces with some pointed references to both weaknesses and strengths as they appear. We should also explain that because we wish to focus attention on audiovisual media operations in this as we have in earlier chapters, and because we devote another chapter to the print-medium program, we shall not include the subject of libraries in the present discussion in a detailed way. We have stressed earlier that facilities for all media can either be combined in one comprehensive service suite or maintained as separate school departments.

Space Needs

The reader should not miss the main point in this section, namely, that in order to provide adequate media services in school buildings, specific functions must be carried out, and to do so operational spaces are essential. This same assertion applies at the school district level, and therefore we shall discuss and illustrate in the next chapter space needs that must be met in planning and equipping school-system media program headquarters. It can be readily understood that space needs for media functions at the district level will be far greater, but even so some of the functions are similar in nature. There is no established requirement for the design of school-building media centers, and their actual size will depend on the degree to which spaces for electronic learning laboratories, CCTV studios,

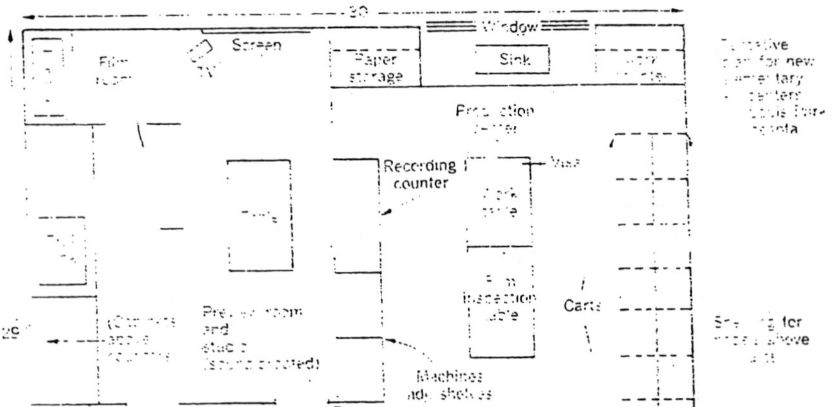

citywide program director to provide minimum-size quarters in a school building for audiovisual media services. Whether constructed in new or old schools this plan should be studied to identify the various kinds of essential functions that have to be carried out *Courtesy Public Schools, St. Louis Park, Minnesota.*

and school library facilities are incorporated in the same suite. Many times, specialised spaces are scattered throughout the school plant according to needs in specific instructional areas. The basic space needs for the school audiovisual media-headquarters operations are suggested in the following list. There should be enough room to

1. Store media equipment issued to or owned by the school.
2. Store media materials issued to or owned by the school.
3. Store audiovisual media supplies.
4. Handle the flow of media materials and equipment in and out of the center.
5. Inspect and clean returned media materials and equipment.
6. Handle and process pre-use examinations of media materials by teachers.
7. Prepare special audiovisual media materials for teaching purposes.
8. Administer the service program.
9. Provide and manage the use of fixed technical installations for the school (such as TV studios and electronic learning laboratories).

Directors of school-system media-service programs need to be aware of these elemental needs for servicing teachers in every school and they should plan accordingly with school superintendents, school principals, architects, school media coordinators, and teachers in connection with all new school-building construction. In the absence of citywide media leadership in the schools, school principals and their school-building media coordinators will have to be the ones to exert the necessary leadership force for planning and implementing, the acquisition of the needed facilities. A noteworthy example of local planning in the new schools of Portland, Oregon, is what is referred to as the school's Instructional Materials Center. In each new school building, and in all others, a large block of space is being provided as rapidly as possible, for centralising the services in connection with all instructional materials. In charge will be a vice principal as a curriculum worker able to help teachers with curriculum problems ranging from books to graphics. This kind of comprehensive service, involving all instructional materials, is characteristic of the Portland system.

How Much Space Is Needed? No easy or pat answer is available for this question. We can, however, identify services to be performed and identify levels of media support for teaching in any given field of instruction on a continuous scale from poor to excellent, weak to strong, minimum to saturation at every teaching station. If we look to common practice, we find some programs of media service operating out of remodelled of media service operating out of remodelled shower rooms; others operate out of book closet spaces where the backs of doors have been equipped with storage shelves for filmstrips. Others, still in cramped quarters for the scope of service, are housed in a conventional-sized classroom that has been carefully planned for some basic services with additional facilities such as electronic learning laboratories and IV studios located elsewhere. In new schools we are more likely to find suites of rooms either for audiovisual media services alone, or a complete instructional materials center where print medium services and audiovisual media are combined. It can be readily understood that when these facilities are combined, the square-footage estimates may strike the naive as being enormous. Referring to the preceding list of basic space needs, it is easy to understand that if a school's media-service center space layout includes a TV studio and related control room and storage areas, and two 50-position electronic learning laboratories, together with a remote-controlled back of programs, the total space requirements would be increased by an estimated 3,250 square feet. The media-service center may in fact have to service special facilities elsewhere in the school, and these we have identified previously, but in cases where classrooms are clustered in such manner as to provide at will a large-group instruction space with a multimedia, rear-projection screen installation, the center's technical staff may have to be on the move to and from such areas on a flexible schedule. Such spaces may be associated with other facilities and hence not thought of as a part of the school's media headquarters suite. Moreover, there are many ways of utilizing floor space efficiently, such as basing floor-to-ceiling storage cubicles, and using the same areas for many uses according to need—for example, using a workroom area for conference groups as well as for the preparation of media for special uses by teacher groups or their aides. Thus, in the light of school size, basic media-service needs, operational level of program, and special-purpose spaces that serve the whole school, we can make some serviceable estimates of space on a square-footage, floor-space basis. We make these estimates for a thousand-pupil school using the previously stated basic needs as follows:

Basic Needs

1. Storage areas for all basic purposes including dead storage (80), media supplies (90), and media equipment and materials (300) for a total of *460 square feet of floor area.*
2. Workroom for processing orders (50), inspecting materials (100), receiving and issuing media materials (50), *totalling 200 square jeet.*
3. Cart garage for holding a dozen ready-to-roll equipment units on mobile stands, *totaling 100 square feet.*
4. Workbench area for checking and servicing equipment units, *totaling 50 square feet.*
5. Area for pre-use examination of materials (individual viewers and headsets for sound carrels or benches, individual small screens for projection of films), *totaling 140 square feet.*
6. Area for preparation of instructional media (see also Chapter) by teachers, teacher aides, and by pupils for special purposes; and area also for duplicators and central duplicating for the school, *totaling 700 square feet.*
7. Area for administrative activity, including leadership (100), and staff space for related operations (100), *totaling 200 square feet.*

   Subtotal, basic need section: 1,850 square feet.

Fixed Media Installations

1. Closed-circuit TV studio for taping and transmitting to intra-school teaching stations: Studio (900), control room (150), storage (100), office (100), *totaling 1,250 square feet.*
2. Electronic learning laboratory (electronic carrels), two 50-position units, and space for remote-controlled banks of programs, *totaling 2,000 square feet.*

   Subtotal, fixed media installations: 3,250 square feet.

Library Needs

1. Complete school library (see for Chapter) facility for print-medium functions, including professional library, *totaling 6,000 square feet.*

   Subtotal for library section: 6,000 square feet.

   Grand total of space estimates: 11,100 square feet.

When perusing such suggested space allocations, the reader should bear in mind that many variables must be considered, and that therefore the figures given must be recognised as tentative in light of school needs and operations. The estimates provided are nonetheless serviceable for discussion purposes. The illustrations should be analysed with care to assess the nature of the services which a given diagram of a center, or its special layout, will support in actually. Wide variety in available space and the ways in which it is used are readily observable.

Some Guidelines for Designing School Media Centers

We shall of course concern ourselves mainly with basic audiovisual media space needs, since in subsequent chapters we include detailed discussions of a number of specialised services that may or not be planned as a part of the school's media-service center. We refer to preparation of media by or for teachers, school library services, television, and self-instruction systems. In each of those chapters additional guidelines and illustrations will be provided that will assist the prospective media leader in the school or city to perceive the possibilities clearly for combining any or all of the many desirable services either in the same location or in several locations in the school.

We may now refer to basic media-service spaces as : (1) storage areas, (2) order-processing and materials-inspection areas, (3) equipment-maintenance area, (4) mobile-equipment (cartgarage) area, (5) media-preparation area, (6) pre-use-examination-of-materials area, and (7) administration area. Each of these areas will be discussed briefly, with the understanding that in the next chapter much additional information will be given to the planning and design of the citywide or district-wide media-service center. First, let us turn our attention to some general consideration.

Some General Considerations: In their notable booklet, published in 1961 as part of a project pursuant to a contract with the U.S.Office of Education, De-Bernardis, Doherty, Hummel, and Brubaker formulated several statements in the nature of broad guidelines for the planning of the instructional-materials center in each school building to meet the needs of both teachers and students. We quote those guidelines as an introduction to the more specific recommendations that follow:

The storage, cataloging, inventory, and distribution of books and of all other teaching materials should be combined in one center, designed to assure coordinated efficient use of its resources. The instructional materials center should be located centrally for the efficient distribution of equipment and materials and for convenient use by teachers and students.

In buildings of more than one floor, elevators or ramps should be provided so that books, materials, and equipment can be transported easily. Floors and entry-ways through which carts must pass should be free of obstructions. Kickplates and jamb-protection should be provided where equipment must be moved through doors.

Due to the weight of materials and equipment needed in the center, and due to problems of handling and distributing supplies and equipment, a ground floor location is preferable.

All features of the center should be planned for flexible arrangement. Storage, cabinets, shelves, and walls (where acoustical considerations permit) should be movable so space may be rearranged to meet the changing functions of the center and make possible multiple uses of space.

The arrangement of the center should provide for isolation of noise-producing areas from classrooms and reading rooms. Those activities of the center that generate noise are previewing, testing and repairing equipment, auditioning, preparing teaching aids and materials,a nd distributing supplies and equipment.

Provisions should be made for future expansion. The ultimate size of any school or school district cannot be foreseen with certainty: neither can the degree of increase in use of new educational media. Therefore, the materials center should be planned so it can be expanded with a minimum of cost and disruption to adjoining areas.

Space requirements for storage, distribution, and preparation of materials will depend on the degree to which these functions are shared between the center and the classroom.

Adequacy of storage is paramount. Long-range requirements for storage of equipment and materials must be considered.

One of the authors of the booklet just referred to was Amo DeBernardis, then Assistant Superintendent of schools, of Portland, Oregon. Because of subsequent formal planning work completed by a coordinating committee of Portland School System administrators including that author, and which was published in 1964 as "Educational Guidelines for Southwest High School," we can trace the influence of the general guidelines previously quoted in the formulation of specifications and also in the actual architectural plans. We, therefore, quote the entire section under the heading *Instructional Materials Center.* The reader should bear in mind that the Southwest High School was being designed for a starting enrollment of 1,200 with plans to expand to 2,400 pupils.

Instructional Materials Center

Effective teaching and learning require many and varied teaching materials and equipment. Books, periodicals, films, filmstrips, microfilms, recordings, programmed learning materials, television programs, models and displays, and data banks are some of the teaching and learning tools available to teachers and students. The school must be organised to make these materials easily available to teachers and students. The facilities must be planned not only to make these tools available but to efficiently store, distribute, and repair them. The instructional materials center is the central focus for the handling of these materials and equipment. It should provide the following services to students and teachers:

To catalogue and inventory all types of teaching and learning materials—books, pamphlets, films, recordings, models, exhibits, art prints, slides, film-strips, microfilms, community resources.

To maintain and service all of the teaching tools used in the school.

To inform teachers and students about new developments in materials, equipment, and teaching technology.

To produce materials which are unique to a specific teaching situation.

To provide assistance in the locating of needed teaching and learning materials.

To assist teachers and students in the use of teaching equipment and materials.

To provide space and facilities for teachers and students to preview, audition, review, and try out various teaching media.

To serve as a comprehensive learning laboratory in which students can learn to use all types of learning materials and equipment.

General Considerations for the Planning. The center should be located centrally so that it can serve the various components of the school. It should be designed to make it easy to change partitions or expand areas such as reaching and storage. Acoustics and ventilation should be carefully planned to take care of the work being carried on in the area. Floors and doorways should be designed to facilitate easy movement of carts, materials, and equipment.

Reading Area. This area should provide the following:

Reading space for 150 students (preferably not more than 80 to 100 in any one area).

Storage space for 15,000 volumes.

Spaces for individual reading and research.

Display space—cases, tackboard.

A browsing area.

Materials Stock Area. This area should provide the following:

Storage for books, periodicals.

Storage of microfilms, slides, films, recordings, tapes, programmed learning materials.

Circulation Area. This area should be centrally located to facilitate checking of materials and supervising of the various spaces. It should provide spaces for card catalog and reference files and be easily accessible from office and work area.

Multi-purpose Area. This area should:

Provide adequate lighting for television production.

Be assessable to the production area.

Provide storage facilities for television camera, lights, console, etc.

Accommodate 120 students for large group instruction.

Provide folding partition to allow room size to be changed easily.

Be accessible from the corridor.

Be adaptable to the production and distribution of closed circuit television programs.

Provide adequate power and outlets for television cameras, projectors, etc.

Conference Area. This area should:

Accommodate small groups of 6 to 8 students.

Be adaptable to use of all types of learning materials and equipment, films, recordings, slides, programmed learning materials.

Be conveniently located to the materials.

Provide for supervision.

Have a folding door to permit combined use of adjacent room.

Have adequate ventilation, light, and acoustical control.

Provide shelving for storage of books and equipment.

Individual Study Spaces. The individual study spaces should:

Be equipped to use all types of learning materials and equipment, books, machines, recordings, etc.

Provide some visual and sound separation from general reading area.

Have adequate lighting and ventilation.

Individual Preview and Audition Spaces. These spaces should:

Accommodate one student.

Have adequate acoustical and ventilating treatment.

Provide space for using recorders, viewers, micro-film readers, projectors, teaching machines.

Provide temporary storage for books, tapes, films, recordings.

Storage Area. The storage area should:

Provide for adequate storage of all types of materials—maps, globes, projectors, exhibit screens, recorders, displays, tapes, carts, etc.

Be located near the general receiving area for the school.

Be easily accessible to all parts of the center.

Be arranged for ease of handling material.

Provide shelving and storage space which can be easily changed to fit new equipment and materials.

Maintenance and Service Area. The maintenance and service area should :

Provide space for the repair and servicing of all types of teaching media such as books, audio-visual equipment, science equipment, maps, globes.

Provide work-bench and tool cabinet.

Provide space for grinder, test equipment, bench drill press and small tools.

Provide storage for equipment needing repair.

Production Area. The production area should:

Provide space for production of all types of teaching materials, such as transparencies, slides, motion pictures, models, charts, dioramas, signs, posters, mock-ups, etc.

Provide space for jig saw, table saw, and other small tools for model making.

Provide darkroom which can be used for production and instruction.

Provide space for artist.

Provide space for storage of paints, papers, wood, etc.

Provide adequate power and electrical outlets to run small shop equipment.

Provide sinks with hot and cold running water with clay traps.

Provide space for editing films, slides.

Provide space for photocopy equipment.

Office Area. The office area should:

Be located to facilitate supervision of the materials center.

Provide space for desk, books, files, and storage space.

Be adjacent to a work area.

Receiving Area. The receiving area should:

Be located near loading area for the school.

Provide doors which allow carts and equipment to be delivered with care.

Provide shelving and spaces for temporary storage of materials and supplies.

Textbook and Supply Area. The textbook and supply does not need to be in the JMC complex, but could be adjacent to it. This area should:

Provide space to house textbooks.

Provide for the distribution of books to students.

Be easily accessible to a corridor and receiving area.

Provide space for receiving, storing, and distributing educational supplies.

Multi-purpose Learning Lab. The multi-purpose learning lab should:

Provide electrical and communication facilities for all types of audio and visual instruction.

Provide seating for 40 students.

Be equipped with 40 student stations with facilities for listening to tapes.

Provide for a master console.

Provide two individual listening rooms.

Providing for showing of all types of visual materials.

Providing for adequate ventilation, sound, and light control.

Provide chalkboard and tackboard space.

Future Expansion and development. All partitions in the center should be of a removable type to allow for future expansion and rearrangement of the space. Power facilities should be designed so that it would be easy to use any type of new electronic teaching device. Lighting and ventilation should be so designed as to allow for the division of spaces into any size from small group to large group.

The final result of such planning was combination of one central instructional materials center for the whole school and eight additional so-called unit-instructional-materials centers, one for each unit school. See Figures.

Some Specific Suggestions for Designing Each of the Working Areas: We shall now give consideration to those space arrangements that contribute to the effectiveness of the media-service program and which may facilitate future changes to meet new developments. We shall make these suggestions in relation to each of the seven basic needs previously listed, and also in direct relationship to the Portland, Oregon specifications which should be borne in mind as the additional following information is analyzed.

Storage Areas

1. Provide five kinds of storage:
   (a) For media materials such as films, tapes, globes and maps, slide sets, filmstrips.
   (b) For media equipment units not on longterm assignment to teaching stations for issue on request. See Figure.
   (c) For media supplies: spare reels, film leader, cleaning fluids.
   (d) For infrequently used equipment units and stocks of accessories, and equipment awaiting trade in, commonly referred to as "dead" storage.
   (e) Bulk storage for summer or other non-use periods.
2. Provide for additional space to store materials used for preparation of media, and spare parts for equipment such as tubes, belts and lenses in or near areas of such activity.
3. Arrange flow diagram of operations and use storage area spaces as sound barriers, and also in line with economy of time and effort to retrieve needed materials.
4. Supply adequate lighting, ventilation, and dehumidification when storing electrical and electronic units that may deteriorate over long periods of idleness.
5. Allow space for workers to move freely when returning or retrieving materials from shelves and bins.
6. Refer also to *The Storage Area* list in the Portland, Oregon, example.

Order Processing and Materials Inspection Areas.

1. Economize on time and effort by locating order-filling and packaging processes near storage and pick-up or delivery areas.
2. Incoming and returned media materials such as films, disks, filmstrips and filmstrip sets, slide sets, tapes and kits need to eb visually inspected for signs of damage and errors in repacking in the classroom. Special electronic and/or mechanical equipment may be required. Such inspection stations ought to be located in optimum relationship to storage areas.
3. Provide electric power for inspection devices, and sufficient space for both worktables on which to lay out materials and mobile carts for returning materials to storage or stacks.
4. Filling orders for filmstrips and other materials becomes an arduous task when shelving units are too close to the floor. Provide convenient to use storage units for efficient handling.

5. Provide space for shelving, or a long table or bench, on which to place packages ready for pick-up and delivery.
6. Media materials should be returned from classrooms to the same location, a central receiving station, where they may be routed conveniently to inspection area.
7. Refer also to the *Receiving Area* and *Maintenance and Service Area* lists in the Portland, Oregon, example.

Equipment Maintenance Area

1. Provide a waist-high work bench equipped with adequate electric power in plug mold, constructed so as to include storage bins for equipment units being worked on.
2. Repair materials need to be handily stored in drawers and bins, and one or more pieces of test equipment may have to be placed on the workbench or on appropriate shelves nearby.
3. Maintenance area needs to be supplied with mobile stands for moving equipment to and from storage areas, or mobile stands each with its own piece of media equipment should be located adjacent to the maintenance bench with easy access to school corridors.
4. Locate the maintenance area in close proximity to media equipment return stations.
5. Refer also to the *Maintenance and Service* list in the Portland, Oregon, example.

Mobile Equipment Area *(Cart Garage)*

1. Provide an accessible row of mobile projection stands each with its projector, tape recorder, portable electronic learning laboratory, stereo tape or record player, portable television display or transmission system, ready for delivery to teaching stations upon request.
2. Locate mobile equipment-stand area near corridor to avoid traffic through workrooms.
3. Locate the mobile equipment storage area adjacent to equipment repair and service area.

Media Preparation Area

1. Special attention should be given to the problem of storing supplies for the preparation process. Stocks of supplies ought to be visible to teachers using the facilities, and good organisation is essential. That is, supplies for a given process such as making Polaroid slides (in either 2 × 2 inch or 3¼ × 4 inch size) ought to be arranged together and

labelled properly. Shelves and cabinets with sliding doors may have to be used in combination.

2. Waist-high workbenches, or flat-top student desks for sit-down processes such as binding slides, should be provided, making possible convenient arrangement of all equipment from copy-cameras to lettoring octs.
3. Provide special working stations where equipment is in a state of readiness for immediate use, with needed supplies nearby or at the station.
4. Refer also to the *Production Area* list in the Portland, Oregon, example, and to Chapter, *Implementation of Media Preparation Services.*

Pre-use Examination of Media Materials

1. Provide flexible area for simultaneous examination of all media by individuals and small groups, by means of small projection screens and headsets for individual or small-group listening.
2. Provide plug-in boxes for sound, and projectors and players arranged on optimum-size tables, Provide possibility for group viewing of a single projection screen and an additional person viewing his own screen using an additional projector.
3. Suggest using nearby classrooms for large-group evaluation of media.
4. Previewing space should be easily unable for other work groups on occasion for recording instructional tapes as an example.
5. Refer also to the *Individual and Audition Spaces* list in the Portland, Oregon, example.

Administration Area

1. Usually, the criterion uppermost in the minds of planners of offices and administration areas, is privacy. This is not generally in keeping with the great need of school-building media center administration activities. Although some planners surround an office area by wall-to-ceiling partitions, it may in fact be far more effective from the standpoint of getting work done to strike a balance between privacy and visibility of as many working spaces as possible. This would be especially desirable when reliance is placed on student assistants.
2. Conference spaces may be associated with office areas and media literature files for professional study-committee use.

3. Far too much space is devoted in general to the office area. When space allotment is at a minimum, the size of the office for the school-building media coordinator should also be at a minimum, and emphasis should rightly belong on the contact with operations as needs dictate.
4. Management activity by assistants needs consideration, and hence desk and file space must be provided in proper relationship to the media coordinator's office.
5. Refer also to the *Office Area* list in the Portland, Oregon, example.

We have presented space estimates in consideration of essential functions, and we have presented some guidelines for designing such operational areas. However, the prospective media-center designer needs for more information than he has received to this point. We, therefore, assure the reader that we shall discuss and illustrate in detail many aspects of media-use operations and needs in the chapters that follow. We ought to stress the point, now however, that not all of the media-service facilities have to be located in one suite. It is often highly desirable to move equipment and materials into substations and also into several more specialised service stations such as electronic learning laboratories and TV studios.

Some Suggestions for Planning Media-Service Centers in Old Schools: It is rarely possible to find large unused spaces in older school buildings that can be taken over for developing a media-service center. The probable alternate methods of providing needed space are to construct an addition needed space are to construct an addition to the building or to take over one or more classrooms. In the former case, the previous general and specific suggestions may be helpful. In the latter case a great deal can be done with imaginative layout of space available in a single classroom, which may provide more than 675 square feet of area. Planners would make a serious mistake if they recommend the use of wall-to-ceiling partitions in such class-rooms. Emphasis placed on work-flow diagrams, over-all administrative surveillance capability, and on maximizing working space for teachers and crew of assistants, plus the location of possible smaller substations and additional cart garages to serve clusters of classrooms on additional floors that older buildings are likely to have will pay dividends in increased service effort.

Further discussion of details and specifications regarding the school-building audiovisual media-service center and its equipment are unnecessary for the present, since the school-system audiovisual center will be discussed in the chapter that follows. Significant parts of that discussion will be applicable to service centers within each school building. Such plans as have been described indicate the kind of service center that each school should be provided with. The instructional programs in some schools demand that these centers be larger and more comprehensive than in others.

Having viewed in detail a number of the pertinent aspects of organising, planning, and staffing good audiovisual media-service centers in school buildings, we should focus our attention finally on a problem that relates to over-all operation, namely, the management of control systems. We need not present such management systems in great detail because it is doubtful that any given system that is devised will be applicable in a universal way to all school programs. We must, however, stress the importance of giving due attention to the nature of the problem, and call for creative and high caliber action on the part of the citywide media program director, the school-building media leader, and the principal.

Management of Audiovisual Media-Service Systems

The difference between leadership and management, and we emphasize here again the great need for professional leadership or perceiving and setting goals and designing good service systems for achieving them. Good management in the implementation of policy is also an essential phase of the on-going, developing media-services program. In preceding sections in this chapter and in earlier chapters we have discussed a number of organisational problems, and by suggesting desirable procedures for the acquisition and distribution of media materials, and deployment of equipment to mention just a few topics, and in the duties that have been listed, we have implied the necessity of effective operational systems. It remains for us at this point to identify some of the systems that should be set up and managed efficiently. We again deal with audiovisual media processes common to the programs in most schools with the knowledge that many variations exist in the degree of media emphasis and comprehensiveness, and that new developments are certain to appear in the future that will require new control procedures.

Distribution of District-and School-Owned Media Materials

Nature of the Problem: Schools that are units within a school district that has an organised, district-wide media-service program, are likely to have available many resources upon which to call, located in central school-district head-quarters. They may also have their own collections of media materials, either on long-term assignment or owned outright, located in the building for daily use. Materials needed by teachers may therefore have to be ordered from the citywide center or from the school-building center, or on a free-loan or rental basis from sources outside of the school system, but this procedure will be treated as a separate system. Such materials must be ordered, delivered to the teacher or teachers, used according to need, and returned to school district headquarters on time. How can this clerical process, that involves high-cost materials, be routinised and handled in a safe manner by other than professional employees?

Suggested Management: Procedures may naturally vary according to local arrangements with a given citywide media center's scheduling system, but the process in rather general terms is clear-cut. Hence the following suggestions may be made:

1. Provide teachers with a statement describing the step-by-step procedures that have been officially adopted by the school and school system, having to do with deadlines, quotas, delivery and return dates, and other items characteristic of the local system.
2. Distribute sample order blanks or odering forms for materials available only from the city-wide headquarters, and remind teachers of deadline dates for submitting orders for materials.
3. Distribute catalogue or specialised listings to each teacher.
4. Collect orders on due dates and forward them to citywide center for processing.

5. Return confirmations of scheduled materials to teachers involved, but a listings is made by dates of use for the entire school for each work, for those media that may have multiple uses by several teachers-for example, motion pictures and tapes.
6. When motion pictures and such materials as are likely to be used by more than one teacher arrive at the media center of the school, they are logged in or checked off on the incoming list and placed on suitable shelves or racks pending delivery and/or pick-up by the teachers who wish to use them.
7. Media titles and/or packages are noted for return according to lists that have already been prepared and then made ready for return to city headquarters.
8. Make some centralised media materials available directly to teachers by special procedures, using a different ordering form. Such materials should be noted by means of carbon copies of original orders, and should be delivered directly to teachers who are to return them to the school's media center for pick-up by school-system's trucking service.
9. Make available school-building-owned materials by using a separate multiple-copy ordering slip. Such media as maps, globes, filmstrips, tapes, may be picked up or delivered to teaching stations, and upon return by the teaching stations, and upon return by the teacher are checked off on the order slip.
10. Organise full- or part-time staff members or students to handle clerical aspects of materials processing. Write out specific instructions and post them, and give copies to personnel concerned.
11. Deploy a staff member to make daily checks on the system's operation.
12. The media leader should make periodic evaluations of all aspects of the process, including analysis of flow diagrams and motion-time observations.

Any system must be as nearly foolproof as possible under the enforced limitations; however, a professional leader must not become enslaved to clerical and menial tasks. Thus good procedure must be painstakingly worked out and delegated to appropriate workers.

Independent Short-Term Procurement of Media Materials

Nature of Problem: In addition to obtaining media materials from district headquarters and from school collections, teachers are permitted by means of budget allotments to make use of materials from sources outside the school system on a rental or a free-loan basis. Because of their high cost, potential value, popularity, and often limited local availability, motion pictures are the most frequently rented medium. Aside from the problem of providing financial support to each school media coordinator for this purpose, the heart of this problem is locating the right film, getting it for use at the right time, and then returning it to the distributor on time to be sent to the next rental customer.

Suggested Management: Since film procurement through rental arrangements is such an important method of acquisition for so many schools, this problem was discussed in Chapter under the topic *Efficient Procedures for Renting and Borrowing Media.* Systems may of course vary greatly from school to school, but nevertheless operational systems are made up of essential elements, and these were set forth in considerable detail in that previous chapter. Therefore, at this point we shall assume that the school is operating an independent system of rental procurement limited by specific budget allotments involved. The following briefly stated suggestions as to management constitute a review of the earlier treatment.

1. Provide check-off lists of previously regularly rented film subjects for teachers, including space for new film requests and dates desired for use.
2. Provide simple ordering forms together with a school calendar that includes vacation periods, marking periods, and other pertinent regulatory information.
3. Maintain card file of preferred distributors with related code numbers included on lists sent to teachers.
4. Use a labor-saving printed form letter for setting up rental orders with distributors.
5. Compile and distribute to teachers involved, the list of rental motion pictures scheduled for each month of the school year.
6. Check monthly master list for rental films (formal log sheet) as soon as films arrive, and fill teacher requests for

equipment and service. Notify teachers if necessary to confirm arrival of expected film shipments.

7. Inspect films in every shipment prior to use to determine print condition, and then place them on the separate, rental-film ready rack or shelf (to avoid mix-ups with district-owned and school-owned media).
8. Locate films, if not returned to ready rack on due date, and inspect them for damage, repackage them in original containers, label properly, and enter on log sheet the return shipment data and post office insurance number.
9. Notify distributor of any irregularities in the film shipment, and save log sheets for handling the bill-paying process.
10. Note evaluations from teachers regarding future film rentals and/or purchase recommendations, filing them appropriately. Refer also to Chapter content included under *The School-System Process of Evaluation and Selection.*

If we scrutinize this process carefully, it can be seen that once the system has been established, only clerical functions are carried out to implement it. Hence, helping teachers to choose and evaluate media in light of their objectives, and evaluating the entire system constitute the higher-level processes usually carried out by the professional school-building media coordinator.

In some districts, the rental film process is carried on only by personnel working in the district-wide media headquarters. In these cases, some of the elements of the above operational system are still desirable, particularly those that have to do with the control of the film at all times while it is being used in the school-building audiovisual media center.

Handling Media Equipment Breakdowns

Nature of the Problem: In any good-sized elementary or secondary school that has a well-organised and supported media program, anywhere from ten to fifty audiovisual media equipment units may be functioning in as many rooms at a given time. Teachers may be operating this equipment or, in some cases, students in the class or assigned student operators from a media service-center crew. What happens when there is a breakdown ? Who will be Mr. Fix It? The teacher? The operator? Will the audiovisual media coordinator be called out of a conference, or even his own class of pupils, to diagnose the difficulty? What operational plans ought to be implemented?

Suggested Management: The answer is not too difficult. If we follow the principles already enunciated, we can see that there are several alternatives, but one thing is certain, the remedy has to be administered fast. Contrary to some common practices, it does matter to a lot of people that time is wasted because of defective equipment of because equipment is sent out in a poor state of readiness. The following essentials should be present in any good system formulated:

1. Send out to teaching stations only those equipment units that are fully ready for use.
2. Organise an emergency operational equipment pool, with standby projectors on mobile stands ready to dispatch to a teacher in trouble.
3. Assign a student technician to trouble shooting and equipment-dispatching duty near the office phone. (Such calls will hopefully be so few that students assigned to this duty may study most of the time.) In larger schools, troubleshooting duty may be handled by full-time technicians who are working regularly in graphics or maintenance, or doing other technical work in electronic learning laboratories, and who may be absent from such a post for a few minutes on an emergency assignment.
4. Undertake to develop organisational plans for locating equipment pools near clusters of classrooms so that standby units are available a large percentage of the time close at hand.

In trouble-shooting situations, especially when technology becomes complex as it does with automatic and remote-controlled equipment, technical personnel become indispensable. Such personnel may then be made available for training purposes, and hopefully teachers and some of the student technicians will be able to handle most, if not all, of the minor difficulties that are almost certain to arise.

Distribution of Media Equipment

Nature of the Problem: This problem is directly related to the problem of procuring media from all sources for use by teachers, and also directly related to the assignment of operators. Once the needed tapes, films, and filmstrip, to name just a few media, are at hand, coordinators are then faced with the problem of providing the right equipment (and operators if necessary) to make possible the effective use of the media. In large schools this problem is a serious one and one that may have to be resolved by placing restrictions on the volume of service. The equipment may have to be operated by teachers themselves when enough technicians or student workers are not available. As soon as teaching stations are equipped with all needed equipment units, and teachers can operate their own equipment, then coordinators will have to deal only with the problem of media delivery and pickup. Hence the problem is one of degree of self-sufficiency of teachers in their own teaching stations. The more self-sufficient they are, as far as media equipment is concerned, the less serious the problem of equipment distribution becomes. Since one of the basic principles to be followed in providing media services is that of timeless of use by the teacher, and since teachers should have materials and equipment conveniently available, we suggest that the equipment-distribution problem be solved without fail.

Suggested Management: As guidelines for media coordinators with similar problems we suggest several essential parts of a system to handle the distribution of equipment units from an equipment pool or substations, as follows:

1. Collect the organise requests for equipment service from teachers, up to the limit of equipment and personnel available, using suitable order forms, sign-up chart, equipment-allocation board, or sign-up sheets for the week posted at the media center, in the office or library or at any suitable location.
2. Assign equipment units as requested entering notations on a master request sheet.
3. Schedule operators, if teachers need them; otherwise deliver the requested equipment at or before the appointed time.
4. Post a daily schedule for movement of equipment units according to assignments and work orders for operators. Provide standby equipment units for substitution.
5. Issue assignment slips to each operator specifying jobs to be done. (Slip to be given to teacher for signature and report on quality of personnel service and operational efficiency of equipment assigned).

6. Pick-up all equipment units that are due back at end of the day for a complete readiness check-up and reassignment to mobile equipment pool, to regular substation, or to the next day's teaching stations.

Unless teachers can operate their own equipment, and this will always be the case a certain percentage of the time, the media coordinator has no choice but to organise a student technical crew, employ full-time clerks and technicians, or work out some optimum combination of supplying the needed personnel services for a predictable number of hours of classroom service each school day. In the Los Angeles City Schools, a simple and workable procedure is recommended in the handbook for audiovisual media coordinators who, in released time from teaching assignments, organise service programs in their respective schools. This suggested six-step procedure is as follows:

A six-step procedure is recommended to achieve this self-scheduling effect:

1. Five teacher sign-up sheets, one for each day of the week, are posted with the confirmation sheet in a central location.
2. Days and periods when service cannot be provided should be crossed off the schedule. Some coordinators note reasons for limitations on service, such as holidays and assemblies.

Projectionist's Report Form

Projectionist's Name————————————

		Yes	No
Film Code————	Punctual		
Projector————	Efficient		
Room————	Cooperative		

Remarks————————————

————————————————

Mark (circle one) A B C D

Teacher's Signature————————————

Date———— Period————

Fig. 7.5 : This check-off evaluation form for the teacher to fill out on each occasion of service, or during selected periods of the month, unknown to the student, if record keeping becomes burdensome, is a model of desirable simplicity. *Courtesy Los Angeles City Schools.*

3. Teachers sign up for film showings on days and at times desired. They should be secure in the knowledge that films will arrive on schedule unless they are notified to the contrary...
4. At the end of each day, the sign-up sheet for the following day is transferred to the audio-visual room...
5. The sign-up sheet is used as a worksheet to program the movement of crows with projectors and films. The coordinator will:
   (a) Assign projectors and crews to rooms where they are first needed during the day...
   (b) Reassign each projector, period by period, for the balance of the school day, scheduling it to the nearest classroom where a film is to be shown...
   (c) Assign a crew a each projector for each period...
   (d) Schedule additional projectors to and from storage areas if necessary.
6. Worksheets are filed as a record of film use within the school.

As the reader studies the preceding six steps, he should consult also the illustrations that show the special forms and processes that were designed to make the system work.

Another part of the equipment-distribution problem is the long-term-loan aspect of supplying classroom needs such as portable tape recorders, filmstrip projectors, individual viewers, headsets, automatic slide projectors with programmed tape accessories, short exposure equipment, and the like. Equipment may be needed for extended period of time, and in fact such unit may either be picked up by teachers or it may be delivered and set up after-school and left for specified periods of time. Request forms, assignment records, and a filing system for due-back dates, at which time the return of equipment units is checked and irregularities noted and action taken, are the essential elements. Limitations in assignments may have to be announced and strictly adhered to for the good of all concerned.

Again it can be seen that the work to be done is largely clerical and technical in nature, and the need for sufficient assistance is self-evident. The media coordinator must find ways to procure needed hours of work, devise a workable plan of operation, assign the jobs to the right people and check on and correct weaknesses in the system.

Maintenance of School-Owned Media Equipment

Nature of the Problem: The problem of maintaining audiovisual media equipment units in a state of operational efficiency becomes acute when they become worn and outmoded. Therefore, all operational equipment ought to be scheduled for replacement according to an optimum time schedule. Essentially, equipment needs to be given regular care and kept in good running order. This demands regular cleaning, a readiness-for-next-use check-up after each assignment, periodic inspection for signs of wear, and an immediate check-up upon receiving reports of malfunction. A stock of spare parts and maintenance supplies should be maintained so that proper adjustments may be made quickly and conveniently. Major repair work should probably be done at the central repair service, or by local equipment dealers, depending on policies. All cleaning and inspection work and considerable minor adjustment work can be handled on the spot in the school's media-center maintenance area. Equipment on loan to classrooms, and all fixed equipment installations, such as multimedia, projection booth, TV studio, and electronic learning laboratory installations must be given the same meticulous care to make possible trouble-free service at the time of need. Such action calls for a good maintenance-management system.

Suggested Management: Elements of an equipment-maintenance system are as follows:

1. Assign technical personnel on a daily basis to check and prepare mobile equipment units for issue. Prepare and issue to personnel involved a list of specific jobs to be carried out for each kind of equipment.
2. Make minor repairs, replace parts as needed, and make notations on equipment-record card for each unit handled.
3. Maintain a stock of repair and servicing materials, using a stock card to describe each item as to part number, source, and price.
4. Maintain a file of service manuals.
5. Post a set of instructions regarding the handling of equipment in need of major repair service (e.g., tag and send equipment unit to central media headquarters; prepare a requisition and fill out a form letter covering shipment to local or regional equipment dealer; or, pull defective equipment out of service and substitute standby equipment,

pending repair in the school's own center by qualified technical personnel working on an overtime basis).

6. Set up a schedule for periodic check-up of all fixed equipment installations, noting action required, substituting replacement equipment units as needed.
7. Using suitable equipment control cards for units issued on a long-term basis to teaching stations, carry out a periodic check-up including cleaning, operational efficiency analysis, and repairs as needed.

This technical work may be carried out by qualified students working after school, but supervision of all operations, including the record-keeping aspects of the work, is essential. Such supervision may have to be given by a specially qualified member of the student crew, but preferably by a full-time technician who may be performing more difficult tasks while student helpers are carrying out routine checks. No professional teacher-coordinator or other leadership personnel should be using time and energy to carry out technical operations on equipment.

Reservation and Scheduling of Media-use Teaching Stations

Nature of the Problem: When fixed media-equipment installations are organised and administered by the school's media center personnel, the media coordinator must set up an efficient control system for the flow of students and teachers on a daily basis. Many schools today have one or more electronic learning laboratories, multimedia teaching stations, large-group TV viewing areas, TV studios, audio production studios, and teaching auditoriums. In some schools, the fixed installation may be an integral part of a cluster of teaching stations, as for example in the Foreign Language Department. In such cases, the school's media coordinator is responsible for maintenance and possibly for operation but not for scheduling. In other cases, as for example the school's auditorium, facilities may be scheduled only through the principal's office, or through the principal's office and the media coordinator's office, personnel in the latter being called in to render service on a routine operational basis. In most of the technological installations, the media coordinator will be involved with not only routine service, but with the scheduling as well, since some limitations may have to be placed on the degree of service that is available on a given day or in any given class period.

Therefore, we can readily see that a management system needs to be formulated.

Using Teacher Sign-up Sheets

One sheet for each day of the showing week is posted so that teachers may sign up for films.

Teachers request films, using code letters appearing on the school confirmation sheet. In the example shown above, the audio-visual coordinator has indicated that he cannot provide service during third period because of an assembly.

At the end of the day, the coordinator uses the sign-up sheet as a worksheet, first scheduling the movement of projectors.

After the projectors are scheduled, he assigns projectionists.

Suggested Management: Essential elements that must be incorporated in the management system are the following:

1. Establish limits on operational service in light of present technical staff for the operation of fixed installations, and distribute procedural statements to all teachers who use the specialised teaching stations.
2. Post sign-up sheets which incorporate the operational service limits for any given installation, that is the number of periods in a day or week that can be reserved, at the media center, and accept telephone orders as staff permits.
3. Arrange schedules of service for operational staff, students, or full-time technicians, and write assignment work orders.
4. Call in operator report slips on the operational efficiency of equipment used.
5. Maintain a log sheet (or use original sign up sheets) of installations scheduled.

Maintaining the Inventory of Media-Equipment Process

Nature of the Problem: In the modern school the number of pieces of media equipment may become enormous. We think, of course, of electronic laboratories where headsets, tape-recording units, and TV receivers may have to be listed separately. We think also of teaching stations where there are individual filmstrip and slide viewers, and teaching machines, and then there are the larger pieces of media equipment that are either assigned to teaching stations or distributed on a mobile basis. Hence, whereas media materials are generally purchased and listed in catalogs, or entered on various types of file cards, equipment units are purchased and placed on shelves for distribution without being listed in the same manner. We therefore face the problem of setting up an adequate system that will reveal what equipment is on hand, where it has been assigned or stationed, and whether it is where it is supposed to be at any given time.

Suggested Management: The management of inventory is essentially a problem of devising and using a control card that carries adequate information and keying each of many cards to an inventory list if such listings are required in the school system. A master inventory may be automated so that print-out processes for each school are periodically possible. In fact, the management of an inventory-control system may be simply the management (may be not so simple either) of a system already established and being implemented on a school-district basis. At any rate the essential elements of a control system are as follows:

1. Log in each piece or unit of equipment as it arrives at the school from a vendor, if purchased, or from the district media center if assigned.
2. Ask the central media headquarters office to supply standard transfer inventory cards, or fill out an inventory card for each unit of equipment received, noting as called for on the card, date of purchase, make, model number, cost, and dealer's name or code. On this card also indicate the school's identifying number, such as MP 15, indicating that this unit was motion picture projector number 15. Refile the cards in appropriate categories.
3. Using appropriate stencils and a paint sprayer, stencil the school's name or code and equipment unit type number, for example, Smith School MP 15. Stencil both the equipment body and the case.
4. Make additions, or corrections as to replacement when appropriate, to list-type inventories.
5. Use each inventory card as a maintenance record card with suitable maintenance check-off lists on the card.
6. Indicate on the inventory card the teaching station assignment, if part of a fixed installation, or indicate equipment pool, as the case may be.

7. Periodically, as is feasible or as demanded by school-system policies, complete an actual unit-by-unit physical inventory, indicating completed date on each card or school list.

Systematizing Routine Processes

A larger number of operations are carried out in a well-organised media-service center than those that have just been discussed in detail, not necessarily demanding a multiple-step control system. Yet, we can think of no better way to manage these operations than to routinise them and develop easy-to-use request or check-off forms. The main idea is to get the work done conveniently and effectively without sacrificing prudence. Every good manager knows that there is a time and place for a specified kind of work to be completed, that deadlines have to be met, and that to get work done, it has to be systematized. We can apply this need to the more extensive control systems just discussed, and we can apply it as well to other operations such as issuing media-preparation supplies to teachers. We will discuss this problem fully in a later chapter, but we should point out here that at least a simple log sheet showing the items issued and to whom issued ought to be maintained. Evaluation forms from media used should be collected and processed for their contributions to purchase and subsequent rental plans. Expenditures against the school's budget allotments should be checked weekly and monthly and carefully noted. Records should be processed monthly for reports and some or all of these processes need to be carried on according to the school calender to maintain proper relationships to system-wide business operations.

The citywide media program director will have a great deal to do with the formulation of workable policies by school coordinators and their respective school principals. He can also help to inaugurate systematic procedures that will assist all people involved. Once again we refer to the supervisory booklet. *Handbook for Audio-Visual Representatives,* published by the Los Angeles City Schools, which urged school media coordinators to carry out specified duties according to a schedule. We quote this schedule as follows:

First week of school

Train projectionists.
Take all equipment out of storage and reinventory.

Acquaint new teachers with available audio-visual equipment.

Acquaint new teachers with ordering procedures.

Establish a calender on which are noted such dates as those for distribution and return of departmental film orders and for mailing IBM film-order cards to the Audio-Visual Section.

Meet with the principal and department heads to establish departmental film quotas.

Daily

Before school:

Check availability of equipment.

Review the day's showing and delivery requests.

At the close of the school day:

Pick up the film sign-up sheets and equipment requests for the following day.

Schedule projectionists and sound projectors.

Schedule the movement of equipment other than sound projectors.

Account for all equipment.

Check security of storage room.

Day Preceding Delivery Day

The following duties often are delegated to students to be performed under careful supervision:

Rewind films...

Inspect films for damage to determine need for additional training.

Make certain that any beginning and ending leaders which have become detached are returned in the proper film can.

Make certain that each film is in the right can. Place the films in their proper bags, and return bags to the established delivery point.

Delivery Day

Supervise the cleaning and inspection of all machines and equipment. (Refer to the *How to Operate* manuals for guidance.)

Supervise the checking of titles of newly delivery films.

Assign each film a code letter which can be used for identification on confirmation sheets and sign-up sheets.

Notify teachers of previously confirmed films which do not arrive in the school.

Delivery Day Plus Two

Duplicate copies of the following week's film confirmation sheet.

Delivery Day Plus Three

Post the following week's film confirmation sheet and distribute copies to teachers.

Post the following week's film sign-up sheet.

Monthly

Assist department heads with departmental film orders.

Process IBM film-order cards for mailing to the Audio-Visual Section.

File IBM order cards when they are returned.

Notify department heads of titles which have been ordered but are not confirmed.

Biannually

Order supplies and equipment.

Last Half of Each Semester

Select projectionists to serve during the following semester.

Begin training new crew members before or after school.

Last Week of the Spring Semester

Collect and store all audio-visual equipment and materials for which you are responsible.

Provide the principal with an inventory of this equipment and material.

Supply information about missing equipment.

Lest the reader assume that we have given consideration to all of the duties of the school-building media program leader, we hasten to point out that this was not our intention. We have dealt with major topics such as in-service education of the staff in earlier chapters, and other chapters follow such as the budgeting process in its entirely, which have a bearing on a number of other processes that involve the media leader in carrying out his responsibilities. We have at this point dealt with a few basic, more or less routine control systems that have to be carried out on a continuing basis. Other systems are bound to be demanded as technological processes become more complex and comprehensive in their application. The school media coordinator will be successful only when he has learned to be a good administrator, for without good management of day-to-day services, the results of his good leadership with teachers will not prosper.

We must point out finally that the optimum balance must be found by citywide media program directors between adequate material and personnel services located in a central headquarters structure, and the capability growing out of the organisation of school media centers to give teachers the technological help they need on a day-to-day basis. What we are emphasising is the major point that leadership energy, that makes the formulation and implementation of adequate systems possible, must be fed continuously in optimum amount into each school unit.

Problem-Solving Activities

1. Just how do you strike a favorable balance between creating and meeting demands for audiovisual media services? What is likely to be the result if a school principal or media co-ordinator oversells his program?
2. Formulate a plan for providing systemwide equipment facilities. Show how you will strive to make use of both centralisation and decentralisation in assigning equipment units.
3. Explain by a series of diagrams how you would deploy the media equipment units in a 28-classroom elementary school in order, for example, to avoid wasting instructional time when a motion picture presentation is desirable? (This question demands that you identify and relate the different ways of supplying equipment to teachers when they need it.)
4. Refer to the section of Chapter relative to the decentralisation of media materials in school buildings and discuss the merits of such decentralisation. Under what conditions would you say that decentralisation would be unwise?

5. Prepare a proposal for a school principal (you choice of elementary or secondary school with the guidance and approval of your instructor). Specifying type and pupil enrollment, lay out in outline form the nature of the desired audiovisual media-service program. Specify the desired: *(a)* need for media services; *(b)* pattern of organisation; *(c)* need for professional leadership and how to supply it. show diagrams of relationship of media leadership to school principal and to city media director.
6. Identify the principal difficulty in obtaining part-time professional assistance for the service media program in elementary schools. State in outline form the ways of surmounting the problem. Be sure to state what the provision must be at advanced stages of media service.
7. Why has it been possible to operate audio-visual media-service programs in the past with such limited professional, technical, and clerical assistance?
8. Identify several basic circumstances under which it would be wiser to separate the library and audiovisual media services organisationally? Under what circumstances ought the two branches of service be combined or unified? Can you cite cases in support of your points?
9. Identify a school system of your choice with which you are familiar and in view of your knowledge of the teachers on the staff and the number of school plants in the district, use the minimum standards for personnel quoted in the chapter to work out the number of professional and technical media personnel that ought to be provided.
10. Analyze the list of professional duties stated by the author under *Nature of the Media Coordinator's Duties (Group 1* and *Group 2,)* and identify the potential contributions of technicians and clerks in carrying them out.
11. Write out a list of specifications for a qualified full-time, audivisual media coordinator for a school principal to use in procuring a professional media coordinator.
12. Write out a proposal for a school principal requesting budgetary support for a complete staff of professional and support personnel to carry on a mature media-service program. Show in this proposal the degree to which you propose to make use of student workers.
13. Sketch in outline form a training program for fifth and sixth-graders in a new audiovisual crew. Develop an apprentice system for this training and show how the training sessions

become progressively more difficult, based on previous learning. Indicate how automated, self-instruction may be employed in the process.

14. You do not have permission of the principal to use student workers because of tight scheduling and team-teaching operations. You therefore have to provide full-time technical help for which budgetary support will not be forthcoming for another year. Explain in a proposal what your plan for action is and how you would execute it.
15. Assume you have been assigned a normal size, 30-foot by 26-foot classroom, in each of ten elementary schools, for remodeling as a school audiovisual service center. Make a scale drawing of your planned layout. Label your diagram fully as to utilisation of the space to facilitate audiovisual services in the building. (Study the illustrations in the text and attempt to avoid in your own sketch any weaknesses you find. Do not use code numbers or letters for identifying your spaces. Use readable labels for quick identification.)
16. Some teachers refuse to exchange class-rooms with other teachers to share darkening facilities. Do you blame them? Is the central projection room the most desirable way to provide facilities for projecting pictorial materials? Defend the negative view by giving at least three good reasons for your opinion. What are the arguments in favour of the projection-room method?
17. (A) You have been asked by your principal to submit a rough sketch of a complete audiovisual media-service center for a new elementary school that will enrol 1,000 students. He wants you to indicate the space requirements and area and to show particularly how the different space requirements are related. Make this sketch and label it. Use words and abbreviations in labels, not a coding system.

    (B) Carry out the same assignment for a 1,200-student high school.

    (This assignment should be carried out by groups of students, each working on a part of the specifications. Some groups should choose elementary schools and other secondary. At the discretion of the instructor, blocks of unlabelled space may be indicated for media-preparation and television operations with the intention of completing the diagrams with special reference to topics in Chapter.)

18. Discuss in class and agree on the space requirements for a modern school library facility as a separate unit from the audiovisual media-service center, for an elementary school for 1,000 pupils and for a high school housing 1,200 students as a starting enrollment.
19. Analyze any two of the control systems that have to be devised and managed by audiovisual media-service leadership and fill in the details in a flow diagram showing the number and kinds of workers required to get the job accomplished. Include the nature of supervisory personnel as well. Label the diagram fully and include notes where essential.
20. In the management of control systems at a media-service center as depicted in this chapter, select any one of the systems depicted and indicate how the system could be replaced—that is, eliminated entirely—by substituting a different set of circumstances. Identify the system and then report the new circumstances that would eradicate the need for the operations.
21. What are the alternatives to building up a strong service system carried on by school-building personnel in each elementary and secondary school? Support your points by diagrams or convincing arithmetic.

References

American Association of School Librarians. *Standards for School Library Programs,* 1960 (Chicago: ALA).

The Audio-Visual Program, Bulletin 218. (Indianpolis, Indiana: State of Indiana, Department of Public Instruction, 1956).

Brown, James W. and Kenneth D. Norberg. *Administering Educational Media* (New York: McGraw-Hill, 1965).

Burgert, Robert H. and Ben L. Gumm. "Keiller Elementary School." *Audiovisual Instruction,* Vol.10, No.2, February 1965).

Cobun, Ted and Hal J. Cress. "North Division, Niles Township Community High Schools," *Audiovisual Instruction,* Vol. 10, No.2, February 1965,

Coleman, Jean and Margie Gonce. "Wilbur Wright Junior High School," *Audiovisual Instruction,* Vol. 10, No.2, February 1965.

Daniel Wanda. "The AV Coordinator on the Rise," *Audiovisual Instruction,* Vol.2, No.4, April 1957.

DeBernardis, Amo, Victor W. Doherry, Errett Hummel, and Charles W. Brubaker. *Planning Schools for New Media,* in cooperation with the U.S. Office of Education (Washington, D.C.: The Superintendent of Documents, U.S.Government Printing Office, 1961).

DeBernardis, Amo, David M. Crossman, and Thomas E. Miller. "Media, Technology, and IMC Space Requirements," *Audiovisual Instruction,* Vol.10, No.2, February 1965.

Educational Facilities Laboratories, Inc. *The High School Auditorium 6 Designs for Renewal.* (New York: EFL, 477 Madison Ave., 1967).

Ellsworth, Ralph E. and Hobart D. Wagener. *The School Library: Facilities for Independent Study in the Secondary School* (New York: Educational Facilities Laboratories, Inc., 1963).

Estes, Nolan. "Valley Winds Elementary School," *Audiovisual Instruction,* Vol. 10, No.2, February 1965.

Faris, Gene. "Tentative Guidelines for Audiovisual Personnel and Equipment," *Audiovisual Instruction,* Vol.10, No.3, March 1965.

Faris, Gene and John Moldstad (assisted by Harvey Frye). *Improving the Learning Environment* (A Study on the Local Preparation of Visual Instructional Materials). In Cooperation with the U.S. Office of Education. (Washington, D.C.: Superintendent of Documents, U.S. Government Printing Office, 1963).

Finn, James D. "Professionalising the Audiovisual Field," *AV Communication Review,* 1:6-17, Winter 1953.

Ford, Harry J. "The instructional Resources Center," *Audiovisual Instruction,* Vol. 7, No. 8, October 1962.

Gardner, Dwayne E. "Prescribing Educational Specifications," *Audivisual Instruction,* Vol. 10, No.2, February 1965.

Giesy, John P. "A Working Relationship,"*Audiovisual Instruction,* Vol. 10, No.9 November 1965.

Glenn, Magdalene. "Organising a Materials Center," *National Elementary Principal,* Vol. 40, No.1 January 1961.

Goldberg, Albert L. and Richard A. Darling. "Is the Instructional Materials Center the Answer?" *Audiovisual Instruction,* Vol.6, No. 5, May 1961.

Green, Alan C.(ed). *Educational Facilities with New Media* (Prepared under a contract with the U.S.Office of Education) (Washington, D.C.: The Department of Audiovisual Instruction of the NEA, 1966).

Greer, Phyllis. "A Materials Center That Really Works," *Audiovisual Instruction,* Vol.5, No.10, December 1960.

Guerin, David V. "Media's Influence on Design," *Audiovisual Instruction,* Vol.10, No.2, February 1965.

Handbook for Audio-Visual Representatives, Secondary Schools (Revised 1965), Los Angeles City Schools, Instructional Services Branch, Los Angeles, California, 1965.

Harcleroad, Fred F.(ed). "The Education of the AV Communication Specilist" (Proceedings of a DAVI Seminar), *AV Communication Review,* Vol.8, No.5, Supp. 2, September-October 1960.

Larsen, John A. and Jewel Bindrup. "The Library Curriculum Center: Hub of the School Program," *Audiovisual Instruction,* Vol.5, No.10 December 1960.

Mannino, Phillip. *ABC's of Visual Aids and Projectionists Manual, rev. ed.* (University Park, Pennsylvania: 1935).

Martin, Ann M. and C. Walter Stone. *A Study of Regional Instructional Media Resources, Phase I-Manpower.* (Prepared under contract OE-3-16-027, with the U.S. Office of Education.) (Pittsburgh: Graduate School of Library and Information Sciences, University of Pittsburgh, 1965).

McMahan, Marie, "Building Coordinator: Professional Partner?" *Audiovisual Instruction.* Vol. 7, No.8, October,1962.

Mesedahl, Leroy K. "The IMC: Contribution to Individualised Instruction." *Audivisual Instruction,* Vol. 10, No.9, November 1965.

Miles, Bruce and Virginia McJenkin. "IMC's: A Dialogue," *Audiovisual Instruction,* Vol.10, No.9, November 1965.

Mitchell, Malcolm G. "What's Going On in the School Library? *Phi Delta Kappan,* Vol.45, October 1963.

Moldstad, John and Harvey R. Frye. "Making Room for AV," *Audiovisual Instruction,* Vol. 2, No.10, December 1957.

Libraries, Vol.13, No.3, March 1964.

Phillips, Murray G. "Instructional Materials Center: The Rationale," *Audiovisual Instruction,* Vol.5, No.10, December 1960.

Pryor, Robert L. "Speedy Repair Equals Good Utilisation," *Audiovisual Instruction,* Vol.8, No.3, March 1963.

Quantitative Standards for Audiovisual Personnel, Equipment and Materials (in Elementary, Secondary, and Higher Education). Developed as part of the Faris-Sherman Study conducted under the auspices of the United States Office of Education, National Defense Education Act, Title VII, Part B Program (Washington, D.C.: Department of Audiovisual Instruction of the NEA, 1201 Sixteenth Street, N.W., January,1966), mimeographed.

Rufsvold, Margaret. *Audio-Visual School Library Service* (Chicago: ALA. 1959).

Sharp, J. Stanley. "Architectural Steps in Facilities Planning," *Audiovisual Instruction,* Vol.10, No.2, February 1965.

Sherman, Mandel. "Training for a Top-Flight Coordinator," *Audiovidual Instruction,* Vol.3, No.5, May 1958.

Taylor Kenneth I. "Instructional Materials Center," *The Nation's Schools,* Vol.66, December 1960.

Waitenberg. Milton. "A Comprehensive Service Center for Randolph High School," *Audiovisual Instruction,* Vol.7, No.8, October 1962.

Winston, Fred and others. *Guiding Students in the School AV Club.* (Washington, D.C.: Department of Audiovisual Instruction, NEA, 1201 Sixteenth St. N.W., 1962).

8

Organizing the Citywide Audiovisual Media Center

Readers may well wish to ask a searching question after painstaking analysis. They may wish to ask, "Why, with well-developed media-service facilities and systems advocated for each school building, should there be a need for a districtwide or citywide headquarters suite?" We must have unitary leadership and responsibility for the citywide media program, and we must also have operational facilities, staff, and financial support to provide those inevitable centralized services that are or will be demanded in light of local needs. We assume therefore that as we build strong school-building service systems, our efforts will prosper because of the energizing action of a strong citywide media organization, which will not remain static in its own development but will alter its service programs at various stages of technological progress.

In setting up an audiovisual media center, the director must blend professional, clerical, and technical services, and must therefore bring to his job a through understanding of appropriate physical arrangements, adequate technical control of materials and equipment, and adequate inventory controls, and he must possess the ability to build an effective staff organization. Therefore, the purpose of this chapter is to aid the prospective director in making wise decisions and recommendations in setting up these processes and procedures.

Emerging Patterns of Media Center Organization

The single most important first step that a school community takes on the route to providing effective audiovisual media services is to create an agency to provide services to the schools as units of viable, citywide or districtwide organization. Hopefully an operational plan such as the one described in Chapter 1 would have been legislated into action as a fitting start for the program of service. However, even though there is universal agreement on the need for citywide service organi-zations, there is not universal agreement on a single pattern and structure. We shall therefore discuss first the need for such centralization of services and leadership and then undertake to describe the nature of the media-service organizations that are presently being established in schools systems.

Need for Centralized Leadership and Services

A citywide media center, as we have pointed out already, is not just a suite of offices that houses the media program leader for the district, plus collections of media, but it is the heart of a system-wide organization. It is also a symbol of the energizing force for external action being taken, and it is the scope and quality of that action which really matters. If we return to Chapter 1 we note that principle number one, first in a series of broad principles for the organization for audiovisual media services, is stated as follows: *The work of organizing and developing instructional media services will proceed most effectively under specialized, centralized leadership, working coordinately with other curriculum personnel and under adequate system-wide financial support for auxiliary staff, equipment, materials, an facilities.*

The alternative to such action, as implied by the *leadership* principle, is to do what school systems without formally organized media programs do—develop a separate media-service program in each school building. The higher cost through duplication of facilities, the wasted effort of innovating individuals who make decisions without sound technical guidance and standardization of procedure, the hodgepodge of operations, procedures, and points of emphasis that develops within a school system (even though the program is carried on under the control of school principals and other administrators talented in other aspects except technology) can lead only to inefficiency and eventual disaster.

No one knows in exact detail what the media-service center in any given district or city oaught to be. How large it ought to be, what services ought to be given, how fast the development oaught to proceed, where it should be located, and how much financial support is required are relative matters that depend on local conditions. We insist that "pipelines" of service and leader, ship energy ought to feed every school-building unit, fulfilling through such units specific obligations in each teaching station or learning area. We do know that the technology for teaching and learning is growing in complexity. We know that many changes will have to take place, some of which may proceed at a steady rate, and others which must be accelerated according to local developments. We know that the planning and design for action and the responsibility for study and recommendation is a vital part of the leadership force that helps groups discover and formulate their proposes, then guides them in the process of implementing changes in good balance. And we know that many of those changes need to be made according to long-term plans in all the schools to benefit all of the learners, and that help for teachers must be organized and implemented according to an optimum schedule. We know also that the needs of learners are paramount and that appropriate technological tools of increasing complexity are increasingly the only means of meeting those needs. Learning situation involving their use in modern-day schools require an extensive and dependable service system for teachers.

Thus we assert that we can see the need for centralized facilities in which a thriving media organization can operate effectively for the good of all concerned. We can also postulate the working principle, based on more than a half century of experience, that a centralization of audiovisual media leadership and services with an ensuing optimum decentralization of facilities, services, staff, and financial support is the right and proper point of departure for audiovisual media development. And it is this particular development with which we shall be mainly concerned in this chapter.

We therefore now turn to a description of the emerging patterns of organization for centers of media services. The base of the organization problem is whether services will include all media, both print and nonprint, within the media service center. We shall not deal in the following pages with a resolution of the issue, mainly because we wish to focus attention on the audiovisual aspect of media services and the unique problems to be faced by those who are responsible for providing them. However, we realize fully that one of the emerging patterns for organization is that in which all media services are developed, both centrally for the district, and then further decentralized in each school building. In the discussions that follow, the reader should also refer to the previous chapter which dealt with the organization and development of school-building media-service centers. In actual practice it is possible that the districtwide center will differ in organizational pattern from those that are developed in each school. For example, the district center may specialize in audiovisual media but one or more of the schools may develop an all media service center including library services. We shall deal first with the pattern of organization that separates the print and non-print media problems and service.

Organizations Separating Print and Nonprint Media Services

This pattern of organization was the first to develop, as we pointed out, and it has continued to serve well in cities and towns around the country. Under this pattern the audiovisual media program director is a coordinate curriculum leader with full responsibility for the development of all nonprint media services including facilities, staff, and planning for financial support programs. Print-medium services, both central and decentralized as units in each school building, come under the jurisdiction of other administrative and supervisory personnel. If we take note of the pressure exerted by special-area supervisors for their own programs, for financial support, additional operational space and staff, we can see that, given a situation where there is an understanding of the urgency for audiovisual media development on the part of Board of Education members and key administrators, rapid advancement of the system-wide audiovisual media program is likely to result under this pattern of organization. On the other hand, as school systems search for new methods to provide administrative control over increasingly complex organizations and services, it becomes feasible to re-group departments and divisions under knowledgeable and skilful leadership. Hence, under this arrangement, all media agencies are likely to be brought under unitary leadership. Department heads or chiefs of specialized services under such circumstances with adequate budgets and staff may proceed to the development of exemplary and comprehensive media services for the enhancement of modern educational programs.

Organizations Combining Media Services

Under recent pressure to change the name of technological service agencies from *Audiovisual Education to Learning Resources, Instructional Media, Instructional materials, or Audiovisual Communications,* and as various professional groups have sought to expand their skills and services, we see a movement toward an all-inclusive media organization. We see great merit in the unification pattern, but we see also the possibility of an unfortunate imbalance in the concentration of effort on one branch of media service or the other. This possibility would be more likely to occur if a bias has developed because of training and experience, or the lack of it. We must note that favourable conditions are needed for each type of media organization, that is, unified or separate, if the release of potential values is to take place.

We can state the situation in summary fashion by pointing out that the media program director, or the print-medium specialist, when possessing required qualifications, ought to be sensitive to instructional needs that demand new or modified services leading to greater comprehensiveness and efficiency. As needed, then, either or both of these qualified teaching methods specialists may be called upon by school-system administrators to

1. Coordinate the centralization of all print-medium processes and development.
2. Coordinate the centralization and decentralization of all nonprint media processes and development.

3. Coordinate the development and operational use of electronic learning laboratories, dial-access systems and other self-instruction systems.
4. Coordinate the ordering, storage, and distribution of school supplies.
5. Centralize and distribute maps and globes
6. Coordinate the use of community resources, including reciprocal activities and field-trip programs.
7. Centralize and distribute museum materials.
8. Provide a centralized and decentralized service for the production of still and motion pictures, charts and other graphic materials.
9. Organized and coordinate a school-owned educational radio station.
10. Coordinate the use and production of closed-circuit television programs for instructional purposes.

All this appears to be a formidable undertaking, but it need not be when staff and financial support are adequate, and if this is not the case, the media program director must use his own good judgment by saying "No" until conditions for success are more to his liking.

The combination of audiovisual media with print-medium services makes possible the broadest unification of media services, and names such as *Curriculum Materials Center* and *Instructional Materials or Media Center, or Learning Resources Center* become applicable.

Such a center in Portland, Oregon was early recognized as one of the most comprehensive of its kind anywhere. "The main idea back of his unification," said the center's director, Amo DeBernardis, "is to provide for the Portland teachers one resource center from which they can obtain any and all teaching aids that fit their instructional needs, and also receive professional help in their use." In Portland, book services not only include a centralized organization for the ordering, distribution, and repair of textbooks and supplementary books, but they also include a library of professional books, periodicals, resource units, and other curriculum publications. Insofar as school supplies are concerned, all school supplies from construction paper to science, music, art, industrial arts, and gym equipment are centralized under instructional materials center management. The point that Debernardis makes regarding the advantages of a unified center are worth-noting.

1. It minimizes the tendency to look upon certain instructional aids as entirely unique and therefore unrelated to the general process of education.
2. It provides better coordination of service functions of purchase, distribution, and maintenance.
3. It has elicited more coordinated effort on the part of staff in the in-service growth of teachers.
4. It makes for greater economy, both in use of materials and in effort by staff and the classroom teacher.
5. It has provided more effective coordination of aids within each school.
6. It has made possible a more efficient inventory.
7. It has made possible a better implementation of the curriculum.

Not all Instructional Materials Centers are really what the name implies. Instead, some centers are little more than audiovisual service centers with limited additional duties involving one or more phases of print-medium service. Those that do have library functions to perform carry them out in a great variety of ways. In some cases textbooks and library reference books of all kinds are handled centrally for elementary schools only, since school libraries and librarians are not available there. At the secondary level, textbooks and other reference secondary school library. Other instructional materials centers exemplify truly unified media-service centers and both selection and supply of reference books and the distribution and use of all other media are coordinated on a system-wide basis, In large instructional materials centers a number of supervisors or assistant directors are placed in charge of the various divisions such as book-services, television, media design an preparation, and non-print-media distribution.

Any media program director should realize that he could easily let himself become, more than anything else, the manager of a warehouse. This will be inescapable if he permits himself to be saddled with extensive media services without necessary increases in staff and budget. Each situation will demand a careful analysis and a wise policy decision.

Location of Media Centers

Some media centers are to be found in new school-system administration headquarters, and others in old and abandoned schools that have been taken over with a minimum of remodelling. Classrooms in outmoded buildings may still serve as film vaults, media production facilities, publication printing shops, and office suites once they have been air-conditioned for year-round comfort. However, for central, closed-circuit television studios and control rooms, such space may be totally inadequate. Other media centers may be located in spaces provided in new secondary schools that can be made large enough to support the media services for the district as well as to support in a sizable area the special school-building services described in Chapter 7. So it can be readily observed the country over, that media directors take their centers to place where, above all, operational spaces are adequate, both horizontal and vertical. But there are many factors that should be considered and which will come to light in later discussion. For the time being we suggest the following scale of priorities.

1. Design the audiovisual media center, or an all-media center, with adequate space, to be housed in a new and separate building, centrally located with reference to schools in the district.
2. Design the audiovisual media-center suite in combination with, or separate from, the system-wide print-medium services as dictated by local conditions, with adequate space, as a part of a district-wide administrative center.
3. Design an adequate district-wide audiovisual media center, or an all-media center in combination, to be housed in a new school building, separated specially and operationally from the school's own media center.
4. Take over as much space, in light of justified needs, as can be allotted in an older building to be shifted from instructional to administrative service in the district, and plan required remodelling activity to adapt the space to be used for efficient audiovisual or all-media services.
5. Remodel a number of classrooms in an existing school building still in active instructional service to meet audiovisual and printmedia service needs.

As media-service programs develop, the focus for service will shift into the individual school, and because of this situation, there is little point in trying to merge the center for a school building with a district-wide center in an attempt to economize on personnel and space. The two services are likely to be vastly different, therefore they should be kept separate. It does not seem right that one school in the district should be given the kind of preferential treatment generally thought possible in connection with the combination of district-wide and school-building service centers, and the prediction is that one or the other is likely to be at a disadvantage. The main, service center should be free for specified services to all schools.

We should not fail to mention that any one, or any combination, of unique circumstances may influence, and rightly so; the decision to move to a lower priority in the preceding list of situations for locating the citywide media-service center. For example, in West Hartford, Connecticut, it was voted to inaugurate an individualization of instruction project by means of what is referred to as dial retrieval of television and audio programs for both large-group and carrel utilization. The installation was planned originally for a new high school that had been authorized by the Board of Education. Since the new high school itself was to be the hub of the project for subsequent interconnections with other schools, it was decided to locate the new citywide media-service center there also, along with the installation of retrieval- and program-preparation facilities in specially designed spaces. To serve the school's own media program, an additional school-building media-service suite was also designed in close relationship to the citywide suite. Such a school-building center could well have been an entirely separate suite, for example combined with the school's library as an instructional media center.

Emerging recently is the pattern of regional services, which, after all, has been in existence for a long time in the large-scale and comprehensive media-service organizations established in a number of county school agencies. Federal and state-supported programs are now appearing that involve a number of school districts. Such regional media-service centers include television and dial-access systems together with computer processes an curriculum and inservice education leadership forces.

It is likely that specialization will develop within such large organizations to carry on those media services that can be handled effectively, but not in any way causing the emphasis on strong school-building services to be eroded. Staff, both professional and technical, and adequate financial support are of course prerequisite to such action. New patterns of service may thus be looming on the horizon where school-building, citywide, and regional service centers may be the only means by which all of the services needed by teachers in the modern school may be available.

Planning the Layout and Use of Audiovisual Media-Service Spaces

In previous chapter we pointed out that there seemed to be no pat answer to the amount of space needed for any given operation because there were so many variables. We assert, however, that even though there are some educated guesses as to how much space will be needed for a given school-building center, it is the nature of the services provided to teachers and the inclusion of special facilities, such as electronic learning laboratories and the entire library facility as well that should determine the layout and amount of space needed. We may ask: How large should a district media-service center be, and how much space is required by each of the component spaces required? We make the same assertions as for the school-building media-service center: The nature and quantity of services will determine the various space needs. Knowledge of the processes by means of which media materials and equipment and assistance in their effective use reach teachers at their teaching stations helps us in making sound judgments as to how much space is generally required to provide any given service. And it is on this basis that we estimate space needs in district-wide audiovisual media-service centers.

Some Observations about the Differences in District and School-Building Media-Service Centers

Except for those situations where citywide and school-building media centers have been combined for special reasons, we can see a number of differences in spaces, services, and functions. Bearing in mind the possibility of special circumstances, we state these differences as follows:

1. School-district centers serve teachers, not pupils. For example, district centers are not generally called on to provide electronic learning laboratory facilities. Nor do they issue books, as a school library would, directly to children. On the other hand, school-building media-service centers are more likely to serve both teachers and provide direct services to pupils as well.
2. District-wide media centers almost always organize and implement television programming services. School-building service centers develop TV studio facilities, and or videotaping and distribution facilities, as a means of expansion. The exception would be a decision to conduct a pilot project, tried out in one or more schools prior to organization on a system-wide basis.
3. District centers are not generally called on to distribute equipment units on mobile stands. Hence little or no cart garage space will be needed.
4. Properly equipped meeting rooms and conference rooms are more likely to be called for by school leaders and by executives for planning in-service education and innovational programs at school-district headquarters. For example, meetings in school buildings are likely to be held not in the media-service center, but in other properly equipped spaces. But district media centers, especially in schools-system administrative headquarters, may have to maintain special meeting-room facilities.
5. District media centers generally require better and larger loading and pick-up facilities.
6. District centers generally need to set up media design and preparation facilities and often combined sign services with the preparation of publications to greater extent than do school-building centers. District centers are more likely to carry on graphic production services that demand support of full-time, sophisticated technicians, but graphic or media-preparation services in each school building are likely to demand teacher work-room space with some technical and artistic support.
7. School-district library services to schools are likely to be administrative and distributive by nature rather than pupil-service oriented as are school-building library or print-medium service centres.
8. School-district centers are likely to demand extremely large storage areas for media materials and equipment in contrast to school-building centers.

9. School-district media centers will generally demand much larger areas for administration and personnel, equipment-and-materials inspection, and for repair, shipping, and receiving areas than will school-building media centers.
10. School-district centers generally require more space for reception and display area, bearing as it does a greater burden for good school-system public-relations responsibility as well as system-wide promotional activity in the field of media.
11. School-district centers generally require more space than do school-building centers for the work of programming and mass-producing audio and vidotape programs.

Looking back over the preceding list, we must insist that the greater the emphasis is on building up services in each school, the less will be the need for space at the central headquarters. However, this generalization is relative, depending on an optimum balance, for as services mount in each school, more and more of the instructional periods in every teaching station with demand media support. Therefore, because of the pressure for increased central services of specific types, the space needs and requirements may still be greater rather than less as the previous generalization would seem to suggest. But the balance at that point would arise from a different set of circumstances. We would then state four guiding generalizations as follows:

1. Optimum space for known service will increase the efficiency of the work done by the available personnel, and conversely, crowding causes working efficiency to deteriorate.
2. Media-center space requirements should be planned to meet educational needs of a given school system for a 15-year growth period.
3. The need for space for any given area depends on the nature and volume of a known or predicted service and the specific operations to be carried out.
4. Until services can be predicted, no valid estimate of space needs can be made.

We have already dealt in depth with the problems of establishing school-building audiovisual media-service centers, and although we need not repeat here all of the guidelines mentioned previously, we shall nevertheless proceed with an enumeration of the space needs in the present section and deal with them briefly. However, we wish also to caution the reader, to apply what he has learned in the previous chapter to the design and organization of school-district media-service suites.

Specific Space Needs and Suggestions for Layout in a District Audiovisual Media-Service Center

In the light of known operations and desirable services to meet instructional needs, the following comprehensive list of spade needs is suggested as a basis for local planning and reference:

1. Reception and display area.
2. Administrative and clerical offices.
3. Storage space for materials.
4. Storage space for equipment.
5. Blind storage.
6. Shipping, receiving, inspection of materials and work space.
7. Loading and pickup space.
8. Equipment inspection and maintenance space.
9. Professional library, committee study, and conference room space.
10. Preview and pre-auditioning space.
11. Graphic production space, including publications.
12. Photographic laboratory and work room.
13. Recording studio and control room.
14. School-system FM radio station space.
15. Closed-circuit, or low-power radiation, system-wide television studio, control room, and storage space.
16. Remote-controlled, system-wide resource bank for audio program tapes and videotapes for use in self-instruction service.
17. Rest rooms.

If it is desirable to change the emphasis from audiovisual media service to a comprehensive media service the following additional space needs should be added to the preceding seventeen items: *(a)* operational spaces for all print-medium services including the school-library program, *(b)* expanded publication production and distribution center coupled with a curriculum laboratory area, and *(c)* space for the possible storage and processing of schools supplies.

In subsequent sections and paragraphs the layout of centers will be discussed in terms of functional groupings of space needs, as previously listed. However, since desirable production, telecasting, and print-medium facilities emphasis will be placed upon the more commonly known facilities that may well have a high priority in starting a service program. Possible future expansion should, of course, be borne in mind when planning current operations.

Layout of Office Space and Reception Area

These areas obviously need to be together so that a member of the office staff can efficiently receive and route visitors to proper people and places as a part of regular secretarial and clerical duties. Sometimes the reception area has to be too small to include display and browsing areas, and in these cases interesting displays at or near entrances ought to be arranged as, for example, in corridors adjacent to the office. A few brief possibilities and adjustments in layout of these facilities follow:

1. The director's office should be close to the center of operations, not on another floor or at the end of a ccorridor away from his staff operations. If possible, his office should provide for privacy, but if necessary he may find a quiet corner in the main office or in the central work rooms, if office, storage, and workroom is a large block of space. In metropolitan centers where there are a number of department heads, the director needs a private administrative suite. Sometimes the director is separated from the center of operations by being located in another building provided for supervisory staff members. In general, this is not recommended, but such arrangements will work if a competent manager for the clerical and technical services is located at the central distribution unit.

2. Where adequate space is unavailable, space priority should be given to working areas cutting the space allotments for reception and the directors office to an operational minimum. In such cases, it is better to combine all functions in one operating area without partitions.

3. Reception areas ought to have a reading table for catalogs and handbooks, and this area could also be arranged to include space for committee meetings.

4. The director's office space should be expanded and arranged to serve as a part of the professional library and committee study area whenever the reception area is extremely small.

5. If other places are available for waiting and browsing, it will be better for the sake of control to have the reception area attractively fenced off, with a gate leading to other offices and operating spaces. Directing individuals to recording, consultation, and study activities on schedule is obviously an important function, since confusion and embarrassment are otherwise unavoidable.

6. In large centers, various divisions such as photographic production and broadcasting and telecasting would of necessity have to maintain their own reception and administrative offices.

7. Provide ample space for assistant director or manager's office and for secretarial and clerical workers according to volume of services.

Space-Need Estimates. Some space-size estimates are as follows : office or desk and work space for the director, 200 square feet; office and work space for the assistant director or manager, 160 square feet; desk and work space for secretary and clerks, 140 square feet for each; space for scheduling and general office work, 200 square feet, and reception space 150 square feet. Most of the estimates presented are minimal.

Layout of Storage and Distribution Spaces

In this section suggestions will be made regarding methods of storage for each king of audiovisual media and the use of available space for the following operations: handling the work of filling orders inspecting materials, packaging, returning used materials to storage, loading and unloading, and issuing equipment and materials. Sometimes it is necessary to issue equipment to users in the same school building where the center is located , and when this is the case, it is essential to provide a convenient, mobile projection-stand storage area with easy access to a corridor. The main considerations in the arrangement of allotted spaces are the efficient use of staff services, and the protection of capital investments in materials and equipment by adequate provision for their storage, care, and handling. The prospective media director must be prepared to adjust this entire operation to local conditions by either improving an existing operation in an old or recently remodelled building or, as opportunity presents itself, by planning a modern media-service center in new construction. Without being pessimistic, he should be prepared to make the most of what space he can get, since actual allotments will rarely be as much as he needs or requests. Basic directions and suggestion for space planning are:

1. In planning space needs for the storage and handling of audiovisual media, the director ought to look ahead ten to fifteen years in order to provide for the type of program realistically envisioned as developing during that period.

2. The director should arrange operations within spaces allotted in terms of a natural flow of work to economize on the time and effort of personnel. The only profitable way to attack this problem is to construct a flow diagram showing the relationships between the essential processes that must be carried on. The first diagram should cover the process of receiving materials, and it must include the following flow of activity, beginning with the rear-door loading zone or the front-door parking area: *(a)* materials are carried or wheeled to a receiving bench in the center's work area where packages are opened and the materials are placed on a mobile table or rack; *(b)* return slips are checked off against original delivery records; *(c)* materials are wheeled to inspection benches for cleaning and repair, and after such processing they are *(d)* wheeled to storage vaults, shelves, or racks, and properly filed for subsequent request.

Another natural flow pattern is the process of filling orders for media. This flow-of-work diagram is a follows: *(a)* media material such as a film, chart, filmstrip, exhibit, videotape, or audio program tape are pulled from storage racks or cabinets and placed on a mobile table; then *(b)* they are wheeled to shipping benches where they are packaged and labelled; then *(c)* they are placed in canvas delivery bags or in boxes marked with the name of the school awaiting delivery; and finally *(d)* they are moved to the loading platform on scheduled delivery days. It can be seen that efficient flow-of-work patterns should be planned in great detail before specifications are stated for amount and shape of spaces being requested.

3. Arrangements for adequate light and ventilation should be made to facilitate the proper inspection and cleaning of materials because matching picture frames and sound tracks

of motion pictures require accurate observation of small details, and some cleaning fluids have annoying orders even if they are not toxic.

4. It is urgent also that film materials be kept at normal humidity and temperature conditions; hence a separate room is advised where humidifiers can be operated to keep the air from getting too dry, as it does for instance, in overheated rooms in winter. Brittleness of film materials must be avoid. Such vaults according to suggestions in (2) should be conveniently located with respect of the inspection and packaging benches. Doors into film vaults should be wider than usual to permit mobile film racks and tables to pass easily. Sliding doors are best for space economy.

5. Equipment storage spaces should be near loading and issuing areas. These storage areas could be in the repair shop, but generally the shop should be free of this storage function. However, equipment should be stored as close as possible to the individuals who inspect it, that is, to those who will check its readiness for the next use. Whenever equipment is stored during damp summer months, ventilation in the spaces is needed, or silica gel must be provided to remove excess moisture from the air. When these precautions are not taken, mildew is likely to damage cases and electrical insulation.

6. Loading and unloading zones should be on ground floors with access to loading ramps, and since trucking carts should be available for hauling packages, floors and floor coverings should be able to stand up under hard usage.

7. Although other than ground-floor locations for storage and distribution are commonly found, they should never be specified unless private freight elevators are available. If necessary, the prospective director should compute the tonnage of materials handled annually, adding both incoming and outgoing materials, to prove his point if there should be conflicting requests for ground-floor spaces.

8. Optimum working space should be provided around the packaging bench, and ample space should be provided around the film-inspecting benches for immobile film racks or tables. The packaging bench ought to be a comfortable height for workers; such benches should be constructed to provide underneath storage space, and should be of such size that

they can serve as table tops for numerous construction activities if other workbench space for these purposes is unavailable. A width of 24 to 30 inches, length of 7 to 12 feet, and height of 38 inches for stand-up work are desirable general measurements for the combination packaging and work bench.

Space-Need Estimates: Some space-size estimates are as follows: Assuming two automatic film-inspection machines for each station, 200 square feet per station, counting access area from and to storage (the more motion picture prints that are used per day or week, the more stations and personnel will be required to get the film-inspection work done); storage of media, such as tapes, films, filmstrips, slides, exhibits, and picture sets may run from 1,500 square feet in a small district to 10,000 in a metropolitan center; for equipment a minimum for general purposes, would be 1,500 square feet; for receiving and packaging, depending on volume, a rough estimate for moving media materials and equipment would be a minimum of 1,500 square feet; and for a loading zone and docking area other than driveway space, minimum of 1,000 square feet, with unoubstructed areas for moving mobile stands and rubber-tired trucks and hand-carts.

Layout of Equipment-Inspection and Maintenance Space

In general, college and university and metropolitan audiovisual media-service centers maintain the largest and best-equipped equipment maintenance shops; however, many small and medium-sized cities provide school shop facilities for inspection, cleaning, and minor service work. A few centers have been fortunate in discovering a technical person who repairs materials and equipment, and who serves as a photographer or in some other capacity besides. Again, the emphasis in this section is upon the spatial arrangement of the shop and not procedures and equipment, since these will be treated later in the chapter. It should be remembered that in the preceding chapter, shop facilities were recommended as a part of the school-building service center, and the reader should re-check the recommendations and illustrations given there. Therefore, the following suggestions and directions apply to the layout of shop facilities in the school-system audiovisual media center, where facilities need to be more complete and the space allotment greater.

1. Because the job of issuing and controlling materials and equipment is not a shop function (although in small audiovisual media centers these functions may have to be combined), the various units of equipment should be stored elsewhere. However, the repair shop ought to be located near the equipment-receiving area to minimize the work of carrying equipment to the shop. If the shop is near the receiving area, all work of inspection in addition to cleaning and servicing ought to be done in the shop space.

2. If mobile equipment carts are available, and day-to-day inspection of incoming equipment units can be done at an inspection station near the issuing and loading zone, the shop functions may without undue hardship be assigned to space located at a considerable distance from the distribution center but always on the same floor.

3. The most efficient flow pattern is: *(a)* inspection of equipment near receiving point; *(b)* to storage for subsequent issue or *(c)* to shop for repair; and finally (d) back to storage for immediate assignment. Another flow pattern could be *(a)* referral to shop from a city school building via receiving room for needed repairs, and *(b)* return to issuing room for cartage to its original school location via regular delivery channels.

4. When laying out equipment spaces, a sink and a separately veined exhaust fan should be provided to facilitate cleaning operations.

Space-Need Estimates: Again, an estimate of space requirement is difficult to make when the variables are unknown. We can say that the equipment-service facility should not only be considered as a world bench well equipped with test equipment, but also as a staff of technical personnel that can move to locations where decentralized facilities are operating in each school building, or to telecasting facilities or important dial-access resource banks where automatic installations may be in need of a periodic check up or emergency service. Hence a good technician needs a tool kit, high-level diagnostic ability, and speedy conveyance for himself and his instruments. We must think of the space for a maintenance area in terms of the amount of service to be rendered, but as a minimum we suggest a range of 400 to 1,000 square feet. A technician ought to have a small desk, to keep his service manuals, equipment-service diagrams, and maintenance records in.

Layout of Blind Storage Space

The importance of so-called blind or dead storage space is frequently overlooked in planning the layout of operational spaces for audiovisual services. Every center should have at least one storage area in the main office and one or more additional storage closets measuring at least 6 feet wide by 8 or 10 feet deep. In new construction, such spaces may serve also as "expansion" space—for example, as additional preview rooms. These storage areas need not necessarily be located close to operational centers, but they could be located off corridors in such a way that they would serve to stop undesirable transmission of sound. That is, a preview room or recording studio could be located between such storage rooms, thus protecting that space from noise. Small blind storage rooms make possible an uncluttered appearance in regular storage spaces, since obsolete equipment units or infrequently used materials may be stored out of sight. It should be recalled that obsolete equipment units may be used as trade-ins on new equipment units—hence the recommendation to store them. If the possibility of deriving trade-in value is remote, outworn equipment should, of course, be discarded. If such storage areas are not possible in the main center, rooms in other school buildings should be found for that purpose.

Space-Need Estimates: The estimated range of space needed for so-called dead storage should run from a minimum for every service center of 1.50 square feet to possibly 700 feet of floor space well utilized by floor-to-ceiling racks in large school-system media-service centers. This space estimate is of course relative to other space allocations in regular equipment storage areas. The more unused space there, the less dead storage space needs to be planned for. Here again, a word of caution is in order. Both central and decentralized storage spaces will be required as media-service centers expand their operations in all schools, and an optimum balance is called for when the build-up of services of in individual schools is emphasized.

Layout of Professional Library and Committee-Room Space

An audiovisual media center must have space to house its professional library, equipment literature, catalogs, and curriculum listings for teachers, as well as its reference materials for the director. In smaller centers these items may be kept in the director's office, a small consulting office off the main office, or an attractive corner of the main office. These materials should be located in or close to the main office area, since materials on file should be subjected to a control system to assume their usefulness at the time they are needed. Some centers have well-developed areas for these purposes, while other have to make the best of a single shelf and a couple of file cabinets.

If it is remembered that the professional library can be an important factor in mass communication—for example, in-service education programme for the school system—it can become more than a reading room for a few staff members. It can become a well-developed service center for teacher groups and planning committees at all levels. If the curriculum-development center is a part of this facility, the space and the personnel involved may be extensive. The job of staffing it and providing space for it would be less difficult if it were only a storehouse for audiovisual media publications.

Space-Need Estimates: If a committee room—or a room we may refer to as a conference room, fully equipped for projection and sound recording—is included in this facility, we must allow considerable additional space. In good-size school systems, especially when audio-visual media centers are located in or near administrative headquarters, a small auditorium should be set up in such a way that conference tables could be installed to suit the purpose of the meeting being held. As a minimum we would estimate the need for, 1,000 square feet in a medium-sized school system for the professional library facility with an additional 500 to 1,500 square feet for a conference room or small auditorium.

Layout of Preview and Preauditoning Spaces

If obtaining space is a problem, the allotment for a large-group preview facility should have a low priority. This viewpoint is not heretical at all because many large preview rooms sit idle a large percentage of the school day. Suggestions and direc-tion for allotting such space are discussed in the following list.

1. Small preview and pre-auditioning rooms are urgent, and two to four of these rooms, involving approximately 36 square feet each, need to be located where sound emanating from them will not disturb other operations.

2. A large preview room seating thirty to forty people is not necessary at a school-system center less it can double as an equipment laboratory, a production center for slides and transparencies and other graphic materials, a picture-mounting workroom, a recording studio, or some other operational area that can be shared by the center and other school agencies.

3. The work of previewing for selection purposes must necessarily go on continuously in every school building in the system, since material need to be routed to teachers, analysed, and reported on in accordance with system-wide plans.

4. A projection room seating ten to fourteen people should have high priority, however, and perhaps one of the small, booth-type projection and sound auditioning facilities recommended in (1) should be expanded into one of these.

5. All preview rooms used need to be located close to equipment and close to center personnel who can operate the equipment and check on fulfillment of schedules and appointments. This means locating such spaces near office and equipment-control areas, at least on the same floor for convenient supervision.

6. When necessary for elimination of noise, listening to audio materials may be done by individuals or small groups using earphones. Infect, we should give highest priority to providing an area seating fifteen to twenty-individuals who could examine films and listen to audio tapes in special analytical situations, possibly looking at ten different films at the same time. Such work may be conducted efficiently only when small projection screens and headphones are available in

a bench-type or carrel arrangement. Such work is required when film clips are being sought in connection with automation and self-instruction systems work. However, here again, not all of this work can go on at the school-system audio-visual media center. Most of it will be carried on in school-building media-service centers as already described.

Space-Need Estimates. In a district-wide audiovisual center we believe that the minimum of space to be laid out according to suggested plans and priorities for use would be 700 square feet.

Layout of the Graphic Production Area

Graphic production departments in audio visual media-service centers often provide diagrams and pictorial illustrations for a wide array of school-system publications, but we think of such departments more particularly in connection with the design and preparation of media for teachers to use in their fundamental professional work. In this modern-day technological development we need to produce or modify and revise self-instruction teaching system, and make in addition, of help teachers make, a variety of media from a 2 x 2 inch slide sequence and audio-programme tapes for an individual study carrel, to overhead transparencies and 8mm single-cartridge-type motion pictures, or even a set of models for a television programme. We have also insisted that each school building have its own media production facilities at a level consistent with central media-service policies.

Space-Need Estimates: The specific programme being developed will, determine the recommendation for space, but it is difficult to envision a media-preparation programme that operates in a facility area less than, 1,700 square feet. We arrive at this figure in the next chapter which is devoted to this important subject of media design and preparation operations in schools and school systems. Photographic darkroom services and facilities are included in that discussion: and in the overall space need estimate.

Layout of Recording Studio and Control Room

Another operational space need is an area where recording work may be done. Today, with magnetic sound motion picture equipment and with the rapidly advancing technology of magnetic tape and its special relationship to telecasting and self-instruction programme, a recording studio and control room merits careful consideration. Such a room, even it if is only 400 square feet, can be serviceable. An adjoining control room with a glass panel and with connector plugs in the partition separating it from the main studio, of 100 square feet minimum, will enable better recording of sound for all purposes. The studio, being acoustically treated, may serve as well to record audio programmes and short talks by school officials in connection with school public-relations programme. Also, the control room may house tape re-recording equipment for preparing multiple copies of tape-recorded materials loaned to the school system for that purpose. The work of re-recording, however, does not demand the special conditions of a studio facility. The location of studio and control room is a critical matter from the stand-point of external and internal noise. Only by an analysis of local conditions can the decision to include a sound recording studio be judged practical or impractical. In designing such space particular attention ought to be given to acoustic treatment, to quiet air-exhaust and air conditioning systems, and to suitable floor coverings. As with the subject of graphic production facilities, we shall include valuable, considerably detailed information relative to sound recording and audio-programme production.

Space-Need Estimates: It has already been indicated that at least 400 square feet would be needed for a small recording studio and this space should be so arranged that a control room of 100 square feet could be provided to give the facility additional flexibility and to increase the sound quality of the eventual productions.

Layout of School-Systems FM Broadcasting Space

The development of magnetic tape technology and new transmission systems has greatly facilitated radio broadcasting, and while FM broadcasting has not generally prospered as an instructional medium, there are many possibilities for significant contributions, some of which may be utilized in the future in large-group teaching activities as a supplement or combined with television components. Space needed for school radio production and broadcast activities must be determined of course, by the nature of present and future programme schedules. Broadcasting on whatever scale, large or small, requires the following spaces:

1. One main studio and control room.
2. One auxiliary studio and control room as a minimum to facilitate rehearsals and taping processes.
3. Main transmitter equipments room (may be located near or remote).
4. Administrative suite and production offices for staff and director.
5. Combination workroom and tape and disk library.
6. Exterior space nearby, of on roof, for FM tower and antenna.

The instructional needs for school-operated radio stations will have to be correctly analyzed, and the wisest possible decisions must be made concerning recommendations as to the best method for meeting them. FM facilities may be combined with an audio programme remotely-controlled audio resource bank, or may be a part of a general transmission facility including television.

Space-Need Estimates: Space-size estimates would be as follows: main and auxiliary studios in combination with a single control room that houses a tape-duplicating process would run from 650 to 1,000 square feet or more; supervisory and secretarial space, approximately 300 square feet; a workroom and map and or disk library space would run to 900 square feet (If an automatic audio and videotape resources bank were included an additional 700 to 1,500 square feet ought to be provided.)

Layout of Closed-Circuit, System-Wide Telecasting Facilities

We have already suggested that school-building units may in addition to central telecasting services maintain their own closed-circuit television studios. And also we have referred repeatedly to videotape services for both large-group and self-instruction activities. At this point we can, for the sake of completeness deal with the layout of telecasting facilities superficially in view of the fact the subject of television services will be dealt with in considerable detail. Again, the envisioned use of television, programmed and used locally and possibly in combination with other school systems in a given region, will determine the space requirements, but we will at this point emphasize the need for some very basic facilities and arrangements. Primary facilities will include spaces for studios and control room, preparation room which may include film previewing devices and the means for preparing visual media in support of good programming, conference tables for planning productions, storage space for sets and props, storage for videotapes, films, slides, charts and exhibits, maintenance area, an equipment storage area for remote equipment, large-screen projection systems for loan to schools, receiving and unloading area, administrative and secretarial areas, and a suite of offices for programme personnel, technicians, and television studio teachers.

Space-Need Estimates. As hazardous as it is to estimate the nature and amount of space needs, we can state some approximations based on the kinds of spaces that are generally needed by school systems that go into television seriously. On the basis of the assumption of a system-wide programme we can suggest the nature of space-sizes as follows: Main studio, 1,650 square feet; auxiliary studio, 800 square feet; control room serving both studio, 500 square feet; programme and media preparation room, 1,200 square feet; storage areas for all purposes, 1,650 square feet; receiving and unloading area (building spaces only, not driveway or truck space), 800 square feet; administrative and secretarial office space, 300 square feet technicians and programme personnel, five desk and operational spaces, 500 square feet; desk spaces for participating television teacher in a professional headquarters, for five studio teachers, 1,000 square feet (approximately 200 square feet for each desk and operational space).

Arrangements for Rest Rooms

Planners unavoidably have to put certain spaces in wrong places. In the case of rest rooms, the availability of water supply and drains may dictate the placement of rest rooms in locations where they obviously do not belong. This word of caution is included for media directors who may wish to provide every convenience for their colleagues and visitors, but who ought also to avoid recording the sound of flushing toilets in their teaching tapes, or avoid subjecting guests to embarrassment by having them walk through storage and maintenance areas enroute. When problems of rest room location arise, it may be expedient to seek usable space off outside corridors but adjacent or near audio-visual media service centers.

As we pointed out earlier, we shall not at this point begin the discussion of the problems of implementing print-medium programmes in school systems. We will devote to this subject, and there we shall include ample illustrations as to layout of spaces and the recommended space allotments for the processes that are required. We shall also amplify fully in the other chapters solutions to problems associated with media preparation and television services.

At this point we need to turn to the problems of providing adequate storage facilities for handling and distributing the media materials needed by teachers and pupils.

Storage Facilities at the Center

Planners of audiovisual centers need to understand that the nature of storage facilities is usually determined not only in terms of available space, but also in terms of the way materials are, or ought to be, packaged. It should be recognized without fail that the way materials are packaged has a bearing on their protection against damage, both in storage and in transit, on the convenience with which materials are inspected after use, and on the ease with which they are returned to storage to be identified again for order-filling processes. Specific suggestions and illustrations for proper treatment follow.

Motion Pictures

Open film racks should be purchased or fabricated locally whenever it is expected that a film library will eventually grow to several hundred reels or more in size. Such racks should be so spaced in the film vault that mobile carts can be brought to within an arm's length of the racks. Metal, closed cabinets are often used to house small film libraries of a hundred reels or less, but cabinet doors are often in the way because swinging space must be provided. Care should be taken that the film separators in the racks are wide enough apart to hold film cans, although some libraries discard the film cans and store just the reels.

When cans are used, labels must be affixed to the outside of each can that match the label on the film leader. When can covers become bent, or are jammed on, film inspectors have a difficult time opening them. Films lost because of being incorrectly placed in film cans may be difficult to find. On the other hand, if film reels are damaged in transit, then coasts for new reels will have to be met, and this offsets the time and trouble saved by the film inspectors when they do not have to open a can first before putting the film on the inspection machines. In most cases the 400-foot cans or just the reels are kept separately in their own racks for convenience in filling orders. Some film libraries keep all sizes stored separately. This is hardly necessary, since all other film cans or reels other than the 400-foot size can be reached and handled easily if stored side by side. Plans for identifying films are many, but in general, cataloging procedures and ordering systems have a bearing on the final decision. Some of the most common systems for locating motion pictures on the racks and identifying them are the following.

1. *Alphabetizing by Title Only:* Write a brief title and the print number on the can, or if no can is uses, write the title on the film's white or coloured leader strip with a felt-nib or nylon-tip pen. Also type up a brief title and print number on a small label and fasten it to the film rack to indicate the permanent storage position of a particular film.

2. *Using a Numbering System:* Write a code number for the film title on both leader and can and possibly again on the rack. For example, film numbers could run from one to a thousand with a prefix of MP. Such code number would then appear in catalogs, subject listings, and of film cards.

Filmstrips

Many ingenious devices have been devised for storing filmstrips, from the commercially available shallow-drawer cabinets to the home-made drawer with separators made of piano were stretched taut after being threaded through appropriately drilled holes in the drawer frame. Other devices range from hanging wall frames to ordinary shelving where filmstrips are stored in cardboard boxes. Many filmstrip libraries are now storing filmstrips in small sets and are distributing them accordingly. Also, the new plastic filmstrip container with unlosable cover is a popular development. A number of libraries dislike filmstrip drawers because of the packaging problems, preferring to inspect and return filmstrip cans to a carboard package, and to store the package on a marked shelf ready for delivery, thus avoiding the separate packaging operation of placing the filmstrips in a suitable carton or carboard tube every time an order is filled. Coding with catalog numbers or other suitable identifying numbers should be affixed to both can and shipping package. Sound filmstrips with their accompanying records need extra coding numbers to indicate disks or tapes that must be packaged separately or in combination. Large fiber cases for records are recommended

Filmstrips can usually be assigned to individual school buildings as a part of a standard collection. The assignment of such collections becomes a local policy matter.

Slides

We should first not that slides of various sizes need different storage treatments. The 4 × 7 inch slide is largely available commercially in connection with short-exposure techniques. Another slide, often referred to as the standard lantern slide, $3\frac{1}{4} \times 4$ inch is now rarely found for purchase commercially. Such slides are made by teachers for special purposes for repetitive use. This size is in fact made by the Polaroid Land camera process using 46L and 146L film. The 2 x 2 inch slide in colour and black and white is the most popular size of slide today because of its frequent use in automatically control slide projectors in television studios. They are also made by teachers from a great many sources, making up as they do sequences for self-instruction use in carrels, or used by teachers in classrooms by means of remote-control processes in front of a large or small group. Black and white Polaroid slides are easily made for use in the 2 x 2 inch size and these of course are made up in a few minutes as the need arises. Other 2 x 2 inch slides in colour are made up by teachers from their own sources and are developed by local or regional commercial processors. Such slides are returned in one to five days depending on the processing contract. Special processing services may be obtained in some metropolitan areas that would return mounted slides in a matter of a few hours.

Instructional media programme directors may choose to store slides in sturdy wooden, car-board, or metal boxes, by topic keyed in topical listings to subject-matter headings, books, and units of work, or they may be arranged by and for teachers in, for example, carousel magazines by topics and given to teachers, or assigned to school-building collections for repetitive use. The days of storing slides in drawers, or in visible file cabinets seem to be gone. The great difficulty is that teachers do not have the time to search long and complicated listings for content for their presentations. Once found, and used, such materials ought to be duplicated and field by magazine, for a given teacher's use or duplicated for each teacher in a subject or at a specific grade level. Appropriate code numbers for available sets of slides should of course be in the catalogs sent to teachers.

The only alternative would be to employ random-access devices that would locate such specific slide topics by means of automatic-selection devices. Slides are extremely valuable in self-instruction, and in large-group processes. Ways must be found to make them available on a long-term custody basis for teacher who key them into their daily teaching activities. It is obvious then that the storage of slides becomes pretty largely a problem of storage in a given school building, or in a teacher's room or television studio. More details about slide-making processes and services are to be found in Chapter 9 in connection with media design and preparation processes.

Study Prints

Pictures distributed by a center should be stored in sets, with the possible exception of large-size art prints. Legal-size filing cabinets or appropriately sized shelves are needed to house the sets, and additional protection must be given by specially fabricated carboard boxes or by according-type folders with tie strings. Tying a set of pictures together and storing them in cabinets with exposed edges and surfaces is not recommended.

Paper-box companies will turn out boxes according to local designs and measurements, using sturdy clasps, hooks or other cover festering devices. Mounting procedures are discussed in a later section on care of materials; however, mounting according to standard sizes of mounting-board material will be a help in standardizing the sizes of transit boxes needed. When individual pictures are distributed, sturdy covers and clasps are necessary for protection.

We should point out that in view of today's technological development, we may well agree to turn over to school buildings sets of pictures urgently needed in their day-to-day teaching. Such use of materials ought not to be left to chance, and curriculum guides ought to stress that such materials are either *basic* or *supplementary*. When it makes little difference whether a given medium is used or not, and if indeed, the use of media is not stressed by those in charge, there seems to be little point in the laborious and expensive processes worked out to get them to the right classrooms at the right time. The days of such laxity with regard to the use of media are about over.

Disk Recordings

Vertical storage cabinets or shelving are easy to fabricate locally, or they may be purchased. Heavy-duty record sleeves should be procured in quantity and used to give records adequate protection. Transit containers may be of the fiber-film-case type with carboard fillers to keep the record from sliding during periods of transportation. If space permits, disks may be stored vertically in their shipping containers, thus providing more room for appropriate code numbers or appropriate labels. If stored as individual disks in original covers, protruding adhesive cloth tabs may be used for identifying members.

At this point of technological development, it seems obvious that teachers who use disks for specialized instruction ought to have them either in their own possession or have access to them in a school-building collection. Again the curriculum guides for a given grade and programme of instruction will determine the need for the expansion of this medium. The convenience (subject of course to copyright law stipulations) of taping a section of a disk, and properly relating it to required instructional tasks—

thus preserving it for repetitive use—is obvious in many fields of teaching endeavour.

An essential service with regard to disk recordings that could be given by a media center would be the continual supply of standard sleeves and album covers so that school-building media coordinators could keep their disk recording collections in the best condition possible. The replacement of album covers together with new labels will make the use of disks by teachers more convenient. Hence the necessary supplies should be stocked in quantity at headquarters.

Taped Audio Programmes and Videotape

Audio-programme tapes and taped television programmes referred to as videotapes are easy to store since regular metal or wood shelving units will suffice. The best way to store tapes of all kinds is to keep them in their original carboard boxes to which explanatory labels may be attached. If there is any chance that tapes may be mixed up in their containers, then each tape ought to be labeled with adhesive-backed labels, commercially available. Since there is no way as yet to examine the condition of tapes without playing them through, or spot checking then by actual playing, extra care must be given to prevent erasure, and mixing up the subjects in their containers. Tapes may be distributed in canvas bags, but care should be taken to keep audio-programme tape packages from opening in transit allowing tape to unwind and become damaged. The larger sizes of videotape reels would not be likely to open up during local delivery trucking periods. Masking tape, or a rubber band may easily serve in the former case as an adequate precaution. Tapes should be stored vertically for easy accessibility during the order-filling processes, and label strips may be easily affixes to the edges of the boxes.

Realia, Exhibits, Kits, Models, and Dioramas

No center should consider distributing such materials without adequate space and staff for proper handling. Mounted animals need specially designed wooden boxes, and dioramas with glass or clear plastic covers need adequate transit cases of sturdy carboard or wood to prevent excessive deterioration. Ample shelving or bins will be needed, and storage in their regular transit cases of all large items will, of course, expedite delivery processes.

Maps, Globes, and Charts

As indicated earlier, models, dioramas, and exhibits need only appropriate storage shelves against a wall. The same arrangement will suffice for globes if they are stored in transit containers of heavy-duty, reinforced carboard or fiberboard with straps. Globes will have to be stored in there fiberboard or corrugated car-board cases and separated from accompanying metal floor stands. Flat maps and charts may be stored either in a series of drawers of suitable size or in vertical slots made by arranging metal or wood partitions 2 to 6 inches apart in a large bin. When vertical storage is used, all flat materials should be placed between masonite or heavy paper covers. If charts and maps are of the roll-up type, whether on spring rollers or not, they may be stored in long, reinforced cartons to the type portable screens come in, or in heavy carboard tubes. Storing these tubes or cartons at the center requires shelving or bins arranged so that code numbers of titles are in full view.

Storage of Equipment

Ordinarily, equipment units are decentralized in the schools; hence, equipment storage-space requirements at a city school-system center are not large. Appropriate metal or wood shelving and bins need to be built into the available space. Consideration should be given to a modular construction of bins that can be stacked up in horizontal or vertical fashion. This is possible if over-all measurements of height, width and depth are accurately figured. The main purpose is to provide shelving against a wall or in tiers of bins back to back in the center of a storage space.

Applicability of Storage Procedures to School-Building Centers

We should emphasize here that storage facilities will have to be planned as for the district-wide center, but it is likely that storage problems will not be as great, nor the space for handling the media demand in a given school anywhere near as extensive.

The previous suggestions, however, will have to apply to school-building centers as well.

Care to Media Materials

Audiovisual media materials must be maintained in first-class condition or their deterioration will accelerate. Teachers lose interest quickly when the materials they receive from central depositories are outworn in appearance, when film materials break during projection, and when materials look dirty. The district media programme director must known what kinds of acre and handling processes to prescribe, and he must be able to supervise operational plans as carried out by workers. In the preceding section proper packaging for transit to and from schools was stressed in connection with storage and ease in handling. In this section the proper care in terms of inspection and processing is emphasized, and specific suggestions are made for each of the basic kinds of media.

Motion Pictures

After a film is projected, it should be tactually inspected, using standard motor or manually operated rewinds, or mechanically inspected by means of automatic inspection machines. Where such machines are used, it is frequently reported that a pair of machines and one full-time inspector is very efficient working combination. Inspectors themselves may be part-time or full-time adult workers, men or women, or students who come to work after school. Women are increasingly being used to get this important work done. Specific suggestions for carrying for motion picture films are discussed in the following paragraphs.

Equipment Needed: It is quite obvious that in cases where film collections are small, less than 600 prints, the expensive automatic, electronically controlled film-inspection machines may not be practical. If the school building or the school system can affort it, however, it would be a matter of great convenience, and perhaps a means of utilizing a one-man technical force very effectively, since the inspection of incoming films from outside sources, and the inspections of films before being returned to distributors outside the school district, are sizable jobs. High-speed inspection machine would be a means of saving the technician's time for other important jobs.

Because inspecting films by hand opens up such opportunity for error in judgement, it is better for the films distributed, regardless of the size of the collection, to inspect them by machine. We therefore urge an effort even on the part of small school-system film libraries to acquire the automatic units that even students can operate with greater certainty of spotting defects in film condition. The machine itself may cost approximately $3,000, and a good quality splicer with high-speed film cement costs an additional $ 175.

In case schools and school systems are forced to use hand film-inspection methods, we suggest that the following equipment be acquired: film rewinds, preferably motor driven; a good quality splicer, preferably a model where the emulsion is scraped off without the application of moisture; a sturdy inspection table where workers may be comfortably seated while working; good overhead lighting; a motor-driven film cleaner, or a small fluid applicator for manual use with the film rewinds; a small light-box for sound-track and frame-matching purposes; and, a magnifying glass. But as we have emphasized the trends is toward machine detection of defects in both large and small film-distribution agencies. Of course, a couple of motor-or hand-driven film-rewind devices may be easy to use for the insertion of replacement film footage sections where soundtracks have to be accurately matched.

Film-Care Supplies: The prospective director needs a few words of advice about supplies. Frequently these will have to be purchased in quantity as needed. Because of possible alteration in characteristics through evaporation, film cement should be purchased by the carton in the smallest container offered that will not allow the fluid to evaporate. Other supplies needed are cellulose pads (commonly used in connection with memo and ditto duplicator machines) for applying fluids manually; coloured "head" and "tall" leader stock; heavy-duty coloured cell or masking tape for fastening down loose film ends; film-cleaning fluids such as Renovex, and Protect-O-Film; and, felt-nib pens and ink for writing on leaders and cans. A word of caution is in order at this point, since not all fluids may be used as effectively as others in the automatic-electronic film-inspection machine with film-cleaning attachments. When such machines are utilized, the manufactures's recommendations should be followed.

Film-Care Processes: The main processes or film-care jobs are as follows: inspecting visually, electronically, and tactually; splicing to eliminate all defects (avoiding notching since notches do not pass through electronic film-inspection machines); cleaning with chemicals; treating new prints before projection; analyzing print condition; replacing specific and general conditions on control cards; and, realising damaged footage. When inspecting tactually, the inspector must be taught to let the film slip through his fingers in such a way that defects in film edges, perforations and film blisters will be consistently detected.

Splicing is, of course, an extremely critical operation and must never be done in a slipshod manner. In general, this task needs close supervision because errors in workmanship lead to more serious damage to the film during later projections. If moisture is used to loosen the film emulsion, the film ends must be thoroughly dried before applying film cement. Another critical aspect of the splicing process is the deft application of the cement by one stroke of the brush, with immediate lowering of the film press into its clamped-down position.

Films may be cleaned while rewinding them, using a cellulose pad dampened with one of the recommended cleaning fluids. As has already been mentioned, inexpensive applicators or motor-driven film cleaners are available, but machine methods are preferable. When films are inspected by machine, defects are automatically detected. When a defect is found the machine stops automatically, calling for personal observation to identify the defect and to take remedial action.

Another essential process is the treatment of new film prints. This process is identical to the cleaning process except that the fluid is applied to the new prints for the sake of pliability, not cleanliness. Since all film prints ought to be projected before acceptance to check physical print conditions, the film-pliability fluids can be added by allowing the film to pass from the feed reel along a loosely pinched, chemical-dampened, cellulose pad. This job is more effectively carried out on automatic machine.

The only efficient way to obtain up-to-date information about film condition is to maintain an adequate film-condition report card in a special file on the film-inspection bench. Each splice and each damaged footage replacement should be recorded, as should each film cleaning. Unfortunately, this is a job for clerks, and clerks and other technical workers seem to be all too scarce.

Replacing footage need not be so difficult a job as generally thought. Actually, the only difficulty is the proper matching of the sound track of the new section with that of the old. This job is made easy by ordering replacement footage in units of whole scenes. Thus the splice may be made by joining the last frame of one scene with the first frame of the new scene, and the sound tracks will then be automatically matched. The light-box and magnifying glass aid this process. When other than scene-to-scene replacement has to be done, the section containing the newly spliced-in-footage should be projected to ascertain if sound and pictorial continuity has been maintained.

Slides

The first essential of slide care is to bind the slide properly between cover glass. No slide in any size is ready for distribution until this has been done. Miniature slides, the 2 x 2 inch size, may be quickly protected by glass, using the special metal, snap-on or insertion-type mounts, or they may be bound by using bulk supplies of clean cover glass, standard masks, and $\frac{3}{8}$ inch binding tape of the plastic variety. Usually a slide-binding wise is needed for this work if it is to be done in any quantity. The second essential is to keep slides clean. This is a tremendous "window-washing" job if the slide library is large, and precautions must be taken by students or others who are employed to do the work to keep cloths just damp enough with water to rub off the fingerprints and smears, and then to dry the washed glass thoroughly. If moisture is allowed to get between the glasses through breaks in the tape binding, the emulsion and hence the picture may be seriously damaged. The third essential is maintaining good physical conditions of the binding. This process demands that cracked over glass and loose or sticky binding be replaced in time to prevent damage to the picture. Whenever possible, binding materials should be standardized and stocked in quantity. The advantages of such a procedure are obvious.

We have already indicated under the subject of storage that slides should be stored and arranged for projection in such a way that they receive a minimum of handling. Cautioning users to handle slides by their edges is hardly sufficient. The way to prevent handling is to store slides in their automatic magazines or trays ready for repetitive projection. Where one or more slides in a single presentation must be repeated, duplicates should be made on the spot or abtained commercially. The kind of care made necessary by selecting sets of slides-for a given presentation or self-instructional exercises, only to break up the selection for return to a master file or storage rack is unworkable in most schools. To facilitate control of slide materials that are subject to reordering, a master file card for each set should contain the number and title of each slide and its source, not only to facilitate replacements in case of loss or damage but also to make a quick cheek-up on the number of slides returned after each use. Slides get mixed up with other sets, or often a slide is forgotten in a slide carrier at one of the schools; hence each slide needs to be correctly coded by set and item number.

Study Prints

The newest and most effective method for taking care of study prints is to laminate the entire picture between two clear plastic sheets. The Audio-Visual Section of the Los Angeles city schools owns its own machines for this process, by means of which the necessary heat and pressure are applied. After trimming to desirable dimensions, the picture are packaged in carboard containers for storage and transit. In the St. Louis audiovisual center, pictures are obtained in sets and then sent to a commercial concern which supplies the plastic-laminating process service. When embedded pictures get soiled, it is an easy matter to wash then off with a dampened cloth. Another way of preserving study prints is the standard mounting procedure that uses mounting stock of suitable colour, weight, and texture, together with photo dry-mount tissue. Such pictures must, of course, be replaced when soiled or damaged. It is also extremely important to show teachers how to use thumbtacks, display hooks, clamps, and tables for displaying instructional pictures properly.

Filmstrips

Although 35mm film splicers are available, this process is not recommended for torn filmstrip. Arrangements should be made with producers or distributors to replace all worn prints at a reduced price. Filmstrips may be visually inspected, but they should be handled by their edges and then rolled up without cinching, since this may result in scratching by dust practicles. Filmstrip cleaners, using the same fluids as for motion pictures, will remove dirt and keep the film base pliable, which of course is essential. When cleaning filmstrips, film fluid should be used sparingly. Jagged corners of torn perforations may be cut off with a film notcher or scissors to prevent further tearing during subsequent use. It is generally true that the job of caring for filmstrip prints is not carried out sufficiently well, with resulting dissatisfaction on the part of teachers and pupils. Since the volume of use of filmstrips is so high, a new and critical look should be taken at this aspect of the media maintenance service in both school-system and school-building media-service centers.

Disk Recording

Disk recordings have to be kept clean or they will soon be worthless for instructional purposes. Visual inspection will generally show when cleaning is needed, or when damaged by scratching dictates immediate replacement. Cleaning by standard chemical cloths that facilitate dust removal by freeing disks temporarily of static electricity charges is recommended. Such cloths, available at any record shop, tend to dry out and deposit a fine chemical dust on the record. When they are in that condition, dampening them with water will usually restore their usefulness; however, they should be replaced when they get dirty. A cloth dampened with warm, slightly soapy water is also recommended for cleaning records. One other aspect of record care is the determination of groove wear that may not show to the unaided eye. When high-quality sound is mandatory, records should be checked by playing them, preferably near their center areas, on a record player in excellent physical condition. Records should be stored vertically without being allowed to remain in a slanting position. Also, disk recordings should never be stored near steam pipes or in direct sunlight.

Tape Recordings

Prerecorded audio-programme tapes should be periodically checked for the distortion that may result from what is called magnetic "print through." This is a slight modification of the original magnetic patterns, made by the interaction of the fields of magnetic force on the adjacent layer of tape on the reel. These transfer patterns have considerable intensity, so that the net effect is a faint echo that may be annoying. "Print through" is less likely to occur in 1.5-mil (standard thickness) tape. It is also less likely to occur, or is less noticeable, if the tape is stored under cool conditions, since it increases proportionately with the temperature.

Polyster base tape is not affected by temperature and humidity as is regular cellulose acetate tape, and therefore this somewhat more expensive tape is recommended whenever tapes have to be stored under other than normal conditions. Best long-run temperature condition for tape storage to prevent embrittlement are 60° to 70° F. and 40 to 60 per cent relative humidity. Another aspect of the proper care of prerecorded tapes is the use of leader and trailer tape to eliminate the gradual shortening of footage due to the almost inevitable breaking off of end pieces. Also, standard splicing tape ought to be used with regular tape splicing machines instead of the regular varieties of plastic adhesive materials.

Videotapes present a different care problem when it comes to splicing. Splicing must be electronically done, using a second tape recorded equipped with an electronic editor, either built into the tape machine or attached as an accessory. A videotape that is damaged will therefore have to be replayed and reedited into a shortened version of the programme originally recorded.

Storage conditions that apply to polyster tape apply to videotapes as well.

Ideal Storage Conditions

It has been emphasized again and again that storage under ideal conditions is a prime essential in safeguarding the quality and life of media materials for classroom use. Dust and excessive dryness will work havoc on some items, and moisture will have adverse effects on others. Hence, air conditioning may prove to be the most important of all care essentials. Properly designed boxes and packages for the storage and transit of kits, globes, realia, and models should be provided, or else the public money spent on the material will be wasted. Media-service programme directors are responsible for bearing in mind these important details and should make sure that appropriate action is taken.

Care of Media Equipment

We must not turn our attention to the job of taking good care of audiovisual media-equipment units. Several recommendations have, of course, already been made that have a bearing on how this work is to be done, and it would be well to recall them before proceeding to specific suggestions. First, it has been recommended that every school plant have assigned to it for the year, and perhaps permanently, as many of the frequently needed projectors, recorders, record players, and other equipment as the school's programme demands; second, that centralized pools of equipment be set up at the school-system audiovisual service center to meet special needs, and even to met regular needs until adequate or complete decentralization is feasible; third, that each school building establish its own fixed media-equipment installations such as TV studios, electronic learning laboratories and the so-called teaching auditoriums with permanent media-equipment fixtures; and fourth, that each school establish its own school-building service center, including a school media programme coordinator and technical service crew. Insofar as adequate care of equipment is concerned, these recommendations.

1. Certain equipment-care essential should properly be carried out in each individual school-building unit, while other

maintenance jobs should be referred to the school-system media center. In this connection, minor operations of cleaning, lamp changing, and other adjustments ought to be done at the school-building center, and all other major repair work should be carried out at or through the main school-system media equipment shop.

2. In cases of equipment breakdown, temporary replacement equipment units should be arranged for, either from the centralized school-system pool of equipment or from the nearest, reputable equipment repair agency.

3. The central equipment-servicing and maintenance shop must be related to the care and inspection programmes in each school building in very definite ways. In this connection it is recommended that the school-system audiovisual maintenance technician be the chief technician for the school system and that the main shop serve as a distribution center for all maintenance of equipment supplies.

Whenever full-or part-time center technical assistants are lacking, the director will have to formulate with his school-building media programme coordinators the best possible plan of action for the superintendent's approval. Such a plan may call for the negotiation of a flat-fee service contract with the nearest instructional media equipment dealer; immediate action by each building coordinator to order repair work to be done by business firms, up to a specified expense limitation for the year; the emergency replacement of equipment by the central service center or by the local equipment dealer; the use, on a part-time or overtime basis, of a school-system electrician, physics teacher, or industrial education teacher, and the use of preventive maintenance procedures by the periodic over-haul of equipment by a reputable service company. Or the plan may call for the use of a talented crew of high school students on a part-time basis to check tubes, lamps, and do other needed work short of a major overhaul job.

The job of caring for equipment is made easier when the kinds of equipment used have been standardized. One thing is certain, if the equipment units that make possible the use of media are not maintained in good condition, then the service programme may just as well be liquidated. Beginning media programme directors must find ways to solve this over-all problem and must check this service-programme aspect continuously if their services are to be held in high regard. The prospective director, therefore, needs to be a technician up to a point. Although he *should not* be a repairman himself, he needs to be able to hire one, he must be able to identify operational deficiencies in all kinds of equipment, and he needs also to be an organiser and overseer of technical services and activities.

Space is not available to undertake a detailed descriptive treatment for the operation and servicing of specific makes of projectors. For this detailed analysis of operation, the reader is referred to the manufacturer's service manual for each specific make of equipment. Such manuals must not be confused with the booklet of operating instructions supplied with equipment units upon purchase. The media programme director will have to write to the manufacturer for them, and this is an indispensable reference file that every audiovisual center shop should have. Such service manual enable the media programme director, or chief technician, to order commonly needed spare parts by manufacturer's standard catalog numbers, enable him to write better technical bulletins for coordinators and teachers, and also serve as the director's self-teaching guide. Actually, such service manuals for each type of equipment owned ought to be in the hands of each school-building coordinator as well. The prospective director needs to see the servicing and maintenance jobs in a general, over-all perspective in order to make proper local decisions. It may be necessary for him to increase his own skill in this connection as opportunities become increasingly available. The next topics deal with general-care essentials for equipment servicing and for setting up shop facilities.

General Care Essentials

Cleaning Lenses of Projectors: Dirty lenses are common causes of defective picture projection, and the only remedy is to set up proper lens-cleaning procedures and routines. Similar optical elements are included in all projectors. These are as follows: lamp reflectors (unless reflectors are built into the lamps), condenser lenses, and objective lenses. Some projectors, such as overhead and opaque projectors, have front-surface mirrors and reflectors. The following procedures and precautions should be noted.

1. Optical elements in motion picture projectors, because of high-speed mechanisms and high operating temperatures, accumulate dust and oil particles rapidly. Hence, the back of the projection lens should be wiped with lens tissue before each use of the projector. Unless this is done, the collection of dust particles and an oil film on the back of the objective lens will cause an objectionable picture-halo of haze.

2. Front-surface mirrors and reflectors pose another problems, since they must be brushed off lightly with camel's-hair brushed to avoid scratching. No lens-cleaner solutions can be used because some of them contain chemical agents that will mar the top surface of the mirror. Fingerprints on front-surface reflectors cannot generally be removed except by a water-dampened cloth; however, seriously impaired mirror surfaces may be replaced at the factory. Regular mirror surfaces may, of course, be washed or wiped off in the manner prescribed for other optical elements.

3. Service manuals published by manufactures should be studied to ascertain the nature and exact positioning of optical elements, so that when they are removed for cleaning, they may be accurately replaced.

4. Regular schedules or routines should be established for cleaning lenses. Except for daily inspection of objective lenses, weekly, monthly, school-term, or end-of-year schedules should be decided upon according to local needs. A spot check by any supervisor student coordinator, media director, or chief technician is needed to see that routines are being followed.

5. Lens tissues and lens-cleaning fluids should be stocked in quantity.

6. The director needs to issue one or more illustrated bulletins on the topic of cleaning lenses. Such bulletins or manuals may be prepared by the director himself, by technicians, or by a committee working under his editorship.

Proper Oiling. Again: the manufacture's service manual must be consulted and exact oiling procedures noted. Record players, tape recorders, blower fans and motors in all kinds of projectors, and so on, should be carefully checked for oiling requirements, since failure to comply with the manufacturer's instructions nullifies warranty provisions and decreases quality of service. The tendency is often to oil either too much or too little, and the only safe procedure is to follow stated requirements by attaching a service card to each equipment unit for a visual check on service or to maintain a file or such cards at each school building. Wherever an equipment pool is based, service cards should be maintained and the director or equipments supervisor must take this job seriously. Strict orders on oiling, and clear instruction on ascertaining if too much oil has been added, should be issued and then compliance noted. In general, motors in new projectors, record players and tape recorders are self-oiling, but this should be definitely ascertained. In the extremely critical case of older models of motion picture projectors where oil cups are provided, oiling at out every month, or if use is very heavy, oiling after every four hours of projection, or every sixteen uses of the projector, may prove to be more satisfactory. When optical elements show excessive accumulation of oil film, or if projectors smoke a little during operation, the amount of oil should be decreased. Proper oilings cans for adding one drop at a time and the recommended grade of light oil should be stocked in quantity by the central shop. New models of mechanical equipment units require little if any oiling, hence the word of caution of ascertaining the manufacturer's specifications.

Changing Lamps. Prefocus base lamps of all types are easy to change, and the only caution is to avoid finger burns by cooling off the burned-out lamp before replacing it. The best way to do this is to run the motor, thus using the blower to cool off the hot glass. It will be necessary in motion picture projectors without the stop-on-film feature to disengage the film before the motor is turned on. Exciter lamps of bayonet-base and pin-type are even easier to change because their operating temperature is low.

The director should take care that correct specifications are given when ordering lamps, since the life of a projection lamp is shortened considerably when line voltages are higher than the lamp was made for. It is recommended that the local line voltage be ascertained and that the lamps ordered should be manufacture for use at slightly higher line voltage than in maintained by local power companies. For example, if the local line voltage is usually 115, then lamps should be ordered that are marked for use on 120-volt circuits. The slight drop in illumination is negligible and the life of the lamp is increased by several hours on the average. However, all lamps should be replaced when they become blackened and blistered even though they haven't burned out.

Adjustment and Alignment of Optical Systems: It was pointed out previously that projectors generally make use of the same kinds of optical elements, and it is obvious that such elements have to be centered and lined up on the optical axis for evenness of the projected field of light. Projecting a focused field of light on the screen permits an immediate visual inspection of defective alignment because dark corners or unusually bright areas will appear within the field. Since as many of the optical elements as possible are lined up and centered in fixed positions, adjustments have to be made at specified points.

Usually trouble arises when the lamp socket becomes loosened in the process of changing lamps and is either lowered or turned clockwise or counterclockwise in its clamp. The first of the two changes in the lamp socket just mentioned will cause a darkening of the lower part of the projected field. The use of asbestos gloves and dark glasses will, of course, be required for the process of loosening setscrews on the socket clamps and raising the socket (while the lamp is burning) to the proper position where the field of light is uniform once more. The turning of the socket, darkens the left or right portions of the projected field of light. The rule to apply here is that the plane of the lamp filament should be parallel to the lens elements. In making such adjustments locally, a light shield should be held by a helper or mounted in such a way that the worker's eyes are protected from the bright light of the lamp.

One other adjustment that may have to be made is the moving of the reflector and lamp socket assembly closer to or farther away from the condenser lenses. This operation must also be done with shielded eyes. Always, the rest is an even, sharply focused, field of light on the screen. Bright center spots, darkened corners, and vertical streaks of light and shadow through the screen are symptoms that reveal trouble with optical alignment. The trend in manufacture is away from all adjustments by users—in other words, to minimize the amount of work by local technicians.

Sometimes condenser lenses are positioned and held parallel by coil springs. In checking for trouble, make sure that even the fixed optical elements are positioned properly as intended by the manufacturer, but sealed-in optical elements should never be opened. Service manuals should never be opened. Service manuals should be studied carefully to note special instructions about optics, but in general it is best not to move the lamp reflector or disturb its distance from the lamp, and none of the lens elements should be touched while they are hot.

Replacement of Optical Elements: This is another equipment-service job well within the usual school-system audiovisual center's service routine. Here again is a case in point revealing the advantage of standardization, since with projectors of only one manufacturer on hand, it is easy to carry a stock of spare lenses and heat-filter glasses. To carry a stock of spares for several different makes and models would be difficult and uneconomical. All that is required is to proceed according to diagrams in service manuals of the manufacturer and replace lens elements according to standard part numbers. Care should be taken to work out a labeling system whereby spare lenses are clearly and accurately marked to avoid later mistakes. A card system for the easy ordering of spare parts as supplies run low is an urgently needed aspect of the *shop supplies* plan.

Testing and Replacement of Electronic Tubes: With an increasing number of record players, tape recorders, and motion picture projectors, all using amplifiers, the job of testing tubes and transistors is an urgent one. It may be done in two ways: Either testing equipment must be purchased that will handle the kinds of tubers and transistors specified in the electronic schematics use, or a commercials audio-radio-television service company will have to test them. In the latter case, electric components should be taken to the local dealer for checking and the replacements purchased there as needed or standard space components kept in stock. If equipment and staff are available, it is best to maintain a stock of components and replace defective ones without delay. Although not all amplifier troubles are caused by defective tubes or transistors, the checking and replacement job is simple and can be done with a minimum of technical training. Searching out other amplifier-circuit troubles is a time-consuming task, and unless the large volume of electronic equipment on hand warrants the addition of trained technicians to the school staff, it is advisable to have this repair work done by audiovisual media equipment dealers who specialize in service to schools.

Equipment Switches and Electrical Cords: Media equipment units demand different types of control switches and electrical cords. Except for battery-powered tape recorders and picture viewers, all have power cords usually fastened to the equipment internally by clamps and soldered connections. Such cords may have built-in-on-and-off switches, and when this is the case, spare switches should be on hand for replacement purposes. A good soldering iron should also be on hand to facilitate arrangements for the quick repair of faulty power lines. Also, because loose connections and broken lines that are such frequent sources of trouble are not easy to discover by visual means, a test lamp with appropriate connectors, and a short speaker line cord with alligator clamps ought to be handy for checking purposes. Since on-and-off power switches and volume and tone control switches often cause annoying trouble, such units should be stocked for fast replacement. Sometimes these switching units get dirty, in which case cleaning them by brushing with carbon tetrachloride may correct the difficulty. This is a job for a full-time or part-time technician, if available; otherwise, for a local repair agency. Proper care of switches and cords is an element of maintenance that makes a big difference in the satisfactory performance of equipment. Many different connectors are easy to make up, or they may be purchased from equipment service companies. Local conditions and preferences for operations will determine the scope of connectors needed. Some schools have developed simple connector devices by means of which automatic slide projectors and other types of equipment may be turned on and off by remote-control switches. Other connectors are for copying disk recording onto magnetic tape. Standardization of equipment and types of connectors for any given operation in the schools will facilitate technical performance by both technical and professional personnel.

Inspection of Equipment after Use

One of the main essentials in taking good care of equipment is the discovery of operational defects before they can disrupt teaching plans in the classroom. Whenever equipment has been used, it should be checked for faulty performance before it is used again. One of the most time-consuming service jobs is the one where technicians have to open up an equipment case, set up the projector or tape recorder, actually try out test materials of familiar pictorial and sound content, and then proceed to clean the lenses, tighten control knobs, repair cords and switches, and so forth. However, this job of readying equipment for the next borrower is a detail of such importance that to fail to get this work done properly is to endanger the whole service programme. The importance of good care of media has been stressed previously, and the care of media equipment is directly related to the prevention of damage to materials.

In order to decrease the time involved in checking media equipment and materials after classroom use, some coordinators and media programme directors require the teacher and/or the operator to fill out a short check-slip, stating the equipment performed satisfactorily and that the material itself was in good condition and was used without interruption. Dependence upon such forms is dangerous, and an inspection schedule must be set up in conjunction with such a reporting system to catch trouble before it catches teachers and pupils. It is this insepction and reporting system that sets in motion the process of referring to school-building or school-system audiovisual equipment maintenance shops the equipment units that need repair services. The discussion of general care essentials has preceded, and now some specific considerations for taking good care of equipment will be discussed.

Motion Picture Projectors

Good care of motion picture projectors involves a few special considerations:

1. Fuzz and dust particles must be removed from the aperture by means of a bristle brush and lintless cloth, taking extreme care that no metal object comes into contact with metal parts of the film channel.
2. Remove excess oil and dirt from around the filmgate and lens barrel. Complete cleaning of these parts calls for a brush, cloths, and carbon tetrachloride.
3. Spring and fiber belts must be repaired or replaced as needed.
4. Sprockets must be checked to ascertain if hard-packed dirt and oil has built up in back of the sprocket teeth. Such accumulation should be removed by a wooden object (never metal), otherwise film perforations will be enlarged and perhaps torn as film tension pushes the tooth and its enlarged base through the opening. Carbon tetrachloride may be used to soften this hard-caked deposit if it cannot be pushed away with a match stick or a hard wood splinter.
5. Jumpy film motion on the screen and noisy operation may indicate that the intermittent movement needs adjustment or that film class have become grooved and need honing down on the under side of the claws. Such work must not be attempted except by expert technicians, but overhaul and repair work of this nature must be carried out on schedule.
6. The SMPTE test film *Jiffy,* as well as other test films, are useful in checking pictorial and sound elements of projection performance. Exciter-lamp focus and speed governors need particularly to be checked, and test films are extremely valuable for this work.
7. Magnetic sound motion picture projectors need to have erase and record heards defined cautiously with lens tissue. Metal objects, as was pointed out earlier, should never be inserted for cleaning purposes where film guides may be scratched.

The extent to which audiovisual equipment maintenance facilities are developed will depend on the size of the equipment inventory and the availability and adequacy of local repair service agencies. Simple arithmetic—comparing costs of repair by agencies outside the school system, cost of cartage, and cost estimates for a center-staff technician and spare parts if a shop facility were to be established—will establish the need for increased facilities. Maintenance costs for motion picture projectors, record players, and tape recorders will be highest, because of their moving parts and electronic components.

Magnetic Tape Recorders

What we have said about amplifiers, tubes, and transistors also applies to tape recorders, but the maintenance of tape recorders requires a few characteristic tasks that may well be carried out in a school-system audiovisual shop. The following suggestions should be considered:

1. Drive and rewind belts and rubber-rimmed wheels need to be checked for proper tension and wear. They can often be replaced by individuals with a minimum of technical training.
2. The squealing of pressure pads on tape can be stopped by cautiously roughing up the matted-down surface of the pads that press the tape against the recording and play heads.
3. Magnetic heads should be wiped free of accumulated iron oxide.
4. Magnetic heads should be checked for proper alignment and for this purpose a test tape procurable from Audio Devices, Inc. is indispensable.
5. Tape recorders need to be protected room dust at all times and all accumulations of dirt around rollers and capstans should be removed frequently.

Record Players

Record players are generally available in large numbers in almost every school system, and it is sad that they are not cared for in better fashion, since damage to disks is so frequently the result. Although the correction of serious trouble in amplifiers is the job of expert technicians, many maintenance tasks can be carried out in the local school and school-system insepction and repair shops. Special suggestions are:

1. One of the first essentials of care is to convert all existing styli and cartridges to the diamond type. Though higher in cost, diamond styli are the most economical in the long run. Stocks of replacement cartridges and styli of the appropriate type should be maintained for ready use. Standardization, wherever possible, is recommended to simplify insepction and replacement.

2. Styli and cartridges collect dust and dirt. A camel's-hair brush is needed to brush away this accumulation. The dirtier the records, the more often this has to be done.
3. A microscope should be used to examine styli for wear.
4. Pickup arms must be fastened down to keep them from banging during transit. Such screws, hooks, or clamps must be continually checked and tightened.
5. Turntable speed checks should be made by means of stroboscopic card-type disks; other audio-test disks are available from Cook Laboratories.
6. Because of moving mechanisms, dust and dirt accumulate in hard-to-reach places; hence special cleaning and inspection routines must be set up to keep machines in good condition.

Projection Screens

Those in charge of the inspection and maintenance of audiovisual media equipment should not forget the projection screen. Whether mounted permanently on walls, or carried as a portable units, screen fabrics and tripods or other support systems need to be kept in first-class shape. Tears, smears, wrinkles, and adhesive tape have no place on a reflection surface, and jagged metal corners, bent support rods, and weakened fasteners are equally objectionable in that tripod or wall-mounting system. A full stock of replacement units and parts, including fabrics, should be on hand to keep screens clean and in good repair. Standardization of screen makes, sizes and types will facilitate inspection and maintenance.

Overhead Transparency Projectors

This frequently used piece of media equipments, the overhead transparency projector, is often assigned to each teaching station and placed in ready-to-project positions on low projection stands or pedestals. Many times there is a separate titled projection screen. This means that it is likely to be assigned to and cared for at an individual school building. Cleaning, installing new connecting cords and fixtures, and replacing lamps as maintenance processes will be done at each school-building media service center. More serious maintenance work will be done at the district media center. Special suggestions are as follows:

1. Lamp reflectors and lamp sockets should be checked periodically and replaced by standard parts.
2. Motors and thermostats that control on-off switches should also be replaces when defects are observed.
3. Thorough cleaning of optical elements should be done at scheduled times.
4. Standard switches and connecting cords should be stocked in quantity and maintained in satisfactory condition for quick replacement.

Electronic Learning Laboratories

District-wide media-service centers may be called upon to provide special services with regard to servicing equipment units operating as basic components of electronic learning laboratories. Although we have already recommended providing the needed technical workers in each school building to take care of such services, we pose it here also as a responsibility of the main media centers. Such equipment may range from a simple passive listening device to a combination of media-use operations involving tape recorder, automatic slide projector, 8mm cartridge-type motion picture projector, and a television receiver, all or some of which may operate by student dialing or by other selection mechanisms. Such learning centers must be the object of periodic insepction on an optimum schedule or be constantly attended by technical personnel and must have immediate attention when mal-functioning of equipment is detected. A maintenance force must be available to report to one or more schools for what we can call continual coverage. Special suggestions for action are as follows:

1. Maintain a stock of spare knobs and control buttons and replace then at once when they are removed by students using the facilities. Students who spend scheduled periods in such facilities are likely to either deliberately, or unconsciously try to remove or loosen such devices. Continuous action of that type results in havoc, and hence in instructional programme to guide students toward better care of the equipment is essential. Teachers who route students to self-instruction must recognise the relation of "equipment destruction" to lack of both general and specific motivation.

2. The best way to service electronic learning laboratory equipment is to provide replacement units, as projectors,

receivers, amplifiers, and recorders and to repair observed defects in media equipment repair shops where stocks of parts and test equipment are available. The value of standardization is again obvious in expediting such work.

Television Receivers

We recognise the need for technicians and adequate supervision in the important work of maintaining media equipment and materials. Television receivers, both for use in closed-circuit systems and for programme reception via master antenna systems from sources outside of the school system, must, like projectors and recorders, be kept in excellent working order. So again, like servicing electronic learning laboratories, an on-the-job-work force must be provided, or sets must be replaced at the first sign of defect and returned to adequately equipped servicing centers for repair. In large-scale programmes the need for trained and qualified technicians in each school-building media programme is an obvious essential. Special considerations are the followings:

1. Provide for the immediate replacement of defective television sets sent to a testing and repair center.
2. Stock spare parts and provide the necessary tube and transistor testing equipment for facilitating service.
3. Arrange for periodic check-ups and an efficient reporting system by teachers as to operational efficiency.
4. Make periodic checks on mountings, castors, and other support systems to spot loose connections and possible weaknesses as a precaution against accidents in classrooms.
5. Defects in television sets may have to be traced to defective television studio equipment: such as cameras, transmiters, and videotape recording units. Thus the maintenance system for television receivers and for electronic carrels utilizing television programmes arising in studios and in automatically controlled programme-source banks must include the availability of qualified studio technical personnel for proper operation and control of complex equipment. (A test film, TV 16,367 feet, $35; a television alignment and resolution slide, AR Slide, 56; and several videotape test tapes for multifrequency and primary audio level are available from SMPTE 9 East 41st Street, New York, N.Y.)

The Media Equipment Shop as a Supply Center and Clearing House

In the foregoing paragraphs the media equipment shop has been pictured as a supply center for spare parts, lamps, styli, screen fabrics, oil cans, belts, switches, electrical cables, special connectors and cleaning fluids. The shop, as has also been implied, is the headquarters for maintenance activity that can be carried on locally. This activity has been implied by discussions under the headings of general care essentials and under additional specific processes and suggestions for a few of the major kinds of audiovisuals media equipment. One aspect of the supply problem has not been mentioned in sufficient detail, and this is the construction by the central technician of supply of needed special connectors. In complicated programmes, such as those conducted in schools today, a variety of connectors need to be made up and supplied to the various school buildings. Short speaker-to-projector cords, cord adapters for various jacks and fittings. "Y" cable connectors for feeding two microphones into one tape-recorder input, and special remote extension code for operating equipment from the front of a teaching station, are just a few of the many items needed in quantity. Also, maintaining a stock of projection lamps and electronic tubes, transistors and condensers is no easy problems to solve. Certainly, a stock-card system is called for to facilitate inventory control and periodic ordering.

Some metropolitan school systems maintain supply depots or agencies known as central stores from which teachers, school principals, audiovisual technical, and professional personnel draw needed supplies that are purchased in large quantities annually. The audiovisual media programme director should take whatever steps are necessary to inaugurate as many economies as are possible by central purchasing. Under central-purchasing conditions, the problem of adequate inventory procedures is eliminated for the media director; however, a system should be worked out whereby appropriate lamps and other supplies may be identified by standard code numbers. Here once more the advantage of standardized equipment lists is made clear.

One other aspect of the media shop activity is the clearing-house function. Equipment inventory cards with purchase dates, repair and assignment data, and serial numbers must be maintained. Furthermore, equipment units that have to be shipped out for extensive repair work ought to be processed by the central shop staff, that is, logged in, sent out for repair according to contractual arrangements, inspected upon return from the repairing agency, and delivered to the school building as originally assigned. This work, when it is handled by the shop as a central routing and clearing-house agency, relieves school-building personnel of annoying details. Much of the extensive repair work, however, should be planned and carried out during months when the schools are not in session.

The director who sets out to organise the kinds of procedures and processes for handling, caring for, and utilizing media materials and equipment described in the preceding pages of this book, must realise the necessity for a clerical, technical, and professional staff that can get the work done in terms of effective teacher service. National and stage organisations are giving this problem the serious attention it deserves.

Staffing and Organising the Audiovisual Media Center

Building a comprehensive staff organisation, not only to carry on the work of the audiovisual media center as a headquarters unit but also as a system-wide service force reaching into every classroom, is a formidable problem, and when reasonably adequate financial support is unavailable for fast-pace development, it may have to be solved in unconventional though hopefully creative ways. We have already mentioned the problem of arriving at an optimum balance between, the development of strong, well-staffed central service facilities and strong, well-staffed decentralized school-building service unit. This becomes a critical issue as technology increases in complexity and scope, and we may postulate the principle with confidence that as instructional technology moves toward newer roles where media make important and scheduled contributions to the process of presenting substantive materials to students and guiding their specified responses, both in large-group and individualized situation, the balance between centralized and local service centers must shift toward decentralized facilities and staffs. In an earlier day, the problem was to create loan services, but now the emphasis is on media installations operating permanently and on firm schedules, where a tenuous loan that may or not be cancelled at the last minute will not meet the teaching requirements.

The citywide media programme director has the responsibility to meet and deal with this problem. This so-called media director as an executive must identify specifically just what work must be performed, how expertly it must be carried out, and then he must seek the help of individuals to exert the necessary effort for the tasks at hand.

Staff for Audiovisual Center Operations

Since we have dealt at length in a previous chapter with the problems of providing staff for school-building services, we can concentrate on staff for the audiovisual media center at the school-district level. But we must remember that smaller school districts have the same needs for media that large school systems have, and they therefore need similar services without being able to affort the media specialists that larger operations demand. We must consider in every case, be it large city or small town the nature and demand for services and the ways to provide them, rather than concentrating on the number of specialists the present budget and the potential tax dollars will support. It appears quite obvious that whether the center consists of one small office or a whole building, or whether the media director of the citywide programme of service is a full-time workers or not, he must acquire a central staff proportionate to an allotted personal-serviced budget. His own time, however little he has at his disposal, must be used to the best advantage, and the way this time is spend will determine the nature and scope of the success of the programme at any operational level.

An earlier reference was made to personnel guidelines for staffing media programme in schools and school districts, but in this regard we can also quote the statement made by the State of Indiana, Department of Public Instruction, in its Bulletin No. 218 relative to initiating and expanding audiovisual programmes, that suggests the following standards for staff:

> Each school systems should have someone responsible for the audiovisual programme. He may be called a director or supervisor. School systems with 50 or more teachers and all counties should have full-time professionally trained audiovisual supervisors...Also, he should be provided with sufficient clerical and technical assistance to permit him to devote his major energies to professional administration and assistance in the utilization and preparation of materials...

It is this citywide media director or supervisor that must systematize and organise personnel forces to the limit of his local resources and ingenuity. It is certain in this stage of development of technology that he will have to bear in mind that his own center staff may have to be deployed in unique ways for services throughout the school system, and also that he can work with school principals in achieving mutual objectives for improving instruction, but that his own center may be the originating point and the only available service center for any given time period. Let us make no mistake about it, however, that it is what goes on or ought to go on in each school that really matters.

Staff for Administrative and Supervisory Functions

First we should consider the range of administrative and supervisory positions of a professional nature. We need to recognise the expanding role of media in modern education, and the increasing need for specialized staff members as smaller audiovisual media programmes expand and as programmes develop in the metropolitan school districts. The need for professional assistants and specialists will be inevitable. Additional staff members beyond the leadership of the media programme director may well be placed in charge of divisions or departments, or they may be given the title of Consultant, Associate Director, or Coordinator to provide leadership energy for areas of activity at the center or to energize system-wide programmes of service. Their functions are to:

1. Supervise media-service activities for each level of instruction as elementary or secondary school activities.

2. Energize selections of kinds of media, such as textbooks and library books, or projected or nonprojected media.
3. Administer and supply leadership for departments or divisions such as radio, television, photographic and graphic production.
4. Take charge as a coordinator of service functions such as in-service education, distribution, business management, and the school-building coordinator programme, and television programming for elementary and or secondary school telecasts.
5. Supervise media-supported teaching systems development.
6. Manage a central facility, such as the instructional materials center.

Positions such as those mentioned may have to be filled by professional people on a part-time basis, making full use of interested teachers who are willing to undergo special training for new duties. Individuals are often anxious to do such work for various types of rewards. The main consideration is that people who are selected must be professionally prepared and well qualified or the duties they undertake.

Staff for Technical Functions

We have only to review the staffing requirements for school-building programmes to realise the need for such personnel working at the district-wide media center. We must recognize that in the present state of development, unless technical personnel are available, such functions as installing and operating and maintaining television studios and electronic learning laboratories of a sophisticated level are out of the question, and any stopgap, intermediate steps may be classed as foolhardily and wasteful of the money appropriated for the organisation of the media programme.

Carrying on the work of a citywide media programme, as we have said before, is largely concerned with providing services to all schools, all teachers, and through them to all learners, but it is the schools as units that must possess fixed facilities and make full use of media materials and equipment assigned to them from media headquarters. The technical work must therefore be oriented not only toward technical work required at the center, but toward the school-building units themselves.

Some of the major functions to be carried on by technical workers are the followings:

1. Maintain media materials and equipment at the center and assist in the schools as demanded by local arrangements and needs.
2. Install, operate, and maintain school-system television studios and assist as assigned with the same function in the school-building TV operations, including transmission and reception.
3. Assist with the installation and maintenance of electronic learning laboratories in school-building units.
4. Prepare media of all kinds at the Center according to specifications and designs supplied by curriculum planners and teachers, and assist with similar operations in each school-building unit according to local plans.
5. Supervise the work of media-center and school-building technicians.
6. Maintain adequate inventory of school-systems media equipment.
7. Maintain in a stock of spare parts for the servicing of school-system-owned media equipment units.
8. Maintain adequate inventory and a stock of media-preparation supplies for use at the center and for issue to school-building units.

As programmes develop, shortages in staff will be inevitable, and when new positions are created it will without doubt be difficult to till them, yet it will be urgent to get work done on time to prevent deterioration of both media materials and equipment. Many centers have turned to the physically handicapped for part-time and full-time work much to their complete satisfaction. However, obviously the work assignment should be one that is appropriate. In addition to full-time workers especially trained for their jobs, the part-time employment of capable students during after-school hours and on Saturdays to inspect media materials and carry out prescribed maintenance procedures is also a possibility. Because closer supervision of the work of part-time workers is generally needed, the director ought to make the most responsible individual of such crews an operational supervisor, inspector, and checker. However, in no case should minors be permitted to work without on-the-spot supervision of responsible adults.

Staff for Secretarial and Clerical Functions

It is little wonder that some schools systems with low secretarial-support budgets have difficulty in obtaining and keeping citywide media programme directors. Professional peoples should not be burdened with the volume of clerical details inevitable in the media-service field. We are not talking at this point of getting out of hard work, but what we are emphasizing is that the leadership force for energizing programmes for the involvement in media-use development must not be cancelled out because available time is not used profitably.

Although it is not recommended because again too much time is required for laying out the work and subsequent supervision, part-time clerical workers may have to be recruited from local high school commercial departments. Students can give good service, especially if the work is laid out with clearly stated instructions, and several students on a well-planned schedule can provide continuous service during most of a school day. Media programme directors who are themselves on part-time assignment ought to arrange, if at all possible, for the employment of a qualified part-time worker (student or non-student) during the period when they are free of teaching duties. But if significant developmental progress is to be made at any school-system or school-building media service center, then adequate secretarial and clerical staffs will have to be provided, in optimum balance with other personnel forces.

Staff for Media Mobility Functions

Although we recognize a wide range of skills and required training and experience within the technical-function personnel, we also see the need for support staff in the nature of a labour force. The main function of such a force will be to make it possible to move media materials and equipment between the center and the schools where they are put to work. Thus the media programme director must see to it that the required labour force is adequate to meet demands for mobility in the light of the local level of utilization.

Custodial services are also necessary, and this part of the labour force may be provided under other budgets, and this may also be true of the trucking units that may operate on a system-wide basis for all divisions and hence may be under supervision of other agencies. The fact is that such services, both trucking for pick-up and delivery, and custodial in nature, are mandatory.

Staff for School-Building Assignment

We have already discussed in detail the problems of school-building media-service organisation, and in this connection great emphasis was placed on the need and procurement of adequate staff members—professional, technical, and clerical. We emphasized the value of adding to the school principal's staff the needed personnel, and when this is done, such personnel certainly would be working with the citywide media programme leader, but would be on the staff and be located at a given school building. In some instances, staff members are located at the media headquarters, but are assigned on a part-time basis, or other optimum schedule, to perform specified tasks at one or more of the schools. In such cases, the understanding is that the service is performed for the school principal for the good of his programme, but not under his responsible surveillance.

Employing Needed Staff

The importance of employing a qualified professional person for media-leadership responsibility can hardly be overemphasized, yet all too frequently too little attention is paid to the preparation of specifications for the position. Once the media director himself has been employed by other school administrators, it will be up to him to prepare adequate specifications for every new position he is able to create, whether professional, technical, secretarial, or skilled or unskilled labour. We shall turn next to this important topic for the emphasis that it deserves.

Specifications for Media-Service Positions: Major duties need to be clearly in mind as a part of any given set of specifications, but they are by no means the only topic to receive attention in a prepared statement of personnel qualifications.

Certainly an applicant wants to know just what he has to do on the job to be successful, and we want to prepare an announcement to locate qualified people and to urge the right individuals to apply and become active seekers for any given position that is open. But we need to state precisely what requirements must be met by the successful applicant in addition to possessing the special abilities to carry on the work described. Thus if we view the problem as one of preparing a written statement that can be duplicated and distributed as deemed advisable then we should include the following information:

1. Position title and description.
2. Major duties and responsibilities.
3. Specified requirements to be met by applicants:
   (a) Desired professional preparation and specialization (including specific courses).
   (b) Desired personal qualification (hobbies, personality, health, habits, and appearance).
   (c) Desired educational experience in the profession and related activities.
   (d) Desired scholastic record level, degrees, and certifiability.
   (e) Desired age and sex.
   (f) Nature and number of letters of recommendation desired.
   (g) Desired social competency, vitality, and character.
   (h) The level of special abilities desired.
4. Salary, and other working arrangements as to time committed, vacations, and to whom responsible.
5. Special job requirements, if any.
6. Instructions for application.
7. Unique inducements for applicants.

Naturally wide variety is found in formats of announcements and in the details of the specifications set forth. One of which covers the employment of a media school-system programme director, another deals with the search for a qualified person to serve as a media specialist working at the elementary school level, but responsible to the school-system audiovisual media center, and the third covers the announcement of a position of television producer-director.

Writing a good set of specifications is not only applicable to the employment of professional personnel. The media programme director who fails to devote adequate attention to the analysis of job requirements and to make use of desirable personnel-requirement policies and procedures is guilty of making some dangerous assumptions. Public school administrators and leaders know well the difficulties and embarrassments of dismissal proceedings. Two additional examples, one from the Board of Education in Hartford, Connecticut, and the other from Geneseo State University College in New York, will show the attention devoted there to the employment of qualified individuals for newly created technical positions. Since the additional examples are related to those preceding, we shall refer to them as Example 8.4 and Example 8.5.

Example—8.1

Board of Education
Stamford, Connecticut

June 14, 1916

Announcement of Vacancy — Coordinator of
Audio Visual Education

It is the intent of the Stamford Board of Education to employ a *Coordinator of Audio-Visual Education* for the year 1966-1967 who shall be responsible for directing and coordinating the programme of audio-visual education and instructional materials for the whole school system by providing leadership in determining the objectives, policies, plans, and programmes for the long-term and short-term successful operation of the audio-visual education and instructional materials programme, in order to implement improvement of the instructional programme.

Major Duties and Responsibilities

1. To initiate and improve the use of audio-visual materials throughout the school system.
2. To inventory and assign audio-visual equipment in the school and classrooms.
3. To work with the teaching staff in the more effective use of multi-media materials of instruction.
4. To be knowledgeable of and be able to recommend specific audio-visual equipment.

5. To conduct in-service courses on the use and operation of audio-visual materials.

Qualifications

The audio-visual and instructional materials coordinator must:

1. Possess the training and experience which will enable him to fulfill his function in the instructional programme. The minimum of a Master's degree is required. At least five years of teaching experience at the elementary and/or secondary level is desirable. Experience as a coordinator or director of audio-visual aids and curriculum materials on a building or system level in desirable.
2. Be a well-versed equipment technician responsible for the selection, operation, inspection, maintenance, and inventory of all equipment and materials.
3. Be able to met all State certification requirement for this position.
4. Have had graduate courses in the organisation and administration of in audio-visual programme; in the proper utilization and evaluation of materials; in the production of materials; in the production and utilization of educational radio and TV programmes; in learning theory especially as it applies to self-instruction; in the fundamentals of curriculum development; and in general supervision.

Salary and Working Conditions

The salary for this position is based on what a candidate would receive as a teacher multiplied by 1.28. The work year is twelve months with one month vacation.

Filing an Application Consists of

Letter of applications detailing educations, experience, and personal qualifications for this position.

Applications for this position must be filled by July 15, 1966.

Note: It is expected that the appointee will provide sufficient notice to his present employer.

All correspondence should be addressed to:

Dr. Joseph B. Porter, Superintendent
Stamford Public Schools
151 Broad Street
Stamford, Connecticut

Example–8.2

Please Post

Hartford Board of Education

Administrative Offices
249 High Street
Hardford, Connecticut 06103

Notice of Vacancy
Media Specialist

A full-time position will be available as a media specialist on September 1, 1996.

Duties

1. Working primarily on the elementary level, grades k-8.
2. Providing assistance to all members of the teaching staff with utilization and production of instructional material both during and after school hours.
3. Providing assistance to other staff members working as Curriculum Materials teachers.
4. Assisting in the design and implementation of in-service workshops for all staff.

Qualifications

Applicants must have or be able to obtain by September 1, 1966, State of Copnnecticut certification as a supervisor in a special subject field, with a recommendation as an audiovisual specialist.
This position is authorized under the State Act for Disadvantaged Children of 1965. The position is approved until June, 1967, and will continue as long as funds are available.

Salary

The salary will be the regular teacher's schedule plus 5%, for the normal school year.

Applications

Candidates should apply in writing to Mr. 'Thomas, H. Skirm, Director of Certificated Personnel, Board of Education Office. 249 High Street, Hardford, Conn. Applications close Jun 30, 1996.

THS:ba
6/21/96

Example–8.3

State University College Geneseo, New York	Position Available:	Television Producer-Director
	Appointment Date:	Apr. 1, 1997 or after
	Date of This Notice:	January 26, 1997
Staff Vacancy Notice	Salary $10, 000 - 11, 000	

Position Available: Television Producer-Director

Appointment Date: April 1, 1997 or after

Responsibilities:

1. Initiating and conducting faculty orientation and training in Instructional Television.
2. Working with faculty members to incorporate multi-media material into their course curricula with a concentration on instructional television.
3. Studio television directing.
4. Training and supervision of student crews.
5. Limited teaching of some broadcasting course segments.

Qualifications And Experience:

1. Masters Degree.
2. Interest in the overall media approach to learning, including programmed instruction, dial access retrieval systems and computers.
3. Preparation and experience in Instructional Television producing and directing.
4. Some knowledge of lighting and set construction.
5. Some teaching experience preferred.

Salary: $10, 000 to 11, 000

Apply To: Send Credentials To:

Example–8.4

The Board of Education
Administrative Offices, 249 High Street
Hartford 5, Connecticut

May 16, 1992

Available Position
Audio-visual Technician

Nature of Work

The work requires skills of a technical nature, primarily in repairing and maintaining mechanical and electronic equipment.

Duties

1. Tests, maintains, repairs, and converts a wide variety of mechanical and electronic equipment and components, such as sound motion projectors, filmstrip-slide projectors, record players, tape recorders, radios, television receivers, and amplifiers.
   (The above duties are performed at the Audio-visual Department or at a school, depending upon the situation).
2. Maintains inventory of replacement parts and tools.
3. Duplicates tape recordings for classroom use.
4. Prepares and produces graphic layouts for instructional use through photocopy or diazo process.
5. Performs related work as required.

Qualifications

1. Considerable knowledge of the technical and operating principles and applications of equipment, tools, and materials and used in the testing, maintenance, and repair or projection, amplification, and related electronic equipment.
2. Ability to read and interpret schematic diagrams of electronic equipment.
3. Ability to repair electronic circuitry.
4. Ability to repair mechanical equipment or have high mechanical aptitude.
5. The following of qualifications are most desirous, though not mandatory:
   (a) Knowledge of graphic layout and art ability.
   (b) Knowledge of photography
   (c) Knowledge of diazo reproduction

Experience and Training

1. Two years experience in servicing and repairing projection, sound, and electronic equipment, preferably in the audio-visual field, and/or
2. Graduation from an academic or technical high school supplemented by technical courses in the theory of repairing sound and other electronic equipment, and some practical experience in this field.

Salary for the Position

This is a full-time position with a salary range of $4200.00 - $6000.00. The starting salary will depend upon the qualifications of the applicant.

In addition, the Board of Education offers a number of fringe benefits in the way of paid insurance and liberal paid vacation policy.

Application Procedure

Applicants should write or contact Mr. Edwin M. Manson, Coordinator Audio-visual Materials, Board of Education, 249 High Street, Hartford 3, Connecticut.

Applicants should be prepared to submit a short synopsis of past training, experience, and places of related employment.

The starting date for this position will be between August 27 and September 1, 1992.

Edwin M. Manson, Coordinator
Audio-Visual Materials

In Example 8.4, it can be readily seen that the media program director entertained the hope that he could locate a qualified person with a combination of abilities that would enable him to broaden the base of his services. He was searching for a person possessing maintenance skills and skill in graphic arts as well Combining functions in one person in highly desirable in small media centers, and in centers just beginning, a program, but as service expands, such individuals must specialize, thus having to choose one or the other of several fields of work. Certainly men and women who possess a wide variety of skills in media work are extremely valuable. Those who have limited skills, but who are willing to learn can eventually serve their school systems or school-building unit more effectively.

Remuneration of Audiovisual Media Center Staff. It is understandable that great variety exists in the pay scales around the country for various types of media personnel, but nothing prevents the estimate of a range in remuneration. IN Connecticut for example, according to a 1965 survey, full-time school-system media program directors, by whatever name they are designated, earned from $9,800 to $14,8000. The acute shortage of personnel in certain to accelerate salary increases for full-time supervisory salary scales. It seems quiet obvious that lower salaries are paid in some small communities where a full-time person is employed without benefit of a supervisory salary differential. Such practices are not destined to be widespread in adoption. We are, of course, well aware also of the range in pay scales for technical workers of various levels of ability and for work of increasing technical complexity.

Example–8.5

State University College	Position	Technical
Geneseo, New York	Available:	Specialist II U-6
	Appointment	
	Date:	Approx, Apr. 1, 1997
	Date of	
	This Notice	February 10, 1997
Staff Vacancy Notice	Salary:	Approx, $7500

Position Available:	Technical Specialist II U-6
Appointment Date:	Approx. April 1, 1997
Responsibilities:	The Language Laboratory Technician is responsible to the Director of Instructional Resources through the TV Chief Engineer and must work closely with the personnel in the Language Department. He is responsible for the day-to-day technical operation of the laboratory, and assists the instructors in the operation and use of the equipment. He is to be responsible for the technical preparation of tape sources and other similar functions related to dial access facilities. He is responsible for the upkeep of equipment and performs repairs where

	needed. He supervises those students a assigned to help him.
Qualifications and Experience :	1. Ability to handle Tape Recorder circuitry, audio circuitry and switching circuitry including those common to Dial Access Systems. 2. Ability to maintain and repair audio equipment associated with the above. 3. Ability to instruct students and instructors in use of equipment. 4. Ability supervise assigned help. 5. Experience in the operation of tape recorders including editing and dubbing. 6. Experience in basic electronic theory and in the use of test equipment. 7. Knowledge of program distribution and retrieval. 8. Experience with basis switching systems and in wiring audio cables. 9. Ability to study and learn new developments in associated electronic equipment. 10. Good personality and ability to work well with others.
Salary:	Approx. $7500
Apply To:	Send Credentials To:

If we refer to statements of pay given for personnel needed in school-building units, we note that technical workers are likely to be paid from $3,500 to $9,000. Supervisors in any given category would probably receive an additional $1,000 or more per year. In addition, we may well find that some combinations of skills and experience would call for adjustments in pay scales that would add several hundred dollars to the announced salary schedules.

Organization of Staff for Control of Media Center Activities

We get a good idea of the system-wide scope of the formal work that has to be carried on. However, a great deal of informal work throughout the system has to be done also. Only the media program director himself can serve as the spearhead for getting this wide variety of formal and informal tasks performed by a relatively large number of participants. Since he can never contrive to do this work himself, he has to elicit the cooperation of teachers and others to get it done. An overview of this informal work required by the media center in its day-to-day operations will be of interest to the reader and is presented in the following list.

1. *The work of Formulating Policy for Recommendation to the Superintendent.* Voluntary participation of members of an advisory council or special study group is essential. Such a council needs to be widely representatively and may include one or two lay participants in addition to one or more curriculum leaders, school principals, teachers, and school-building media coordinators.
2. *The work of Analyzing Media-Use Needs.* This valuable work is called for by the director on a voluntary, individual-response basis through school principals and other curriculum specialists. In addition to deriving data from questionnaire methods, school-building or system-wide committees may have to be organized to study and compile relative information.
3. *The Work of Selecting Materials* . This colossal work load demands considerable individual and group effort. Since this vital group activity need to be formalized, staff for the selection panels or committees ought to be recruited for definite periods of time and made a part of an important professional organization even though the work is done voluntarily. The selection of instructional materials is such important business that other supervisory leaders must also bring influence to bear in getting this job done expertly. The procedural basis for this work was described in Chapter 3.
4. *The Work of Selecting Equipment.* This technical work calls for a group of qualified individuals to participate according to need in solving equipment problems. Participation should involve a definite term assignment and should provide for continuity of personnel.
5. *Other Work Needed.* Many other individuals and committees will be needed on an intermittent basis to do the work of writing manuals, preparing lists of materials, preparing handbooks of instructional procedure and to do the work of teaching colleagues as recommended and described in

earlier chapters. Such services will be entirely voluntary, and the media program director need but ask for it. However, he must always see to it that proper credit is given for the completed results . In some cases experts outside the school system will have to be called in. Some of these experts should be paid, while others need only to be reimbursed for expenses or entertained locally, depending on the circumstances.

From the preceding discussion, it can be observed that the system-wide staff organization is based at the media headquarters, and that some staff members are organized formally in a highly structured way, that other staff members are loosely organized in an informal way while they are working for varying periods of time—under media leadership—on vital school problems. Thus we need to caution, the media leader to examine his lines of control and to keep on the one hand from developing an autocratic climate that will block creative participation and service by others unless he himself can command it personally at each step of the way, and on the other from starting so many things and having so many processes and projects going that he music nothing. This letter kind of loose control is unproductive and dangerous. The good administrator will therefore seek patterns of structure that will expedite the accomplishment of his goals and yet will maintain, through a combination of delegation and check-up on action, up-to-date information about what is going on, by whom, and at what quality level. The following suggestions are made as guidelines for appropriate action:

1. Define the duties of each staff member in light of the processes to be carried out, and delegate them officially by duty charts or other official communication. Through conferences, work out detailed specifications and check on accomplishment.
2. When two or more people are at work on similar processes, delegate supervisory responsibility to one of the two or more workers, and while maintaining wholesome contact with all workers, call for and get control through the supervisor of the process involved.
3. Create divisions or departments by grouping similar or related duties, as soon as specialization is feasible.
4. By working with principals, the school superintendent, and curriculum leaders, establish several working groups with

defined responsibilities. Set the lines of responsibility to properly appointed steering committees, and to the delegated chairmen. Steering committees with their respective chairmen should be responsible to the media program director or his delegated supervisor. In-service education programs for innovations and selection panels for media materials are examples.

5. Set up a school-building media program coordinator council for supervisory functions, and if program expansion warrants it, appoint a supervisor for each division, elementary and secondary, making the supervisors, or the council chairmen responsible to the media director.
6. Write out official plans with the approval and endorsement of the chief school administrator, and delegate by authority, the responsibility for the actions taken under assignment. Write out the description of the problem to be solved and also the letters of appointments to groups, to be sent by school authorities, and follow through to send bulletins of detailed instructions, and assist in laying out suggestions for final plans.
7. Sketch out in attractive format a clear and precise chart showing the formal organizational relationships, and show in plans for action that recognition of and credit for will be noted and reported to cognizant officials. Duplicate and distribute, and make necessary revision as needed and redistribute, to all involved.
8. Write up in as attractive a manner as possible a recommended policy statement for all assistants, participants, and authorities, obtaining the approval of chief school officers before publishing it.

Such involved suggestions without a final and specific program in mind or on paper may appear to be irrational, yet implicit in the list is a sensitivity to the people, goals, and processes for accomplishment. It may appear that one goal is to fabricate a program of activity that eliminates any arduous mental or physical work on the part of the media director. Nothing could be further from the truth, for if we now reconsider the earlier chapters we see administrative problem in their true light, and the director must find ways to budget his time for important professional leadership activities. We have already discussed the desirable nature of administrative duties and have shown that *designing, planning, proposing*, and *deciding,* are the hallmarks of top-level action.

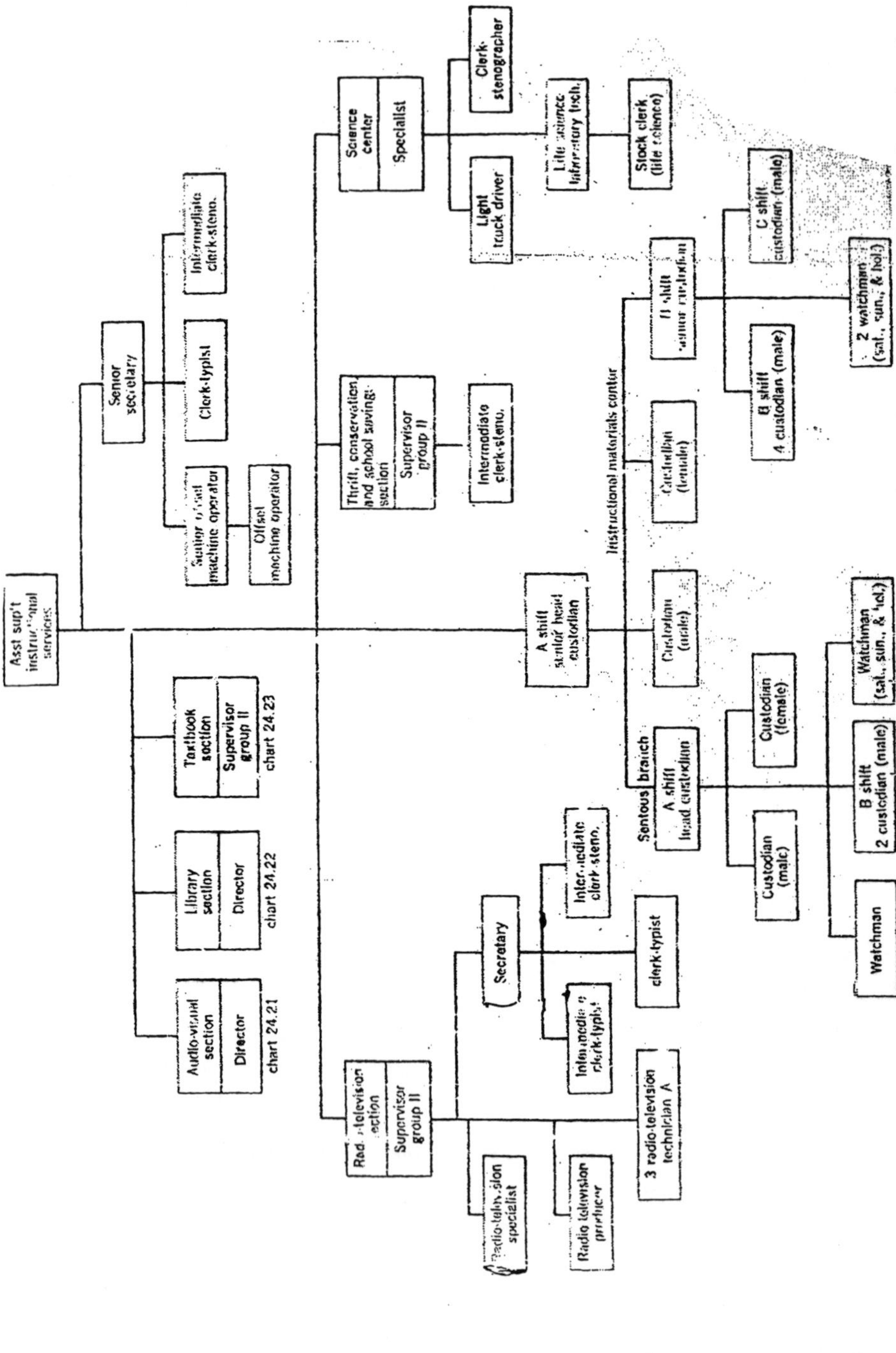

Fig 8.1 : These two organization charts contain clearly marked out relationships and functions existing at various

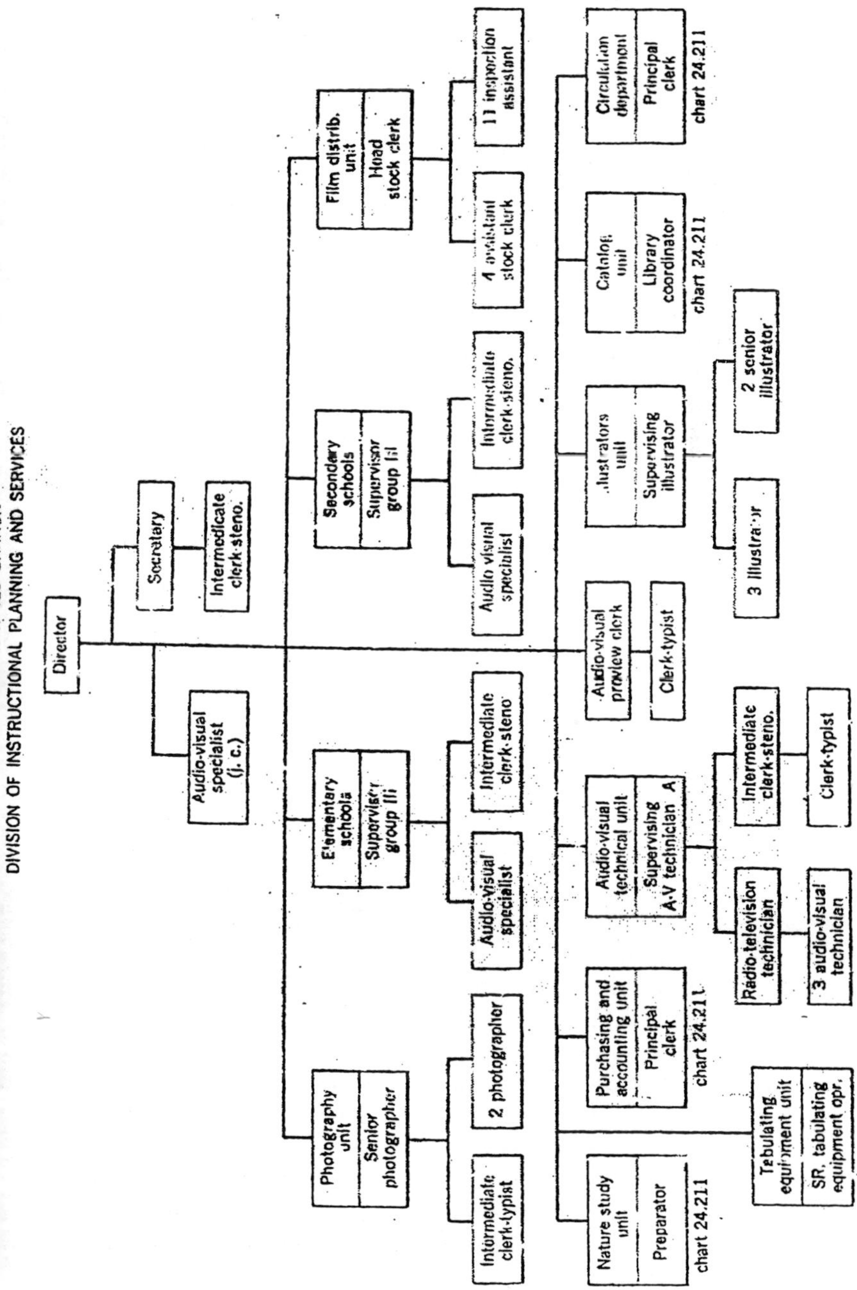

Audio-visual Section Instructional Services Branch Division of Instructional Planning and Services

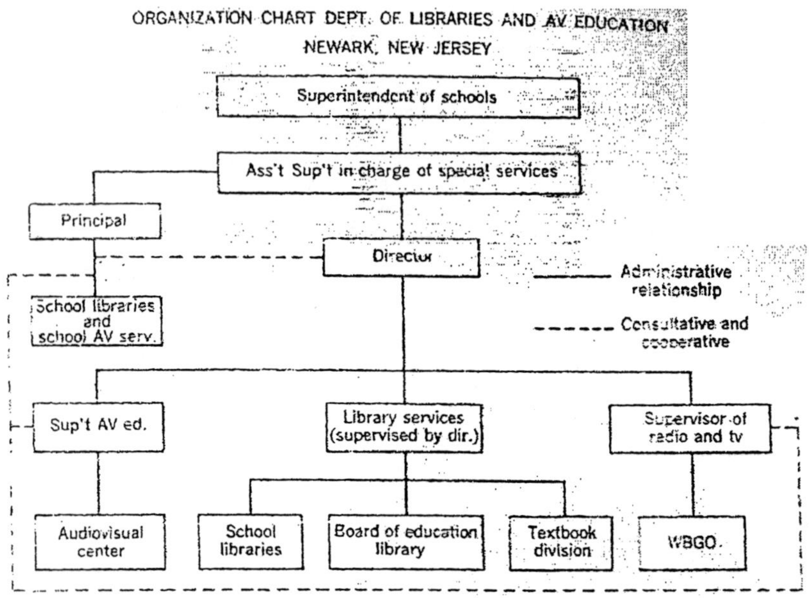

Fig. 8.2 : This organization chart was redrawn from the original appearing in the official handbook of the department. Questions relative to salient features of the chart should be referred to in the text.

At this point we need to show a number of cases where the media program leader relates his own activity to the structure he has created for his own system-wide operations. To do this we turn to several examples of actual cases where operations are sufficiently complex to show the problems that exist. First, let us turn to Los Angeles, admittedly a large, complex, and comprehensive media organization, for a diagram and brief comment. Before studying the Los Angeles diagrams in Fig. 8-1, the reader should know that the administrator of the Instructional Services Branch has the rank of Assistant Superintendent, and is directly responsible to the Head of the Instructional Planning and Services Division. He works coordinately with the chief administrator of Curriculum. In this organization we focus attention on salient characteristics and unique features by means of the following questions to be pondered by the reader:

1. How many sections are identifiable in the chart? How many of these have a Director in charge? How many have a Supervisor Group II in charge?
2. Does the Chief Administrator of this branch act as supervisor of both professional and technical personnel? In which case is the supervision direct instead of indirect?
3. Does the Administrator and all Section Directors or supervisors appear to have adequate secretarial personnel?
4. Why do you suppose the Library Section in separate from the Textbooks Section ?(Function? Scope of service to over 500 schools?)
5. Refer now to the detailed chart that shows the Audio-visual Section operationally organized under a Director. Note that although not provided here for analysis, still other charts have been made to pinpoint staff relationships.

Next we shall examine the organizational structure that marks out the pattern in operation at Newark, N.J. See Fig. 8.2. The reader is asked to answer another set of questions that points up unique features of the plan of organization:

1. In the city of Newark, as shown in this diagram, are all instructional media services combined under the leadership of a single professional person?
2. Is the Director of the Department directly responsible to the Assistant Superintendent of Schools? Does he work coordinately with school principals?
3. What are the three branches of the Library Services section? in this instance who acts as the head or supervisor of the Library section?
4. What school official is in charge of the school-building libraries and audiovisual services?
5. Are the ranks for TV and AV Section Heads equivalent?
6. What flexibility exists in this organization with regard to the talents and experience of the Director? Would the Director have to be a specialist in library science?
7. Does Newark have an audiovisual center? Is a professional specialist in charge?
8. Does it appear in the chart that all media are combined in school-building media-service centers? Who is directly in charge of such units? What is meant by consultative and cooperative relationships with the principals and with the school-building media-service centers?

Before leaving this problem for additional creative thought by the reader, we should examine a few additional samples of structure that represents both medium-size and smaller city school systems. We therefore turn to the organizational patterns is effect in the public schools of Portland, Oregon, Colorado Springs, Colo., Pawtucket, R.I., Penfield, N.Y., and Great Neck, N.Y. See 8.3 and 8.4, to note their status of development and salient features.

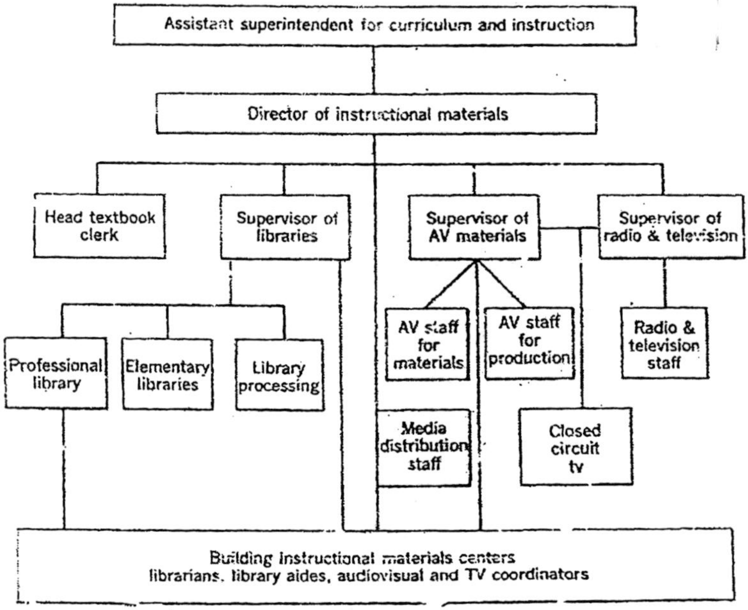

Fig. 8.3 : This is the organization chart for the comprehensive instructional Materials Center for the Public Schools in Portland, Oregon. Using the same of similar questions as were raised in connection with Fig. 8.1 and 8.2, study the staff specialization in this system. Note the joint effort implied between the Audiovisual and Television sections with regard to CCTV. Make some comparisons between the Newark and the Portland charts relative to functions being carried out.

The present discussion of citywide media-service headquarters, provide content in abudance to stimulate readers to develop administrative insight into media-use problems– which is the nature of this book. Media directors must realize the sweep of development in the past decade and must look ahead to vast implementation, even as new developments loom on the horizon. The fact is that we must note trends in media activity in response to teaching needs, and continuously, analyze the nature of the system-wide contributions being made to instructional effectiveness. Therefore before we leave these problems to attack others, we should emphasize the importance of keeping vital records of services rendered and problems identified in day-to-day routines. The next section discusses this aspect of the media center organization and activity.

Media Center Records and Reports

Prospective and practising media program directors need to realize the importance of keeping their superiors well informed about the services, activities, and trends of their organizations. Most chief administrators will demand periodic reports but if they don't, the media administrator who fails to submit them regularly each year misses a great opportunity for piling up evidence of need. Furthermore, he fails to place squarely where it belongs the responsibility for failure to take action on pressing needs. Although this may be of little consolation to a harried director, it is nevertheless wise tactically. Moreover, effective reporting inspires confidence for future action. An effective reporting process, however, requires an adequate record-keeping system, and some suggestions for keeping records are therefore discussed next.

A System of Records

It would be an easy matter in a media center to keep so many people busy checking on what the others do, that other important work would go undone. What kinds of records are likely to be useful? This question is difficult to answer because future needs for information can only be predicted. Records may actually, however, make the difference between success or failure, or they may go unused for a decade. In general it is the uses to which records are put that must be the basis for the decision to keep them. To be worthwhile, some of these uses would have to include: *(a)* historical reporting, *(b)* reporting growth and development, *(c)* predicting outcomes and identifying trends, (d) evaluating contributions, *(e)* providing publicity for developing community understanding and support, *(f)* identifying instructional and personnel needs, *(g)* obtaining additional staff and budget allotments, and *(h)* good business requirements.

The director needs to decide what records will be likely to be significantly useful, and then he needs to set up a process for summarizing them monthly and annually. Cluttering up the files and wasting valuable hours of labour on unnecessary figures is an unpardonable error. The media director will do well also if he keeps in his desk an out-of-sight summary sheet for each month on which to note important major decisions, meetings attended, and unexpected developments. At the end of a term or year, such notes become valuable. The media leader is also urged to develop his system during his first year on a new job, or at any rate, as early as possible, to provide maximum continuity of the data based on the operational level in effect at the time of his arrival or appointment. The following suggestions merit consideration:

1. Preserve original organization directives, annual budget expenditures, records on classrooms darkened in each school, inventories of media equipment units and materials, purchase requisitions, and other vital information such as employment and work records summarized in man-months of service or in some smaller unit of measurement.
2. Tabulate for each month the total number of media orders received from each school building in the system.
3. Make a tabulation of the number of each kind of centralized item distributed for each half year to each school.
4. Set up a tabulation of the use for each month for those media materials that are decentralized in each school and ordered from the coordinator's office by teachers. (Coordinators report this information to directors.)
5. Set up a summarization system in each school through the school-building media coordinator for the projection requests in order to tabulate the average number of items for each projection order. Such records are to be totaled at end of year or term as average length of the projection period, number of times classes were combined, and names of teachers who reveal highest competence in using materials. (These records are to be kept at the school coordinator's office only).

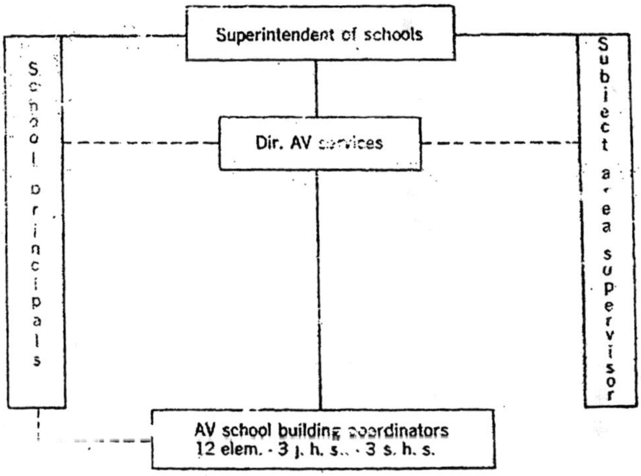

AUDIOVISUAL SERVICES ORGANIZATION CHART
PUBLIC SCHOOLS, COLORADO SPRINGS, COLORADO

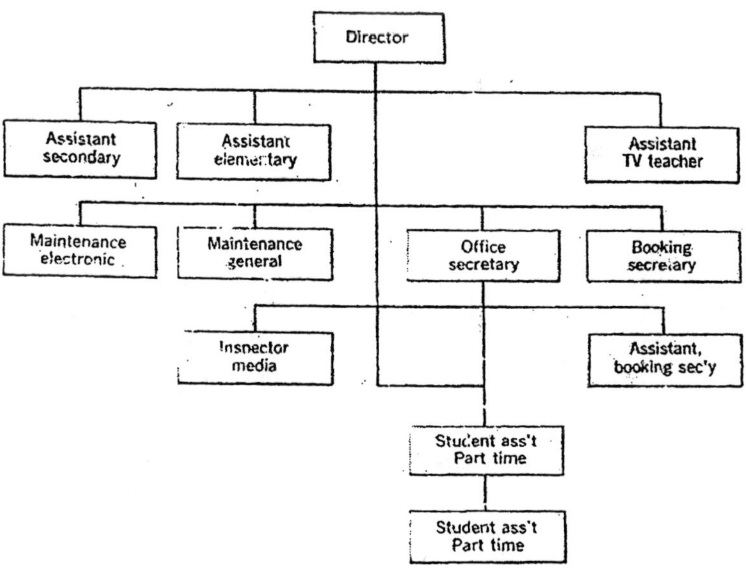

(a)

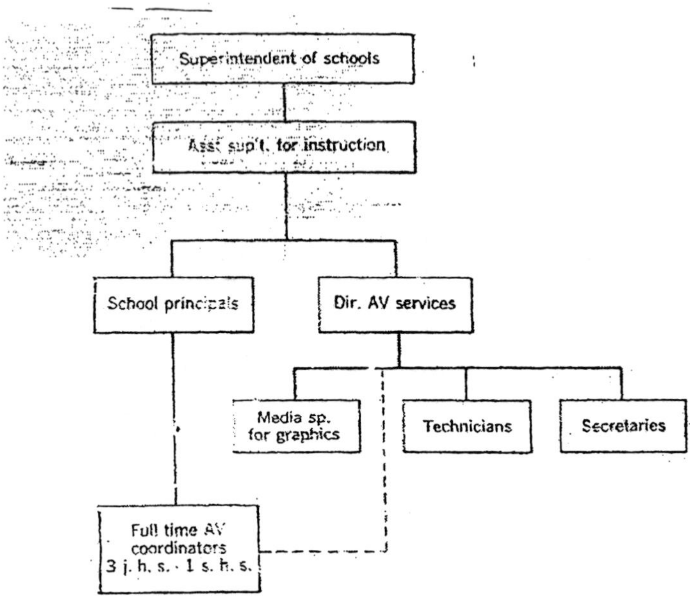

PENFIELD ORGANIZATION CHART—PENFIELD, N. Y.

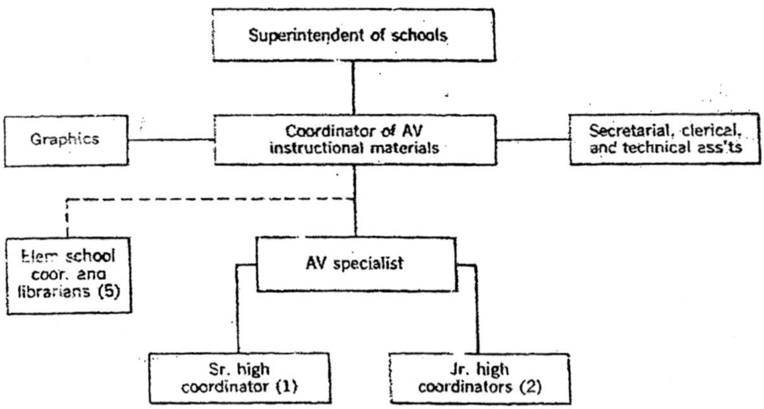

Fig. 8.4(b) : Organization charts for the following cities, arranged in order of population ranging from 80, 000 to approximately 18,000 Pawtucket, Rhode Island, Colorado Springs, Colorado, Great neck, New York, and Penfield, New York. The directors of these program are responsible for audiovisual media services only. All of the charts have been resketched.

6. Also in each school building obtain a tabulation of the times each term or year that non-projected audiovisual materials are utilized such as bulletin-board displays and audiovisual production activities involving tapes, transparencies, slides, and models.
7. Make monthly estimates of the number of pupils using electronic laboratory facilities as fixed installations, and such other media uses as regular participation in school-system, closed-circuit telecasts.
8. Maintain accurate records of school meetings conducted for in-service education purposes, including location, attendance, and nature of participation and action.
9. Maintain a listing of individual and group service projects completed as contributions to a program in a particular school and also to the system-wide program.

The media director needs also to consider unique ways to obtain qualitative evidence of the use of materials, and although this is a responsibility of other supervisory personnel as well, he needs to tackle the problem in his own area of operations. It can be seen in the foregoing lists that tabulations of qualitative data are set up at the school-building level where continuous observation may lead to reliable evidence. Of course the preceding items of information may be handled and summarized in various ways. Some may never be made use of other combinations of data may be added. It will be interesting to the reader to study a number of recent listings of types of data collected and utilized of types of data collected and utilized in school-system media centers. Several examples follow.

Example–8.6

In the audiovisual media center at Niles Township Community High School, North Division, Skokic, Illinois, data collected and tabulated for use in the Annual Report are as follows:

1. Number of teaching periods during the day, month, and year.
2. Number of periods various kinds of media equipment units were scheduled, day, month, year.
3. Number of machines available.
4. Per cent of periods using audiovisual media equipment.
5. Number of pieces of instructional materials produced at the audiovisual center.

6. Total volume of specific kinds of audiovisual media used by teachers.
7. Number of in-service education programs offered.

Example–8.7

In the audiovisual media center at Colorado Springs Public Schools, Colorado Springs, Colorado, data collected and tabulated for subsequent use are as follows:

1. Number of in-service meetings held.
2. Number of television and radio programs produced and telecast each week.
3. Number of TV Program brochures distributed.
4. Number of kinds of audiovisual media produced for elementary and secondary schools.
5. Number of teacher evaluations of media items completed.
6. Number of consultative meetings held with teachers.
7. Number of consultative meetings held with administrators.
8. Number and kinds of audiovisual media used in secondary schools.
9. Number and kinds of audiovisual media used in elementary schools.

Example–8.8

In the audiovisual media center at Penfield, New York, data collected for both regular and special reports are as follows:

1. Number of media material titles distributed to each school during ten-week intervals.
2. Number of media material titles distributed to each school for the school year.
3. Number and kinds of media items produced for teachers.
4. Media utilization by departments and grades.
5. Number of in-service education meetings held with records of teacher participation.
6. Degree of use of fixed media installations in school buildings.
7. Number of staff visitations to schools for media purpose.

Such data are particularly useful, when summarized and tabulated by years, in showing trends and rates of development. Systems for keeping records are, of course, indispensable in connection with programs for public understanding and support and in connection with evaluation activity.

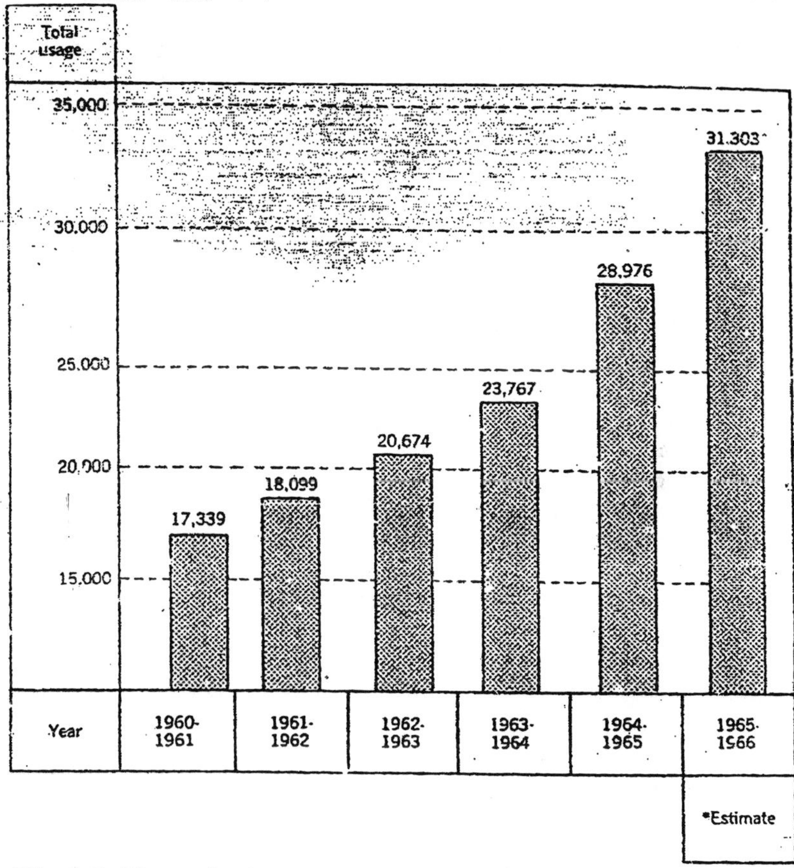

Fig. 8.5 : We need to improve our reports and proposals, both verbally and visually. One way to enhance this communicative impact is to use our design and operational skills. This chart was easy to make because the appropriate data had been collected and processed regularly.

Audiovisual Media Center Reports

A record system should be based on well defined uses, and one of these is, of course, reporting to all who are concerned. Reports to the public, as well as to the staff organization spread out among the various school units, are of great significance, but the reports considered here are the reports made specifically to the chief school-system administrators, who is turn use them as needed for their own analysis and reporting purposes. Reports to administrators should be factual, terse, succinct, graphic, comparative, free of errors, and attractive in format. The use of a summary check-off sheet for the media directors' desk has already been mentioned as an indispensable item in the record system because the director needs to show clearly his own efficiency as well. His annual report may, of course have to conform to local requirements, but the following suggestions as to procedure may be helpful:

1. Set up a novel introductory section, emphasizing some major highlights of activity.
2. Report major changes in policy.
3. Report vital statistics according to media materials and processes of distribution in comparison to figures for a base year, graphic or tabular in format. Continue such comparisons during a five-year period; then subsequently report the current year with base year and preceding year only.
4. Organize a section of the report to deal with the two following major aspects of operation, namely, *special needs* and *continuing needs.* Include under each of these the date on which the need should be met, and also include the progress made toward meeting it in the current year. Special needs have to do with pressing personnel problems, urgent new facilities, new demands that have appeared, and how such demands should be handled. Continuing needs are the year-to-year problems like improving the media-center quarters, increasing the size of equipment and material inventories, installation of fixed technological facilities such as outlets and light-control systems in classrooms, and the problem of appointing and training additional school-building media coordinators.
5. Set up a strong concluding section for the report, one that summarizes important aspects already mentioned or makes a strong recommendation pointing to the over-all operational progress for the year to come.
6. Use graphic illustrations.

Although these suggestions may apply in many ways to other administrative uses, they are specifically intended for audiovisual media-use reports. Telling the media-service story to the public necessarily involves other points for emphasis and other techniques. The media director is advised not to wait until reports are called for, but to set up a record system and reporting process at once. The media expert must be prepared to facilitate the thinking of top administrative officials by providing sound proposals and recommendations for action.

Problem-Solving Activities

1. An older, two-story school building has been taken over by the school department as its administrative headquarters. You, the director of grøwing audiovisual media-services program, have been assigned three classrooms at the rear of the building on the first floor. Your classrooms are adjoining and on the same side of the corridor. Each measures 32 feet long by 26 feet wide, You are told that this space assignment will have to last for the next ten years. Television service programs are envisioned, but textbooks and other reference services are handled by other agencies. You have been permitted to build an addition to the building to house television facilities. Partitions separating the classrooms are load-bearing walls that cannot be removed, although opening may be made in them. On the basis of the operations described in this chapter, prepare: *(a)* a labelled scale drawing of how you would remodel and use this space and the building addition; *(b)* a labeled scale drawing showing your layout of furniture, cabinets, and so forth, to control the flow of work for the inspection, storage, and distribution area, and indicating the relationship for the present of the television addition to the total media center; *(c)* study the commercially available storage facilities mentioned in this chapter or as shown in catalogs, and then specify their location in another scale drawing of the storage areas; *(d)* make a list of the furniture that would have to be built for the new facilities (do not include photographic darkroom furniture in this exercise); and *(e)* prepare detailed construction specifications for any two of the major items listed in item.

2. As time permits and your needs demand, engage in a thorough study of the main types of audiovisual equipment to develop operational and adjustment skills. Use the manufacturer's service booklets for each piece of equipment, and plan a time schedule for what you need most to do.

3. Outline procedures for an effective stock control, ordering, and inventory process for the audiovisual media-

center shop. Make a list of the major supplies that will have to be stocked if schools are going to be well served.

4. Assume that you have been appointed to the position of media program director in a small city where there are ten school buildings. Assume further that you have a reasonably sized audiovisual media-service center in the high school where your own office is located and that you have been hired to develop a system-wide organization. Sketch out your plan to develop this organization as to full-time staff, duties, service units, use of student crews if deemed necessary, and advisory councils. Draw a line-of-responsibility chart for the organization you have established.

5. What characteristics would you like your media school-building coordinators to possess? What recommendations would you make regarding their training, services, and remuneration?

6. Why should directors be concerned with maintaining adequate records of activities and services? Why should a record system be devised soon after a media director's appointment? Formulate the kind of record system you believe would be of maximum helpfulness.

7. Examine a number of annual reports as prepared by media directors, and identify their strengths and weaknesses. Of what value are annual reports to the media program director? Would you write them even if not requested to do so? Why, or why not?

8. After studying what conclusions do you draw about the prime responsibility of the citywide media program director in terms of his ultimate accomplishment? What shift in balance between central and school-building center as to facilities, staff, and media budget, do you envision? What organizational structure to achieve this goal would you need to develop in light of modern roles of media?

9. How will decentralization of media collections in school buildings be likely to reduce recommended storage areas at media headquarters?

10. Describe in a succinct summary the nature of professional and technical duties carried on in a *centralized* print-medium service area as it would exist in relation to a citywide comprehensive instructional media center.

11. State clearly in an itemized listing several major ways in which citywide and school-building media services are likely to be different.

12. Make a listing of generally needed media-service center areas, as presented in this chapter, and total the estimates of required space for the functions given. If you wish to take issue with the total square footage you have discovered, make adjustments in terms of your own specific recommendations. Report this to the class and see if your colleagues will agree.

13. Formulate a plan in outline format for the system-wide maintenance of conventional projection equipment. Be thorough. Do not *fail* to take into account personnel, stocks of spare parts, and central and school-building service programs.

14. Suggest a method for handling technical control and maintenance of fixed electronic carrels and TV studios in school buildings to guarantee continuous readiness for use.

15. Sketch out one employment specification sheet for one media position of your choice. (Each member of the class group should do one of these announcement-of-position and job-specification sheets. All should then be turned over to the instructor and an editing committee for final polishing, rewriting, and duplication for issue to classmates as a package.)

16. You are employing one new assistant media director for the center, and one new maintenance supervisor for system-wide functions. Suggest your plans for screening and interviewing as follow-up procedures to the use of the announcement and job-specification sheet you prepared in a previous exercise.

17. Criticize the pay ranges-presented in this and the preceding chapter for required professional and technical personnel in citywide and school-building media centers, and up-date them in light of local or changed conditions. Make your own estimate of need and cost for media personnel in any situation you name.

18. On the basis of discussion and guidelines developed in the text and in class make a list of the kinds of data about audiovisual services and processes that you as a media program discusses would recommend keeping for the purpose of preparing annual and interim reports.

References

The Audiovisual Program, Bulletin No. 218, State of Indian, Department of Public Instruction, Indianapolis, Indiana 1956.

Brown, James W. and Kenneth D. Norberg. *Administering Educational Media.* (New York : McGraw–Hill, 1965).

Cobun, Ted and Hal J. Cress, "North Division, Niles Township Community. High Schools," *Audiovisual Instruction,* Vol. 10, No. 2, February 1965, pp. 36–137.

Cohen, Samuel (Interviewer). "What Does Audiovisual Mean to You?" *Audiovisual Instruction,* Vol. 9, No. 1, January 1964, pp. 40–60.

—."The Import of the Wantagh Interviews and a Modest Proposal for Next Steps," *Audiovisual Instruction,* Vol. 9, No. 1, January 1964, pp. 61–63.

DeBernardis, Amo. "Portlands's Instructional Materials Center," *Educational Screen,* Vol. 28, No. 1, January 1941, pp. 13–15.

DeBernardis, Amo, Victor W. Doheerty, Erret Hummel, and Charles W. Brubaker, *Planning Schools for New Media,* in cooperation with the U.S. Office of Education (Washington, D.C.: The Superintendent of Documents, U.S. Government Printing Office, 1961).

DeBernardis, Amo, David M. Crossman, and Thomas E. Miller. "Media, Technology and IMC Space Requirements," *Audiovisual Instruction,* Vol. 10, No. 2, February 1965, pp. 107–114.

Faris, Gene. "Tentative Guidelines for Audiovisual Personnel and Equipment," *Audiovisual Instruction,* Vol. 10, No. 3, March 1965, pp. 201–204.

Faris Gene and John Moldstad (assisted by Harvey Fyre). *Improving the Learning Environment* (A Study on the Local Preparation of Visual Instructional Materials). In cooperation with the U.S. Office of Education (Washington, D.C.: Superintendent of Documents, U.S. Government Printing Office, 1963).

Fordd, Harry J. "The Instructional Resources center", *Audiovisual Instruction,* Vol. 7, No. 8, October 1962, pp. 524–526.

Geriach, Vernon S. The Professional Education of the Media Specialist," *AV Communication Review,* Vol. 14, No. 2, Summer 1966, p. 185.

Glenn, Magdalene, "Organizing a Materials Center," *National Elementary Principal,* Vol. 40, No. 1, January 1961, pp. 28–30.

Goldberg, Albert L. and Richard A. Darling. "Is the Instructional Materials Center the Answer?" *Audiovisual Instruction,* Vol. 6, No. 5, May 1961, pp. 194–195.

Green, Alan C. (ed.) *Educational Facilities with New Media,* (Prepared under a contract with the U. S. Office of Education) (Washington D. C.: The Department of Audiovisual Instruction of the NEA, 1966).

Handbook for Audiovisual Representatives, Secondary Schools (Revised 1965). (Los Angeles: Los Angeles City Schools, Instructional Services Branch, 1965).

Lehman, Frederick M. "A Study of a small Audiovisual Community," *Audiovisual Instruction,* Vol. 9, No. 1, January 1964, pp. 37–40.

Martin, Ann M. and C. Walter Stone. *A Study of Regional Instructional Media Resources, Phase* I—*Manpower.* (Prepared under contract OE–3–16–027, with the U.S. Office of Education.) (Pittsburgh: Graduate School of Library and Information Sciences, University of Pittsburg, 1965).

Mesedahl, Leroy K. "The IMC: Contribution To individualized Instruction," *Audiovisual Instruction,* Vol. 10, No. 9, November 1965, pp. 705–706.

Miles, Bruce and Virginia Mcjenkin. "IMC'c : A Dialogue," *Audiovisual Instruction,* Vol. 10, No. 9, November 1965, pp. 688–691.

Mitchell, Malcolm G. "What's Going on in the School Library?" *Phi Delta Kappan,* vol. 45, October 1963, pp. 44–47.

Moldstad, John and Harvey R. Frye. "Making Room for AV," *Audiovisual Instruction,* vol. 2, No. 10, December 1957, pp. 270–271.

Nicholson, Margaret E. "The I.M.C." *School Libraries,* Vol. 13, No. 3, March 1964, pp. 39–43.

Phillips, Murray G. "Instructional Materials Center: The Rationale" *Audiovisual Instruction,* vol. 5, No. 10, December 1960, pp. 326–332.

Pryor, Robert L. "Speedy Repair Equals Good Utilization," *Audiovisual Instruction,* Vol. 8, No. 3, March 1963, p. 153.

Quantitative Standards for Audiovisual Personnel, Equipment and Materials (in Elementary, Secondary, and Higher Education). Developed as part of the Faris–Sherman Study conducted under the auspices of the united States Office of Education, National Defence Education Act, Title VII, Part B, Program (Washington, D.C., Department of Audiovisual Instruction of the NEA, 1201 Sixteenth Street, N.W., January 1966), 18 pp. mimeographed.

Sample state Certification Requirements" (A collection of reports). *Audiovisual Instruction,* Vol. 10, No. 10, December 1965, pp. 787–794.

Sharp, J. Stanley, "Architectural Steps in Facilities Planning," *Audiovisual Instruction,* Vol. 10 No. 2, February 1965, pp. 101–103

Stone, C. Walter (ed.), *The Professional Education of Media Service Personnel.* (Pittsburg: Graduate Library School, University of Pittsburg, 1964).

Taylor, Kenneth I. "Instructional Materials Center," *The Nation's Schools,* Vol. 66, December 1960, pp. 46–50.

9

Implementation of Media Preparation Services

When a school or school system provides its teachers with convenient facilities for the preparation of their own slides, transparencies, tapes, films, and other instructional materials it may be said that it has reached a high level of maturity in the development of its audiovisual media services. Unusually skillful teachers today are adding to their communicative skills the power to select, arrange, construct, photograph, visualize and record ideas that help teach more effectively. Fortunate indeed are teachers who have in their schools the necessary supplies, equipment, and the assistance of media coordinators, principals, or talented colleagues to carry on high-caliber planning and preparation of creatively conceived materials, and infinitely more fortunate are their pupils. Such teachers have a greater impact that stems not only from increased pupil understanding, but from the increased-teacher-pupil contacts, as for example with tape-recorded instruction that can be presented to one group while the teacher is working face-to-face with another. We must quickly point out also that such teachers are the ones who will be most likely to utilize locally prepared materials, in combination with ready-made, ones, in the newer teaching roles of media which are generally referred to as instructional systems.

The truth is that all of us ought to accelerate our progress towards this maturity in media services. In the light of overall teaching needs, however, we need first to build our media-service program for teachers on the solid base of adequate facilities for ready-made media for then, since we will have at hand the needed equipment units, we are at least partially equipped to use the various materials produced locally. We need to work next or concurrently toward facilities for the preparation of unique materials planned and made by teachers themselves. Some teachers are fortunately working in situations where materials such as 2 × 2 inch color slides, Polaroid slides, acetate transparencies, together with spirit masters and stencils, are available and upon order will be prepared and delivered according to schedule. Such services provide teachers with either centralized or school-building technical personnel who serve as consultants and producers, thus freeing teachers for other creative planning activity. However, a great many teachers the country over would feel privileged indeed were they permitted to make the materials on a do-it-yourself basis, if the supplies and facilities were in their schools.

As teachers learn to select and prepare their own instructional media materials, they invariably develop new insights and skills that are increasingly being associated with the best modern-day teaching methods. Today's technology makes such maturity possible, but maturity of this caliber arises at two levels. First, there is the operational level of maturity, that is, a level of maturity residing in the teacher who strives to execute his or her ideas about instructional media. Second, this maturity arises at the administration level in the school system that strives to organize and maintain facilities for teachers to use. These are the basic levels of maturity without which team teaching, automation, large-group instruction, and instructional television will never fulfill their promise, since their successful use is uniquely tied to effective communication.

In the face of the rapidly developing technology for the local preparation of media, and because of the newer roles of media that demand systematic and scheduled use of media in combination, we assert, that one of the significant problems that a school-system or school-building media director will have to deal with effectively is the organization and implementation of media-preparation services. We therefore turn to a discussion of the problems that will have to be met and solved. To view the media-preparation problem in perspective we present the following questions which we shall attempt to answer: Who needs locally produced media materials, and why is there such an urgency for media-preparation facilities? Who should design and prepare special-purpose media—teachers or supporting technical staff? What spaces for media preparation facilities are required? Should media preparation services be centralized at media headquarters, or decentralized in each school building, or should an optimum combination of facilities and services be organized? What control systems need to be set up for providing media preparation services? What in-service education programs will be needed? What new staff members will be required to provide needed services?

Nature of the Need for Local Media Preparation

Who Needs Locally Prepared Media Materials?

We have already pointed out that teachers are in large part the ones who have need of media in order to communicate effectively with their students—either in large or small groups or with individuals. But we must not overlook the need for in-service education media for use by curriculum specialists and by school administrators. Administrators throughout the school system often require specialized materials for use with both lay and professional groups. Hence we can readily see the need for a wide range of media from television programs to audio taps, and from slides to charts for a wide variety of school-system purposes.

Why Are Media-Preparation Services Urgently Needed?

Expert teachers who develop keen insights into their subject-matter specialties, often need to prepare up-to-date media that reveal recently formulated relationships. Talented teachers also wish to present content in diagrammatic and pictorial form to supplement commercially prepared media to make specific local applications. Such efforts to improve communication have been increasingly put forth by teachers in schools everywhere with the aid of rapidly developing technology. However, in recent years the appearance of new media and the increasing emphasis on new arrangements and conditions for teaching and learning have brought a new urgency to the need for local media-preparation facilities. We shall explain how a few of these changes and developments have a bearing on the need for unique media.

Large-Group Instruction and Team Teaching: Although large-group instruction is generally a part of any team-teaching operation, we can treat both items as separate changes. In large groups, students simply cannot see what is going on during classroom demonstration with apparatus, and are sometimes lost during referral to charts and maps in the front of a large teaching station. Means for enlargement area necessity. Therefore, either television or other display systems become a prime necessity. A teacher can hold up for inspection a crystal, a flower, or a skull, but students in back of the first few rows, even if they have 20/20 vision, cannot make the observations required. See Fig. 1. Thus we see a new urgency in presentations in front of large groups for projection techniques with close-up views made possible by 2 × 2 inch color slides, for example, of any content desired. Also, diagrams can be drawn and displayed by means of television receivers arranged so as to give every pupil a front row seat. In team teaching we not only have large-group presentations that demand attention-holding media materials but the teacher making the presentation is likely to be an expert in a particular field and hence will be in a position to use an combination of commercially available and locally produced materials, carefully worked out in the light of desired objectives and required pupil responses. Furthermore, media that control the presentation of content and guide the responses of the pupils (even when the teacher is at work elsewhere) will as a rule have to be locally adapted, or made locally in their entirety.

Television: The widespread use of closed-circuit television programing in schools, either on a system-wide, groups-of-schools, or subject-matter and grade-level basis, demands the kind of studio-teacher performance that is richly communicative. One of the great new reasons for providing media-production facilities is to build the kind of television programs through creative media use that will accomplish goals effectively. Although many potentially valuable commercial materials are available for this purpose, television teachers insist that they have a wide variety of media with which to get their message across to students.

Self-Instruction and True Individualization: The development of programs for teaching machines, and the use of pictorial and audio media in carrels for individualized teaching demand locally produced media from video and audio taps to slide sets and film clips. In fact, as will be pointed out later, both pictorial and audio media may be combined in programs recorded on videotape and transmitted to both large and small groups and to individuals.

Multimedia Presentation Techniques: Multimedia or multi-image and multi-screen-presentation techniques, using either front or rear-projection surfaces, are also likely to demand sophisticated local media-production resources. We except that in the future many such presentations will be comercially prepared and packaged for local use, but we believe that when such installations are available in schools, unique use will demand the power to organize or reorganize and combine up-to-the-minute local media for teaching the groups involved.

Teaching Systems: The modern teacher is no longer enslaved from hour to hour by the need to confront a group of students and control them second by second. There are newer ways to present content and elicit desired responses of an interacting nature. The modern teacher turns over to media, properly produced, structured, and presented, a number of burdensome though vital teaching tasks. Even though teaching kits and instructional packages will be commercially available in increasing quantities, it is obvious that in a great many cases, teachers will still need to use their own personally designed and structured media as a part of modern instructional systems.

Administrators and Their Public-Relations Programs: The desire of school leaders to communicate effectively coupled with the expectancy of the public to receive messages by up-to-date technology, demands that public relations presentations be enhanced by specially prepared media. We must also consider, however, in addition to personal appearances of school speakers at public or executive meetings, the wider audiences that should be reached through audio and television programs and through effectively illustrated school stories in the press. Such uses of special media productions constitute another aspect of the urgent need to inaugurate media-preparation programs in the schools and to expand them according to demonstrated needs.

We can therefore see that for both conventional and new roles of media materials and equipment, the need to organize and implement local media-preparation services is of prime importance. Media program directors will have to take action in this vital area and struggle with problems having to do with policies, staff, supplies, financial support, and in-service education. One of the most important policy matters has to do with the amount of technical service to be provided to teachers. That is, should teachers be expected to spend time planning their own media materials, or should technicians and student crews make the materials for teachers? Perhaps there is no pat answer to this question. To answer it we need to explore the nature of media-preparation processes, and a number of other important questions.

Nature of Media-Preparation Processes

Considering the speed with which technological processes in the preparation of media are advancing, many of the processes referred to in this section will probably be outmoded before this manuscript goes to press. However, this section does not need to be a penetrating analysis of the state of the art, nor does it have to include a handbook on preparation techniques. What we must point out is the nature of the processes we could necessary in any school-system media design and preparation program. We therefore wish to present a basis, however incomplete, for the purpose of the identification of problems and the implementation of program plans.

Two Basic Aspects of the Media-Preparation Process

Before we present more details relative to the state of technological development for media preparation, the kinds of a media needed, and the processes, required for their production, we ought to set forth two aspects of the process, the understanding of which will help the reader think more clearly about these problems. These problems involve content and design, as well as the mechanics of making the medium, the operation of the equipment involved, the way supplies are used, and the artistic quality and physical excellence of the final result. We shall discuss each of these main topics briefly to give needed direction to subsequent suggestions.

Visualization and Design: When a set of slides, overhead transparencies, or an audio program on tape for business education or biology is produced locally, it is quite obvious that it is the teacher—the professional—who ought to be responsible for the content. Teachers must decide first what concept or process needs to be visualized, and this decisions must be made in the light of specific objectives as they are being achieved in the teaching-learning environment. What is diagramed or printed on a transparency involves decisions about the effect or impact of the message on the learner—and the impact on the learner is a function of his personal responses. Basic, then, to the process of media preparation are the decisions of the teacher who must bear the responsibility of his professional activities. It is he who identifies a specified need in light of an instructional situation. The design of the message and often the medium selected will depend on the advice of a number of curriculum workers, who may be involved because they themselves will use the medium in subsequent presentations. The design of a given message will obviously depend on the nature of the roles to be played, what the learner already knows, and what he is supposed to do when he perceives the content of the medium. These are complicated professional matters and therefore we can separate them from the often complicated but non-professional activities referred to as operational techniques.

Operational Techniques: This aspect of media preparation involves equipment units, devices and supplies, mechanical skills, wide knowledge of processes, difficulties, adjustments, and the ability to make judgements in the light of the limitations inherent in any given medium or combination of media. Many of the operational techniques such as exposing a master with diazo-coated film and developing it in an ammonia-filled "pickle jar" may be performed by a fifth-grade student. Other processes like making an overhead transparency of a chart constructed on logarithmic graph paper that is 12 × 14 inches in size is an entirely different matter. Thus technicians need to be widely skilled, and problems often arise that require unusual insight as to how a message can be presented to obtain the reaction desired and clearly set forth by the teacher in pre-construction conferences. We see in any graphic center both the operational side of media preparation and the message-and-design side of the whole process.

Because of these two basic aspects of the process of media preparation, there will always be a number of people involved, some professional and some not. At times, teachers who are willing to struggle with content-and-design problems may need a professional media specialist (experienced in teaching methods) to counsel him on matters of message and design. After the critical decisions have been made, the actual operational work should be turned over to an artist-technician for completion.

A View of Media-Preparation Technology

We have shown the basic aspects of a process involving both teachers and technicians, and in preceding sections we have shown the need for an organized media preparation service. We shall now introduce a view of current media preparation technology.

Kinds of Media Generally Needed in the Modern School: When we consider the many roles of media in the modern school, we can easily understand why teachers, especially those who have developed maturity in communication skills, have need for specially prepared media. With increasing frequency, teachers who have been able to concentrate their efforts and energies at high levels of professional activity are engaged in creative planning-and-design activity, and are finding easy to turn over to media several direct teaching tasks. Little wonder then that teachers are facing up to the need not only to use ready-made media, but are designing their own for a variety of roles in the teaching process. We therefore state that many kinds of media are being prepared locally in the mot advanced media programs around the country, and we can list these commonly reported types of media as follows :

1. Printed matter; instructional sheets, booklets and school publications.
2. Photo enlargements.
3. Overhead transparencies.
4. 2 × 2 inch color slides.
5. Polaroid slides, 3¼ × 4 inch.
6. Filmstrips.
7. Audio programs on tape.
8. Television programs on videotape.
9. Motion pictures, 8 mm cartridges and 16 mm film footage.

When we consider this array of media production by schools in their media-preparation programs we can perceive the underlying content and decisions that are faced by teachers as they either explain to others what to make, or make the materials themselves. We now turn to a specific aspect of the operational process, which we need to consider because it emphasizes the preparation of source materials that are often the basis for the media-preparation process.

Making Masters for Media Production: When teachers wish to have sets of slide transparencies made up that are based on their unique needs, the first step is often the making of source materials such as graphs and pictorial arrangements which will then be photographed in color, or converted into multi-color overlays in overhead transparency form. This work must be done either by teachers themselves or by other audiovisual specialists and their supporting technicians. These processes of making what we may refer to as *masters* involve a number of specific operations and often a great many supplies. We shall list the following operations as examples :

1. Use lettering materials, such as pens, brushes, scribers, drawing boards, inks, crayons, and pencils.
2. Use pressure-sensitive sheets, tape, symbols, patterns, and other drawing aids.
3. Use stencils, stamps, and pre-cut letters.
4. Use assorted papers and acetate sheets.

Operational Techniques with Equipment: In any well-organized and comprehensive media-preparation program it is possible to observe many kinds of equipment that must be operated in carrying out the basic constructional steps required in the making of instructional media. We shall now list some of the common operational techniques.

1. Make overhead transparencies from masters by the
   (a) photocopier method
   (b) diazo-ammonia method.
2. Duplicate print-medium masters (spirit-master and mimeo stencils).
3. Use photography to produce still-picture media:
   (a) use regular and Polaroid Land cameras
   (b) copy masters (handmade flats, layouts or paste-ups)
   (c) make negatives
   (d) make film and paper positives
   (e) make slide duplicates and alter camera angle and light values.
4. Use photography to produce motion pictures :
   (a) 8 mm cartridges, both sound and silent
   (b) 16 mm footage, with magnetic or optical sound tracks.
5. Mount instructional material on paper by dry-tissue methods.
6. Laminate instructional materials in plastic.
7. Mount slides in frames and between glass plates.
8. Mount transparencies using suitable cardboard frames.
9. Put film footage in cartridges and on appropriate reels.
10. Record sound on magnetic tape.
11. Record television programs on videotape.
12. Program pictorial and sound components.
13. Select, sort, splice, and edit film and tape.

This listing of operational techniques, partial though it may be, constitutes a formidable number of skills for any teacher or audiovisual specialist and his supporting technicians to possess. Yet in modern programs, these and many more increasingly sophisticated skills are essential. We therefore ask the question: What personnel in any given school system should prepare the media required by the instructional program?

Who Should Do the Work of Preparing Locally Made Media?

In their report of a national study of the local production of media by school personnel, carried out by Indiana University in cooperation with the U.S. Office of Education, Faris and Moldstad answered this question using opinions expressed in their interviews with a sampling of teachers. They summarized their findings as follows:

The classroom teachers had differing opinions concerning the best method of getting visual materials prepared. Approximately one-third preferred to prepare their own materials if given adequate time. The remaining teachers preferred that someone else do the actual production work. When asked who this production person should be, they tended to prefer the audiovisual supervisor or student assistants.

All of the television teachers interviewed expressed a preference for engaging a specialist to prepare the visual materials desired. The great majority thought that a hired artist should be employed to do the work while a very small proportion preferred an audiovisual specialist. In no instance did a television teacher express a desire to do his own production work.

It is very interesting to note the major deterrents as reported by the same authors, based on a questionnaire and also on actual interviews with teachers as follows :

...respondents to the nationwide survey indicated that lack of time to prepare materials was the greatest deterrent to an expanded use of local preparation facilities. The classroom teachers confirmed this finding with thirty-four of the fifty-six teachers interviewed indicating lack of time as the greatest deterrent and lack of knowledge or ability to produce materials as the second greatest deterrent. Television teachers placed lack of time as the second greatest obstacle with lack of knowledge or ability to produce materials as the greatest.

It will be up to the media program director for the school system, or the media coordinator in a single school building, to formulate workable plans in line with principles already stated in connection with needed services for teachers and pupils. Teachers ought to be brought into the planning deliberations, their roles in local production discussed, facilitating equipment purchased, space allotted, and optimum staff in light of local media-use development employed and deployed. This means that if we consider such professional processes as deciding on what needs to be produced, how and when it is to be used, how it will be designed and what media are selected, we know that teachers will have to be involved in some of the preparation work. But teachers may or may not be willing to devote hours of work to such routine technical processes as lettering, exposing, printing, duplicating, binding, and the like-Optimum balance, therefore, between professional work and the semi or nonprofessional work is the key to effective programs of media-preparation services. We therefore conclude that if there is no media program director in a school system to organize central media-preparation facilities, staff, and materials, and advise teachers as to professional ways of meeting their special needs for media, and no media coordinator to carry on the media-preparation work at professional levels and to organize supporting technician services, then media preparation activities will not be feasible. School-building and centralized media services, the need for technicians, artists, and film and tape editors is an urgent one, and both full-time and part-time adult employees, some of whom may be teachers with reduced teaching to loads, as well as student crews, may have to be utilized if school instructional programs of modern, technological character are to develop and prosper.

Space Needs for Media Preparation

The difficulty in specifying the amount of space needed for media preparation lies in the number of variables that have a bearing on the operations that have to be carried out. The list would be too large to deal with here, but we ought to point out a few of the items as follows : the degree to which operations are carried out in more than one place; the number of people who will be working simultaneously in any given location or on any given process; the degree to which media prepared have to be used by teachers throughout the school system on schedule, or the quantity required; the speed with which the media must be produced; the complexity of the technological situations in which the media are to be used, as in television production, electronic learning laboratories, or in multimedia presentations; the degree to which equipment units are ready for immediate use; the number of teachers desiring to use the services (the volume of the total demand); the commitment on the part of media program directors to giving adequate services; the degree to which ready-made media become systematized; and a host of other factors as well. Therefore, the estimates space requirements are based on a number of factors, experience with actual operations, or predicted needs as school programs become more complex and teachers become more sophisticated. Knowing then that this discussion is neither precise nor comprehensive in scope, we present in both text and illustration the nature of space requirements that are likely to have to be met by media coordinators as they embark upon programs of media preparation. We shall refer to space needed for both specific media operations and service areas such as photographic darkrooms and general storage area. We shall turn first to a discussion of the amount of space needed to prepare 2 × 2 inch color slides, Polaroid slides, overhead transparencies, audio-program tapes, and videotapes.

2 × 2 Inch Color Slides

When 2 × 2 inch color slides are made by teachers, or by technicians working to carry out slide-making processes at their direction, space must be available for a camera mounted on a table or bench, on which can be placed a stand with separate or attached lights. Also needed will be space for source material such as magazines, books, and periodicals, and also space for a box or case the size of a book, in which to store copying lenses, filters, adaptor rings, and attachments. In some schools, instead of laying a book or magazine flat on a bench under the camera, a camera is mounted on a tripod and the source material is placed on a shelf or tacked on a wall and photographed in an upright position. This procedure maybe necessary in copying large charts and posters. The working space for two people in front of a bench would be normally the same as for the bench and camera itself. *Hence we estimate that an always-ready photographing unit would require a minimum of 15 square feet and working space for personnel would be an additional 15 square feet for a total of 30 square feet.* Not included is normal access space for moving up to and away from the equipment unit. Access space is best provided by locating such operational units in an optimum-size general service area or workroom. The estimate of 30 square feet for a copy-camera unit could then be considered in light of a need for mass production, the degree of decentralization and centralization in the school system, and the number of teachers and pupils that need to work on the equipment. There would be a minimum of one such camera for each school-building unit in any media-preparation program envisioned, and in a central-headquarters-type of organization, multiple units with full-time workers would have to be provided.

Polaroid Slides

Because the Polaroid slide process requires no darkroom operations, many schools have need for such a rapid, on-the-spot process. Where 2 × 2 inch slides in black and white are a necessity—as in television—the larger Polaroid Reflex copying units would be required. A special lens is require for making an image of an 8 × 10 inch picture of diagram on film small enough to fit a standard 2 × 2 inch mask-and-slide mount. *The total operational space requirements for such a unit would be a minimum of 36 square feet.*

Overhead Transparencies

As with other media-preparation areas, when we discuss overhead transparencies we are forced to make assumptions as to the nature of the equipment. We shall therefore limit the equipment to the following types and assume that together they constitute an operating unit: a dry-process photocopier unit to make transparencies directly from single-sheet source materials, one similar unit for the production of transparencies from sources appearing in books or booklets, and one set of equipment components for exposing and developing diazo-coated acetate sheets for multi-color *static* or overlay transparencies. These three kinds of equipment could obviously serve three persons simultaneously, and each would require bench or table space over which or under which there could be an on-the-spot storage area for needed operational supplies. This bench space for equipment and working room would amount to 12 square feet for each of the first two components and 18 square feet for the third. The room for personnel in front of the three components would be a minimum of 42 square feet. *Therefore the total space requirement on an operating-unit basis would amount to 84 square feet as a minimum.*

Audio-Program Tapes

Magnetic tape has become the workhorse of the electronic learning laboratory, and has served as the basis of dial retrieval systems in individualization programs at all levels of instruction from first grade through college. Teachers who use audio-program tapes need not only write the scripts and add the sound effects, but they need to record them and then often have them duplicated in quantity for all the teachers of any given grade or subject. Where can these operations be performed? It is quite obvious that teachers can make their recordings in their own homes, in their classrooms, or in the ideal environment of the recording studio either in their own school centers or at media headquarters for the estimates that appropriate equipment is available and it must be further understood that we are considering only minimum operational space to record a studio teacher with adequate media-support facilities. This means then that we ought to provide at lest one small studio, one control room in which the videotape recorder would be operated, and in which such media as slides and film clips could be combined electronically as needed by the studio teacher. It should be emphasized, even in this superficial treatment of the subject, that adequate storage space and media-production space must be included in the plans for any desirable studio facility. We should therefore include in this special videotaping unit, which might well be a part of a large-scale television production and multichannel transmission center, areas for listening, viewing, and editing, plus preparation space and storage. This videotaping unit in any broader scope of service would have to be vastly increased in size, but here we may consider the possibility of incorporating this estimated space as a unit in several elementary and secondary school buildings in a school system. We shall now make some hazardous estimates of what the space needs of a minimum unit would amount to.

1. A small studio accommodating one teacher as a presenter, with simple set capability and with media-support facilities, would demand *a minimum of 200 square feet.*
2. The required control room housing console, camera controls, videotaping units, multiplexer for slides and film would demand an additional *200 square feet as a minimum* for simple videotaping operations.

3. For a minimum area in which to set up a workroom for editing, viewing, and media preparation for a specific program, the requirement would be *approximately 180 square feet.*

Thus for this limited-use television-taping operation the total space need would be 580 square feet.

Multi-Purpose Working Area

In any media-preparations program, either centralized or decentralized in each school building, there is need for multipurpose working space. We have already pointed up the process of making masters for many media-making process, involving various lettering materials and devices, but also there are the important processes of design and layout, binding, and mounting, programming, sorting, and selecting. Some processes such as editing, listening, recording, and copying have already been discussed in relation to specific process with audio-program tapes and videotapes. But we must be sure to consider in addition to the specific space needs already identified, the urgently needed areas to serve in support of such equipment-operating stations as slides and transparencies, together with the arrangement of pictorial displays, printing and duplicating processes, and the production of motion picture film cartridges and clips. Hence we must provide space for drawing boards, flat-top tables, workbenches, a sink or two, and a small desk and chair for each of the technicians and staff artists. Presumably the leadership staff would have office space provided in other areas of the school's or school-system's media-service center. In this general service area we need also to provide adequate storage for hundreds of items of bulk supplies. The necessity of providing storage areas is often lost sight of in the plans to meet other operational needs. The lack of storage areas located in good relation to the functional uses of the available space may actually to be so serious as to cripple media-preparation operations. We shall therefore give this need the prominence it deserves. It has already been pointed out that along with each equipment-operating station there should be shelf or table space for the supplies that have to be used as a part of the actual operation, but the storage supplies, and the necessity of having a space to be used as an issuing center or stock room constitute another problem.

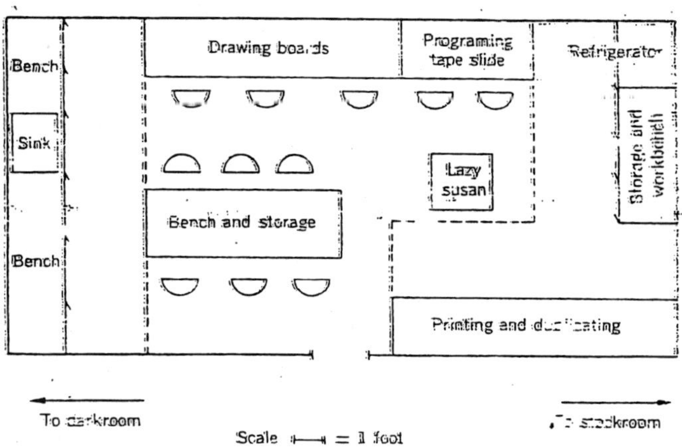

STORAGE ROOM FOR MEDIA PREPARATION SUPPLIES

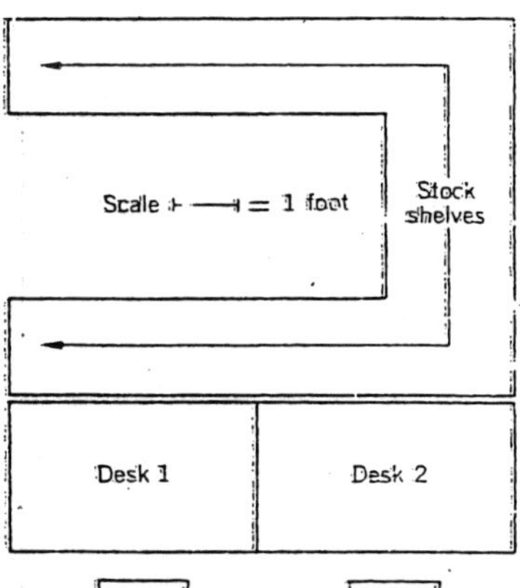

Fig. 9.1 : One of these author's sketches indicates minimum space allotments for working areas that are needed in connection with the use of basic media-production equipment units. The lazy Susan is suggested as a means of putting needed supplies for basic processes in a conveniently accessible place. The other shows a simple diagram for arranging a stockroom for bulk supplies that would be conveniently accessible to the main working areas, but which could be kept locked.

Now, as we contemplate this kind of planning, we see again the relationship of comprehensiveness of media-preparation programs to the number of teachers desiring services, and also the degree of decentralization among the various schools. We shall again seek to depict space needs in light of predicted functions and operations and then further in the light of a number of teachers and technicians at work on the processes in question. The estimates of required space for this general service and working area are as follows:

1. A work bench with space for three drawing boards and operational area. *36 square feet.*
2. One slide-selecting, sorting, and programing bench space and operation area, *25 square feet.*
3. Multipurpose workbench (pedestal type with storage underneath) and two-side working area, *64 square feet.*
4. One binding and mounting workbench with sink, plus working and access area, with underneath and overhead shelf storage areas, *66 square feet.*
5. One working and access area for refrigerator and workbench space largely for printing and duplication processes, with storage underneath and on overhead shelves, *35 square feet.*
6. Space for locating spirit duplicator and mimeo machines, offset , printing press, plus working-access area, *45 square feet.*
7. Lazy-Susan type storage rack, five feet tall, with access area for choosing labelled supplies for prescribed processes, *15 square feet.*
8. Two desk-and-chair for technicians, *45 square feet.*
9. One stock room with floor-to-ceiling shelving and bins for bulk supplies and film stock, *44 square feet.*
10. Space for one 2 × 2 inch slide duplicating and modifying unit (Heiland Repronar or similar) and access area, *30 square feet.*

Summary of General Service and Working Area: Operations in the working area that were identified in the preceding items would amount to a total of 400 square feet. See Fig. 9.1 for a checkup on the generalized space arrangements to show the requirement for personnel space in relation to equipment and materials operations.

Photographic Darkroom Services

In discussing the general service area we have not yet mentioned the need for a photographic darkroom suite in relation to all of the processes we have identified. There is always the possibility that darkroom procedures will be eliminated by the use of commercial photographic laboratory services. Later when we discuss the possibility of designating which media-preparation functions may be assigned to media headquarters and to school-building media-service centers, we may feel compelled to call for a critical decision as to whether or not in school-building centers it is essential to provide complete darkroom services. However, we can point out that there are a number of significant contributions on-the spot that darkroom operations can make. Such processes, for example, as making Kodalth negatives and positive film prints, or sharp high-contrast pager prints as parts of masters from which 2 × 2 inch slides are made, are vitally important. We should also mention the production of photo enlargements and the possibility of contributing to the process of illustrating school publications. Naturally all color film developing ought to be processed by prepaid commercial mailers. But this has been emphasized before. What we need to do now is to specify some space needs based on reasonable standards and functions.

The reader should bear in mind that we are considering operational a space needs instead of giving procedures for carrying out specific tasks, and also that we are not concerned with where such darkroom services should be made available. We now face the question as to who will use the darkroom. We assert that if darkroom services are to be made a part of media-service centers, either in each school-building or at school-system media centers, technicians ought to be available to carry on the required operations. We can no more recommend that a professional media coordinator or director of a media program spend his time in a darkroom developing film rolls and making paper or film prints than we can recommend his spending a whole day or more probing a sound system amplifier for a defective circuit.

We believe that in any large-scale media-preparation program at a school-system center a photographic darkroom service suite should be planned and staffed. If the decentralized program is sufficiently well developed then each school may also need a smaller darkroom service suite, yet as we have already pointed out, some significant media-production processes may be carried out by means of commercial photofinisher companies. We have in mind the duplication of sets of 2 × 2 inch slides, for example, for twenty or thirty science teachers in any given grade, all of which may be needed at the same time. Therefore, a whole range of possibilities opens up for photographic facilities at both central and school-building media-service headquarters. This subject will, however, be discussed in a later section. For the present, what are the possibilities for getting photographic work done?

Some Plans for Photographic Operations: The plans given here start with those most desirable operationally from the director's standpoint and end with those that provide a minimum of continuous, high-caliber service, and hence are least desirable.

Plan 1. Provide a photographic laboratory suite consisting of workroom for dryers, mounting, presses, and so on, and at least two small darkroom to facilitate simultaneous developing and printing work by more than one person at a time.

Plan 2. Provide one darkroom, approximately 9 feet by 12 feet and a small adjoining workroom consisting of a central workroom 12 feet by 20 feet (including two drawing-board tables, storage workbench, photo dryer, and workbench for picture trimming and mounting).

Plan 3. Provide a small darkroom, 9 feet by 9 feet, with an adjoining workroom of about the same size.

Plan 4. Utilize on an arranged schedule the darkroom in a new school building as close to the central media or school-building headquarters as possible.

Some Example of Photographic and Graphic Facilities: Several methods for arranging facilities were implicit in the possible plans for action in the preceding section. Basically it is the teacher who ought to have a high priority for photographic and graphic services. Hence, media-service centers in both elementary and secondary school buildings ought to include at least ones small photographic darkroom together with working areas.

In planning such photographic laboratory spaces, the following items are critical and need careful description :

1. Lighttight characteristics of the room, including proper light locks.
2. Electrical cutlets near workbenches and near sinks.
3. Exhaust fans with proper light traps.

4. Regular lights and safe lighting.
5. Running hot and cold water, and sometimes, sinks ought to have double-mixing valves and double drains.
6. Equipment such as trays, tanks, thermometer, timor clocks, enlargers, printer, light table, dryer, mounting press, sinks, and storage cabinets need to be selected and specified by make and size.

Even though the planner of the photographic suite may have the good advice of an architect, he should be forewarned that :

1. Two small darkrooms rather than one large one are needed if developing and printing processes need to be carried on by more than one person simultaneously.
2. Large print demand more handling and sink space.
3. Ventilation is a necessary feature.
4. Stainless-steel sinks are recommended.
5. Formica covering for dry benches is serviceable, but maple wood with a coating of wax is preferred by some.
6. Floor coverings of title with surfaces that are impervious to moisture are desirable.
7. A space-saving type of light lock ought to be designed and incorporated as an essential.

Space Requirements. It is conceivable that a school system would have demands for a large volume of photographic developing and printing with all the necessary related work of drying, trimming, mounting, and labelling, for various instructional uses. Hence the space requirements estimated here may have to be considered as totally inadequate for such an operation. Rather, we are considering here a suite that may be considered as minimum operational unit to be expanded as the volume of demand increases. In any event we may say that providing darkroom space is not enough. Additional space is generally needed as a working area for photographic darkroom services. We have already described the need for space in which to make masters, mount, bind and select, sort, and label, and a part of this general service area could be located in such a position as to be handily used by darkroom technicians. Thus if we already have a general service area of adequate size for media-preparation work, we need not provide a completely separate working area for the darkroom. Yet for the purpose of this estimate, we must include the workroom in order to give the need for daylight working area the emphasis it deserves. We therefore estimate the space requirements to be as follows:

1. One darkroom of 9 feet by 12 feet minimum.
2. An additional working space also of 9 feet by 12 feet for a *total of 216 square feet.*

This recommendation is essentially the same as described in *Plan 2* in the preceding discussion, and this plan may be considered as the minimum for incorporation is plans for media services in every school building. We of course see this minimum facility as an integral part of a media-service center, and not as a science club suite to be used by groups. When such use is envisioned, greatly expanded and multiple-use spaces will be required.

Motion Pictures

As we consider space needs for he school and school-system production of films, both 8 mm and 16 mm—possibly employing both magnetic and optical sound tracks, depending on the intended usage—it is easy to visualize the completely equipped and spacious commercial film production studios for television and the movies, and to make some startling though expected comparisons with the cubbyhole spaces used by some schools. It would seem obvious that schools need not go into the kind of film-production operations envisioned in comprehensive, large-scale film making. Yet we must face the need for making film clips and film cartridges for a host of teaching situations from special films for chemistry laboratory introductions to automated self-instruction systems, where media play direct teaching roles. We should also recognize the fact that in most audiovisual media centers there are spaces such as television studios, audio-program recording studios film editing and inspection stations, equipment storage, vaults for storing films, photo-service darkroom, and general service areas, all of which may contribute space for the many processes of film making. Although this situation makes it difficult to state what the minimum space requirements are, we shall attempt to itemize some of the operational needs for space even though such space may be available in other sections of a media-service center. One more fact we should note before estimates are given, namely, that according to predicted school needs some of the footage needed will be shot in outdoor places, possibly at the bank of a polluted river, in a slum area, or at a town meeting. Studio sets will also be needed, and animation stations as well, but space for shooting will be shared with the world outside the school.

Specific Space Needs in Relation to Operations: The space-need operations listed include basic indoor filming and related activities, based on the assumption that processing, printing, and sounding are done by commercial laboratories. Estimates are as follows :

1. Indoor filming activity under lights, *400 square feet.*
2. General service and working area for lettering, mounting, and chartwork; for storage of filming supplies, and for storage of cameras, accessories, and lighting equipment, *400 square feet.*
3. Space for the preparation of animation sequences, isolated from other operations to permit maximum exposure control, *40, square feet.*
4. Viewing of workprint footage, *40 square feet.*
5. Editing, splicing, and conforming footage, and for packaging footage for laboratory shipments, *54 square feet.*

Summary of Space Needs for the Production of Motion Pictures: Totalling up the operational spaces specified we see that such a minimum-sized facility as seems reasonable for predicted school-system needs would be likely to amount to *978 square feet.* We point out more that the specified operational spaces are often combinable creatively in carefully laid plans.

Grand Total of The Space-Need Estimates for Media Preparation

As soon as we total up the various estimates that we have made, the reader is likely to observe that such needs as we have indicated seem unreasonably large and generally unattainable. This is of course not true. If we point to industrial plants, we may assert that the only industrial plants that are operating under crowded and inadequate space limitations are those that will soon be going out of business. This observation naturally applies to the entire media-service areas in each school, not just for media-preparation processes. Just what is the total of our estimates? We add up the specific space-requirements as follows to answer the question :

1. 2 × 2 inch color slides (a single operating unit), *30 square feet.*
2. Polaroid slides (a single operating unit), *36 square feet.*
3. Overhead transparencies (a three-process unit), *84 square feet.*
4. Audio-program taps, *384 square feet.*
5. Videotapes, *580 square feet.*
6. Multipurpose working area, *400 square feet.*
7. Photographic darkroom services, *216 square feet.*
8. Production of motion pictures, *978 square feet.*

   Total *2,708 square feet.*

The reader may now review the space need for a school-building media-preparation area and conclude that the estimate of 700 square feet indicated there as a minimum is woefully inadequate. We should point out, however, that the estimate given was for what is referred to as basic needs, not inclusive of additional fixed and special-purpose facilities.

Possible Use of the Space Estimates: Naturally all of the space estimates made are relative to special and local needs. If a school system has inaugurated a program of rear-screen multimedia presentations as a part of firm plans for using instructional systems, them media-preparation facilities for specified types of media preparation must be provided on a priority basis. If a school has a dial-retrieval television or an audio-program tape system, then facilities, staff, and budget considerations for audio programs and videotape preparation will be necessary. Moreover, any one of the estimates may have to be increased radically, and other space estimates in the list decreased by a factor that is arrived at by balancing the many demands. For example, it may be realistic and necessary to increase single-station estimates by a factor of three or more depending on the number of personnel (teachers, teacher aides, pupils, and graphic technicians) to use them during a given school day. If a comprehensive media-preparation program is to be provided, the total space estimates suggested should be considered as a minimum requirement for the district media center with additional media facilities required in each school-building service area.

Combining Functions to Reduce Space-Need Estimates: Before we discuss the possible combination of operational spaces for multipurpose uses, we should point out that the estimate for space to prepare videotapes should not be included because such a suite would naturally be a part of a larger television program-production complex; however, we have already stated the assumptions underlying the need for videotapes as perhaps separate from television programming in the usual sense. Yet, if television activities in any given school system are comprehensive in nature, it may well be the headquarters for the special videotaping processes as well as the general program-producing capability. We can also point out that the motion picture production space, stated as a minimum of 978 square feet—which is less space than is usually allotted to a fairly large classroom is an elementary school—could be in part combined with multipurpose working areas, with film splicing and packaging areas, with viewing and listening area, with office space areas, and with television studios provided the spaces are already available and can be spared for sufficient time to accomplish the work that needs to be done within the specified time limitations. Thus it may be feasible to increase certain operational spaces to accommodate additional functions, or to provide additional conveniently accessible equipment-storage space, so that equipment units needed for a given operation may be assembled and placed on available workbenches and then dismantled and put away in designated places for the next assignment. We must not lose sight of a condition already stated, namely, the possibility of including the entire media-production facility in the plans for a large school-system television facility, where we have already suggested that the preparation area should be as large as 2,000 square feet, thus serving general as well as specific needs. The problem of combining functional spaces into workable arrangements is not an easy matter. Each case is unique and no pat answer is available, but planners may well consider the following guidelines :

1. When full-time technical personnel are employed, fewer operational spaces will be required. This means that part-time personnel, such as teachers and students, will not have to be working simultaneously at a greater number of stations. And additionally, various equipments units will

not have to go unused for many hours during a given school day. That is, each available equipment station or working area will be used more efficiently.

2. When teachers, teacher aides, pupils, and part-time technicians must use equipment units and working spaces during the school day, the greater will be the number of equipment units and working spaces that will have to be provided, and the more equipment-operating stations maintained in a state of readiness.
3. The fewer the equipment stations that are in a state of readiness, the greater will be the waste in productive capability on the part of technicians and teaching personnel, and the less the desire on the part of teachers to participate or use the services.

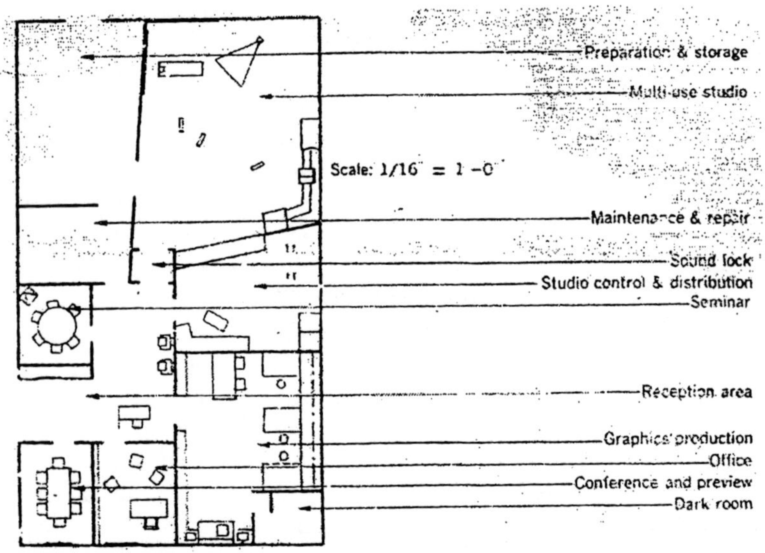

Fig. 9.2 : Note the multiuse studio in this sketch from the book by Green, *Educational Facilities with New Media,* published by DAVI of the NEA in 1966, usable for television, audio and motion picture production. Note also that this sketch does not include the other spaces that we have stressed in connection with the school's broad media distribution and use program. It is likely that some large school plans in the future will include such a media-preparation facility; it is possible that such a comprehensive facility at this sketch depicts will be more applicable, for the time being, to school district organization.

4. The fewer the ready-to-use equipment stations available in media-preparation suites the greater will be the need for storage areas.
5. When work spaces assigned for specific functions are available only by appointment, and when media-preparation projects in process cannot be left in a secured state conveniently for later resumption, the less the chances are that vital needs will be fulfilled.

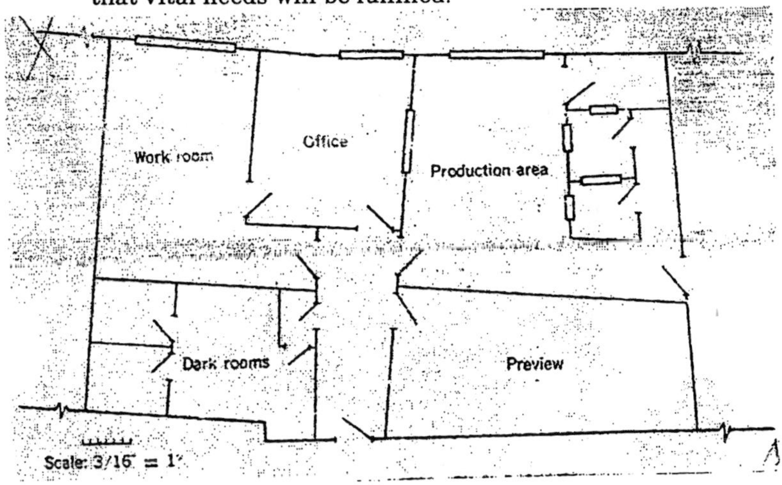

Fig. 9.3 : This is the floor plan of the audiovisual media service center at South Junic. High School, Great Nec, New York. Note an allocation of space of the media preparation program.

Organization of District-Wide Media-Preparation Services

As we look at the problem of organizing media-preparation activities on a district-wide basis, we need to focus attention on the many different kinds of services than media-preparation centers are frequently called upon to give. The following list is not comprehensive, but is presented in rather broad outline to exemplify the possibilities.

1. Produce study print pictures in sets for classroom, distribution, such as local pictures of historic sites and manufacturing processes.
2. Produce slides and filmstrips on topics needed for school use but unavailable for purchase, such as materials for social studies, language arts, business skills with local

adaptations, and materials for science-laboratory skills, including emphasis on media in self-instruction systems.

3. Make motion pictures of special processes for classroom teaching purposes such as are needed for musical processes and techniques, and athletic-skill development, including film sequences and cartridges for self-instruction processes.
4. Produce pictorial materials for student diagnosis and remedial work, such as materials needed for improving reading and speech skills.
5. Produce pictorial and graphic material for more effective communication at public-relations meetings, and also programs for radio and television.
6. Handle picture-mounting processes for all pictorial materials acquired for distribution.
7. Produce study displays, and exhibit material such as dioramas.
8. Make up illustrations for school publications, including improvement in design of mimeo bulletins as well as formal printed publications for wider circulation.
9. Offer advisory and consultative services to school media coordinators, to school-club groups, and to teachers for their own photographic, graphic, and self-instruction projects.
10. Microfilm important records.
11. Provide such photocopying services as are needed for the school's record-keeping system.
12. Provide photocopier services to include paper and reflex spirit masters for instructional worksheet applications.
13. Prepare overhead transparencies.
14. Make photographic plates for photo-offset printing processes.
15. Make mimeo stencils and provide duplication services.
16. Plan and produce audio-program tapes for electronic learning laboratories at all levels of instruction.
17. Duplicate audio-program tapes in quantity.
18. Plan and produce videotapes for transmission to all schools via closed-circuit facilities for both large-group applications and individual uses in electronic carrel situations.
19. Mass produce printed labels for media items to be distributed to all schools.
20. Provide photographic darkroom services to meet school-building instructional needs.

Location of Media-Preparation Facilities

Where should the services we have mentioned be performed? In the preceding section the various spaces were described in relation to specific media that teachers need, but we must be quick to recognize that there are also what we may refer to as administrative needs, and a glance at the foregoing list will reveal such items. The issue is, to what degree should media preparation services be centralized? To what degree should they be carried on in school-building media-service centers? We turn to a discussion of this cluster of problems, with attention devoted first to the centralization pattern of organization.

Organizing Media-Preparation Activities at Headquarters: Since media-preparation programs are common, although differing as to scope and volume of service, a large number of administrator and media people have come to grips with the problems of where to locate facilities and how to get the work of media-preparation accomplished. One of the patterns of organization for getting this work done is to locate the facilities at the district wide-media-services center. The main advantage of this placement falls to the district office staff, since overall district problems are more easily given highest priority. Under this arrangement, services for specific instructional needs for specific teachers and specific schools may not be as easily or speedily met. In other words, it appears that when media-preparation services are set up in central media headquarters it is easier to control the processes that get priority, and also those that do get highest priority are likely to be the ones that meet general needs that may or may not be purely instructional in nature. The following examples will make this clear.

1. General services like photostating and microfilming school records, making up illustrations for school publications, catalogs, and curriculum guides, making photographic plates for photo-offset printing processes, producing media for public-relations meetings, making sets of slides for self-instruction processes on a system-wide supply basis, and handling production of study-prints for a given curriculum topic for distribution to all schools are all district-wide media services that may choke off many other vital needs for specific uses.

2. When a citywide school system has inaugurated a special program such as dial-retrieval television, media-production programs may be so controlled as to give complete staff and financial support to one kind of medium to the exclusion of others.

3. The citywide center is likely to be less conveniently accessible to teachers who need to discuss specifications for media sequences, therefore the headquarters program is likely to function on a longer time-lag basis between request date and fulfillment date, or not function at all in relation to specific teacher request.

Need for Central Media-Production Services: The generalized listing of common media-production services indicates many activities that are best carried on by centralized facilities, staff, and responsibilities. We can identify such specific operations : (1) supplying photographic darkroom services in connection with school-system and school-building instructional needs; (2) providing an advisory and consultative service to school-building media coordinators; (3) mass producing media items in sequence for all schools; (4) systematically producing videotapes to meet overall curriculum plans; (5) providing mass duplication of audio-program tapes for electronic learning laboratories in all subjects where the use of this medium has been systematized and scheduled firmly as in individualization programs; (6) producing media for administrators' presentations; (7) handling the work of printing school publication, including preparation of illustrative materials. There are also many other uses, some of which have been indicated at the beginning of this section. All of these generally applicable services are vital, and it would appear that many of them cannot be feasibly handled by school-building media-preparation centers. It seems quite obvious then that in the face of burgeoning technology, a centralized media-production facility is inescapable. The problem in this case will be to supply the staff and facilities needed to expand services to the point where specific teacher needs are being met in addition to those district-wide services that are generally available.

Organizing Media-Preparation Activities in Each School Building. There are many who insist that the only way to get specially prepared media items for pinpointed uses in each school building is to organize media-preparation services on the spot. Then and only then will teachers as individuals get the fast service needed. Teachers say, "We need to be able to make our own media, and if the necessary supplies are at hand we can make them as soon as we can design them in response to a specific need." In the preceding section space needs were discussed in light of known operations and in this connection we must note that teachers may have to have convenient arrangements under which to work for short periods of nonteaching or nonscheduled time. Student crews and even full-time technicians and clerks, as teachers aides, may never get what they need if they have to submit request through media coordinators to media headquarters. This is especially true in extensive metropolitan areas. It appears simply impossible to consider 500 school-building staffs calling for specific media-preparation services on a day-to-day or week-to-week basis. Yet it also seems next to impossible to set up 500 media-preparation suites staffed with technicians and stocked with supplies, but it may not be impossible after all to develop arrangements where most of the needs can be met. We ought to consider the nature of the school-building media-preparation service needs. Teachers, as we have already pointed out, want others (students, the media specialist, and coordinator) to make their slides and transparencies, and one can hardly blame them, but we also know that many teachers will carry out their own media-making operations if the environment is conducive. Therefore, we have the responsibility to provide a climate in which teachers can and will participate at an optimum level in this necessary instructional activity. On-the-spot facilities and assistance constitute one route to such desirable participation.

Some Important School-Building Media-making Operations by and for Teachers: Earlier we considered media-preparation services and related them to centrally operated facilities. Now we consider several of those services that seem to be best carried out at the school-building level. Some of these are as follows :

1. Make transparencies according to day-to-day or week-to-week needs, such as would be made by teachers themselves, or student helpers or technicians, or by teachers' aides in team-teaching situations.

2. Design, make masters, and run off instructional sheets using reflex spirit masters, or other duplicating stencil or master processes.
3. Plan and prepare 2 × 2 inch slide sequences for visual presentations using current events, maps, and pictorials.
4. Use lettering devices to make posters, captions, display titles, as parts of student research and creative project work.
5. Plan and produce audio-program tapes for electronic laboratories, and for classroom multi-group activities.
6. Plan and produce videotapes for school-building closed-circuit television transmission, using inexpensive equipment for special self-evaluational purposes, or more sophisticated taping equipment for classroom or school-building studio-recording situations.
7. Plan and make sketches, diagrams, mounted pictures for use with classroom television-display (or image-magnification) system.
8. Mount pictures and caption materials for classroom displays.
9. Produce audio and visual materials to meet specific teaching needs both for large and small-group use for exchange with other teachers of similar grade and subject interest, such as bulletin board display, audio-program tapes, slide sets, transparencies, and instructional sheets.
10. Use motion picture cameras for making film clips and cartridges.

Need for School-Building Media Preparation Services: As team teaching techniques develop, and as electronic learning laboratories and other technologically supported teaching methods become a firm part of the daily teaching process, we shall have to face up to the need for media-making facilities, staff and supplies. We have already pointed out the effect of newer roles of audiovisual media on the urgent need for special-purpose material which take on new significance when teachers communicate with large groups of students. Nor do students go into carrels today just to read a book, but also to listen to audio-program tapes, or to study a videotape, or to be programed through a set of slides that teaches them how to carry out basic skills. Without school-building facilities, many of the week-to-week instructional needs for media will not be met. As we have said before, the availability of the right climate, close at hand, means that teachers can learn new teaching methods and try their fledgling wings until a new desirable security develops.

Optimum Decentralization and Centralization. If we blend the ingredient operational processes of the foregoing centralized and decentralized patterns of organisations we have the answer to our problems for making media for modern teaching needs. It is obvious that most centralized media-making programs cater to general school-system needs, or generally get lost in them because of lack of financial support. It is equally understandable how school-building media-making facilities and programs cater in concentrated fashion is week-to-week teaching needs of the school's professional staff. When these basic patterns are blended in optimum balance, school-system media centers concentrate or district needs and on the needs that can be met for all schools according to carefully laid plans, and leave to schools, after facilitating the development of adequate services, the operation of programs designed to help teachers carry out their various instructional tasks. Such localized programs may therefore put proper emphasis on both teachers and their presentations and on pupil needs as well, to make sure that the carrels and machine rooms are properly supplied. How best to separate the services that are to be given will depend on the states of local technological development, on budgetary support, and on the innovative needs of a given school system. Priorities will have to be established in the light of valid plans, with additions of new services being made year by year as the means become available. Although we shall not rule out the possibility in our own deliberations of a strong and comprehensive, centralized, media-making center, we shall now look toward an optimum balance between the assignment of media-preparation functions to media headquarters and to school building media-service center. The media program director has a difficult job on his hands to set up this balance, and an even more difficult task to obtain financial support to implement his plans. When this has been accomplished, he may move by appropriate stages toward the acquisition of the needed equipment and staff, and undertake the in service education programs that will speed teachers on their way to desirable change.

Acquisition of Needed Equipment for Media Preparation

Since the purchase of equipment units goes hand-in-hand with local instructional needs and available operational spaces, we need not set up at this point a massive listing of desirable equipment and supplies. Instead we shall stick to some high-priority items in line with generally needed media for school uses, concentrating attention on visualization processes rather than on audio-program and videotape preparation. Audio-program production, which is generally related to single-medium audio presentations, is often tied to visualization processes through tape cartridges or by means of tape-slide programmed sequences. In Chapter 10, videotape processes and needs will be added since that chapter will deal with implementation of television-program services.

Mounting

Dry Mounting Press
Laminating Equipment
Mounting Cloth (Muslin or Chartex)
Materials for Framing with Tape
Mounting for 3-D Materials

Coloring

Air Brush
Commercial Adhesive Materials
Plastic Inks
Other Inks
Slide Crayons
Tempera
Water Colors

Lettering

Mechanical Lettering Devices
Cut-Out Letters
Felt-Point Pen
Rubber Stamp
Primary Typewriter
Stencil
Paste-Up Letters
Embossograph

Photography

35 mm Camera
4 × 5 Camera
Enlarger
Polaroid
Darkroom
Copy Equipment
16 mm Camera
2¼-2¼ Camera
Filmstrip Camera

Reproduction

Reflex Copy
Other Copy Processes
Mimeograph
Ditto
Diazo
Silk Screen
Multilith
Line-O-Scribe
Xerox

The Nature of Equipment Needs for Media Preparation Services: In their national survey report, published in 1963. Faris and Moldstad reported that, "The most frequently produced visual instructional materials for classroom or television use were 2 × 2 slides, photographs, graphic materials, mounted pictures and overhead transparencies." As a part of this survey, the authors developed a listing of categories and items indicating the nature of equipment and supplies that merits restatement here to focus attention on some of the basic media-preparation operations being carried on by schools.

No listing for purposes of our discussion, least of all an index of the technological state of the art, can be formulated that would state with any degree of certainty the relative merits or priorities for acquisition by schools and school-system centers for their proposed media-making services the list just quoted is no exception. We have already pointed out that darkroom services may be neither necessary nor feasible, since so many desirable processes can be carried out without on-the-spot film developing and printing. Also in the quoted list, several of the processes and materials may be eliminated or substituted in favor of local production needs. For example, small offset printing presses, and such operations as silk-screen and multith reproduction may be or possibly ought to be handled centrally. Under photography processes, schools may wish to add a slide duplicating unit, and eliminate all except 35 mm, Polaroid, and the 16 mm motion picture cameras.

One of the values of the list is its categorization of processes, for any school system or school-building media-making center will inescapably be engaged with some of the processes mentioned under each of the categories. Another important point to keep in mind while studying the list is to treat each equipment item or process as a category for listing specific items of supplies that would have to be procured and kept in stock to carry on the processes. For example, what kinds of supplies would be needed for making use of the dry mounting press, the 35 mm camera, or for reproducing transparencies by the reflex process?

Since we are focusing attention on instructional needs rather than on how the functions will be assigned to either (or both) central or decentralized media-making service centers, we ought to make a straight equipment list without including at this time any reference to supplies or the media to be made. With the list, we have provided a cost estimate—with the knowledge that prices may vary greatly. The following list is an arbitrary one, excluding darkroom equipment entirely, but will nonetheless be helpful, especially in the light of everyday instructional needs of teachers.

	Equipment Items	Cost Estimate
1.	35 mm Single Lens Reflex Camera, plus adapter rings and close-up lenses, direct-reading light meter, blue filter, suitable copy stand with lights.	$ 280
2.	Polaroid Industrial View Camera, plus extra lens for 2 × 2 inch slide images, copy stand and lights.	800
3.	Polaroid (Regular Copymaker) Camera, plus stand, lights, and close-up lenses (3¼ × 4 inch slides).	250
4.	Slide Duplicating Unit (such as Heiland Repronar) and accessories.	360
5.	Reflex Photo-Copier, single sheet unit.	400
6.	Reflex Photo-Copier, book copier unit.	380
7.	Diazo-Coated Film Transparency-making Equipment (one operating system complete).	300
8.	Mimeograph Duplicating Equipment Unit (electrically operated) and stand.	450
9.	Spirit Master Duplicating Unit (electrically operated) and stand.	370
10.	Primary Typewriter, manual.	250
11.	Dry-Mount Press (24-inch min. model, open on three sides).	300
12.	16 mm Motion Picture Camera and three-lens turret, plus suitable tripod.	750
13.	Two Paper Cutters, one 24 inch, the other 15 inch. Two units.	80
14.	One Set of Lights (consisting of five reflector type flood lights each on a tripod).	100
	Total	$ 5,070

In the foregoing listing we have omitted audio-program and television-program taping equipment. Neither have we indicated items such as special lettering pens. These we shall refer to later under supplies. The equipment units just listed seem to be the most necessary items for a media-making center in each school building. Reference to the space-requirement sections will reveal an estimate of how much space will be needed for these items.

General Equipment Selection Problems: It can readily be seen how the purchase of equipment has to be specified in light of special needs and operations. Hence in some instances multiple units have to be purchased and installed, while in other situations but one operational unit of a kind such as a 35 mm camera and stand needs to be specified. Centralization and decentralization policies will strongly influence equipment-selection decisions. It seems almost certain that the equipment needs at media program headquarters will include at least one each of the basic items of equipment to meet the needs of media leadership personnel and for curriculum and administrative staff members as well. It is doubtful that smaller media-producing school-building centers would or should be called on to divert their specific need programs to handle additional services for headquarters. Media program directors will doubtlessly have to develop printing press and sophisticated illustration-produccing units, very possibly also sophisticated and comprehensive darkroom and motion picture production, services. Hence we see the need for a wide variety of equipment units, and the additional vexing problem of finding enough space in which to arrange and operate them.

Acquisition of Supplies Needed for Media Preparation

The Nature of the Media-Making-Supplies Problem: In preceding paragraphs we have discussed the need for equipment units and space in which to operate them, but we have barely mentioned the most burdensome problem of all. This is the problem of providing the raw stock items out of which media materials are fashioned. Providing needed raw materials is a burdensome problem for it is complex, continuous, and very expensive. Even when a good system has been worked out for purchase there is the ever-present problem of inventory and safeguarding against theft and waste. It is not generally realized by teachers, principals, and other administrators, how expensive high-volume use of transparency film, photographic film and even assorted papers is. It is relatively easy to locate a unit of equipment on a table in a production area and schedule its use, but to supply the unit with raw stock from a bulk-supply stockroom, or order weekly supplies from a central warehouse using correct identification codes, and to keep waste to a minimum, are operations that need to be worked out with care. Media program directors and school-building media corrdinators should be aware of the cost relationship that frequently exists between a given equipment unit and the supplies to keep it operating. Using reasonably highquality equipment, such as a $140 (low bid quote) single lens reflex camera solely for 2 × 2 inch slides, and a $ 400 reflex photocopier (dry process), used solely for transparencies as examples, we can predict that each year the cost for but one kind of basic supply item for each equipment unit will equal or exceed the original cost of the equipment.

Identification of Needed Supply Items: Media program directors for school systems are faced with the job of identifying raw materials for making special media for distribution to each of the school-building producing centers as soon as they are organized for service. If his own center is organized to produce media as needed for all techers, the director must identify itmes and stock them in appropriate quantities at headquarters or in a central school-system werehouse. If school-building media coordinators are themselves in charge of ordreing their supplies, using budegted allotments for the purpose, then they must identify those items that are essential for meeting the basic needs of the teachers under their guidance. The mistake is sometimes made of identifying a wide range of itmes to make possible variations in procedur, many different color combinations, many styels and sizes of letters, many sizes, colors. and patterns of pressure-sensitive tapes, for making masters and flats as are essential for transparencies and 2 × 2 inch slides. The point is that it is better to maintain an adequate, continuous stock of a smaller number of basic items, than to try to have on hand great variety but be out of stock at critical times. Another example would be stocking color film and processing mailers for making 2 × 2 inch slides. It would be far better to stock a generally serviceable 20-exposure roll of film and an equal quantity of prepaid processing mailers than to stock many different kinds of film for color slides. Also, it may be unwise to stock for general use black and white 35 mm film for the 2 × 2 inch slide process, since in this case darkroom services to make negatives first will be a necessity. When the immensity of the list of supply items is recognized, it will become obvious that resturctions of one kind or another may become necessary in light of basic operational needs at both citywide media headquarters and at school-buliding media-preparation centers. We now turn to some lists of supplies related to basic operations; however, the reader should not think of this listing as generally applicable to all school situations. Furthermore, new items will have to be added and other items substituted from time to time. Also, the reader should recognize that not all of the specifications and information needed for reordering are included. The reader may note that since the present listings are based on actual inventory cards, a categorization process is displayed that may not flt other situations.

Lettering Supplies and Devices

This category contains 101 specific items including scriber pens, ruling pens, speedball pens, commpasses, heat-resistant adhesive-type letters and numbers, adhesive patterns and symbols, stencils, inks, nylon-tip pens, LeRoy templates, Wrico templates, Wrioc bursh and manuscript pens, grease pencils, Keuffel and Esser transparency marking pencils, tweezers, scissors, rulers, triangles, and assorted styli.

The foreging list indicates the content on one card for each item mentioned, for eight of the fifteen categories in this particular system. Each card has a seriatim number and also a category number. Within each category a decimal numbering system is used. Stock cards can then be truned over to a typist in any grouping according to need and then resorted for filing in the inventory card box. The other categories in the system that has been excerpted are *Flannel Board process, Darkroom Supplies, Display Suppiles, Dispensers, Sprays, Cements and Thinners,* and *Equipment.* Care must be taken to not duplicate inventory cards in any system devised, and thus since some items are used in many ways for a number of purposes, it seems best to categorize multiple-purpose item under useful headings such as *paper, tapes, lettering supplies* and the like where materials have several characteristics in common.

Citywide media program director and the media corrdinators in school-building centers cannot help but realize that unless the right supplies are on hand at the right time, little if any media-preparation work will be completed. We shall turn our attention to several management problems a little later, but right now we ought to bring up again the matter of obtaining staff members to give needed assistance in the media-making program. We have learned by observation how complex the problem is of getting the right supplies for the right processes, and we know that media directors and coordinators themselves will not be able to devote more time than that required for supervision of a system already designed and established. Therefore we must look for help from a number of people who may possess varying degress of talent in the media-making process.

Staff for Media-Preparation Activities

As teachers begin to increase their used of media, and even begin to design and fabricate thier own, they will not be backward in making known their demands. This is true regardless of the level of instruction. When the writer organized a do-it-yourself media-preparation program at the university level, not only instructors, but full professors came to learn how to make their own slides and transparencies. Teachers at every level will do the same-not all, but some will. Sometimes professors said, "Let me send my graduate assistants, I am busy on research and teaching. Won't you make these slides for me? May I send my secretary?" We know that even though some teachers would make their own media, they prefer to get help, the more the better. Television teachers, because of their sophistication in media-use techniques and the time-consuming nature of the TV program, demand more insistently and more consistently that artists be assigned to their support. we have already pointed out the findings of Faris and Moldstad in this regard. They found in their survey that 37 per cent of the teachers queried would make their own media, 41 per cent felt the most satisfacory arragement would be to have the audiovisual specialist make them, 14 per cent would accept the work of students as a satisfactory arrangement, and the remaining 8 per cent believed that a hired artist would be the best plan for getting their media-making work done. By comparison, all of the television teachers wanted full media-making support, with 77 per cent being in favor of having an artist do their work.

The reader is well aware after the discussions that modern-day media service programs simply cannot be operated by a one-man combination of leader, manager, technician and clerk. Personnel standards have been quoted and emphasised. But now we reiterate that to embark on a media design-and preparation program without staff assistance, especially in light of the other duties already set forth, is sheer nonsense. So we wish to state what some of the possibilities are, bearing in mind the various levels of activity and possible patterns of organization.

1. Organize first a media-making center at headquarters and employ a media design-and preparation specialist, in a professional position. Supply him with a graphic technician to handle darkroom and other technical operations in providing needed services. Employ a crew of part-time high-school students on an after school basis. Make as many services as possible available to all schools.

2. Organize a central media-making facility, and carry on limited district-wide services at headquarters. Organize additional media-making facilities, equipment units, and staff in each elementary and secondary school, and expand school-building operations at an optimum pace to the following satisfactory levels:

(a) Start with services to teachers who will make their own media, with a part-time technician, or preferably a teacher released from half-time teaching to head the program. Such a staff member would train a crew of student workers and personally assist the teachers with the work of designing and planning media, and with equipment operations and supplies. Hopefully teacher aides may be trained to carry on routine processes under this arrangement.

(b) Move to a level of operations involving a part-time graphics technician who will expand the service program from a do-it-yourself to a we-will-do-it-for-you basis, restricting available operations to such commonly needed media as overhead transparencies and slides. Teacher aides where normally available will assist specified groups or teams of teachers as needed.

(c) Develop a high-level program using a part-time or full-time professional person to aid teachers in their design and planning work to develop special instructional systems, using in addition a full-time technician in large schools to carry out equipment operations, maintain inventories, and meet standards of quality. A part-time secretary will work as a part of this staff-to handle clerical operations. Teachers will handle design, planning, and sequencing work after school or during free periods, and the technical staff, assisted by available teacher aides, will handle routine construction on work during times when the preparation areas are relatively free. The media program coordinator for the school will provide leadership and managment services, and maintain proper connections with the citywide media program director. The media program leader at headquarters and the school-building media coordinator will have to make sure that all phases of the media-perparation program are being balanced in light of system-wide curriculum needs, such as the need to mass produce audio-program tapes and scheduled multimedia presentations. They will have to arrive at an optimum balance in separating media-preparation functions at their respective centers.

Such plans are proposed in light of burgeoning technology. Electronic learning laboratories in each school, large-scale and comprehensive television-service programmes, and the scheduled use of media-supported instructional systems, opeating for individualization as well as large-group presentations, are all a part of a new and seemingly inescapable environment. We have already indicated the problems that will attend such technological advancement in schools from the standpoint of providing facilities, equipment, materials, and staff, but if teachers are to make their own media, or design and plan media materials for technicians to produce, then the implementation of in-service education programmes will have to go hand in hand with the solution to the other problems mentioned. We have of course already discussed the significance of this aspect of the media programme director's duties in general. Now we turn our attention to the need for in-service education as it is needed by media-making activities and programmes.

In-Service Education for Media-Preparation Activities

Technological mindedness does not come easy to some teachers. We discussed the *change* process earlier in this volume, and emphasised that teachers who undertake innovative methods either of their own volition or as a result of encouragement from supervisory personnel, need continual assistance. When we look at the nature of this assistance we recognise at once the need for instruction on the one hand and environmental facilitation on the other. Inviting facilities to undertake new kinds of activity appeal to many, and although we once felt that all we had to do was to help the willing, this may have been a way of saying that it really didn't matter if innovative methods were used or not. We should look therefore to effective methods of in-service education that pin-point the objective to be achieved in all who by some previous agreements are to engage in any given new process.

Pinpointing Needed Performance: When facilities, supplies, convenient arrangements, and a service organisation are provided for carrying on a number of operational processes, then it is essential to analyse the processes to determine the skills that are needed by teachers. In any of the operational processes for making media, there are difficult and highly professional skills, and simple constructional skills easy enough so that they may be developed by fifth-graders. If, for example, we consider the making of overhead transparencies, or Polaroid and 2 × 2 inch colour slides, should teachers be taught to concentrate on the professional job of selecting and visualising ideas and relationships and on the making of *masters* and *flats*—or taught mainly to carry on routine equipment-operation processes? When a crew is made available for the routine processing, then of course teachers as professionals may put more time in on the former instead of the latter. This means, then, that in in-service programmes an optimum inhance will be developed between needed creative work and the routine work of equipment operation. Under these conditions of balance, demonstrations of equipment operation for the purpose of showing results and standards will suffice in a great many cases. Teachers need to work together on image-changing activities, the most fruitful of all of which will be creative work on masters and flats and the creative work of selecting source materials and arranging symbols. Many teachers will need help in the process of designing visual presentations, for these in essence are the stimuli that elicit pupil responses. This process calls for extreme sophistication when the stimuli and response phases are arranged by the teacher to operate apart from overt teacher control. When only those teachers who will consent to do their own work are entitled to use a media-making facility, then of course the two instructional goals must go hand in hand. This is the kind of skill identification that must be carried out by planners of in-service programmes, but this and other kinds of vital action have already been given the emphasis. However in this specific framework of reference we ought to deal with the identification of in-service education target groups.

Pinpointing in-Service Education Groups: In this vital process of instructing teachers in new methods, in-service education planners must make decisions on a priority basis. In-service education in media-making processes may have to proceed along priority lines within groups of teachers of a given grade or subject. Such priorities are of course arrived at by effective cooperative action between media-programme and other curriculum and administrative personnel. Hence, although we need to instruct teachers in general, groups may have to be arrange and taught in an established sequence, marshaling all of the available capability to inaugurate innovative programmes of wide application in the curriculum. Curriculum revision in science and social studies programmes, or the inauguration of video-tape production demanding heavy media support, or the activation of multimedia presentations for large-group instruction in both elementary and secondary schools are good examples of processes that may demand priority arrangements. Such needs may not exist one year, but may burgeon the next with the completion of new school buildings containing hitherto unavailable spaces requiring new procedures.

Increasing the Impact of Media-Making Activities Through Exchange: In-service education planners and teachers have not yet widely applied methods for gaining maximum benefit from in-service education in the field of media-preparation activities through cooperative exchange efforts. The need to buy ready made media will of course become acute in the years ahead on an unprecedented scale, but this is also true of the process of making audiovisual media for special purposes. Thus we emphasize the need for the coordination of teacher efforts along priority lines. Teachers and in-service education activity planners may, great if they choose to organise such cooperative efforts, make great gains in the availability of special-purpose media. Audio tapes may be rerecorded easily, slide sets may be duplicated inexpensively, and once the masters have been made, additional sets of transparencies may be produced in quantity. Such media production may, through in-service education planning, be made by different groups of teachers or by several teachers working as individuals, and thus one teacher may make five transparencies for a unit in third-grade science and get back fifty for the remaining units in the subject, all of which may be coordinated with the same subject in the next grade. Or as another example, each teacher in the group of ten sixth-grade social studies teachers, after appropriate planning activity, could make five masters for subsequent colour-slide photography. The slides could then be combined into the originally planned set, duplicated and given to each teacher permanently as a set of fifty 2 × 2 inch colour slides in a carousel projector tray ready for repetitive projection. The possibilities are many, but the process demands leadership and management skill, coordination, and willing teacher cooperation. As we have said, technical assistance in carrying on the routine processing is essential, otherwise such valuable projects bog down and get lost, not for lack of professional creativity, but for hours of routine drudgery. As we have also mentioned before, we need to move toward the stratification of teaching talents, and the foregoing example is one way of emphasizing high-level professional activity and adding to it the massive cummulative effect of well directed cooperative endeavor.

Some Observations on Cost

We need not treat the subject of cost in precise detail, nor can this be done, since there is no standard by which we can predict what a media-making programme will cost a school system. The variables seem infinite. Yet there is no reason why we should not continue the process so frequently used of making a reasonable estimate based not so much on common practice, but on some conservative views of the future. We ought to be forgiven if we: (1) eliminate from consideration the cost of operational space in a school building, (2) assume that each school will devote enough space in which to operate the basic equipment units listed earlier, (3) assume that the citywide media-programme headquarters has twice the equipment and materials allotment and twice the staff for media-making purposes as each of the school building centers, (4) assume that each elementary and secondary school would have equally extensive media-making programmes with equal staffs, (5) assume that the volume and comprehensiveness of operations are equal in all schools, and finally if, (6) we use a media-making facility in a school building as the base unit on which cost is estimated, thus making possible a total estimate for any school system of a given number of school plants.

Cost Per School Operating Unit: We shall now make estimates for each of the following basic types of expenditure.

Equipment and Supplies

Operating equipments units (one each) as previously listed, plus two additional 35 mm SLR camera units, one additional Thermo-Fax photo-copier unit, and one additional spirit duplicator	$6,400
Bulk Supplies for media-making processes	$5,000
Subtotal	$11,400

Staff

(a) Media Coordinator, 1/4 time	$2,500
(b) Secretary, 1/2 time	$2,100
(c) Graphic artist and technician full time	$7,000
(d) Part-time helpers, students, hourly, basis, after school	$1,000
Subtotal	$12,600
Grand Total of Initial Expenditures	$24,000

Now we can at least approximate the cost of reasonably sophisticated operating media-preparation unit. According to our original assumptions, we might reason that the headquarters unit would pay out $12,800 for its equipment, going more heavily into publication printing activity or into other special forms of media-preparation work, with the recurring annual expenditure of $35,200. In the school-building estimate, equipment would cost (according to our estimates and assumptions) $ 6,400 with a recurring annual cost of $17,600.

Such estimates in may be shocking to some school administrators and even to prospective media programme directors and coordinators. Media preparation costs need not be disturbing at all, and probably wouldn't be, except for the fact that until recent years, any increase in school-operation costs was cause for alarm and preventive action on the part of the so-called citizens and finance-control boards to keep the taxes down. We of course have not attempted to be a source of shock to anybody; but rather we set out to probe the future quite realistically, even though we did exceed perhaps the present central tendency. Now as we look ahead to a school system and count the cost for operating media-making centers in 500 schools plants, or 20, or 10, we can come to grips with ideas of over-all costs. Whether in actuality media-production costs will be over or under the figures we arrived at is a matter of variables in the day-to-day operation. We have said before that trained staff members, equipment, and materials are no inexpensive, but in the biggest and most crucial business in our time we had better not be lacking in vision.

Management of media-Preparation control Systems

Any school-building or citywide media program leader will soon realize that media preparation services may prove to be the tail that wagged the dog as far as time and work schedules are concerned. This is why we have repeatedly emphasized that this media program leader cannot allow himself to tackle another burdensome job such as media preparation is, without adequate support. Those who believe that a media leader can spent hours operating graphic equipment, lettering instructional media for teachers. or assisting teachers make their own, posses little if any innight into the difficulties of meeting a broad spectrum of demands for service. We therefore now consider some of the managemnt processes for media-perparation services that the director or coordinator must organize and implement. First, we shall consider the control system that restricts the degree of choice in different media that can be made, or the processes unable in any given media process.

Control System for Restricting the Range of Media-Making Processes

Nature of the Problem: Earlier we attempted to provide an opportunity for the reader to develop an idea of the tremendous number of items that have to be stocked in order to carry on media-Perparation activities. Even though we conisder factors other than expense in connection with supplies, it is not always feasible to provide teacher with every known material. We can use as an example, the case of a teacher who wants to make quickly a transparency of a single sheet or map from a periodical. We shall assume that she will use the dry-process photocopier. Should she be provided with blue negative Them to-Fax Type 128; black line on blue film background, Type 129; or black line on colorless background, Type 127? Take as another example, The case of a teacher who wishes to copy a black and white diagram in a book, making it a 2 x 2 inch slide. The teacher normally makes up color slides. Now since the color film employed may generally be used to make a satisfactory black and white slide by the regular color reversal process, the use of black and white film requiring darkroom processing and printing from negative to positive may well be denied. We may well also ask the question as to whether both diazo-coated film and dry-process transparencies ought to be made available as basic processes, and if diazo-coated film is made available, how complete should the stock be ? polaroid film for slides, the types of marker pens, the size and style of lettering sheets, kinds of slide-binding frames and mounts, all may have to be limited in availability. Once the identification of specific items has been made. Sufficient stock must be maintained to permit wide use under quality-control conditions.

Suggested Management: The school-building media coordinator, and the citywide media director should take joint action on this plan, The citywide director may implement such plans for limitation on a system-wide basis. He would have to set up, in this case, a plan to standardize a stock list. Once such a list has been created, the media coordinator at the school-building center will issue the stock as needed. The coordinator may, of course, be in a position to make his own selection, basing his decisions on the advice of key teachers and assistants. The implementation of such a plan is dependent on a number of factors, such as financial support, the number of technical and clerical assistants available, and the degree of sophistication of teachers in design and visualization.

System for the Control of Media-Making Supplies

We now turn to another problem in control that must be solved, namely, the control of media-preparation supplies.

Nature of the Problem: The most vexing problem of all in connection with media-making activities by teachers or technicians, is the handling of supplies. To order, arrange, inventory, issue them to teachers constitutes a clerical job of such magnitude that to disregard it or treat it lightly is to bring the program to ruin.

Suggested Management: We shall indicate a number of steps that can be taken by leadership personnel which may constitute a suitable plan of action. Actually, the steps imply the kinds of conditions that must be maintained if the problem is to be solved,. The essential steps are as follows:

1. Install shelves on open walls near operating equipment units to provide a limited supply of needed items.
2. Maintain one or more mobile carts with an assortment of supplies for specific media-making jobs.
3. Provide for bulk storage that can be under lock and key. The most desirable way to do this is to provide a stockroom cage, or other room set aside for the orderly arrangement of supplies. such arrangments as separate stockrooms are usually found where programms are characterized by comperhensive and high-volume services.Under these circumstances, however, there has to be a stockroom clerk. Without the clerk, a responsible individual has to unlock the area for resupply of equipment units.
4. Inventory cards, one for each item must be typed out with full information for recodering. Such cards may then be turned over to a secretary for ordering. Content on the cards would be copied on order forms and sent to media supply

headquatters or to the schools system central warehouse. Suddenly running out of stock is an ever-present problem that must be solved by setting up a workable inventorying process. Schools may not for a while build up their support personnel to the point wherein the media-production-center inventory control will be 100 oer cent effective. Arrangement of items in stock so that visual surveillance is convenient, helps, but a rigorously followed system of periodical check-up on the available stock, especially insofar as key items are concerned is a prime essential. To this end, a running inventory may have to be maintained on log sheets posted in a central place, so that when film rolls, for example, are issued, the quantity is indicated together with the remaining number of items in stock at that issuing point.

5. Media-making supplies should be arranged so that similar materials are together-for example, pressure-sensitive tapes, lettering pens, and paper. Such plans for arrangment and storage make it possible to develop a high degree of neatness control as well.
6. Stock item arrangements, both bulk-storage and operational-station supplies, such as Thermo-Fax type 127 transparency sheets in readiness at the photocopier machine, have to be checked once or twice daily.
7. Set up strict policies for issuing media-making supplies. For example, a set of rules and regulations, as simple as possible for execution by technicians and clerks, ought to cover the conditions under which rolls of colour film will be issued. One suggestion is that cameras and rolls of film are not to be issued for use outside of the media-making center. A possible exception to this rule could be the use of a camera for field-trip expeditions or for pupil productions under the immediate supervision of the teacher. Saleguards should be set up a against the abuse of equipment and especially unauthorized use of materials and equipment.

Control System for Providing Assistance to Teachers

Quite apart from inservice education programs, such as special workshops, there is a need to set up a control system to give assistance to teachers.

Nature of the Problem. Teachers need a number of different kinds of assistance. They need help in operating equipment units, and they need to be guided through processes that sometimes they do not do frequently enough to maintain speed and error-free performance. In order for teachers to do high-quality work when using media-making equipment, the units must be in a state of readiness. The need for continual adjustments on the equipment ought to be kept to a minimum, Also, clearly stated step-by step directions for procedure ought to be posted near each equipment unit. Unless these conditions prevail, there is liable to be high percentage of poor-quality work and excessive waste. Another aspect of the problem is the need to give assistance, on a priority basis, to specified groups or teachers who must meet teaching schedules in specified programs. large-groups presentations, media-preparation work for television, multimedia presentation commitments may give rise to problems in giving all the help that is needed to meet deadlines. Also teachers who are competent at equipment operation could work alone, but may find that space is not available, or that the equipment is in use.

Suggested Management: In order to maintain the effciency of the media preparation facilities and meet instructional needs, we suggest the following kinds of action:

1. Make an analysis of each equipment operation station and write down specific lockactions, even to posting a photograph of required arrangements for stock items and pieces of equipment. Students and technicians will then follow the directions at each station when checking through the entire media-preparation suite. Such readiness check-ups must be made daily, and preferably following the use of the equipments station by each teacher. This cheek-up work must also be carried out for all shelves on which media suplies are arranged. Use tape printers to make tables for the location of supplies on shelving units or on readiness tables.
2. Make plans to post specific step-by-step directions that will help teachers recall previons action taken. Label operational parts in full view.
3. Set up an appointment system to handle priorities, or make schedules after geting advise from the staff, for hours for work by specific groups at specified stations.
4. Post samples of work done as standards for performance, and also show samples of defective work as a result of common errors.
5. Assign members of operational technical staffs to specific jobs. Write out instructions to technicians as well as for teachers.
6. See that proper check-ups are carried out by the right personnel as assigned.

There are other control systems that may be worked out according to local conditions and situations. Although they should recognize the need to cut red tape for teachers, media leaders need also to recognize that without controls of such complex and often understaffed establishments as media-preparation facilities, the program of srevice may suffer. Regardless of the problems that usually attend media-producing activities, we can assert, that since media are playing newer and increasingly important roles in greater volume, media leaders will have to find ways to lmplement these inescapable and essential media-preparations services.

It is not by chance that the chapter dealing with the important, system-wide implementation of media-perparation program has been completed at this particular point in this box. It is generally recognized by all who understand new uses for audiovisual media in both television programing and as direct teaching components that special-purpose media have to be produced on the spot by a wide variety of operatlonal techniques These uses of media will be abundantly clear as we move ahead into the following chapters, the first of which deals with television and the second with self-instruction systems.

Problem-Solving Activities

1. Identify several teaching processes such as large-group. presentaions, self-instruction systems, and television programing, and prepare for each one you name, a brief statement descrioing the relation the process bears to the media-preparation services needed by teachers that are involved.
2. State the old and new roles of media as repeatedly mentioned thus far in this book and explain the need for local media-preparation services in relation to these media roles.
3. Why is the visualization and design aspect of media-making processes so important ? How is it related to communication by the teacher or by the meduim itself ? How is it related to informatiion theory ? How is it related to instructional objectives ? To the nature of the learning process ? To the goals of puipils ?
4. What is the role of the graphic artist in visualization and design? Is it educational ? Purely technical ? If media are being made *for* teachers, what duties must teachers themselves carry out ?

5. What basic media generally need to be produced by school sysytems today ? How does your list differ from the one supplied in this book ? Can you agree in class, or in a group of teachers, on a listing of media arranged in order of priority, as may be necessary when inaugurating a new media-preparation service ? Do you agree that restrictions may have to be placed on what kinds of media, and how many varieties of cach kind, can be made in any given media-making center ?
6. Your school superintendent has asked you to write him a letter to inform him how many square feet of floor area in the system-wide media-service suite in the new school headquarters building you will need for media -preparation activities. Write him a two-page proposal in which you state the following: *(a)* a listing of specific operational space needs, if all forty schools in the school district are to be served, and *(b)* an altrenate plan for decentralizing the media-producing process to carry on specific operations in each school. List each of the space needs in square feet for the operations to be handled at each school, and *(c)* supply a revised listing of space needs for the centralization plan, or add the new and reduced figures to be listing prepared in *(a)* under the heading " Centralization with Optimum Decentralization."
7. Prepare a floor-plan sketch to scale showing generalized space needs for basic media-producing operations for a school-building media center as follows: *(a)* label to show equipment-operation stations, *(b)* show how each station is related to the general access and working area, *(c)* base operational space needs on estimates given in this book, *(d)* indicate the various operating area figures and also the total area allotted, and *(e)* indicate by arrows flowdiagram patterns as from stock supply to working spaces. (Note: Try to economize in space wherever possible without eliminating specific cperations, or unreasonable crowding.).
8. Using the generalized space-need figures for operations identified in the sketch completed and, make a new sketch of operational spaces to the same scale after having been ordered to submit a new plan for each school in the district limiting the media-producing area to 600 square feet. Label clearly and again indicate a flow diagram and show relationships of equipment operation stations to work areas. (This sketch calls for a combination of specified functions and dratic limitation of operational space. In cases like these, what media do you produce ? what media-producing

processes, can be carried on in teachers' classrooms ? what kits of media-making materials may be supplied to teachers ? what personnel can be allowed to use facilities and when ? How could full-time paid staff members compensate for reduction in operational spaces ?)

9. Your proposals for operating media-producing facilities in each school building have been turned down in favour of a centralization scheme. You know what the disadvantages of such a plan are, but you must write a new proposal outlining a plan for central media-making facilities in light of new staff-space-service relationships. Include in your outline-format plan the following: *(a)* a statement as to the possibllity that extra technical staff working full time can produce more media in less space per hour than in school-building centers, *(b)* a statement as to the possible effect that teachers will not visit and consult with artists and technical staff to the same degree that they would visit school-building units, *(c)* an estimate of the volume of media items that may have to be produced at the central headquarters, *(d)* a stafement that cost of supplies may be reduced for an equal number of media due to waste reduction. since more full-time technicians will be handling the materials rather than teachers and students, and *(e)* a listing of operational space needs in terms of the required central staff to carry on *all* media-producing services.
10. In tabular format, identify basic criteria and make comparison to show advantages and disadvantages of centralization versus optimum decentralization of media-producing processes as a basis for recommending adoption of school district policy.

References

Bowers, Kenneta L. " Filmstrips for Local Needs," *Audiovisual Instruction,* Vol. 9. No. 3, March 1964, PP. 179-180.

Brown, james W. and Kenneth D. Norberg. *Administering Educational Media.* (New York: McGraw-Hill, 1965). Darkroom Construction. (Rochester, N.Y: Eastman Kodak Co., 1951).

Faris, Gene and John Moldstad, assisted by Harvey Frye. *Improving the Learning Environment* (A Study of the Local Preparation of Visual Instructional Materials). Carried on with the cooperation of the U.S. Office of Education pursuant to a contract under Title VII, Part B. (Washington, D.C.: Super-intedent of Documents, U.S. Government Printing Office, 1963).

Frye, Roy A. *Graphic Tools for Teachers,* 3rd ed. (Austin, Texas : E. and I. Printing Co., 1965).

Gaskill, Arthur L. and David A. Englander. *How to Shoot a Movie Story.* (New York: Morgan and Morgan, Inc., Publishers, 1960).

Johnston, Roy J. "University of Miami Learning and Instructional Resources Center," *Adiovisual Instruction,* Vol. 11, No. 2, February 1966, pp. 91–93.

Kemp, Jerrold E. *Planning and Producing Audivisual Materials.* (San Francisco : Chandler Publishers, 1963).

________. "Planning for Local Production," *Audiovisual Instruction,* Vol. 8, No. 5, May 1963, pp. 296–298.

Kemp, Rodger L. and Clarissa Sunde, "Video Tapes for Teaching the English Language," *Audiovisual Instruction,* Vol. 10, No. 4, April 1965, p. 303.

Liechti, Alice O. and Jack R. Chappell. *Making and Using Charts.* (San Francisco: Fearon Publishers, 1960).

Magnetic Recording for 16 mm Motion Pictures. (Rochester, N.Y.: Eastman Kodak Co., 1958).

Mascelli, Joseph V. *Five C's of Cinematography.* (Hollywood, California: Cine/Graphic Publications, 1965).

McVey, Gerald F. "Multimedia Instructional Laboratory," *Audiovisual Instruction,* Vol. 11, No. 2, February 196, pp. 80–85.

Minor, Ed. *Simplified Techniques for Preparing Visual Instructional Meterials.* (New York: McGraw-Hill, 1962).

Morlan, John E. *Preparation of Inexpensive Teaching Materials.* (San Francisco: Chandler Publisher, 1963).

Roberts, Alvin B. and Don L. Crowford. "Multiscreen Presentations: Promise for Instructional Improvement," *Audiovisual Instruction,* Vol. 9, No. 8, October 1964, pp. 528–530.

Veenandaal, Wilfred L. "The Visualisation of an Idea," *Audiovisual Instruction,* Vol. 2, No. 9, December 1952, pp. 260–262.

Weisgerber, Robert A. and Warren Rasmussen. "A Teaching System for Music Listening," *Audiovisual Instruction,* Vol. 11 No. 2, February 1966, pp. 106–109.

10

Implementation of Television Services

Because of its tremendous potential value in achieving instructional efficiency, because of its unique capabilities, because of its many application to large-group as well as individualized instruction, and because of its potential as a vital component for the teaching methods referred to as instructional systems, television is a medium that every media specialist should gain experience with. This chapter cannot be a guidebook or even a major resource for those who want to learn about the many past present, and future uses of television, or for those who seek to develop penetrating insights as they set out to become television specialists, what we desire to a accomplish in this chapter is to prepare prospective media program directors and school-building coordinators for some sound thinking about the curriculum contribution instructional television can make, the way it fits into the stream-of-learning activity, and the problems that must be faced before the medium can be used comprehensively, or even in limited ways, by school systems or in individual school buildings. We need to understand the problems we face in using this medium—problems of personnel. New equipment, the rapid strides being made in the technology, the space required for television programming activity, the possible costs, and the patterns by which television is being put to work around the country.

One of the problems we ran into at once is whether or not we can invest in television equipment one year without having the equipment become obsolete the next. We may be discussing the ways of using video-tape one year only to find that a new technology of videodisc recording has replaced or may replace it. We may find some entirely new and more convenient ways for the transmission of programs to where the learners are waiting. We may find in the copyright laws some blocks to our highly desirable electronic reproduction of materials for classroom uses. So as this chapter is being sent to press, we hazardously refer to studio equipment, table copying and editing equipment, and show pictures of operational uses of television on both closed and open circuits, knowing that the state of the art is an ephemeral condition. We do not apologize therefore for the presentations we make, for we realize that it will become a necessity to retool our operational establishments again and again and continually find solutions to problems as they arise. We need most to point the way to some promising solutions to a presentday cluster of problems that have to do with implementation of television services. When prospective media program directors move into their new positions, they must assess their local television situation in the light of existing needs and operations. They may be called upon to make recommendations for the future, and of course may have to procure the help they need from experts in mapping their future aspirations. They may thus inherit the mistakes of others, or they may have the good fortune to find a thriving, and effective organization in full swing. It is the wisdom for guiding change in promising directions that we earnestly seek.

Television and its Teaching Uses

We shall first identify the unique characteristics of the medium. Many who discuss this topic tend to confuse unique characteristics with possible effects of the medium when used certain ways for instructional purposes. We must separate the communicative effects of any given program on an individual who reacts to it from the basic characteristics of the medium as differing from any other medium.

The Television Medium

Unique Characteristics. When we refer to the unique characteristics of television, we must, as we have just urged, separate program content from television technology. Thus we must mention basic capability of television as a vehicle for communication, display, and transmission, to use a few of the terms commonly used to describe what television does for those who use it. Looked at in this light we can point out three special capabilities:

1. The television medium through what is called electronic reproduction may combine visual and audio components of other media such as motion picture films, slides, and photo enlargements into a single display system.

2. It possesses the capacity to reach an audience of unlimited size, simultaneously for all viewers.

3. It possesses the capacity to transmit program content immediately from the point of occurrence to the point of reception.

Taking a closer look at each of the three characteristics of the transmission system, we can give an example that involves them all. A studio teacher explains a difficult concept for all classes in social science in grade five meeting in thirty different school buildings. The voice and views of the teacher, the pupils' television teacher, provide verbal explanation; and then as a novel experience is needed, takes students on a journey into hot, desert lands by means of a motion picture clip, then identifies the area by means of a map slide, and provides opportunity to make observations relating the slide to the previous film scenes. The television medium has thus served to combine two different media with audio and visual stimuli from the teacher, has served to reach all pupils in the total group at the same time, and whatever the teacher did was transmitted immediately from the point of program origin to the receiving area. Thus these three capabilities open up to the school systems the means to apply in many ways the medium of television to teaching-learning processes. We shall discuss general patterns of uses as have appeared in schools around the country and also point the way to some future possibilities, but first let us identify several basic aspects of television operational technology that have a bearing on its educational applications.

Some Basic Aspects of Operational Technology: The medium of television as a system may operate in classrooms in many different technological ways.

1. Each classroom may have its own television transmission system under the control of the teacher for special and general display purposes, thus producing programme content on the spot to provide immediate visibility of the teacher's behaviour.
2. Program content may reach schools from remote sources outside of the local school system, thus making use of open-circuit transmission, for direct reception by individual school buildings.
3. Each school system may own and operate its own television systems with origination and reception capability in any or all regular and special teaching stations.

In addition to such basic arrangements for utilizing television in the school, we can also identify a number of specific aspects of operational technology such as the following, some of which greatly enhance television's instructional contributions.

1. The capability to preserve television program content for repetitive use by means of low-cost, easy-to-operate video-tape equipment (with other processes in the offing).
2. The capability of editing videotapes electronically as an important adjunct of television production processes.
3. The capability of automating the retrieval of preserved and stored program content.
4. The present capability, made possible through video-tape and other recording processes, to transfer and/or commune source material from a number of audiovisual and print media to whatever video storage system is most conveniently usable in a given education application.
5. The present capability of transmitting television programs by a number of transmission systems, each with its own unique characteristics.

The application of such basic operational technologies will be explained in later discussions and illustrations regarding program production, transmission and viewing at teaching stations. We turn now to television and the curriculum.

Teaching Uses of Television

Most of the nation's educators have not yet been willing to experiment with television in teaching. This unwillingness is certainly typical of education's traditional response to new ideas but anyone who is familiar with the history of instructional television knows that this instructional innovation was launched first among educational decision-makers, with an unprecedented financial support for centres of experimentation throughout the land. Not all of the experimental centers gave rise to permanent and comprehensive programs of television utilization in schools of the area, yet television has nevertheless prospered to a degree. It has by no means, however, resulted in the television establishment, non has it had the educational impact dreamed of in an earlier decade. Murphy and Gross, in *Learning by Television,* had this to say:

That televised instruction has achieved even its present modest success is, perhaps, a miracle. The achievement has taken massive pump-priming from private foundations and government. The Ford Foundation alone has made grants in the neighbourhood of $100 million to all phases of educational television, at first through the Fund for Adult Education for educational television stations and programing, and later through the Fund for Advancement of Education to schools and colleges. The federal government's support has added approximately another $100 million in equipment to the country's ETV facilities.

In the face of burgeoning media technology, a new feeling toward change on the part of both professionals and the lay public and in face of the changing image regarding education and education's processes, television may be viewed in a new climate of activity. To catch a glimpse of this new future, not only for television, but for other media as well, we turn to the preface of the book just mentioned for quotations from a statement by Alvin C. Eurich:

> ... the use of television in the classroom for a decade and more has demonstrated incontrovertibly that students can and do learn quite as well from television as they do from conventional instruction. However, the practical experience of school and college educators with the television medium has been quite mixed. As a result, televised instruction has not taken a central position in education. Rather it is still a marginal enterprise....

As applied to education thus far, television has largely put, current modes of teaching on the screen. The result has been widespread disenchantment as the mediocre level of much instruction has been exposed to professional and public scrutiny for the first time. The need for imagination, ingenuity, and innovation in the whole process of education has been forcefully demonstrated.

The primary goal of ITV in the future must be to raise quality and improve classroom utilization. Here, as elsewhere in education today, mere expansion of present practices is not enough. The way forward is necessarily a new way. To create the new some of the old must be constructively destroyed.

> ... television now stands at the most significant crosswords in its history. Recent developments--governmental, technological, educational- have set the stage for advance to a new level of usefulness and excellence. Opportunities have opened to apply television fruitfully with other new media, and to undertake new experiments with augmented research funds.
>
> ...We are now ready for the next stage, which calls for a thorough, dynamic effort to improve the quality of instruction, not just over television, but throughout our entire educational system with television as one of the many instruments that can be used to give each child, wherever. He may live, the opportunity to become all he is capable of being.

Millions of students around the country have been under instruction by television methods. And it is because of this use of television in teaching that we can identify several patterns for putting television to work formally in the curriculum of our schools. Some of these patterns will doubtlessly continue to make contributions of major proportions in the schools of the future. The patterns we have identified, and we are purposely attempting to separate one from the other for purposes of clarity, are as follows:

1. The use of an outstanding television teacher to make direct presentations to pupils in conventionally organized classes of approximately thirty pupils in specified curricular subjects and to guide the regular teachers for the participating groups in their implementation of teaching plans in direct relation to the firmly scheduled telecasts on a required-participation basic.
2. The use of an outstanding television teacher to make direct presentations to pupils in reasonably large groups of 75 to 100 students, in specified curricular subjects, and to guide the participating teachers in each group (possibly two teachers and one teacher's aide) in their implementation of

teaching plans in direct relation to the firmly scheduled telecasts on a required-participation basis.

3. The use of an outstanding television teacher to make direct presentations to pupils in formally organized large groups of 300 to 500 students in specified curricular subjects, and guide the participating teachers (usually two or more) at the viewing stations in implementing their teaching plans in direct relation to the firmly scheduled telecasts on a required-participation basis.
4. The use of an outstanding television teacher to teach a specified course in the school's curriculum to all organized classes in large groups of 300 to 500 students, meeting at scheduled teaching stations, giving direct guidance to pupils for study and preparation of assignments, with guidebooks, textbooks, and assignments to be handed in as required for grading by assistants. A supervising teacher, and a clerical aide to serve as managerial assistants to the television teacher, with final examinations being taken as scheduled at designated stations.
5. The use of television programmes from sources outside the school system broadcast into the classrooms or participating, regular teachers, who use the programme content as a resource on a voluntary basis. Such programmes may be single programmes or programmes in a series as a part of a course. The differentiating factor is in the degree of control over the programme presenter. In this pattern, the originating agency has control over the presenter, not the receiving school system. The school system may arrange to take all programmes on a series or course basis, paying a per-pupil fee, and by internal agreements may have all teachers in a system make use of the series, carrying on agreed-to procedures.
6. The use of automatically controlled television programmes that are maintained in a state of readiness for retrieval by individual students in electronic carrels or on call by teachers for instructional use by the whole class. In the case of team teaching, large groups may be called together for viewing programmes especially prepared by the teacher or programmes that had been previously produced, described, and announced for use by teachers in specific grade levels, subjects, and units of work.
7. The use of television facilities to transmit to specified teaching stations- special program content to expedite administrative processes in school and school systems. An

example would be the administration of a testing program where a specialist or an administrator assumes control of groups to give directions, such as for testing procedure, or makes a series of significant announcements, and has arranged for assistants at the receiving stations to supervise the prescribed operations.

8. The use of television facilities to deliver audiovisual media presentations- such as motion picture, film strip, overhead transparency and 2 × 2 inch slides-to selected teaching stations on demand as teaching and learning resources according to predetermined schedules, thus eliminating the need for projectors, light control systems, and operators for projection equipment.
9. The use of television equipment in a given teaching station to ensure that diagrams, pictures, realia, and instructor demonstrations with small objects and apparatus are visible to all viewers in a large or small group. This process is referred to as a classroom television display system, or an image-magnification system.
10. The use of television facilities to present programmed sequences to specified groups of students, calling for individual responses on group response-measuring instruments. Thus verbal frames may be presented with reference panels displayed and student responses called for and either measured immediately or computerized for later printout for teachers' records. Such programs may be in video-tape format and individualized as described previously.

The ten patterns of television usage in schools around the country are by no means a definitive and inclusive listing, nor are they a guide to the future roles of this medium. We do, however, see in some of the patterns already discernible, strong possibilities for new and greater impact in teaching-learning activities of the future.

The Future of Instructional Television

Although we need not gaze too earnestly into the crystal ball, it may be revealing to explore more fully the thoughts and hopes previously expressed by Alvin C. Eurich. But we dare not make the often-made mistake of treating television as a gift to the schools by technology and then asking, " Here is TV, what shall we do with it?" we should ask instead, as Alvin Eurich asks, what are some great needs of the curriculum of our time that television technology can help educators meet? This is not an easy question to answer. So we go back in our thinking to a solid base of desirable learning activity. We may ask what kinds of activities do youngsters need inorder to build into them selves the insights and abilities that the technological climate of our time demands? What will suffice to help our present-day learners come to grips with the massive changes that lie ahead? How can youngsters come to grips with the explosion of knowledge and keep abrest of the changes in concepts once they start their formal learning process? To put the question another way: what do teachers need to do every day to teach the insights, abilities, attitudes, and commitments that their professional duties demand? Indeed, let us put the burden on the teacher, and thus onto his curriculum leader and chief administrator, for proper and adequate action. If we assume that the study of our society and its problems, our philosophical outlook and value system, enables us to decide on what we ought to do, what are the resultant processes like? To answer this question, we shall pose a listing of teacher activities that seem inescapable.

Some Inescapable Generalized Teacher Activities

We have often asserted that before teachers and curriculum leaders and planners can decide how to use audiovisual media, or any medium for that matter, they have to be able to take the teaching process apart, then stand off and look at the components objectively. When we can engage successfully in such analytical thinking. We can begin to pinpoint our choice of media. We can then proceed to build systems of combinations of media and the teacher in proper relationship to elicit the responses of pupils the will achieve instructional objectives. The list we pose does not have to be complete to fulfil our purposes, but we must be sure of the teacher takes. The reader can use his own experiences to add to the following list.

1. Provide real and vicarious experiences in natural setting for purposes of operations inference, and generalization.
2. Display illustrations.
3. Provide information to : give detailed directions for action; explain difficult concepts; demonstrate processes; present and define problems; make assignments; ask questions; present case studies and tell stories.

4. Enlarge an illustration or object for all to see.
5. Move learners elsewhere for looking and listening.
6. Give personal guidance to another pupil, group or several groups simultaneously.
7. Motivate students for sustained activity.
8. Provide a common, standardized experience for analysis and evaluation.
9. Get pupils to work independently on creative projects using desirable behaviours.
10. Give continuing guidance to each student.
11. Evaluate the work of students.
12. Prepare media or supervise their preparation.
13. Organize pupils into cooperative groups.
14. Organize reference libraries and facilitate access to them.
15. Organize optimum working conditions that are safe, clean, and wholesome.

We have, of course, not even mentioned one of the most important of all of the professional tasks and that is to formulate valid teaching objectives as a basis for planing action at any teaching station-small-group, large-group or in an electronic carrel. Looking back over the list of the processes that teachers need to carry out every day by one means or another, we perceive that instructional television possesses the potential to give some strikingly important assistance to teachers. We shall turn to a prediction and an elaboration of what some of these major roles might be in the following section.

Some Promising ITV Roles in the Curriculum

Curriculum Needs as a Basis for Television Services. We know now that the year 1971 is not likely to usher in the full fruition of the instructional developments and uses predicted ten years earlier for instructional television. Men who tried to foresee the future for the television medium then, appear to have been somewhat over optimistic. But there can be little doubt that ITV can and will move toward more significant contributions toward curriculum fulfilment in the years ahead, although just what the format will be is difficult to predict. Such predictions as we care to make are based or what we have stated regarding the kinds of performance that teachers have to engage in, or that school administrators have to prescribe for them in light of system-wide instructional designs and programs, and also on the long-term view of changing philosophical concepts of American education. In making the following statements, we hold the reader responsible for wide sensitivity to a number of curriculum relationships. Let us first state a few very important need at all levels of instruction:

1. The pressing requirement of making the most of each pupil.
2. The urgent need to deal with each individual in a personal way, to individualize instruction, some aspects of instruction, such as diagnosis and remediation, and to free pupils for in-depth study.
3. To provide a wide range of experiences in near and far places.
4. To provide challenging opportunities for each student to engage in problem-solving activity, to inquire and question.
5. To provide opportunity for stimulating co-operative endeavour in producing, testing, and evaluating.
6. To save hours of time for teachers in which to give needed guidance to pupils.
7. To provide a range of resource experts in various disciplines, such as mathematics, social, physical, and biological sciences for demonstrations, explanation, refining issues and problems.
8. To motivate students to study independently in a wide range of situations in electronic carrels, laboratories, libraries, at home.
9. To expand the range of the curriculum according to local needs.
10. To establish contacts with rich sources of content, regional, statewide, and beyond.
11. To give needed preparatory information, directions for action to expedite work of students.
12. To free teachers from the drudgery of routine, repetitive teaching of needed factual content and the checking for mastery of conceptualization processes.

Uses for Television to meet Curriculum Needs. As we look toward changing concepts of education, particularly along the lines of priority mentioned earlier in Chapter 4, we can envision the use of the television medium by itself and in combination with other media, and with one or more levels of face-to-face teacher guidance. However, we must not fall to specify the particular instructional need that is to be met, and to `subject that need to critical scrutiny. As new uses are predicted in the following list. We must also bear in mind the advancing technology that, in light of the present state of the art, is reflected in later sections that deal with operational processes and facilities. We must also caution the reader to beware of possible complexity in a simple statement of a possible use of television in the curriculum, because we see new sources of content from business concerns, museums, city gardens and parks, and libraries, all outside the school. We also see new transmission systems for such taped and stored content, but we must emphasize the ways to integrate such new content with the processes by which students interact and learn. Hence in our suggestions, although we do not dear with each in detail, many relationships of the various television techniques employed in and at our teaching stations are implied. The reader is again help responsible for supplying a wide range of examples, and is also urged to devise combinations of the uses presented as well as new and detailed curriculum applications of his own. Our suggestions follow.

1. Use superior teachers in special programs to get large groups of students (300 to 500 or more), in any field, grade, subject, unit, or stage of work, ready to undertake independent study. Such programs would be designed to expedite work in libraries, laboratories, open up problems and issues, organise students if necessary into cohesive working groups or small teams and task forces. Programs would be fully supported by needed media, could be taped for repetitive use, would be in a daily series of perhaps forty minutes or longer, three or four sessions, to enable students to then move in to blocks of work lasting three to five weeks, meeting in smaller groups for guidance, and in the total group again for the next phase or unit. This would appear to be the use of a television teacher as a member of a team, in which facilities for learning were used as components to maximize the use of rational powers.
2. Use television in new courses for large group with massive efforts on crucial areas of needed change such as communications and mathematics, which call for the work of truly superior teachers in special fields. Such programing would demand intensive efforts to organize independent study according to needs with available staff qualified for the type of guidance activity called for.
3. To make experts available in various disciplines who are able to give guidance in a series of programs to aid pupils in coming to grips with problems in special areas of

endeavour according to existing weaknesses in local teaching staffs. Programs may take the form of whole courses, parts of courses as in item (1) preceding, or may be introduced to give guidance in initiating creative, problem-solving activity in supplementing good teachers already available in mathematics and sciences, for example.

4. Video-tapes may be replayed as parts of new curricula as components of whole courses, in any desirable sequence, with the television programs contributing any identifiable part of a specific teaching process from motivation to preparation for laboratory action, explanation of difficult concepts, defining issues, freeing teachers from the repetitive job of presenting basic content.
5. Use television more widely in team teaching presentations for all pupils in the total group, using existing staff and school building television installations-thus permitting replay for some groups needing reteaching and make-up work because of absence.
6. To make available to students in large groups programmed instruction in the form of presentations calling for individual responses in varied written formats and/or by means of group response systems. Such content may be presented to large groups as a means of releasing a number of teachers from information-giving phases of instructional systems.
7. The use of television as a means of individualizing instruction by dial retrieval of special programs stored on video-tape and/or disks, tied expertly according to need into teaching stations for both formal and informal relationships with learning activity. Interconnected schools increase range of coverage by content for both elementary and secondary schools.
8. The use of television to procure and preserve for immediate and/or delayed use, sources of content from regional, statewide and national sources as by means of communication satellites, or by other linkages ending in closed-circuit uses of the content to meet curriculum need, on a large-group, small-group, or individual basis.
9. Use television to accelerate the program of youngsters in any field of need according to curriculum surveys, employing creative programing to make assignments, giving directions for self-study work, and to organize both school and home activities on appropriate time schedules. Large-group as well as small-group programing are both implied.

10. Use television in packaged in-service education programs to update teachers in new curriculum developments and to teach teachers new roles in using teaching systems, for example.
11. Use television facilities for administrative processes such as conducting mass testing programs, compilation and viewing of pupil records, orientation and guidance activities, and facsimile transmission.
12. Use of the medium as a channel for personal contact by school leaders with both pupils and teacher for improved communication about the values and purposes of education, and about new arrangements, plans, and schedules. Such program content would involve both central office and school-building personnel.
13. Use television programing for updating postgraduates in vocational retraining activities, as parts of night-school program using school building facilities and other community resources. Develop methods for using the potential of television for presenting informational aspects, but utilize other means for guiding the use of rational powers.

Some significant Aspects of the Suggested Uses. Repeatedly in the forgoing list the following crucial aspects or television have been stressed explicitly or implicitly:

1. The use of television in proper relationship to other supporting media during and after the programs.
2. The assignment to television of these aspects of the teaching process that can be handled by that medium, with other assignments being made to additional personnel or to media and machines in other locations for the accomplishment of valid educational objectives.
3. The imaginative use of people in television program content, for valid instructional objectives.
4. The breaking away from teaching as usual.
5. A swinging away from the erroneous concept of learning as absorption and memory to the use of rational powers: problem solving, productivity, evaluation.
6. The increased emphasis on independent study, improved interaction with what has been presented and with resulting spheres of activity.
7. The valid use of television in or as one of the components of teaching systems.

8. The valid use of the medium of television to expand the range of school curriculum, to provide experience, and to stimulate and guide organized learning activity.
9. A move away from the lock-step television programing leaving large groups of learners as sitting ducks to waste time on "fill-in" activities.
10. Increased use of libraries and laboratories. (libraries will have to expand their services to teachers and pupils far beyond anything we have dreamed of in the past)

Some Observations About ITV facilities. We must point out that when television uses such as we have suggested are implemented, we shall have to recommend great flexibility in production, transmission, and receptions; capabilities. It is obvious that there will have to be not only centralized, citywide capability, but also several school-building production and transmission centers, otherwise such massive uses as we have mentioned cannot be scheduled as needed, as for example team-teaching presentations with several schools interconnected. Great use may be made of videotapes (or other newly developed technology for storing programs) for the immediate retrieval of these program sources when the required equipment is provided. Moreover, as we shall discuss in the next chapter in connection with self-instruction systems, computer capability may have to be used in several phases of the instructional process. We therefore turn next to a discussion of operational facilities for production, transmission, and reception. But once more we must stress the basic concern that it is the curriculum that must determine the uses of the medium, and not the reverse.

Operational Facilities and Equipment : Program Production

Media program leaders will almost certainly be called into action in any insightful deliberations over curriculum change involving television. We have stressed these important curriculum decision as a basis for the use of all media, not only television, but we should point out that a highly qualified media program director may indeed be the school- system staff member who can best explain how ITV can serve the specified curriculum needs. Therefore, he ought to be considered as an indispensable member on the team of curriculum leaders and school administrators. Once agreements are reached the media director must be prepared to give sound advice on the nature of operational facilities and equipment by means of which desired results can be achieved. The recommendations for implementing television services in all or a part of a school system ought to be worked out as a unified and carefully integrated plan for production, transmission, reception, and viewing of programmes. We emphasize this total solution to these problems lest a specific problem such as transmission pose difficulties so great as to jeopardize or preclude successful operation of the instructional television system for the school district For the purposes of this discussion we shall deal first with operational facilities and equipment for the production phase of the program.

In dealing with these operational problems of production we shall attempt to point out from time to time some of the technological developments that seem to be on the horizon but we shall have to suggest reasonable plans in light of the present technological capabilities. It will be a responsibility of the media director to see to it that he keeps informed and seeks advice from both professional and technical specialists in the field before final decisions are made. We cannot overestimate the importance of getting assistance from qualified specialists before prescribing a given package of equipment. It may be far safer to employ a qualified consultant to check thoroughly the preparation of specifications and to supervise installation it with these basic implementation techniques in mind that we now present a number of possibilities for producing, or procuring, and handling the presentation of the programs, up to the point to transmission. Since not all programs are presented *live*, nor do all of them originate in the local system, the aspect of preserving or the handling of program content in the sense of storage or availability must be treated in this phase of program production.

Providing Instructional Television Program Capability

The heart of any instructional television system is the program content. The patterns for putting such content to work in the minds of learners, as well as all aspects of the content, are vital curriculum matters. It is obvious that we face monstrous needs for program material, and because of this we turn to all available sources for desirable programs. We organize facilities, staff, and supporting media and produce programs locally, and we link up with many sources, already alluded to in earlier discussions, external to the school system, in order to meet identified needs. Therefore in a real sense we face the most crucial problem of all in the processes of program production or program availability. We properly refer to all of the means by which we provide needed programing as program capability, and the prospective citywide, or school-building media leaders must consider all phases of such activity in order to recommend the appropriate facilities and equipment required in any particular instructional television system. Basic program capability is generally achieved by organizing and equipping one or more local studios, and by procuring additional productions, from agencies outside the school district. Ordinarily then, program capability may be developed by one or more of the following program-producing arrangements and processes:

1. *The Central Studio:* A central studio generally implies the transmission processes in addition to production. However, we must concentrate our attention on the process of producing television programs for immediate use *live,* or for storage in a desirable form for retrieval and use according to local plans, both automatic and manual—that is, to be transmitted on schedule to all schools or to a selected circuit of schools, or to be delivered in the form of videotapes, for example, to specific school-building television-service units for use over their own cable transmission circuits.
2. *The School-Building Studio:* As a supplemental program-originating unit, the school-building studio also produces television programs, along lines already suggested, possibly for team-teaching purposes, and also for possible system-wide use among selected schools, grades, and student groups. Such programs may be transmitted *live* or may be also preserved and stored for replay according to local plans, either at the school building, at the central studio storage facilities, or at both.
3. *Teaching-Station, Program Recording Units:* Without the use of studios in the usual sense of the word, classrooms may be equipped with movable recording, viewing, and transmitting units that record off-the-air television presentations for subsequent instructional uses. With the

addition of a television camera for image magnification and another camera for viewing the teacher, programs that combine a number of program-content sources can be taped and stored.

4. *Procurement of Programs from External Sources:* When we consider the program capability process, we must look to rich sources that lie outside the school system. A few of the possibilities are videotape (and, as it appears, video disk banks also) for exchange purposes, filmed television programs, and program content from regional state, and national television services, live, or from stored sources.

What operational spaces and equipment are needed if the program capability we have defined is to be made available to teachers? We shall attempt to answer this question in light of each of the foregoing program availability processes as a means of aiding the prospective media program leader to analyze the problems he must face and solve if television is to fulfill its promise in the curriculum. We anticipate that with the great strides being made in technology new and radically different processes will also be forthcoming.

Program Capability at the District-Wide Studio

Reduced to its simple terms, the process of making and preserving an instructional television program, regardless of how it is to be distributed, or under what conditions, would generally demand two television cameras, a film chain, one videotape recorder, lights, microphones, a control console plus the related operational parts and controls, including audio tape recorder and audio amplifier and mixer control units. The space requirements for better control over quality would be for two separate but adjacent and connected rooms, one to serve as an acoustically treated studio and the other with glass panels for direct visual surveillance to be the control room. As we have already pointed out, studio facilities will also have transmission equipment units. In any studio process, whether *live* telecasting or videotaping, supporting services are required such as graphic production for media support. See Figure 10-6. Also the presenter will likely wish to use apparatus, perform demonstrations, work at tables or desks, and refer to books, maps, and realia. It is therefore essential that adequate workroom and storage spaces be provided.

In the preceding chapter estimates were given that would indicate that limited videotaping operations might be possible in a studio suite of 580 square feet. However, it was also pointed out in that connection that a system-wide comprehensive-service, instructional television studio may need to be as large as 9,200 square feet in area. The variables being so many in local situations, it is not possible to prescribe a standard area without specific information at hand. However, we can make some estimates in terms of the volume of programming needed to meet some of the ccurriculum needs discussed earlier, and in terms of space needed to carry out known functions. If one program is to be produced each day and transmitted later, a minimum-size suite can be used to good advantage, but if four programs are to be planned, rehearsed, and recorded in one day, additional spaces, a larger studio with room for several separate sets and lights will be a necessity. It is also obvious that if the load on a central studio is heavy, the area will have to be greater, and cases where central studios are already large, optimum decentralization to permit special uses of instructional television at individual school buildings will be necessary. If we assume further that the central studio and the school-building supplementary studios will operate videotape resource banks on an automatic retrieval basis, then additional spaces will have to be planned, recommended, and justified.

When central studios are transmitting programs simultaneously, as when several videotape players are feeding multiple channels in cable connections to selected schools, it is obvious that either additional space is required in a central control room, or such videotape machines will be operating with necessary modulators and booster amplifiers in a separate transmitter room. With this brief overview of operations possibilities in mind, we shall now turn to separate treatments of such problems as space needs, equipment needs for both production and preservation, and program-retrieval processes.

Some space needs: Of necessity the estimates of spaces required in which to carry on operational processes are generalized estimates. For our purposes we shall assume fairly comprehensive multichannel television services rather than deal in limited, superficial, and crowded environments.

1. *Three Studios.* Three studios will permit several program-producing activities simultaneously. Videotaping, transmitting a *live* program, taping a presentation for later transmission, the evaluation of a given performance by the presenter, and rehearsing the next program are good examples. Such multiple studios coupled with film and slide chains would permit combination of media with presenter using videotape equipment in the control room. *Estimates:* Studio A, 1,300 square feet; Studios B and C, 1,000 square feet, with a three-studio total of 2,300 square feet.
2. *Control Room.* This space would service three studios and serve as headquarters for all videotaping and transmission, providing also space for consoles, transistorized camera controls, audio control, three multiplier units, space for maintenance work, and would provide space for automatic-relay equipment for the retrieval of stored programs. *Estimate :* 1,950 square feet.
3. *Media Support Preparation Area.* Operations in this area include videotape editing and playback; audiotape editing and playback; film footage search; slide making, sorting, and sequencing; and chart and model making. (See Chapter 9 for media preparation.) This space may also serve some dual media-making purposes on a system-wide basis. See Figure 10-6. *Estimate :* 1,950 square feet.
4. *General Storage Area.* This area is vitally needed to store sets and properties, re-usable media, video and audio tapes, and serve also as a blind storage area. *Estimate :* 900 square feet.
5. *Videotape and Other Forms of Program Storage.* Such storage shelves as are used for videotapes and disks and for ITV film programs should be located adjacent to control room area, so as to provide ready access. Shelves could be located on the walls of an access corridor. *Estimate :* 200 square feet.
6. *Library and Workroom for ITV Teacher.* Such space should be conveniently adjacent to media-preparation area. *Estimate :* 460 square feet.
7. *Ready Room for ITV Teachers.* This space should be equipped with desks and some lounge furniture and work or conference tables. *Estimate :* 460 square feet.
8. *Two Rest Rooms. Estimate :* 100 square feet.
9. *ITV Director's Office. Estimate:* 250 square feet.
10. *Two Offices for ITV Technical Staff, Estimate :* 380 square feet.
11. *Office for Secretaries, Estimate :* 270 square feet.

Summary of System-wide, Comprehensive Service, ITV Space Needs. When we total the space estimates, name on a functional basis we arrive at a figure of 9,210 square feet. Needless to in connection with other school facilities, it may be possible to combine some of the recommended spaces with other space needs. However, again and again we must insist that the space-pinching days of the past, insofar as education is concerned, are or ought to be over. In connection with the analysis of space needs just completed, the reader should refer to a plan formulated by the author in support of the claim for operational space. It is presented here not as the planner who studies a specific location, but as a challenge to the prospective media director to apply what he knows about television operations to a criticism of the generalized needs identified. See Fig. 10.1 and also Fig. 10.2.

AUTHOR'S ESTIMATES OF GENERALIZED ITV SPACE NEEDS

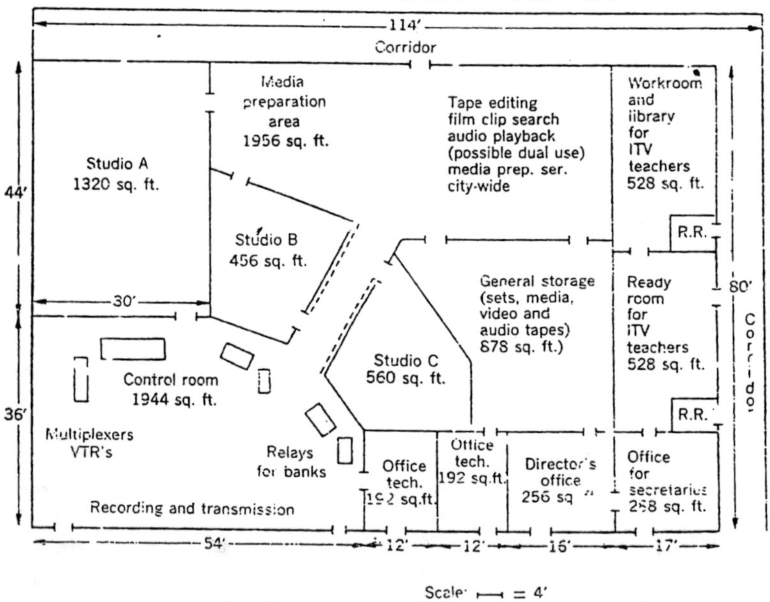

Fig. 10.1 : This is the author's sketch of space-need estimates for a thriving ITV organization at the district level. Many school-district ITV centers have far less. Space is needed in relation to the rate of program production and transmission.

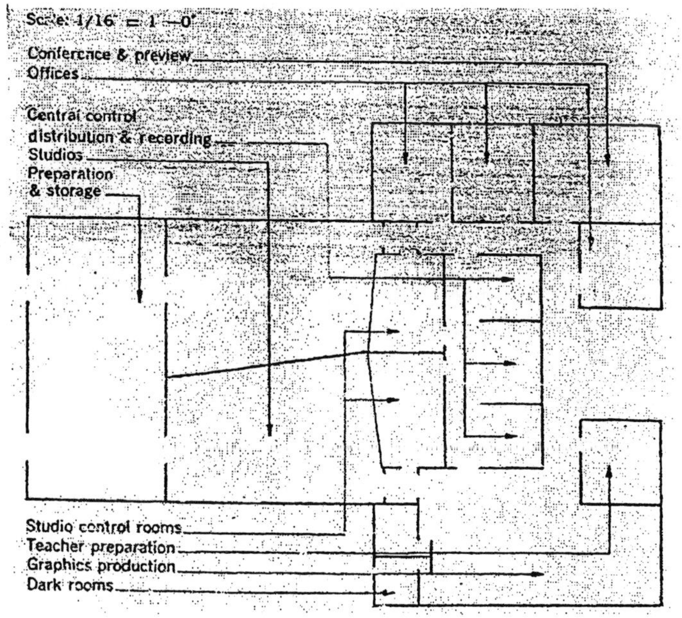

Fig. 10.2 : We present in this illustration the analysis of space needs as it appears in *Educational Facilities for New Media* prepared by Alan C. Green and his group and later published by DAVI of the NEA. This sketch indicates an extensive district center for the media preparation support of instruction. The serious student of television processes will do well to study this diagram carefully.

A Few School-System Examples: Before we finish with the section on equipment and the illustrations, we shall understand that some rather simple methods may be used to produce, procure, and distribute instructional television programs. In fact, some kinds of program content of great value may be made up and stored on videotape without a sophisticated studio. But now since we have discussed in a general way what the nature of the space needs are like for instructional television operations, we ought to temper our demands by referring to the reality of a number of actual examples of school-system operations Hence we turn to two school systems—Elmira, New York, and Plainedge, New York—examine the nature of their production spaces and perhaps refer as well to some related operations such as, for example, transmission systems (although this problem will be the topic of another section). We turn first to operations in Elmira, New York.

Example 10.1 : Operations at Elmira, New York

In this example the instruction television facilities are housed in the Beecher school as a part of the audiovisual center. In-school programs are sent by microwave and cable owned and operated by the Elmira Video Company, the local community antenna system (CATV). The school-system television programing plan involves local experienced teachers whose presentations are videotaped and stored for later transmission on one channel of the cable that the company has set aside for exclusive use by the school districts. J. Gerald Loughling former school principal, director of Elmira Instructional Television and the Audiovisual Center, has this to say about his present facilities : "Our studio is equipped with three General-Electric vidicon cameras, a film chain, and two Ampex 2-inch video tape recorder. Although somewhat crowded, we find it possible to set up for three four programs simultaneously, if necessary." Director Loughlin has also reported the following space allocation: Studio production area 900 square feet; and control room, recording, and transmitting area, 150 square feet. Additional operational spaces include staff offices, storage and program-preparation area, 900 square feet and an audiovisual media-production center of 630 square feet, a space that also serves citywide general media-preparation services. Mr. Loughlin has also reported the addition of three one-inch videotape recorder units for placement in schools not yet reachable by cable connections.

Example 10.2 : Operations at Plainedge, New York

The Plainedge school district television plan has been operating for a number of years on the FCC-established Instructional Television Fixed Service that became effective in 1963. This service utilize the 2,500-2,690 megacycle band (also referred to as megaHertz) for on-the-air broadcast of fourteen programs weekly to Plainedge schools. The transmitter sends out a private television signal that is received and converted at each school. We shall be concerned with transmission system in a later section, thus for the present we shall identify the nature of the operational spaces and the equipment units by means of which the program capability is developed. In the Plainedge system, the Director of Instructional Television reports that the total area is about 1,500 square feet. Of this space about 200 square feet make up the control room, and one end of the program production studio is a media-preparation and workroom area. The transmitter is located in a nearby auditorium stage area storage closet amounting to about 40 square feet, and additional general storage space is found in the studio area. Thus we can see that the total operational area amounts to a total of 1,540 square feet, and there is only one main production studio. Lights are suspended and are controlled by means of a switchboard for the lighting circuits.

The Plainedge instructional television programing capability is maintained by making videotapes of the programs and then transmitting them on an announced schedule. The various equipment units include :

- *(a)* Two Sarkes Tarzian Vidicon camera chains, lenses, tripods, console, and video monitors.
- *(b)* One film chain with motion picture capability only.
- *(c)* Microphones, audio tape recorder and mixer and audio amplifier.
- *(d)* One Ampex broadcast quality video tape recorded and modulator-amplifier.
- *(e)* One 2,500-2,690 mHz band transmitter for one channel operation.
- *(f)* Lights and control board.

According to reports of additional activity, the Plainedge, Plainview—Old Bethpage, and three other school districts (Bethpage, Farming-dale and Massapequa) are combining their instructional television services in a five-districts, South Oyester Bay, Long Island, New York television project. Thus rapid expansion of services in the area seems assured.

We have seen in the two examples limited, one channel ITV services, operating in crowded and far from ideal environments. Yet we must recognize the value in such endeavors to experiment and gain valuable knowledge and experience for future expansion.

Some Equipment Needs for Program Capability: The nature of the uses made of instructional television and what is done with any given ITV program during or after it is completed, determine the kinds of equipment required. As we have said before, we are concerned in this instance with program availability from a central studio facility and our equipment needs are being estimated in that specific orientation. The following list indicates the required equipment units grouped under operational functions.

Producing Instructional Programs for Live Transmission, Minimum for One Studio

1. Two television cameras, broadcast-quality vidicon, with electronic viewfinders, lenses, and tripods.
2. Camera controls, console, 3 video monitors.
3. Microphones, audio tape recorder, audio mixer and amplifier.
4. One optical multiplexer for 16 mm film and 2 × 2 inch slides.
5. One RF modulator and transmitter unit for combining video and audio for RF transmission on a given channel frequency.
6. Lighting equipment and a control board.
7. Headsets and intercom system.

Additional Equipment for Program Presentation

1. One broadcast-quality videotape recorder.
2. One modulator for combining video and audio signals for transmission on a specified channel frequency.
3. One additional video monitor for the videotape unit.

Additional Equipment for Videotape Program Editing

1. One broadcast-quality videotape recorder with modulator.
2. One electronic editing accessory (preferably built into one of a pair of recorders).

Additional Equipment for Simultaneous Transmission of five ITV Programs

(For example, one *live* program, three videotape programs, and one film program)

1. Two additional videotape recorders, video monitors and modulators. (Assuming that at least one of the two VTR units listed previously ought to be free for other recording and playback activities.)

2. One additional film chain, video monitor,, and modulator-transmitter-amplified unit. (This assumes that the previously listed film chain will be used during the *live* broadcast.)
3. Amplifier for each modulator for feeding each of four extra channels.
4. External cable and connections from audio control room.
5. Two additional broadcast-quality vidicon camera units with zoom lenses, lights, camera controls, console controls, microphones, audio-control mixers and amplifiers, and additional video monitors for at least one additional production studio for rehearsal and actual, simultaneous, program-recording activity. This additional studio would be a minimum essential to produce programs for a five-channel transmission plan.

Additional Equipment for Remote Pick-up Programing

1. Two portable vidicon cameras, electronic viewfinders, lenses, portable switching unit.
2. Portable lighting units.
3. Microphones for videotape recorder.
4. One one-inch videotape recorder, portable model.

Additional Equipment for Off-the-Air Videotape Recording

1. A high-quality television receiver for tuning in an off-the-air RF signal.
2. One or more high-gain antenna systems feeding one or more of the videotape recording units.

Additional Equipment Units for Automatic Retrieval of Stored Programs

1. Dial-access system involving telephone-type relay circuitry.
2. Automatically activated videotape players arranged in program resource banks (or other recent automatically controlled transmission units).
3. Transmission equipments units for supplying all receiving stations in a given school, selected schools, or in the school system.

Considering again the space requirements stated earlier, we can see that as additional processes are added and the volume of programing activity increases, meeting the need for multiple studios, media preparation space, workroom and service areas, rehearsal and readying space, becomes essential. When centralized television services must carry a full citywide programing load that involves the use of several channels, the space-need estimates given should be considered as minimum, not maximum. The equipment units listed should also be considered as minimum for the functions indicated. Also, it is essential that all equipment components be interconnected to provide flexibility and ease of control. For example, four videotape recorders could be interconnected so that video and audio outputs could be switched by means of a patch board to the modulator for another desired channel.

Program Capability as the School-Building Instructional Television Studio

We now turn to discussion of school-building ITV program production spaces and equipment. Since we must be prepared to make creative uses of the television medium in the curriculum, one of the first essentials for planning an internal school-building cable-distribution system is to make sure that two-way service connections are installed. Such two-way closed-loop installations will permit the origination in and distribution from any given classroom or school-building studio. Thus we point out that while we may refer to a program production and transmission studio as a supplementary unit, we may also refer to any number of connected classrooms that may serve as improvised studios for a number of different program production jobs. For the time being we shall consider the school-building studio as an operating center for the school's production and distribution activities.

Some Space Needs in the School-Building ITV Studio: In earlier paragraph we have indicated the need for school-building studios and therefore we need not repeat this justification. In the next section we shall point out that program capability may also be enhanced by the use of improvised classroom originating facilities for special purposes. For the time being we indicate some estimates of space needs assuming that the local program demands such expansion into school-building units. We face two situations in recommending studio space in any given school building. In one situation we think of remodeling a classroom turned over to the audiovisual media-service center for operating television services, and on the other we think of recommending space for a new school that is being planned. In both cases the actual space needs would be the same, but in the latter case we might be hopeful of getting a larger and more suitably arranged area. For our present purposes, we shall assume that we are dealing with a classroom unit that has been made available for remodeling, hopefully one that has at least a twelve-foot ceiling. We can also assume for our purposes that the classroom would be in an elementary school where the nature of activity usually calls for a somewhat larger classroom measuring 36 feet by 28 feet. Thus we have as a total area a little more than 1,000 square feet of space. As we think about the utilization of such an area, we may also assume that other departments in the audiovisual media-service center will be able to give certain kinds of special support such as making slides and transparencies and providing film clips for programing uses. With these assumptions in mind we list some estimates for good use of the available space indicated as follows:

1. *Studio Presentation Space:* This area would be the main program production center providing good quality sound and lighting. The limited size of this area would permit only minimum camera maneuverability, but it is assumed that a zoom lens will be available on one camera. Two separate program sets may be utilized, if urgently needed one being used for limited action such as narration for combining and/or transferring other media to videotape. The studio area may have to be diminished by some 70 square feet for media-making activities plus a small area for a shelving unit or metal cabinet for supplies. *Estimate* : 480 square feet.
2. *General Storage Area:* This area ought to be curtained or partitioned off from the rest of the studio. It is needed to store extra sets and backgrounds, rear-projection screen unit, over-head projector and low mobile stand, special charts, and apparatus that needs to be maintained in a state of readiness for ITV use. *Estimate :* 80 square feet.
3. *Workroom and Ready Room for Teachers and Office for Secretary:* This space may be needed for a part of full-time secretary, teachers' aides, or for study and work space for

teachers to use prior to making presentations to be taped. A few library-type carrels, a worktable and a typing desk for a secretary or for teachers to use. *Estimate :* 112 square feet.

4. *Control Room Area:* In this space there should be room for tape storage, taping operations, the film chain with both slide and film projectors, media table near the multiplexer, the cameras control racks, transmitter equipment if separate, a maintenance workbench and underneath storage. The console for both video and audio control would be elevated to provide visibility of the studio area. *Estimate:* 336 square feet.

Some Observations About the Estimates for School-Building ITV Studio Spaces: We refer the reader to Fig. 10.3 where he may study the relationships of the spaces identified in the preceding items and draw his own conclusions about the limitations that a small-size studio places on its potential volume of operations. As we pointed out earlier, the total space for this particular analysis of functions amounted to only 1,000 square feet. As we can readily see, the studio under operating conditions would be cramped, yet given time to get ready, a number of separate programing and transmitting operations could be carried on simultaneously, such as:

1. Transmitting a live presentation as for total-group instruction by a teacher in mathematics or communications to three large groups in a school.
2. Taping the live presentation simultaneously on one recorder for subsequent, repetitive use.
3. Making a videotape recording of an off-the-air program for subsequent and repetitive use, as from a regional network for schools.
4. With additional equipment units such as a videotape recorder, a separate program on tape could be sent out simultaneously with the live presentation, but this would require also a two-channel cable operation with an additional modulator-amplifier unit for the second channel.

Such operations as we have mentioned are meant to be recorded only as possibilities, although they may be valuable supplements to ITV system-wide utilization plans in the modern media-oriented school. We must emphasize the important possibility that the school-building studio would not only be used to increase the program capability in direct relationship to the school's own teaching purposes, but such facilities as we have listed would greatly enhance the production capability of any system-wide studio operation as a programing resource. We are not saying that each school in any given system would have to have a studio facility such as we have just discussed. However, it would be highly desirable to organize, as a minimum, one such supplementary studio for each level of instruction—elementary, junior and senior high schools, and junior or community colleges. As volume of ITV programing increases, as the use of ITV on both firm and flexible schedules makes major curriculum

DIAGRAM OF SCHOOL BUILDING ITV STUDIO LAYOUT

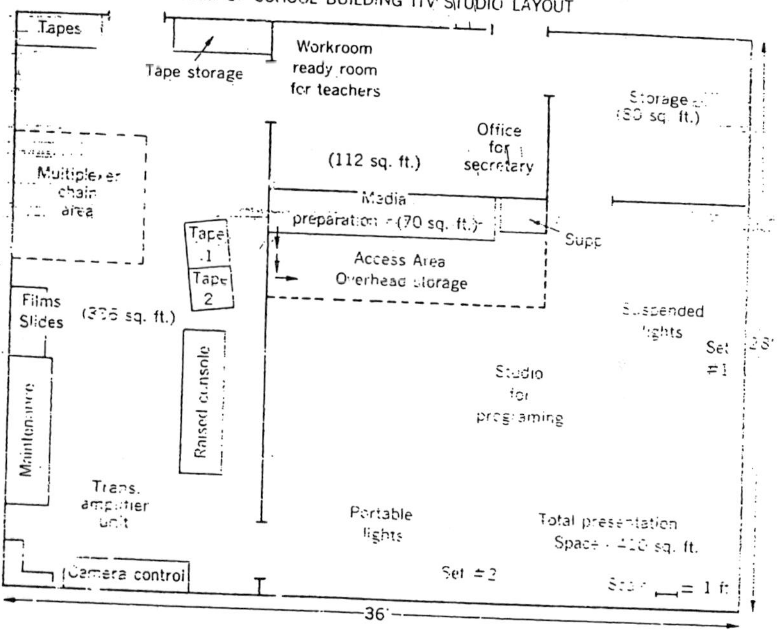

Fig. 10.3 : In contrast to Figure 10.1, this author's sketch is an analysis of space needs for an ITV studio at the school-building level. We assume that the media center will support this ITV endeavor with assistance in many ways, even to supplying leadership and staff and being responsible for its operations. We believe that for serious and mature programing efforts at the building level on operational area of 4,400-5,300 square feet would be a more realistic requirement.

contributions, and as teaching systems demand the use of videotapes or programed instructional television sequences, the ITV district-wide plans will have to encompass decentralized as well as centralized program capability.

Some Equipment Needs for ITV School-Building Studio Unit. For the kind of capability desired in a school-building studio, we can suggest that if school-system needs are also to be met on a contributing basis by such programing, then broadcast-quality equipment ought to be specified. At any rate, every effort ought to be made to provide maximum quality from equipment units that are compatible with the schools and district's purpose. Later on we shall discuss transmission system and we emphasize now the need to provide maximum quality throughout all phases of the television operation from production to reception. The equipment units we suggest as a minimum are as follows:

1. Two broadcast-quality vidicon camera chains with electronic viewfinders, lenses, tripods, console, and video monitors.
2. Microphones, audio tape recorder and mixer-amplified at the console.
3. Optical multiplexer chain using film and slide projectors.
4. Suspended lights and a switchboard control.
5. Headsets and intercom system.
6. Two videotape recorders with electronic editing feature on one of the units.
7. Appropriate modulator for RF transmission and supplementary transmitters and amplifiers for multi-channel operation.
8. An antenna receiving system for receiving and taping programs from external sources.

Program Capability by Means of TV Equipment at Teaching Stations

We have come to look upon teaching stations as a means of supplementing program production for instructional television purposes. We note first the possibility of connecting a videotape recorder, for example a high-quality, one-inch tape recorder, to a classroom receive which may be viewed by some thirty pupils. Since the tape recorder in this case is equipped with a modulator unit a number of receivers can be supplied with the taped program, thus making possible the effective use of the unit by a large group as a total group in team teaching presentations. With the addition of the appropriate amplifier or amplifiers, and the needed splitters, the tape-recorded program can also be transmitted throughout the school on the internal coaxial cable system generally used for programing from the school-building or school-system studio facilities. We see in this process the capability of receiving via the school's master antenna system, off-the-air program content from many different sources of supply. Videotapes of such centralized local, regional, state, or national sources, could also be distributed to the school building for transmission within the school unit as scheduled.

Mobile units of conveniently packaged classroom receiving, recording and transmitting equipment, may be moved, for example, from one science room to another, or from a nearby social science classroom for special program production uses. The packaged units may also be equipped with a camera that may be moved or fixed in a classroom where lighting is adequate and be used to record a particular presentation by a teacher. Such presentations may then be combined later with film clips and slides at the main studio as a part of a teaching system that will be copied and used repetitively and even exchanged with other resource banks. Teachers who use television display or image-magnification systems in their classrooms to make use of minute objects, a wide variety of diagrammatic content, or demonstrate laboratory techniques, for example, may also combine views of themselves and the illustrative material they utilize on the videotape of the classroom unit we have just discussed. We have not yet mentioned that in classroom situations, teachers may make presentations that are immediately transmitted to other classrooms, but we have repeatedly emphasized the value of repetitive use of a presentation by videotape recording methods. When ITV programs are good they are good because of what they do to pupils. When they are preserved, they may be used again and again with equal results, provided that the systems under which they are used are valid, and the conditions for learning are optimum. For examples of processes and equipment packages.

Some Observations About Space Needs for Classroom Television Program Operations: It can be readily understood that in a studio situation we can engineer quality control over programming efforts. We cannot generally match either the audio and video quality achieved in the studio in the classroom program production activity. However, with installation of a camera, pre-set and fixed lights, and teacher controlled camera-switching devices (to permit switching from one overhead camera for diagrams and apparatus demonstrations to a camera that shows a close-up view of the teacher), some highly desirable programs may be recorded that will serve valuable uses in the curriculum. If we have a desirable teaching station to begin with we can say that little if any extra space will be needed for developing the kind of programing capability that we have just described. If we consider equipment units such as Tri-Video, Tele-Center, the Ampex Videotrainer, and the Neuclo TV School Master, it becomes obvious that space in front of a teaching station area would be approximately 25 square feet if camera and lights are mounted in the ceiling. If the camera is on the floor some 20 feet of additional space would be needed and if we figure 15 additional square feet for portable lights, the total space requirement for the equipment would be on the order of 60 square feet. If we assume that a teacher is working part of the time with an image-magnification television camera mounted on a six-foot long table as an additional component, then the total would be increased by 30 square feet. We now have a total figure of 90 square feet taken up by classroom television equipment. All of this may or may not be in addition to space used by the teacher normally.

Summary of Classroom TV Equipment Needs: At this time a good case could be made for classroom use of ITV equipment as a supplement to other centrally located studios. We must add that the several available ITV record-playback systems vary in price, but for the level of sophistication we assume in general, the cost would run to $6,500 including a viewfinder camera. The front-of-room image-magnification system would of course be in addition. The various classroom equipment units envisioned are as follows:

1. One closed-circuit TV and videotape recording-playback system (with the possibility of using the TV camera in suspended fixed-mount position).
2. One image-magnification television camera with fixed lights and accessories, located on a demonstration table.
3. Additional transmission and amplification equipment to take care of long cable runs to various classrooms and to make possible the use of several splitters as would be necessary to supply classrooms with one or more receiving sets.

Program Capability Through Procurement from External Sources

This is the fourth aspect of potential program capability. We have mentioned rich sources from regional, state, and national agencies and distributors, and when schools are properly equipped, these sources can be readily made available. We can summarize these means as follows :

1. Regional telecasts on appropriate schedules from museums, other school systems, and from statewide networks, *live* or already on videotape.
2. Using videotape (or other program capsules) that are distributed as units, or in series, as parts of instructional packages, directly to school-building and school-system studio transmitting facilities.

We have mentioned earlier the possibilities just listed, but we have not yet afforded them the attention they deserve. We can point out, however, that if such sources are to be useful, school-building, district-wide, and classroom videotape playback facilities will have to be provided and used to the fullest extent. School-building and classroom transmitting centers will become obviously more important and even indispensable for meeting specific needs when multiple-channel operations and crowded facilities at central studios begin to interfere with curriculum needs. Facilities and spaces in addition to capabilities already described are not required for procurement and use of programs from external sources. However, such procurement demands master antenna systems or other transmission and reception systems. In fact we cannot consider the use of ITV programs from outside the school unit we have the capability to receive them off the air or via cable, or until agencies send them by parcel post to telecasting agencies in the schools.

Some Hints for Design of Studio Spaces

Before we leave discussion of programing capability in general and the subject of studio spaces specifically, we ought to suggest in summary form a number of major critical recommendations that should be made regarding the design of these program-producing areas. We have referred to both centralized and decentralized studios and have mentioned the use of space in old buildings. We wish now to highlight a few factors that should be borne in mind when discussing studio-space specifications regardless of where they are located.

1. Floor-to-ceiling heights in studio programing areas should be at least twelve-feet and preferably even higher. In other than studio areas, excessive heights may be converted to overhead storages areas, or mezzanine office and other auxiliary spaces.
2. Lights should be suspended on tracks or grids to provide unhampered mobility of cameras and to increase the amount of operational floor space for programing activity.
3. Acoustical treatment should be provided to improve sound quality.
4. Air conditioning installations that employ low-level motor and fan noise are an essential in both studio and control rooms.
5. Studio floors should be smooth and hard. Soft tiles may become pitted from table legs and camera tripods, thus interfering with ease of camera handling.
6. It is essential to provide sufficient AC operating power, and to also provide a sufficient number of outlets for present and expanded uses of any given facility. Such power requirements should be identified specifically.
7. Optimum access areas to multiple studios, in which to carry on auxiliary services of related operations, are necessary for flow of activities and personnel. Doorways should be wider and higher than normal.
8. Studio and control room must be related specially to provide visual surveillance, with proper connectors for camera cables and audio lines, located in the walls that separate them.

9. Provide for intercommunication between television programing, control, and auxiliary spaces. Elevation of console will not only provide better direct visual control, but will enable the program director to operate the console himself as needed.
10. In plans for new construction, specify a four-inch raceway, or trough, covered by a metal plate along the base of each wall of the control room and as required also in studio spaces. Conduits for power ought to be considered additionally. Floor troughs are essential, particularly in control rooms where large cables and connectors tie console, camera controls, multiplexer, videotape recorders, audio lines, and transmitter lines together for both safety and convenience.
11. Suitable backdrops of gray and blue ought to be mounted on traverse systems for use in areas of the studio where programs are to originate.

An often difficult and vexing problem for the media director to solve when planning to make use of television, especially on a citywide basis, is that of making a wise decision on the adoption and implementation of a television program transmission system. Regardless of whether the ITV programs are to be scheduled for large-group use, or dial-selected by individual learners, one or more systems must be employed in transmitting the program from a studio site, or from a videotape resource bank, to the viewing station. A thorough discussion of the facets of such a problem lies beyond the scope of this book, but we shall discuss the main systems that are presently in common use. In this discussion we shall consider the delivery of ITV programs from the output of the transmitter in the main studio to the input of the building where it is received. We shall also discuss in another section the problem of reception, distribution, and display.

Operational Facilities and Equipment: Transmission Systems

Before we proceed to a description and a brief analysis of some of the main possibilities that are commonly used for ITV systems, we will provide the reader with a summary listing of a few basic facts about the nature of television transmission. We can then emphasize the nature of the problem that the prospective audiovisual media director will have to deal with before deciding what system to recommend. Some of these main facts and considerations are as follows:

1. Television programs (television signals) are ordinarily made up of two separate components, the picture signal from the TV camera and the audio signal from the microphones.
2. Video and audio signal components may be combined and transmitted on signal carrier wave. When this is done the signal is called an RF signal (radio frequency) and this signal can be transmitted through space by means of broadcast or open-circuit procedures, or it can be transmitted by a coaxial cable.
3. Standard television receivers are generally used in classrooms to produce both picture and sound.
4. RF signals may be transmitted over long distances by cable, but amplifiers along the way must be employed to maintain signal strength. A number of factors need to be considered in any transmission and distribution system. What is the length of cable? How many schools and their receivers are being tapped off from main coaxial lines? What is the quality of the devices by means of which the incoming signal to a school is split? What is the quality of the modulator-transmitter unit? How many channels are being used?
5. A cable handling RF transmission will carry all of the 12 VHF channels, simultaneously with each channel signal operating on its own pre-set frequency level. Thus each program source, *live* or taped, will require its own modulator-transmitter unit,. Several so-called sub-channels may currently be activated because-transmitters and amplifiers are available for controlling the frequencies. Special receiving equipment may have to be used, however, if the best possible image resolution is to be obtained.
6. The video component alone, coming directly from a TV camera, may be transmitted over a cable directly to a television receiver. Such video signals are understandably of highest possible quality. Since they are not tuned to any particular channel, the entire coaxial cable issued solely for one video program at a time. Television monitors have to be used for receiving such signals, or a regular television receiver has to be modified to eliminate

or bypass other circuits such as the audio, for example. Thus when a cable is used for video transmission only, it has to be scheduled, or a separate cable has to be provided.

7. When the video signal is transmitted over a coaxial cable, a separate audio component line has to be provided from the microphone to an audio amplifier and thence to a loudspeaker or sound distribution system at the viewing station.
8. Intercommunication cables are not coaxial. They are essential for communication between studios and classrooms or between crew members, and have to be separate from the coaxial cables that carry RF signals.
9. RF broadcast transmission may be so controlled (low-power broadcasting) in its radiational effects that it becomes to all intents and purposes a closed-circuit system as does the coaxial cable system. This is particularly true of the point-to-point control possible in line-of-sight transmission with microwave equipment.

In the light of these basic facts and conditions, we shall proceed to a brief description of some of the generally available transmission systems being used by schools for their ITV programs.

Transmission by Coaxial Cable

We turn first to coaxial systems of transmission and to the ways in which, this system is likely to be handled. We have already mentioned in other connections the fact that coaxial cable systems provide two-way RF signal capability when classrooms are looped into a continuous circuit, and in the preceding section the general applicability of the RF system was pointed out. It is also important to emphasize the reliability of the cable method and to note that no FCC license is required for such transmission linkages. It should also be borne in mind that the main transmission cable may possess a wide range of capability characteristics so that it may function in an ITV transmission system in a number of different ways. We are suggesting that new uses for RF signal cable may be developed that will not only link up computerized operations, but utilize additional channels as well for unusually high-definition content with special receiving equipment.

Some Advantages of Cable Transmission: Since the Bell System cable-leasing plan is one of the two basic and reasonably available transmission possibilities open to school districts, we ought to deal at least in summary form with its advantages. The following list of advantages for this transmission system has been complied by Deuel.

1. A consistently high-quality signal at all locations independent of distance or terrain.
2. Facilities which can provide large numbers of TV channels operating at the same time and under most situations, and which are also capable of handling color transmission.
3. Inclusion of all repair and maintenance in the monthly charge, on a twenty-four hour basis, if necessary.
4. Facilities which require no license or regulation of any kind to operate.
5. A private system which is not subject to interference due to obstructions, buildings, or external signals.
6. Freedom from engineering and right-of-way problems, which are the responsibility of the Telephone Company.
7. Experienced personnel locally who are readily available to serve the systems on a moment's notice.
8. A system which does not require the construction of towers or antennas on school buildings.
9. Provision of facilities constructed to the highest technical standards and maintained with the latest type of test equipment.
10. A minimum of capital funds required to establish an effective system, thus making funds available for other school projects.

It is with these advantages in mind that we regretfully note that coaxial cable as a commodity is expensive in the sense of stringing up and using a twenty-mile network, for example; the need for amplifiers over long runs is essential; and the technology of transmission, maintenance, and reception processes is not only complex, but is undergoing rapid change and development. Since the media program director in a city school system can rarely get permission to string a coaxial-cable line on poles owned and operated by other agencies, even if his school system desired to have him do so, he has little choice but to lease TV cable-transmission services, and to these possibilities we now turn.

Leasing Coaxial-Cable Facilities from the Bell System: With the Bell System all needed equipment units, cables, and connectors tare supplied installed, and maintained by the local telephone services companies for a monthly rental charge. Price estimates have to be based on cable distances, number of channels utilized on the cable, number of connectors at the school sites, and other factors that have to be determined locally. Even though technology is changing rapidly, and costs are too, a generalized rate table (subject of course to change for specific situations) will be helpful to reveal the nature of the process as well as to give some idea of the method by which price estimates are figured as shown by the chart on the following page.

Having pointed out the basic items generally used in a arriving at cost estimates, we must now reiterate the fact that technological advancements dictate the development of an entirely new rate scale on a 12-channel basis that in specific situations may prove to reduce these rates by 50 per cent. Even though prices may change drastically, we can see that given a specific number of schools, the number of classrooms to be served, and the airline miles between each school-building unit, this rate table could be used to develop approximation of cost. In light of included maintenance to provide trouble-free service, low capital-equipment expense, depreciation, and replacement costs, the case for cable-leasing arrangements appears strong. We shall discuss one other cable-leasing possibility, which may not be generally available, and then proceed to describe a low-power broadcast system that is nevertheless referred to as a closed-circuit operation.

Main Cable Monthly Rental Charge for One Quarter Airline Mile of Each Leg Between Schools

1st channel,	$15.00
2nd channel,	5.00
3rd channel,	3.00
4th channel,	3.00
5th channel,	2.00
6th channel,	2.00

Cost Estimate for a $2,000 Modulator at Each Signal Source

Monthly Rental Charge for Each Channel :

1st channel,	$45.00
2nd channel,	35.00
3rd channel,	30.00
4th channel,	20.00
5th channel,	20.00
6th channel,	15.00

Cost Estimate for Each Output at Each Receiving Point

Monthly Rental Charge for Each School Served :

1st channel,	$10.00
2nd channel,	5.00
3rd channel,	3.00
4th channel,	2.00
5th channel,	1.50
6th channel,	1.00

Cost Estimate for the Connector Outlet in Each Classroom

Per Classroom per Month, $1.25

Leasing Coaxial-Cable Facilities from the Community Antenna Television Company: The possibility of leasing a cable-transmission facility from Community Antenna Television companies may not be legally permissible. Yet, in the case of the ITV program of Elmira, New York, Public Schools, this is the method by which twenty of Elmira's twenty -two schools receive ITV service. It has been reported that the Elmira Public Schools System has contracted for the exclusive use of one of the Elmira Video Company's channels at an annual cost of $5,000. However, according to FCC controls governing their organization and operation, Community Antenna Television companies are organized solely for the broadcast of commercial programs, and therefore may not offer facilities on a lease basis as a common carrier would do, for other purposes. State legislation in the various states may also prevent the rental of cable space by CATV companies, and moreover, state public utility commission may set up rigid controls over transmission conditions within and across their borders. Unique situations have of course arisen around the country, and hence some exceptions to basic rules have apparently been made. Just what turn these matters, will take in the years ahead cannot be predicted, but it seems highly improbable that what has come to be known as CATV will enter generally into the common carrier field unless some drastic changes are made in the technology of handling electrical power and telephone cables on poles or running them through trenches or tunnels. If and when school districts organize themselves into corporate agencies for inaugurating CATV system for their own ITV transmission activities, they are likely to encounter some major problems in suspending or buying their cables. AT the present time it is common practice for CATV organizations to either rent poles from utility and common carrier companies, and then string their own coaxial cable linkages or lease the cable they need from the Bell System companies.

In view of the preceding discussions, it seems obvious that a school district has two main possibilities for interconnecting schools for ITV programing, namely, leasing cable from the local Bell System company, or owning and operating its own 2,500 mHz FCC-controlled, Instructional Television Fixed Service transmission system. Under this system, an RF signal is radiated on a maximum of four channels, using repeaters and microwave point-to-point transmitters as required to reach all of the schools in a given school district. We describe this transmission possibility next.

Transmission by Instructional Television Fixed Service

The FCC-assigned frequency band for this service is 2,500-2,686 mHz in the microwave portion of the spectrum. The frequency of this band is much higher than the familiar UHF channels in which the highest channel is only 890 mHz. Since the FCC has assigned this band for educational use only, this portion of the spectrum is in a sense a private band with its transmissions not being receivable on TV sets using regular channels. One of the difficulties in the use of this broadcast band is that the signal has to be telecast in a line of-sight path from the transmitter antenna to the receiving equipment, and hence, interference by terrain, buildings, and distance limitations have to be considered and accurately surveyed. Where distance is too great, for example, beyond an obstruction-free twenty-mile path, repeater stations have to be set up, or new paths set up around obstructions, or a point-to-point microwave link constructed.

The system operates by transmitting an RF signal through space in direction-controlled areas at something like ten watts of power. Special receiving antennas pick up the signal at each school building, convert it to VHF television channels and then distribute it via a master antenna coaxial-cable distribution system to all classrooms. The main advantages of such a system are as follows :

1. Up to four channels may be used simultaneously.
2. The system is private.
3. The system operation requires only a second class FCC technician license, and participating teachers and students may need only a third class license.
4. The system is owned outright by the school district and claims are made that cost for the system when schools are widely separated is much less than for cable linkages.
5. Each new school in the area of the transmitted signal may be added to the system by providing the antenna and the distribution system.

As we have already pointed out, interference may result from obstructions, and installation costs may be unusually high when sites for repeater towers have to be acquired, roads constructed for servicing, and pre-construction engineering surveys carried out. Competitors point out that all long-term expenditures should be figured in before net costs are established. FCC licensing may or may not prove to be a disadvantage, but the fact remains that a maintenance staff is essential. It seems obvious that there are significant advantages that could accrue, but as with any proposed transmission system, the decision must be based on thorough study. It is doubtful that teachers and student ought to takeover any great portion of the technical operation of such a situation. Teachers have significant professional work to do that takes a high priority, and even though some students might find valuable experience in such technical work, full-time personnel are recommended so that most of the time of students can be given to serious study activities.

Some Examples in the Schools: Considerable experimental work was carried on in the Plain-edge, New York, public schools by the Adler Educational Service. It was there that the low-power broadcast system was successfully demonstrated on June 14, 1962. Subsequently, the FCC established the Instructional Television Fixed Service in 1963. The cost of the Plain-edge transmission equipment amounted to approximately $28,000 for the one channel in operation. Six elementary schools, two junior high schools, one senior high school and the central administration building (seven airline miles of cable) were within the transmission area at the time. Added to this figure is the maintenance cost, for either a permanent technical staff member or for a private maintenance contract with a commercial company. The cost for Micro-Link Systems' (Varian Associates) installation of a four-channel system for the Mifflin County school District in Pennsylvania, serving 340 classrooms and 10,000 pupils, was $264,195.

Just outside of Houston, Texas, the Spring Branch independent school district is operating a 24-school, 2-channel, 2,500 mHz network. Studio and transmitting equipment amounted to approximately $70,000. The cost for each school's receiving antenna, signal converter, distribution circuit, plus 325 television receivers in the classrooms amounted to $142,000. Rochester, New York, also transmits instructional programs over three channels to 46,000 pupils in 52 city schools. Rochester's television studio staff includes an executive producer, producer-director, director, chief engineer, technician, artist, and a secretary, all full time. Part-time workers include six production assistants, six cameramen an artist, and a typist. For field maintenance work, the crew includes a field maintenance supervisor and two television repairmen. The 2,500 mHz system of Newburgh, New York, transmits instructional television programs over two channels to some 500 classrooms in 25 public and parochial schools.

Also in its first stage of development, the Frenso County 2,500 mHz system serves 47 schools within sixteen miles of the country seat of Fresno, California, Repeater sites will be developed as the service is extended to all schools in the country.

The Jerrold Electronics Corporation in its valuable booklet for school personnel makes the following generalized estimates for 2,500 mHz fixed service installations:

	Cost Range
Transmitter, Tower, and Antenna, One Channel (depending on height)	$15,000 to $30,000
Each Additional Transmit Channel	$10,000
Each School Receiver-Converter, Antenna and Mounting (assuming 20 feet above roof)	$1,250 to $1,500
Maintenance (for ten years, per year percentage of initial cost) amounts to 5 per cent.	

It is recommended that an independent consultant conduct a site survey...A budgetary figure for this service can be estimated at $50 per school and would include path profiles, sketches, and necessary photographs...The survey will determine the best location for the transmitting antenna; which schools will receive satisfactory signals with standard equipment; and which might require more powerful receive-converter units, larger antennas, higher towers, or alternate arrangements.

As we have emphasized previously, the citywide media director has several vexing problems on his hands, the solutions to which may be anything but easy. Thorough study at the engineering level will be needed and he will also find the cooperative effort of many other colleagues to be of inestimable value in formulating recommendations for action.

One other operational aspect of using ITV in the schools remains to be discussed, insofar as equipment and facilities are concerned, and this is the aspect of reception and viewing.

We look at the process of reception as picking up a received signal at the school by whatever means it comes, and distributing it, after optimum electronic treatment to teaching stations or to individual study carrels, for planned and significant viewing.

Operational Facilities and Equipment: Reception and Viewing

We are aware at this point of the various sources of program content and the mean by which they are transmitted to the school in any given district. Thus we visualize one kind of antenna for the 2,500 mHz fixed-service transmission, and another type of antenna for transmission via statewide broadcast facilities. Of course, no antenna at all is required in cases where transmissions are received by coaxial cable. In the former, case, we need two different types of antennas, each of which may feed signals into its own converter, then out to a mixer where they are subsequently split and distributed to receiving sets. When coaxial cable, is used we have a directly usable signal that is amplified and split, and then amplified again as required during long cable runs to all sections of a school building. This situation leads us to treat first the topic of reception by a master antenna system, referred to as MATV.

Reception via MATV

Regional and statewide educational television stations generally have large school populations that use their programs which are almost always broadcast on either UHF or VHF frequencies. Schools that use these programing services must install one or more receiving antennas, must convert UHF signals to VHF signals by means of a converter, and must then mix signals from various channels to supply a composite signal throughout a coaxial cable in a school building to each classroom receiver where a given participating teacher tunes in. Other teachers in other classrooms would similarly tune in the same program on the same channel or tune in another program coming in on another channel in an entirely different subject field. Now, just what facilities are likely to be needed in the operation of such a reception linkage? We can answer this question in considerable, yet not complete detail, since information about conditions such as local signal strength, number of channels available, directions of the various sources, and interference with transmitted signals is lacking. However, since the media program director must sense the need for expert advice, and must himself make some sound recommendations, it is most important to have knowledge and insight into how the process works. He should get any extra help he needs from dealers, state department of education consultants, engineers, and technical specialists as to just what special arrangements are required.

The Basic MATV Equipment Arrangements. We shall start fist by assuming that we have coming in at a given school building at a given hour of the day one UHF channel program and three VHF channel programs. We shall further assume that the three VHF programs originate from different sources and are of different strengths, hence need transformation and separate amplifiers (a strip amplifier instead of the broad band type) for better signal control. We now start with the antennas and show the component parts needed for reception and a two-way distribution loop to all teaching stations as follows:

1. One UHF antenna with a transformer (balun) and a converter to change the incoming UHF signal to an appropriate VHF signal, to be carried by an appropriate channel, and a strip amplifier. (UHF signals suffer such losses in strength on coaxial cable as to preclude their use.)
2. Three single-band antennas, one for each VHF channel, properly rotated and fixed for optimum signal strength, each with a transformer (balun) and an appropriate strip amplifier. (Signal strength on each channel must be equal for the system.)
3. One coupler for the system by means of which the four VHF signals (originally one UHF and three VHF signals) are mixed, split, and fed to the coaxial-cable loop.
4. A complete coaxial-cable linkage system for connecting each classroom with every other classroom and with the main coaxial line on a two-way basis, with additional line amplifiers as required.
5. Each classroom to be equipped with a two-way ITV connector, such as the Jerrold J-Jacks so that each teaching station can become an originating as well as a receiving

station for ITV programs. The so-called *closed loop* hook-up makes this possible. One teaching station would originate and distribute on one channel while another classroom would receive a program simultaneously on a different channel.

6. One or more standard television 23-inch receivers in each classroom.

Looking at the preceding list of components, we can now suggest that under different transmission circumstances such as equal signal strengths and with channel sources lying in the same directions, it is likely that a single broadband VHF antenna and broadband amplifier could be substituted for the three VHF single-band antennas and matching strip amplifiers in the preceding list. The UHF channel would require a separate antenna and a converter and amplifier as listed previously. Otherwise the components would be largely the same. Broadband amplifiers amplify the signals of all VHF channels equally, and this action may preclude their use in some situations.

Reception via 2,500 mHz Television Fixed Service

Since this system of transmission has already been discussed, we have but to relate the reception system to the MATV system just described. If we assume that all of the components in the preceding list have been installed, then we have only to add the special school-building 2,500 mHz antenna, tower, and converter which changes the low-power channel to a specific VHF channel signal. This signal is then fed into an appropriate VHF strip amplifier and on into the coupler for mixing, splitting and routing to the school's coaxial-cable loop. This antenna would therefore operate in the system described much as the UHF antenna-converter unit would work. When two to four channels of low-power radiation are being employed, the composite signal on the school's antenna has to be converted to the several VHF channels, each sent to a strip amplifier or to a broadband amplifier and thence into the coupler and to the classroom cable.

Reception Via Coaxial Cable

We have already noted the advantages of transmission by coaxial cable and considered its possible high cost for widely separated schools. We now point out that when signals arrive by cable to the school building being served, they need no conversion since they are already being transmitted on appropriate VHF channels. Such signals are directly usable at the teaching station outlet. Some amplification may be needed along the coaxial lines but such systems may have already been installed as a component of an MATV reception system. The problem of receiving such signal at the school signal input is the mixing of school-district produced signals with MATV sources. Antenna received signals would be mixed with cable received signals in the coupler-splitter equipment unit. If only cable signals are to be received into the school, no additional equipment will be needed with the possible exception of supplementary booster amplifiers. When such systems are leased on a monthly-fee basis, the cable and auxiliary equipment, such as tap-off and J-Jacks connectors are included, much as is the telephone instruments in the school's central offices.

Equipment Units and Arrangements for Viewing ITV Programs

We come now to that operational aspect of the citywide or school-building instructional television process that is the reason for it all viewing by the learner. If we mention trouble-free equipment, solid-state circuitry that requires but a 5 per cent outlay for maintenance, or if we debate at length the disadvantages and advantages of a given transmission system, it is to make the viewing so free of distractions that the program can have its intended instructional effect. In this discussion we must limit ourselves to equipment and arrangements for its use since what learners do, or how they react, because of what they see and hear on television is a curriculum matter that we have already dealt with. We therefore present three categories of equipment arrangements at teaching stations namely, for individuals, for small groups, and for large groups.

Viewing by Individuals: To provide this kind of viewing or display capability we must visualize an individual learner in an atypical environment, namely, at a teaching station prepared for one person. This means a carrel or booth in which he can receive a special program that meets his unique needs. Technology has been developing rapidly to meet such individualization needs, and there are vastly different way by which the display can be effected, through scheduling, dialing, or some other form of selection process. In fact, as we shall point out later, media other than television may be desirable and essential. The programs may have to originate in the school building itself, or at central studios and resource banks. In the latter case, transmission systems, involving multiple-channel RF and straight audio-program taps have to be developed, and we shall mention these possibilities in the next chapter. For the present we must point out that viewing stations for individuals must be arranged in special rooms, in viewing areas of the school's library, or in selected classrooms according to grade, subject, and learning activity, or even set up in especially adapted corridor spaces in old school building. Wiring for ITV-viewing carrels poses some problems that may be difficult and costly to solve because of the complexity of inter-connected cables that are required. Therefore it may not be feasible to spread them out in widely separated locations. Electronic learning laboratories fully equipped with television receivers and headsets, as well as with audio-program sources and other pictorial sources, may prove to be the most feasible means of meeting special needs within a given school building. Thus the television-viewing devices may be only a part of a total media capability for individualization applications.

Some general Considerations for ITV Viewing: Before arrangements and equipment units are specified it would be well to list some of the major viewing conditions that should be borne in mind when making decisions about the classroom use of instructional television. The physical environment for the use of audiovisual media, but we have delayed our discussion of matters pertaining to television until now. In fact, we must not proceed even now to consider television only, for then we shall certainly make some hideous errors such as blocking a rear-or-front-projection surface with one or more television receivers suspended from the ceiling. We therefore must balance the recommendations for ITV usage in optimum fashion against the urgent need for a wide variety of learning activities. The facts and conditions in the following list twill serve as a basis for later decisions and recommendations.

1. No viewer should sit farther away from a television screen than approximately twelve times the width of the image. This means that for a 20 inch wide. TV image on the tube the last row of seats should not be farther away than approximately twenty-feet. The 6W rule for projected images can be altered to 12W for television viewing. (However, this modification assumes close-up video composition.)
2. The rule for the minimum distance is that the viewer should be seated not closer than approximately three times the width of the image. Also, based on unobstructed viewing by learners in a row, the maximum viewing angle (the angle the normal eye level line makes with a line from the viewer's eye to the top of a television screen) of the closest seated viewer should not exceed thirty degrees.
3. The total included horizontal viewing angle may be as high as ninety degrees, that is, forth-five degrees on each side of the axis perpendicular to the television screen. This is approximately the same viewing angle permitted by matte screens, although the nature of content may preclude the placement of viewers within such wide viewing angles.
4. The nature of the learning activity determines the amount of space required for seating a given number of pupils. Thus television receivers may be required in laboratories, and in both large and small teaching stations, where furniture may range from a tablet arm chair to a desk and flat-top work tables. With normal seating in front of a 24-inch receiver, using desk and chair furniture in a five-foot front to rear spacing, thirty-four learners could be accommodated.
5. Television receivers should be elevated for unobstructed viewing. The height generally recommended is a minimum of five feet from the bottom of the television screen to the floor. Actually, if the students are arranged in a row, the bottom of the screen must be above the normal four-foot eye level of an adult. Thus it is recommended that heights up to seven feet from bottom of screen to floor be used, and moreover, when ceiling heights cannot accommodate the proper placement of receiver, that risers be used to

elevate students seats, or that seats be arranged so that viewers do not have to sit in rows directly in back of a each other.

6. In teaching stations where television is being used, closing regular light-diffusing shades or blinds and turning off overhead lights provide acceptable light-level conditions.

With these basic insights in mind, media specialists can plan the kinds of installations in schools that will facilitate the effective use of instructional television. We turn now to several typical arrangements of equipment in various kinds of teaching stations.

Viewing by Small Groups: In accordance with generally accepted standards for television viewing, which of course may change radically in the years ahead we can assume that for a great many conventional-size classrooms in both elementary and secondary schools, one 24-inch receiver, placed either in a corner or at the front, center of the room, will be the minimum arrangement. This television receiver may be mounted on a side wall, on a suitable high mobile stand with 4-inch, rubber-tired castors, or it may be suspended from the ceiling. In many situations, a mobile stand will be desirable so as to make room for one or more projection screens. Mobility may be very important in those situations where the space is to be used for multi-purpose activity. In learning space where small and large-group arrangements are possible and desirable additional small, portable television receivers may be usable and the addition of headsets and a plug-in strip will permit listening and viewing without distracting other groups. But the means by which programs are to be repeated, or new programs called for, must be precisely defined before such recommendations can be made. For example, one to four students may have need to retrieve a program from the central or the school-system's bank of video tapes, or several carrels may be available in the teaching area, with the possibility of two students making use of each one.

Viewing by Large Groups: By the sixties, the need for large-group teaching stations became obvious. Teaching auditoriums became common, and clusters of smaller classrooms surrounded total-group instruction areas as for team-teaching operations. Many early instructional television teaching stations seated 300 to 500 students, and even auditoriums were divided and especially equipped for formal multimedia presentations. Television could serve large groups seated in one place or it could serve them seated in an unlimited number of conventional size classrooms. We must reiterate the need to provide viewing capability for all learners in these large groups without sacrificing the capability to utilize other media in any desirable sequence. We therefore recommend a variety of mounting for 23- and 24-inch receivers, including mobile stands, permanent floor-pedestal mounts, and ceiling mounts. Such multiple receivers should be interconnected by means of a panel at the front of a teaching station sot that the teacher or technician may turn them on and off, switch to video-channel reception from RF, and use intercom circuits to talk to studio personnel. Sight lines to all receivers must be ascertained to avoid obstruction. When up to 25 TV receivers may be required for a group of 450 to 500 viewers, the advantage of a single large-screen viewing process becomes obvious. This advantage will be fully realized when quality in projection television is assured. Such projection-television systems require critical light-control arrangements adequate sound, and expert technical surveillance. Advancing technology may soon bring about a substantial increase in the popularity of this method of large-group viewing. Scurrying about a 500-seat auditorium to make find adjustments to 25 TV receivers in time for a telecast is one chore we can eliminate with a projection-television unit. The use of this process by means of rear-projection screens will doubtlessly become increasingly important.

One problem that needs special attention is the provision for high-quality sound. In present day media-supported presentations, it is more essential than ever to provide audio-distribution capability for large groups. In small groups a single television receiver with adequate sound distribution from front-mounted speakers may be sufficient. However, in large-groups situations, either well-spaced multiple receivers will have to provide this same coverage, or an auxiliary high-fidelity sound distribution system will have to be planned and installed—for example, throughout the ceiling area. The use of sound from the multiple receivers would have the effect of a low-level sound system that is very effective generally. High-level systems that operate from one central source may not provide the quality needed, especially for instructional television presentations. When teachers switch from one medium to another—as to an overhead projector—it is necessary that they use a lavaliere or yoke microphone to project their voices out over a large group of learners, and in these cases, the sound system employed may be the one already set up in the television receivers. Care must be taken that such use of audio components follows a careful check-up to ascertain that amplifiers are compatible.

Some Standards for School Television Receivers: Increasing emphasis needs to be given to the purchase of high-quality television receivers for school applications. However, more than a high quality receiver is required to effect the improvement of picture definition. Advancing technological development will make such quality possible in all of the components involved. To summarize a few major characteristics a good school television receiver:

1. Has maximum resolution capability commensurate with transmission and origination systems.
2. Produces high-quality sound.
3. Has its loudspeakers located in front instead of on the sides.
4. Has been designed for school use: has sturdy construction, is electrically safe, and easy to maintain.
5. Has safety glass features.
6. Is titable.
7. Is equipped with simple, permanent, operational controls, properly placed for convenient action.
8. Is equipped with a variety of safety-engineered mounting frames and cradles.
9. Has been adapted for school closed circuit wiring systems.
10. Includes jacks and switches for audio distribution adaptations.

Such television receivers, especially on quantity purchase may be obtainable for $150 to $200 in the 23-inch size, with the most inexpensive though acceptable mobile stands starting at approximately $45.00.

Formulating Local Instructional Television Policy

We have placed great importance throughout this book on operational procedures based on sound policies. We have suggested a variety of study committees for formulating recommendations for policy adoption by those who are held responsible for making decisions, and as we contemplate such programs as audiovisual media services that involve major department such as instructional television, media preparation, and media distribution, we need to formulate realistic policies that apply to all phases of their operation from curriculum contribution to staff and finance. It is in this process that we seek to use the combined experience of teachers and school leaders in the application of *administration* and *change*-process principles. It will be these decisions that will determine the direction, comprehensiveness, and uniqueness of the contribution of television services to the school district's instructional program.

In this section we shall consider several aspects of the policy-formulating process, that will emphasize promising routes to success of the program, but such advice will of necessity have to be general inasmuch as the number of variables is too great for a full analysis. A specific and detailed analysis will have to be an essential of the local study and action process. Media program leaders must not ask to be excused from deliberations because the school system is so small that television services will not be feasible. Neither must they say that the pattern of organization and implementation of such programs ought to be patterned after metropolitan school-district operations. We advise a search for a unique approach to the television-service plan with such equipment units and staff as can be procured. With this general innovative and courageous attitude in mind, we turn to the critical areas of operational policy formulation.

Using Curriculum Needs as a Basis for ITV Plans

The strongest base upon which to formulate television policy is instructional need. Anyone who seeks to participate in the planning process must first be able to determine the needs that exist. If television can neither meet these needs nor make major contributions to the process of meeting them, then it would be a wise decision to use other means. Therefore we recommend as a basis for planning activity the study of curriculum and a succinct statement of the way the television medium will fulfill its promise along these lines. In light of this guideline, we suggest that the audiovisual media program director refrain from listing the facilities and equipment needed until he can relate them to a valid basis for thinking and action. We have already given proper emphasis to the curriculum basis for thinking and planning earlier in this chapter.

It is obvious that the thinking about curriculum matters involves not only the school curriculum leaders, principals, and teachers, but the superintendent and board of education members as well. The plan for system-wide involvement in this process may involve participation of several varieties that will not only develop interest and insight but also commitment to action. Visitation, demonstrations, program production, videotape recording activities, large-group and small-group meetings with staff and specialists should be organized and carried out. It may be wise to initiate a pilot ITV usage project before reaching a major decision to adopt its use on a specified level of comprehensiveness. Effective ways should be found to elicit the participation we advise, and out of such participation should come the broad outlines of operational policy regarding additional staff and their duties the acquisition of facilities and equipment (both centralized and decentralized), the provision for required financial support, and the relationship of such program to the existing audiovisual media services in the district.

Planning for Operational Staff members and Organizational Relationships

When schools and school districts plan for instructional television programs, they move rapidly towards firm and scheduled use of the medium in a vital relationship to the curriculum. Plans for operations involve many teachers, not just one, many groups of students, not just one isolated class, and the technological equipment units employed for such presentations demand the kind of adjustment and control that calls for technical training and know-how that is continuously available. This applies not only to the more simple television equipment packaged for use in a single classroom, but also to the sophisticated studio equipment packages that are involved with transmission to teaching stations and buildings on a district-wide basis. In addition to the technical staff, we readily see curriculum workers at a number of levels of involvement. It is inescapable that as instructional television programs move from limited to comprehensive scope the planning for full-time personnel becomes essential. Moreover, this vital need encompasses both professional and technical supervisory personnel, we see, for example, the need for a supervisor of district-wide television services who is a professional worker in the sense of his background of teaching ability and insight; and we also see a technical supervisor who takes charge of the additional technicians. In some cases, a television-process supervisor may not be a teacher at all, but a television specialist who has wide experience with television production perhaps having worked widely with teachers. In any case we must see clearly that it is not the television-process supervisor or manager who makes decisions as to content and teaching pedagogy, but curriculum and teaching personnel. Thus the problem is to provide both professional and technical capability for the programing, transmission, and display process to reach curriculum objectives, and to solve this problem we must seek unique solutions in light of local media-development conditions and resources. At any rate, we must determine what staff members we need and how they should be organized and supervised.

The Need for Staff Members Based on Functions: Since variables are so numerous in instructional programs and services, it is difficult to treat specifically the need for staff members, hence we shall, as has been done earlier in this book, use function as a basis of making suggestions. These basic functions with suggestions for providing staff are as follows:

1. *The Teaching Function:* Select and use unusually talented teachers on the staff to handle program design, preparation, and telecasting, or employ special television teachers to act as supervisors of program-design and utilization processes, according to need. Massive programing projects may demand temporary full-time personnel to plan and produce taped programs write guidebooks and instruction sheets. Only expert teachers can be used for this critical work.

They will have urgent and continuing need for supporting personnel. The salaries for ITV teachers and curriculum supervisors, however, hardly need to be charged to television-operation budgets.

2. *Administration Function:* Leadership and management function may be handled in various ways depending on size and scope of the services tendered. A full-time administrator will of course be essential in metropolitan, organizations, and in these cases his title may be director, coordinator, or supervisor. This staff member may or may not have had teaching experience, but if not, then arrangements for program decisions of a teaching nature will have to be handled by personnel with such experience working with him as team members. An overall television-services administrator maybe a part-time position in the sense that the audiovisual media director would supply the needed leadership an exercise the required administrative control. In other cases, work loads and the qualifications of present staff may be such that the demonstration of the instruction television service ought to be a separate organization with its own part-time or full-time administrator, responsible to the districts curriculum director or assistant superintendent of schools. The need for such leadership and management, exists at each central or decentralized service facility. Qualified teachers who have developed special interests and skills along these lines may serve admirably in many of these positions, and in addition, assume other programing functions. A number of organizational plans may therefore be developed at various supervisory levels that would involve city wide media directors, school principals and others.

3. *Production-Direction Functions:* It would be well to treat such important functions as production and direction separately from administrative leadership. However, under some school-district conditions, it is necessary to combine some of them. We must recognize the needs to coordinate production activities and to direct cameramen, floor, managers, and audio-control technicians in telecasting a live program or taping it for later use. Once a significant instructional program has been designed and scripted, producing it according to high standards of technical quality

is of course another essential. Teachers may carry on such activities on a part or full-time basis, thus calling for a readjustment in their regular teaching assignments. Experienced technical personnel may also, and most frequently do carry on the production activities. Staff must be provided for such activities in every studio, large or small, at headquarters or in school-building facilities.

4. *Equipment Operation and Control Functions:* There is little point in purchasing equipment units for instructional purposes unless they can be installed, controlled, operated, and adjusted for optimum performance. We therefore must provide staff members whose training and experience are primarily technical in nature. Some types of equipment under control of the FCC must be maintained by licensed personnel. WE cannot recommend the control and operation of ITV equipment except by people with the right skills and insights, and we may need to think of chief technician, and a group of assistants, fully qualified to handle the technical operation of all required equipment items including cameras, videotape recorders, amplifiers, transmitters, and related testing apparatus. There are many who still believe that students may be the only technical and operational personnel needed. Nothing could be further from the truth. We have already discussed these matters in an earlier chapter. Part-time technicians may be available from audiovisual media-service centers, and technicians with proper qualifications may be obtained to give over-all technical supervision of electronic learning laboratories, audiovisual media equipment, and television studio and control room equipment. Expert planning must be done to assure that the needed technicians are employed for specific operational tasks. Under appropriate supervision, some students may work on a voluntary basis or on an hourly basis after school.

5. *Media Preparation Functions:* Teachers who are responsible for program production realize the essential character of media preparation for good communication. They know also how much time is required for design and production, and therefore they insist that a graphic artist be employed to give this special service. We may also refer to the need for graphic technicians who can develop the skills for carrying out

routine reproduction processes in connection with slides, transparencies, and charts. Students may have to be used in some capacities for this work, especially when audiovisual service centers are in each school building. Technicians may also expand their scope of service by developing photographic skills as well as electronic skills. In comprehensive programs however, such combinations of functions are not likely to be required.

6. *Secretarial and Clerical Functions:* Unless the secretarial staff of the school-building or central headquarters media centers can handle additional duties in connection with their television programing services, separate full-time or part-time staffs must be arranged for. It is possible that secondary schools with secretarial training programs can supply part-time typists to alleviate the usual shortage of clerical workers, but certainly such assistants would require a full-time secretary who could give on-the-spot supervision. Secretarial-worker pools for a school or for district headquarters may be the source of needed activities yet the volume of work due to scripting, bulletin preparation, and the writing of guidesheets for teachers is likely to be heavy.

Minimum Staff Requirements: It may be helpful in analyzing staff needs to consider the make up of a studio crew that handles the actual telecasting or videotaping of an ITV program. We shall assume that the television teacher is the principal presentor and that he is supported by a variety of media. Members of the on the job operational crew are as follows:

1. Chief technician to start, check, and adjust all parts of the equipment system, including the transmitter; operate the camera controls at the console; operate the optical multiplexer; start the videotape recorder if the program is being recorded; and, punch up the cameras using the fader and special-effects amplifier and other equipment as required.
2. An assistant technician to carry out on-the-spot technical assignments or to relieve the chief technician at the console if unexpected adjustments have to be made; assist with handling slides and film clips for use in multiplexer projection equipment; and, primarily, to operate audio tape recorder, audio mixer, and maintain adequate audio control.
3. One cameraman-technician for operating camera 1.

4. One cameraman-technician for operating camera 2.
5. One floor manager, linking the program director with presentor, and assisting with needed changes on the floor in ways dictated by the director.
6. One program director, to direct all operations according to production plans, including control of console cameramen and all video and audio effects.

If, for example, three programs are being telecast *live,* or are being recorded simultaneously, then we must insist that something like a nonteaching crew of eighteen people would be required. Now, it is true that not all television programs call for this kind of action. Some programs are made up of film clips, slide sequences, or combined with instructional narrative. Others may be made up of one film, as would be the case where audiovisual media are being "delivered" via cable. Thus varying degrees of need for crew members exist depending on the program. But what about the need for other staff members who may not even have to be present when a given program is produced? We refer, of course, to the leadership and curriculum supervision personnel as well as to the external maintenances staff members if, for example, the school system's transmission is by the low-power radiation method. Certainly such personnel must exist in optimum amount and capability. Another way to examine the problem of minimum staff requirements is to consider the number of hours it takes to plan and produce an ITV program. Diamond has reported an example of such an analysis, with specific reference to half-hour ITV program for elementary school science, as follows :

	Hours
Television teacher	22
Producer	13½
Director	12½
Visualization specialist (graphic artist-photographer)	20
Engineer*	8
Student Asistant#	15
Total	91

* Time includes setup and teardown of set.

Includes two cameraman, floorman, and assistants for the visualization specialist.

Perhaps we ought to be bold enough to ask how much time a science teacher spends in preparing to teach a regular class. How much time would lie spend preparing face-to-face large-group presentation using a set of ten self-prepared color slides, a 200-foot film clip, and four overhead overlay transparencies? As we ponder such questions and seek their answers, we should also ask ourselves what we consider the teaching process to be. Only when we have determined this can we identify the character of the staff members we will recommend for a particular local situation.

Some Suggestions for Solving the Problem of Television Staff Organization: The media program director may be asked to make recommendations relative to a feasible and promising organization for the operation of a district-wide instructional television service program. Up to this point we have been considering the need to acquire a qualified and talented operational staff on the basis of required functions. However, the media director himself should be ready to decide what organizational structure is possible. He may be asked to take over the leadership function himself, or his superiors may bypass him, and rightly or unwisely place the responsibility for organizing the ITV program in the hands of someone else. There are many possibilities for organizing such services, and one of the crucial issues involved is whether the media director is qualified at the time the need for leadership arises? But even if he is, there are still unique conditions that may militate against the appointment, which may or may not be desired by a given individual. Sometimes, even though such an appointment is desired, the pressure of present work may be so heavy that to devote any significant amount of time to a new program would be difficult if not impossible. In such cases, and they are frequent, it is urgent that the media director arrange to be relieved of some of his routine duties so that he may devote adequate time to planning and implementing the new program. This, of course, may or may not be feasible. But modern administration demands a number of unique arrangements, not all of which depend on the addition of a specified number of new and permanent people. Hence, we see the need to be ready to undertake innovative tasks, to be willing to tackle new projects and reorganize present assignments and work loads to permit emphasis on new activities. In such instances, should the present director be released to plan the new activity, or should a new person be brought in to do it? Many times this question is answered by chief, citywide, educational administrators who may have their own convictions about these problems. The media director may not get his own way all of the time, but he can be ready with a proposal. In the following list we have summarized some of the possibilities and we ask the prospective media director to consider the consequences of each choice in light of his local conditions.

1. Make the ITV process a branch of the audiovisual media-service organization, and provide a supervisor of the centralized as well as decentralized television facilities and operations. The supervisor as the chief ITV administrator would then be responsible to the media program leader. In the school-building units, the media-service coordinators could also be involved, as would school-building technicians, in carrying out over-all service policies for optimum balance in the instructional program.

2. Separate the audiovisual media and ITV services into two service units, making both leaders coordinate workers in curriculum under the assistant superintendent of schools in charge of instruction. In such cases, it is likely that media preparation services for scheduled television programs would take the highest priority in the audiovisual graphic-production suites. ITV studios could also develop their own media-reparation capability, and the kind of television-teacher demand that we have mentioned earlier may be just the pressure needed to add full-time graphic artists as essential service personnel, either under ITV control, or under control of the district media director.

3. Organize the audiovisual media-services center and the instructional television unit under a citywide instructional television media director who is also responsible for libraries, who in turn would work under an assistant superintendent for instruction. We face in such situations the need to stratify the various directors at a level of responsibility that will attract creative personnel into the various media sections.

All of the possibilities mentioned may be directly related to the size and comprehensiveness of the ITV program, and the previous importance attached to the curriculum contributions by conventional audiovisual media. In smaller school districts, we see similar types of control and coordination, but using interested and qualified personnel from the teaching ranks on a part-time basis. Such part-time positions may be less easy to organize at the elementary school level than at the secondary, yet the possibilities do exist under staffing arrangements. In many ITV programs the inter-service use of technicians, graphic artists, and student crews will be essential, and the kind of organization that facilitates that cooperative endeavor is recommended. Again we must consider ITV services at two levels, namely, district-wide control, and school-building supplementary services to meet specific needs. Decisions regarding the nature of the ITV organization should be made before, not after, staffing procedures have been inaugurated.

Planning for the Acquisition and Installation of Equipment

We have repeatedly emphasized the relationship of equipment needs and specifications to curriculum plans. Planning for instructional television involves identification of stages by which these plans will be carried out, and equipment procurement should then follow these requirements. Committees charged with responsibility for preparing basic plans and recommendation should consider and treat in detail the following aspects of equipment acquisition and installation.

1. Identify and arrange for the specific locations in which each equipment unit will be placed and operated. This means that studio and other operational spaces, in both centralized and decentralized service centers, will have to be designated, procured, remodeled, and readied for the work of installation.
2. Employ a consultant to give advice relative to needed space, to assist with the work of preparing detailed, written equipment specifications, and to serve as a supervisor to check and certify that installation has been carried out in terms of the specifications.

3. Assess the quality levels of equipment being specified in the light of curriculum services by means of committee observation of actual operation of equipment under studio conditions. Thus visits to observe operations which include transmission of both *live* and recorded programs to reception areas will be essential.
4. Stress present and future compatibility of various components of equipment packages.
5. Whenever possible, require in the requests to bid that the vendor install and demonstrate successful use of the equipment specified for the intended curriculum purposes for completion of contract.
6. All phases of the ITV equipment-purchase program should be identified in order to insure that production, transmission, and reception systems will operate as needed under existing local conditions.
7. Identify the stages by means of which the various equipment packages will be procured, in light of the various contemplated service functions.

Planning for Financial Support

No proposal for the inauguration of an instructional television system in a school district should be presented until the required financial support is specified. Hence, community study and planning activity may have to proceed through several stages until the school board takes official action. Special bond issues may have to be floated, additional taxes levied, or school-district appropriations. Increased to match state and federal grants. Regardless of the nature of local action that has to be taken the plan for capital outlay and the plan for providing continuing support for the ITV programs can be implemented. Although the educational need must be specified first, some estimate of the cost must be given early in the deliberations in order to determine if local resources can support the program. It may be proper to plan for financial support in stages, specifying special capital outlay for facilities and equipment to carry out first-stage curriculum services, then specifying financial support in the second stage for temporary staff to speed up earlier phases of implementation, permanent staff for long-range operations and allotments for heavy production costs as the program gets underway. The third stage might cover the expansion of central facilities to include multiple studios and additional channels for district coverage. The fourth stage could specify financial support for school-building studio facilities, equipment and staff to bring the proposal into full operation.

Some Estimates of Cost: Although we have used the term *package of TV equipment* we do not mean to imply that there is a standard television-equipment system that we can specify for all studio or classroom situations. In offering cost estimates, we are aware that prices differ from place to place and that equipment models change over the years. Nevertheless, many readers may find use for cost estimates, for the sake of comparison and for making their own plans based on general school needs. We shall therefore use information gleaned from price lists and estimates of manufacturers, and from personal experience. The price ranges indicate range in quality and are also used to prevent readers from placing too much confidence in the preciserless of the estimates. The items are given in a variety of ways enabling readers to create their own equipment systems for special purposes. In no case should these figures be quoted or used for precise planning and proposal activities without confirmation from local dealers. We suggest the following items and cost ranges as shown in the chart on the next page.

Hazardous as it may be to use the preceding estimates, they do give a general idea of the capital outlay that may be necessary to provide comprehensive ITV services in schools. When plans for equipment use have been formulated, dealers in the systems specified, should be consulted for general or specific confirmation.

It seems quite obvious that adoption or expansion of instructional television poses some large-scale problems for the media program director. On the one hand, there are specific curriculum needs that television can help meet in significant ways, and in meeting those needs with television, some radical changes in the organization of both teachers and pupils may be in the offing. On the other hand, there is a vast and complex television technology to be identified and used to achieve instructional objectives. We have dealt with several main problems in the preceding sections, but by no means all of them. We therefore suggest that the implications in previous chapters for formulating television policy for the schools be carefully considered.

In response to the need for insightful planning for the intelligent, professional, and discriminating use of instructional television, a new field consultant service has been established by the National Association of Educational Broadcasters. The full name of the project is National Project for the Improvement of Televised Instruction. Its activities are financed by a grant from the Ford Foundation. The objectives of the Project are to relate instructional television to sound learning-based theories, improve skills and insights of existing television personnel in the schools improve preservice training programs for television practitioners, and to provide information and assistance to schools and districts about the organization and use of instructional television. The project will pay honoraria and travel expenses of the consulting teams, and the requesting institution will be responsible for the living expenses of the team members while visiting and working in the schools. The NPITI plans to implement a program of national seminars, regional workshops, and publications, and a program of cooperative action with related organizations.

We should not move on to the next chapter before we emphasize our conviction that television is the most awesome teaching medium of our time. We must face the fact that it is very doubtful that we have yet learned to use it wisely and in ways that will fulfill its potential. But television can, if we plan it that way, keep people central, and in optimum relationship to each other. Once we have a teacher and his message on tape, we can use television to deliver that message to the people who need it over and over again. Hence we have the greatest multiplier of professional effort, energy, and communicative content of our time, but this does not mean that we have learned to make it work in the right ways. To do this we must study the teaching process more thoroughly and make perhaps some rather starting decisions. We need to take seriously, before we leave the subject, the good advice of James M. Spinning, given a decade ago.

Item or Package	Cost Range
1. One Vidicon camera chain, complete with audio controls, tripod and dolly, intercom system, video monitor.	$5,000 to $9,000
2. One Vidicon or Plumbicon camera chain, complete chain, complete with stand, light bar, monitor, and accessories.	$2,000 to $5,000
3. Two Vidicon camera chains in a studio package complete with all related operational equipment.	$16,000 to $24,000
4. One videotape recorder complete with modulator.	$3,000 to $9,000
5. One videotape recorder (½-inch, non-broadcast).	$750 to $1,200
6. Two videotape recorders, complete with modulators, and one electronic editor on one of the recorders.	$7,000 to $17,000
7. One film chain, complete with two projectors (one 16 mm film and one 35 mm slide).	$9,000 to $14,000
8. One classroom TV receiving-recording-playback unit (without TV camera).	$4,000 to $6,000
9. One complete lighting package for one studio with control panel and circuits (suspended system only) installed on mobile track system.	$7,000 to $15,000
10. One telecasting, recording, and tape-editing studio and operational ITV unit, as a complete unit in a school building, or as an addition to centralized ITV facilities.	$55,000 to $70,000
11. Master antenna system for a 26-room school including cable and two-way outlets into all rooms.	$2,000 to $3,000
12. One television projection system for single-receiver, large-group auditorium viewing purposes such as the Kalart Co. Tele-Beam equipment unit.	$2,000 to $4,000

13. Television receivers, audiovisual model, 24-inch, on either pedestal, mobile 5-foot stand, or ceiling-suspended cradle, installed.	$2,00 to $4,00
14. Twelve-channel cable transmission system, Bell System Lease, to each school in the district (depending on the air-line distance from program source and related equipment) per month.	$4,00 to $5,000
15. Four Channel low-power 2,500 mHz radiation transmission system from central transmitter (cost for ten years, not including depreciation, but including maintenance and cost of money). See next item for related per school cost.	$50,000 to $60,000
16. Cost per school to install 2,500 mHz low-power radiation reception antenna and related units, not including wiring and classroom outlets.	$1,250 to $1,500
17. One dial-retrieval system for videotape programs for both large-group and individual use per school Basic relay-control and playback center with 12-channel capacity and 100 video-equipped carrels.	$100,000 to $300,000

When it comes to the essence of teaching, it must still be the teacher as person, as person to person, who is central...We need to adapt television to education, and only as we get a good crack at it, can we do that. But, at the same time, we need to adapt ourselves more completely to education. With or without television, we should take some of its virtues into our thinking, give more attention in all our teaching to the kind of planning and order, the sense of structure, the eye-and-ear appeal, the precise timing, and the over-all impact which are special musts for television.

We must not fail to give due consideration to the fact that it is the most natural process imaginable to apply television to education, one of the most pressing problems in our society. It is as natural and meaningful as it is to apply assembly-line technology to the making of automobiles. Television is so deeply involved with the communication of our time, and with the technology of our society, that it cannot help but become an extensive aspect of our education. We must not forget either that just as the learner and teacher on opposite ends of a log, and a group of learners with their teacher in a room with a scroll between them constituted educational images in their time, the environment has changed and new images of man's preparation for life must be developed. Television is almost certain to emerge as a major component in future instructional systems.

Problem-Solving Activities

1. Select any five of the ten patterns set forth in this chapter for using television that have been developed around the country, and identify the particular contributions ITV makes to the curriculum. Make an evaluative judgment about the magnitude of the value that would accrue form each contribution.
2. Using your own image of what constitutes desirable teaching processes, identify and write out the specific components of teacher activity. Then *(a)* mark your list of items with an asterisk in each case that you believe television could make a significant contribution, and *(b)* select the most significant item, in your view, and show what re-organization of pupils and teachers you would recommend if you were to inaugurate a comprehensive instructional television service program.
3. Looking at the problem from a broad curriculum viewpoint, what could television to foster the central values of the Educational Policies Commission of the NEA. Just how is the rational power of an individual developed in his school program? Based on your answer, name one role of : *(a)* a library book, *(b)* a motion picture in a class presentation, and *(c)* a dial-selected videotape.
4. Outline a specific and significant need in the curriculum that you believe is highly significant. Amplify your outline sufficiently to show the various aspects of the need you have identified. (Do this work as a part of a later exercise to plan

for implementation of plans using television to meet the need, or make a valuable contribution towards meeting it. This outline plan should be completed before operational technology is studied, but the possibility of using television should be borne in mind.)

5. In the light of the curriculum need specified in formulate a proposal for providing the required ITV service facilities and equipment. Keep this plan on a broad and general scale indicating only the nature of the program capability in either or both central and decentralized studios, plus classroom program origination. (It is not necessary to deal with specific equipment units needed, or the problems of transmission and reception at this time.)
6. Assume that you are going to plan a central ITV studio large enough to provide all schools with comprehensive service—large enough and sufficiently well equipped to transmit six programs simultaneously (four videotape, one program *live*, and one motion picture film) and still preserve for continuous use one studio for making programs on videotape. Now, study the space layout and make a new sketch showing modifications in it to make that capability possible. Cut it down in size if you can find ways of doing it.
7. Using the conditions as a basis, prepare a detailed list of the equipment necessary to carry out the proposed program of services. Use manufacturer's catalogs and price lists, and specify model numbers for each piece of major equipment and its accessories. (*Alternate problem:* State your own ITV functions and specify equipment units to carry them out at a high-quality level, or work with a task force on a specially assigned set of functions, pooling your results with others to make possible a duplicated composite list for the entire planning group.)
8. Would you be in favor of setting up a centralized videotaping studio, free of all additional transmission and scheduling activity?
9. What would be some advantages of decentralizing several studios in school buildings for production of programs for specific levels, grades, and subjects?

10. The superintendent of your school system has just turned down your proposal for a 9,200 square foot production and transmission facility, and has asked you to trim your program back for a pilot program with a maximum of two channels for transmission. He has set a space maximum of 3,600 square feet of floor area for your central studio facility. The preceding list of space needs as guides, make a new rough sketch showing space allotted for specific functions Label fully to show potential activities.
11. How does the existence of a master antenna system affect the cost and use of a school-building program producing studio?
12. State the advantages and disadvantages of each of the major ITV transmission plans now open to schools.
13. Can you name other feasible transmission methods for school districts that own and operate their own ITV facilities to use besides leased coaxial-cable, and school-owned-and-maintained, low-power fixed-service, 2,500 mHz radiation? If you can identify them, state what obstacles would have to be surmounted before adopting them.
14. Identify any school system with which you are familiar and for the number of schools involved and their distances from each other and the studio, make a cost comparison for the two methods mentioned.
15. Make several diagrams of specific ITV viewing situations using 23- or 24-inch receivers, as follows: *(a)* image-magnification facilities and equipment at a large-group teaching station (100 pupils); *(b)* a 500-seat teaching auditorium; *(c)* a 30-seat classroom; *(d)* using a television-projection system in a 500-seat teaching auditorium. Label all diagrams fully.
16. Make a plan in outline from for organizing and implementing the study of ITV in the curriculum for any school district identified. Using the guidelines for implementing change, identify study committees and stages of action, from possible interest-getting activities to recommendation of the plan by the superintendent of schools and its adoption by the board of education. Deal with all essential aspects of the final plan, such as

curriculum needs, required staff members and their organization, cost of initial facilities and equipment, the transmission, plan and its cost, and school-building ITV equipment units and their costs. (Members of the group should break the problem down into its major parts and then write plans and prepare reports and cost tables cooperatively, arranging for subgroups to study each phase of the plan and to report to the class with handout sheets.)

17. Identify two or more school districts presently providing district-wide ITV services, and by methods that are as easy as possible for the local ITV staffs (such as a personal visit to the site for on-the-spot study and picture-taking), prepare two visualized presentations for group analysis. (Organize two task forces, one for each visitation and report.)

References

Bretz, Rudy. *Techniques of Television Production,* 2nd, ed. (New York: McGraw-Hill, 1962).

Bronson, Vernon and James A. Fellows, *Standards of Television Transmission.* (Prepared under auspices of Office of Education, U.S. Department of Health, Education and Welfare, in connection with an NDEA contract, OE-2-16-027.) (Washington, D.C. :National Association of Educational Broadcasters, 1964).

Brown, James W. and Kenneth D. Norberg. *Administering Educational Media.* (McGraw-Hill, 1965).

Clarke, R. Walton, 1966 *Schoolman's Guide to ETV Communications.* (Philadelphia : Jerrold Electronics Corporation, 401 Walnut St., 1966).

Costello, Lawrence F. and Georege N. Gordon. *Teach with Television,* 2nd ed. (New York: Hastings House, 1965).

Diamond, Robert M. (ed.). *A Guide to Instructional Television.* (New York: McGraw-Hill, 1964).

Educational Facilities Laboratories. *Design for ETV* (*Planning for Schools with Television*), prepared by Dave Chapman, Inc., Industrial Design. (New York: Educational Facilities Laboratories, 477, Madison, Ave., 1960).

Educational Policies Commission. *Education and the Spirit of Science.* (Washington, D.C. : The National Educational Association, 1966).

Erickson, Carlton, W. H. *Fundamentals of Teaching with Audiovisual Technology.* (New York: Macmillan, 1965.

Griffith, Barton L. and Donald W. MacLennan. *Improvement of Teaching by Television.* (Columbia, Mo. : University of Missouri Press, 1964).

Hillard, Robert L. Writing for Television and Radio. (New York : Hastings House, 1962).

Institute for Communication Research. *Educational Television, The Next Ten Years.* (Prepared and published pursuant to a contract with the Office of Education, Department of health, Education and Welfare.) (Stanford: Institute for Communications Research, Stanford University, 1962). (Out of print.)

Jones, Peter. *Technique of Television Cameraman.* (New York : Hastings House, 1966).

Lewis, Philip. *Educational Television Guidebook.* (New York : McGraw-Hill, 1961).

Milerson, Gerald. *Technique of Television Production.* (New York : Hastings House, 1961).

Murphy, Judith and Ronald Gross. Learning by Television. (New York : The Fund for Advancement of Education, 477 Madison Ave., 1966).

Nisbitt, Alec. *Technique of Sound Studio.* (New York : Hastings House, 1962).

Reid, J. Christopher and Donald W. MacLennan. *Research in Instructional Television and Film* (U.S. Office of Education, a publication of the Bureau of Research). (Washington, D.C.: Superintendent of Documents, U.S. Government Printing Office, 1967).

Roe, Yale (ed.) *Television Stations Management.* (New York : Hastings House, 1964).

Russell, James E. *Change and Challenge in American Education.* (Boston : Houghton Mifflin, 1965).

Schramm, Wilbur and others. *The Impact of Educational Television.* (Urbana, III. : University of Illinois Press, 1960).

Smith, Mary Howard. *Using Television in the Classroom.* (New York : McGraw-Hill, 1961).

Spear, James. *Creating Visuals for TV.* (Washington, D.C. : Division of Instructional Service of the N.E.A., 1962). (reprinted 1965.)

Stoddard, Alexander J. *Schools for Tomorrow, An Educator's Blueprint.* (New York : The Fund for the Advancement of Education, 477 Madison Ave., 1957).

Sylvania Electronic Products, Inc. *Equipment Guide for Classroom Television.* (New York : Sylvania Electric Products, 730 Third Ave., 1965).